TIMOTHY PICKERING
AND
THE AMERICAN REPUBLIC

TIMOTHY PICKERING
and the
AMERICAN REPUBLIC

Gerard H. Clarfield

UNIVERSITY OF PITTSBURGH PRESS

This book is dedicated to the memory
of Walt Scholes who was my friend.

Published by the University of Pittsburgh Press, Pittsburgh, Pa. 15260
Copyright © 1980, University of Pittsburgh Press
All rights reserved
Feffer and Simons, Inc., London
Manufactured in the United States of America

Library of Congress Cataloging in Publication Data

Clarfield, Gerard H
    Timothy Pickering and the American Republic.

    Includes bibliographical references and index.
    1. Pickering, Timothy, 1745–1829. 2. United States—History—Revolution,
1775–1783. 3. United States—Politics and government—1783–1809.
4. Statesmen—United States—Biography. I. Title.
E302.6.P5C553   973.4'092'4 [B]   79–24326
ISBN 0–8229–3414–0

Contents

Preface

WHEN I BEGAN THIS BOOK, some thought I was simply being perverse. Did I seriously intend to resuscitate the historical reputation of one of the principal villains of early American history? At the time, I freely admit, I thought it would be interesting to try. However, the sources so convincingly demonstrated that Pickering deserved his reputation that I soon gave up the notion. I might have stopped research at that point but for the realization that these same sources suggested that I had uncovered the archetypal *young man on the make* of the revolutionary generation. The twist in Pickering's case was that he never made it. I began to wonder whether it might not be of some value to explore this other side of the coin, if only to suggest that for every Washington or Adams there must have been a hundred, perhaps a thousand, Pickerings. I was encouraged too, by my certain knowledge that studying Pickering would never be dull. Driven by ambition, frustrated by repeated disappointment, and completely lacking in self-awareness, he easily could and repeatedly did turn violently against those he blamed for his endless frustrations. His astonishing volatility and outrageous self-righteousness further attracted my attention. I wanted to know more.

As I probed further, I became increasingly confident that a biography of Pickering was justified. Most students of the era know that Pickering served in the cabinets of two presidents. Most also are aware that as a senator and congressman he spoke for an extreme brand of New England Federalism. Few, however, are knowledgeable about his full career, despite the fact that from the time of the American Revolution until the election of Andrew Jackson, Timothy Pickering was involved in an astonishing variety of matters, many of them of great moment. Ironically, his failures drove him from one activity to another,

vii

broadening his career. Had he been of a more practical bent, he might have stayed at home during the revolutionary war, become involved in privateering as many of his friends and relatives did, made the fortune he always craved, and lived a more prosaic and less interesting life.

I hardly know where to begin in expressing my gratitude to those who over the past several years have contributed to the completion of this book. The American Philosophical Society and the Research Council of the University of Missouri—Columbia both deserve my special thanks for the financial support they provided. Nor can I forget the many librarians and archivists who gave so unstintingly of their time and expertise. I would also like to thank my colleague Noble Cunningham, who read the manuscript and who has proven a constant source of intellectual stimulation to me. A word too must be said about Mrs. Marie Scholes, whose astonishingly conscientious reading of an earlier draft of this book saved me from many a slip. Finally, and most profoundly, I would like to thank my wife Julie, who has read the text more times than either of us cares to remember, and whose editorial skills have proven almost as valuable to me as her loving encouragement.

TIMOTHY PICKERING
AND
THE AMERICAN REPUBLIC

ONE

From Loyalist to Whig

SOME TWENTY MILES from Boston on Massachusetts' North Shore lies the town of Salem, today one picturesque component of a great metropolitan community. There was a time, however, when Salem had an identity that was clearly its own. Two hundred years ago and more, her harbor was busy with the commerce of the world. The tall ships at anchor and the pervasive smell of "fish flakes" in the air, the bustling, cluttered streets were more than ornamental indicators of a way of life: they were signals of a prosperity that made Salem by the 1750s a distant second to Boston among the towns of the colony. Resembling more an overgrown village than a thriving commercial center, she was of course both. The houses of the town, with their deep lots and gardens behind and between, conformed to an older agricultural pattern, while some of the more opulent dwellings, homes of merchants and sea captains, reflected the commercial prosperity Salem enjoyed and gave a clue to the fundamental business of life there. Wedded to the sea, she would prosper or decay according to the state of her commerce and trade.[1]

By the middle of the eighteenth century the Pickering family already had roots sunk deep in Salem's past. The first of the line, John Pickering, a carpenter, had come from England during the great migration and was admitted an inhabitant of the town in 1637.[2] Although the earliest Pickering amassed no great fortune, he nevertheless acquired enough landed property to form the basis for a prosperous estate. Indeed, the house he built with his own hands reflects a degree of wealth extraordinary for the time. Modeled upon a style popular in England in the middle of the seventeenth century, the many-gabled, half-timbered house still stands, testimony to the skill of its builder. But it serves too as a reflection of his social aspirations and economic accomplishments. It would be an exaggeration to suggest that it was the home of a country gentleman. Yet it is more than a farmhouse and must once have been an impressive sight standing alone amidst well-cultivated fields.[3]

The generations of Pickerings that followed expanded the original estate and, by the early eighteenth century, had established for the family a place in the town's leadership. The original settler's grandson, another John Pickering, was not only chosen a selectman in 1709, but also served as one of Salem's representatives to the Massachusetts General Court.[4] The older of his two sons, Theophilus, attended Harvard College and later became a conservative Congregationalist minister in nearby Chebacco Parrish.[5] The younger son, Timothy, inherited the family home and farm in Salem. A most competent farmer, shrewd businessman, and pious Christian (he became the deacon of Salem's Third Congregational Church), Timothy Pickering, Sr., worked doggedly at enlarging his landholdings. He married Mary Wingate of New Hampshire and raised nine healthy and unusually long-lived children. The younger of Deacon Pickering's two sons was born in the ancestral home on July 17, 1745, and named in honor of his father.[6]

For Timothy Pickering, Jr., growing up in Salem at midcentury undoubtedly had its pleasures. There would have been happy moments in shady woods and sunlit fields or walks along the waterfront where fishing boats and merchant ships lined wharves scattered with an accumulation of nets, cordage, and other paraphernalia of the sea. Perhaps too there were contemplative moments among the gravestones on the old burying hill just across from the ancestral home where three generations of Pickerings lay buried. But if such moments there were, they were few, for the Pickering household was a tyranny ruled by the deacon in God's name.

There was hardly a town in New England that did not boast a character such as the deacon who somehow failed to discern the dividing line that separated the pious from the self-righteous. In public he was an outspoken critic of his fellow townsmen, constantly reassuring himself of his own virtue by denigrating theirs. At home he mistook miserliness for godliness. Though there was plenty of money, he provided only the essentials.[7]

Most of Salem's townsfolk cordially disliked the deacon, for he was an abrasively self-righteous moralist whose constant crusading often proved more than they could endure. He quickly earned a reputation for hypocrisy and sham that lasted years after his death. John Adams, on meeting the elder Pickering while in Salem on legal business, was instantly antagonized:

This man famous for his writings in newspapers concerning church order and government, they tell me is very rich; his appearance is perfectly plain, like a farmer; his smooth combed locks flow behind him like Deacon Cushing's though not so gray; has a quick eye like _____: he has an hypocritical demure on his face like Deacon Foster; his mouth makes a semicircle when he puts on that devout face.[8]

A generation later, an unknown observer rendered a less harsh judgment. Pickering, he wrote, had not been "so bad a man as he is depicted." He seemed rather to have been "like a good many others who think themselves 'Godward all right' and who are 'manward rather twistical.' "[9]

To those who shared his views the deacon seemed an earnest social reformer, but to those who felt the lash of his tongue or the sting of his barbed pen, he seemed either an overbearing eccentric or a self-serving hypocrite who cloaked himself in righteousness in order to enjoy more fully the discomfiture of others. Had he been poor, Deacon Pickering would probably have been ignored. But no matter how quarrelsome he became, how vituperative or personal his attacks, he commanded attention because he was a man of means. As a church deacon, sometime moderator of the town meeting, and omnipresent spokesman for all manner of social and economic reforms, Pickering certainly deserved his reputation as the town's leading controversialist.

Listing among his various causes inflation, which he was against, and church reform, which he supported, the deacon reserved the larger portion of his energies for the struggles against slavery and drunkenness.[10] Ironically, it was the American Revolution, an event he abhorred, that led to abolition in Massachusetts. Yet if the old man viewed the final triumph over slavery with mixed feelings, it was at least a victory. His prohibitionist efforts, however, were without the least significance.[11]

Curiously, Pickering's unsuccessful campaign against alcohol tells us more about the man than do his antislavery sentiments, for his character is more clearly revealed in defeat than in triumph. Or perhaps that is not quite the right way to put it, for victory and defeat have implications of finality that obscure the man's incredible tenacity. Indeed, it is unfair to suggest that the deacon was defeated in his battle against drink; he simply ran out of time. An insistent absolutist, he viewed unceasing struggle against entrenched immorality as preferable to either compromise or surrender. Whatever else may have been said of him, no one ever accused the combative deacon of lacking determination.

Life in the Pickering household was something like living in the eye of a hurricane. The old man thrived on controversy and seemed to enjoy it most when he stood alone against his enemies. The extremes to which he was willing to go are nowhere better demonstrated than by his forty-year battle for control of Salem's First Congregational Church. Pickering supported the Reverend Samuel Fiske who, after more than eight years of conflict with an influential group of "aggrieved brethren," lost control of the church. With the approval of an ecclesiastical council, the Massachusetts General Court, and the colonial governor, the rebels replaced Fiske with the young Reverend John Sparhawk. Pickering, Fiske, and about twenty loyal supporters built a new meeting house but refused to admit that theirs was not the First Church of Salem. When, years later, another generation of churchgoers agreed that the confusion and enmity created by having two first churches should be ended and the schism recognized as accomplished fact, Pickering demurred. In a series of published essays he attempted to muster support for an ecclesiastical council to correct this error. His efforts failed, for where he saw sin, others saw only a move to restore harmony among Salem's Congregational churches. Carrying his logic to extremes, Pickering seceded from the church rather than continue in communion with a congregation that had so egregiously sinned. Ultimately, in 1771, he accepted public censure by his minister rather than submit to the church's ecclesiastical authority.[12]

Capable of acts of querulous extremism, the older Pickering was simultaneously a dedicated parent whose impact on the intellectual development of his younger son was very great. He was committed to the old Calvinist virtues of frugality, good work habits, piety, and the constant pursuit of righteousness, qualities that young Timothy came to revere. There is nothing exceptional in this, for New Englanders traditionally sought to inculcate these values in their children. Yet in the Pickering household there was a difference, for Timothy Pickering, Sr., was a man of spectacular intensity. He taught his son that there were absolute truth, justice, and virtue; that eternal salvation depended upon the determined pursuit of these; and that to compromise, to settle for less than what was just and right, was immoral.[13]

At maturity, Timothy Pickering, Jr., often found himself in disagreement with his father, particularly with regard to political and religious questions. Yet he was his father's son. He accepted as axiomatic the view that to live righteously in a less than righteous world required great moral fiber; that one must ultimately be true to oneself and must never compromise on matters of principle. What he could not perceive was the difference between being righteous and self-righteous; that pride, ambition, and sometimes blind prejudice can obscure a man's perceptions. Also, he sometimes failed to see that a man might honestly believe he was serving the cause of truth when instead his own prejudices and psychological needs had so perverted his understanding that he was no longer capable of discerning where justice left off and personal feelings began.

Although the deacon was careful with his money, he nevertheless had a practical appreciation for the importance of a college education. And so, in the summer of 1759, following three years at the Salem Grammar School, young Timothy, scarcely fourteen years old, set off for Harvard College. He carried with him a pound of chocolate, some coffee, tea, a few other supplies, and a firm parental injunction to work hard, obey college rules, and above all remain pious.[14]

Harvard, in those years, was anything but an imposing place. There were only four buildings on the campus, Old Harvard Hall, Massachusetts Hall, Stoughton Hall, and Holden Chapel. An influx of students, reflecting the general prosperity enjoyed by the colony during the French and Indian War, had overcrowded the college. Some ninety students, the entire freshman and sophomore classes, had to find room and board in Cambridge. Living in town had its advantages, however, for it meant the younger students could avoid eating in the commons. Sixty-five years later Pickering recalled with great distaste the daily routine at the Harvard Commissary. The students marched to their tables in groups of six, each carrying his own knife and fork. Invariably the main dish was "fresh baked beef" though now and then a hard Indian meal pudding was added for variety. Once each quarter, a baked plum pudding was also served. At the end of the evening meal, in what must have been a remarkable mass performance, each student carefully wiped his silverware clean on the tablecloth and departed. Fortunately, at least as far as Pickering was concerned, students prepared breakfast in their chambers. Butter, milk, eggs, and other groceries could be purchased from the butler whose offices were located in the southeast corner on the lower floor of Harvard Hall.[15]

When Pickering entered, the college was enjoying something of a renaissance under the leadership of Dr. Edward Holyoke, former Congregationalist minister from Marblehead. Holyoke modernized the college's entire approach to higher education by encouraging greater freedom of inquiry.[16] He improved the tiny faculty, too, with the addition of John Winthrop, Hollis Professor of Mathematics and Natural Philosophy, "the first important scientist or productive scholar on the teaching staff."[17] In the face of serious opposition, Holyoke also managed to retain the brilliant but controversial Hollis Professor of Divinity, Edward Wigglesworth. Later, he appointed Wigglesworth's son to the same position, thus helping ensure the success of the movement toward religious liberalism in Massachusetts. Another of Holyoke's more significant contributions lay in undergraduate education. Before he retired, specialization of teaching assignments among the tutors became the rule, and texts were modernized to reflect the progressive orientation of the academy.[18]

As a student, Pickering seems to have been well behaved and able. Aside from an occasional small fine for missing prayers or returning late from vacation, common offenses, he was never in trouble with college authorities.[19] Schooled to obedience, he pursued his tasks without complaint. Nor did he find the work overly difficult. His academic performance was well above average. In fact he was one of four members of his freshman class to win an award for scholarship.[20]

It is nonetheless clear that for the youngster from Salem the years at Harvard were not a time of intellectual stimulation. Indeed, he would later describe the education he received there as "miserable."[21] And perhaps the young man's perceptions had some validity, for it was his great misfortune to arrive at Harvard before Holyoke had instituted his most far-reaching reform, the specialization of teaching assignments. Pickering's four years in Cambridge were therefore spent under the stultifying direction of one unimaginative tutor. Dr. William Kneeland ran the boys through a standard course with emphasis on the classics. Equating learning with memorization, he required his students to memorize and recite long passages from such works as Tully's *Select Orations,* Virgil's *Aeneid, The Greek Testament,* Brattle's *Logic,* Gordon's *Geography,* and John Locke's *On Human Understanding.*[22] At the age of eighty-two, Pickering could still remember Gordon's description of ostriches as "birds that were as tall as men on horseback." Having been required to commit to memory large portions of Locke's *On Human Understanding,* he heartily sympathized with the cry of one of his classmates who, after torturing himself for some time in a futile attempt to memorize a lengthy passage, slammed his book closed shouting, "The inhabitants of Hell, I can't read it!" Kneeland was not a teacher but a destroyer of minds, according to Pickering. His methods "saved both the tutor & scholar the trouble of thinking, one to ask, & the other to answer questions on the author's doctrines."[23]

Nor was Pickering impressed with the teaching of the great John Winthrop. It was with particular distaste that he allowed himself to be shepherded up to the second floor of "Old Harvard," where Professor Winthrop kept his laboratory. There he and the other students would watch while the eminent scientist performed his experiments. Pickering had no doubt that Winthrop was an extremely knowledgeable man. But he was no teacher. He hurried over matters elementary to him but difficult for the students, in general leaving them as uninformed as if they had never been present in his classes. Pickering's judgment was severe: "We derived no benefit from his remarks." For him, this statement may well be applied to almost his entire four years at Harvard.[24]

Pickering's recollections of Harvard are in striking contrast with those of some distinguished contemporaries. John Adams, for example, found Holyoke's Harvard an intoxicating place and John Winthrop "an excellent and happy teacher."[25] Where Pickering found only meaningless proforma recitation, Adams discovered a deep intellectual excitement that sent him reeling off into a lifetime spent devouring writings on history, politics, and legal theory. It would be sheer foolishness to suggest that either Adams or Pickering remembered best what Harvard was like. Indeed, there is no reason to discount either man's observations, for each had a different perspective. Clearly, however, Pickering's was the more ordinary mind. If he did not find intellectual stimulation within Harvard's walls, it was because he was by nature a restless activist, not a scholar. During a long lifetime, he took little pleasure in things intellectual.

Although Pickering treated Harvard more as an obstacle than as an opportunity, the degree was nevertheless a passport into the inner sanctum of Salem's elite. He returned home in 1763 an ambitious boy of eighteen in search of a future. But where did the future lie? At length, though none of the professions open to him had any particular appeal, he decided upon the law, for even then he was politically ambitious. He took a job with John Higginson, town clerk and register of deeds for Essex County, and studied law too, probably with Salem's leading attorney, William Pyncheon.[26]

Young Tim Pickering, now beginning to make his own way in Salem, was almost six feet tall, an angular, awkward youth, already balding and bespectacled. The young ladies of the town found him unattractive and he knew it. Yet, no matter how shy and diffident he was, or awkward socially, he persevered in his efforts to make a place for himself in Salem society. When William Turner, a dancing master late of London (or so the advertisement proclaimed), came to Salem, Pickering quickly enrolled in his class. For three dollars on entering and six for an entire quarter, he learned the minuet in excruciating detail. It is genuinely touching to read the pages of closely written notes this gangling, self-conscious youth took while learning to dance, or to consider him carefully observing that when "shifting from one position to another the right knee is to be bent in an easy and careless manner."[27] Alas, "easy and careless" would never describe Timothy Pickering. He was never comfortable in purely social situations and throughout his long life deplored a "frivolity" he found impossible to enjoy.

Even in his earliest adult years Pickering was as aggressive in politics as he was retiring in polite society. A young man fresh out of Harvard and anxious to get ahead, he cultivated Salem's influential few. These gentlemen became his models. He sought their company and conversation, studied their opinions and transformed them into his own, for he saw in these men what he wished to become himself, a provincial gentleman, a local leader. It was for this reason, despite the fact that he could ill afford the extravagant membership fee, that in May 1765 Pickering joined Salem's exclusive Library Society.[28]

The Stamp Act and the crisis that it spawned dominated conversation in the Library Society during 1765. There, where loyalism was the rule, Pickering routinely and without giving any serious thought to the long-range implications of his behavior, denounced Boston's popular party. Later he would explain his early loyalism as the result of youthful inexperience.[29] There is, to be sure, a good deal of truth in this. He was at the time only twenty years old, a stripling clerk studying law, and anxious to succeed. Awed by the older, more wealthy and powerful men whose circle he had joined, Pickering parroted their views, amplifying them with his own natural enthusiasm. Of course, what Pickering would not later remark upon was that his vehement antiradical stand paid immediate political dividends both in Salem and in Boston. Governor Francis Bernard, recognizing a young and promising "friend of government," commissioned him a lieutenant in the Essex militia in 1766.[30]

Not until 1768 was Pickering forced to rethink his earliest political credo. Then, in response to the implementation of the Townshend Acts, a conservative and very respectable Whig faction led by Richard and Elias Hasket Derby emerged in town. With their own newspaper, the *Essex Gazette,* printed by Samuel Hall, Salem's Whigs fractured the old political consensus.

The extent of the change that had overtaken Salem became clear in July 1768, after the General Court voted 92 to 17 to reject the ministry's demand that it repudiate the Massachusetts Circular Letter promulgated five months before.[31] Salem's representatives at that legislative session, William Browne and Peter Frye, acting in defiance of a strongly held opinion in the town, had voted with the minority. Salem seethed with discontent and the selectmen, anxious to restore calm, convened a special town meeting. It was a warm July, and the Town House on Main Street beside the First Church, crowded as few could remember it, was hot and stuffy. After an acrimonious debate, the majority passed a resolution repudiating the vote of Salem's representatives and endorsing the action of the General Court.[32] The minority, many of them Library Society members and friends of Pickering's, refused to endorse the town's action and instead drew up and signed a protest.

Sensing that the town's old leadership was losing its influence, Pickering sought the middle ground. He refused to sign the minority statement. Yet in spite of growing differences, he did not immediately break with his Tory friends. On the contrary, he retained his membership in the Library Society and in 1769 accepted a promotion to the rank of captain in the militia, even though it must have been evident that Governor Bernard was using his patronage power in an attempt to ensure the allegiance of a waverer.[33]

Eventually, Pickering did sever relations with Salem's loyalist faction. It is difficult to pinpoint the event that precipitated this final break, whether it was the military occupation of Boston or the ensuing "massacre." Whatever the case, by the spring of 1770, he had completed his political metamorphosis and was attacking Salem's Tories with as much gusto as he had earlier denounced Boston's patriots. His public vehemence must have been intense, for when a series of columns calling for the total suppression of the Tory faction in Salem began to appear in the *Essex Gazette,* it was widely assumed that the author, *Nauticus,* was none other than Pickering. Another anonymous author, *Y,* recalled that not too long before Pickering had himself been a "friend of government." With pungent sarcasm, *Y* accused Pickering of the lowest form of political opportunism and hoped that he might fully "enjoy the wished for applause and reap the virtuous satisfaction of having bartered honesty for interest." Pickering's anonymous tormentor warned that someday soon the public would come to its senses and that opinion would again shift. It would then be "amusing," he wrote, to see Pickering cringe before those he now berated and threatened. "I leave you forever," *Y* concluded, "to the uninterrupted possession of that happiness which can result from a consciousness of having stooped to the lowest fraud for the vilest purpose, sincerely wishing you every reward that divine or human justice shall annex to successful perfidy."[34]

Ironically, Pickering was not *Nauticus.* His denials, however, only encouraged others to taunt and denounce him until at length he felt compelled to publish a long vindication of his character. No radical, he nevertheless appreciated the power of extremist Whig rhetoric and used it to his great advantage. In each colony, he charged, there was a group of "great and powerful" men who sought to rule without the consent of those governed. These persons were too few to impose their will upon the people of America by themselves. However, they looked for and found support from a succession of ministries in London that "over the past five or six years" had been working to forge the "shackles and chains of slavery" for the colonies. Together the Tories and the ministry formed a powerful coalition, with the former willing to submit to bondage in exchange for "the emoluments of office" and the privileges involved in serving as the instruments of ministerial tyranny.[35]

Even as he once more denounced the Tories and reaffirmed his commitment to Whig ideals, Pickering writhed, struggling to defend himself against the turncoat charge. He admitted having denounced "the wicked, selfish motives of some popular leaders." Nor would he retreat from what he had said. Mob violence was wrong, and the cynical, power-hungry men who used such mobs to achieve their own private political purposes were demagogues. However, he insisted, he had come to recognize that there was a difference between "the cause of American liberty and the pretended patriotism of [some of] its advocates." There were unquestionably among the Whig leadership those who deserved "the name of villain." It would be wrong, however, to judge the movement by such a standard. And it would be equally foolish to support the so-called friends of government simply because they opposed mob rule. If the worst of the radicals were ambitious, even dangerous, men, their counterparts at the other end of the political spectrum were equally bad. The true friends of government in America were those Whigs who resisted an unjust ministry and fought for the preservation of the rights of Englishmen. The king had nowhere in his dominions, Pickering averred, any more loyal followers than the American Whigs.[36]

In this way, seeking justification for the complete political reversal he had executed, Pickering crawled out on a political ledge that in 1770 was still broad enough to support him as an opponent of ministerial policy and simultaneously a loyal Englishman. In the next few years, however, a period during which he emerged as a prominent figure in town affairs, that ledge would narrow until ultimately he was cast off into the abyss of revolution.

In Salem, as in so many other towns in Massachusetts, the political battles of the mid-sixties left scars, took victims, and altered the old political structure. Loyalists were swept into political obscurity to be replaced by new men. One of these was young Pickering, who was blessed with many of the assets needed for political preference. His Harvard background and his membership in the Massachusetts Bar marked him as a young man of promise. Family connections helped, too. The Pickerings were important in their own right. Moreover, his sisters had married well, creating a network of relationships that linked him to a number of New England's prominent families. Finally, his brother John preceded him in local politics, and as one of Salem's representatives to the General Court, a frequent moderator of the town meeting, and a member of the locally prestigious school committee, paved the way for his brother's advancement. When, in March 1772, the town meeting elected Pickering a selectman, it was simply a public affirmation of what had already become clear. At twenty-seven he was one of the town's influential conservative Whig political leaders.[37]

Pickering's early political rise was not accompanied by any substantial improvement in his economic status. Whereas most other town leaders had established themselves as merchants, farmers, or in the professions and from there moved on to take a part in local political life, Pickering had not. Nor, if we are to take the disinterested way in which he pursued his law practice as any indication, did he intend to do so. Law was pure drudgery for him. He was unable to muster the energy or determination to make it a career. At frequent intervals throughout his long life he questioned whether the sacrifices he was making in public service were justified. Often, especially after the Revolution, he revealed a deep sense of bitterness. He had served while others profited. But Pickering was deceiving himself, for he was by no means the victim of some misplaced sense of *noblesse oblige*. He was, rather, from his earliest adult years, a captive of his own political ambition.

In the autumn of 1772, after a two-year hiatus, a new crisis in imperial relations materialized. This time rumor had it that the ministry was intent upon undermining the independence of the colony's judiciary by paying the salaries of Massachusetts' five Superior Court judges from crown revenues. When Governor Thomas Hutchinson refused to convene a special session of the General Court to consider this matter, Boston's town meeting reacted by organizing Massachusetts' first Committee of Correspondence and setting in motion a plan that soon led to the organization of a network of similar committees throughout the commonwealth.[38]

During the earliest stages of this movement Samuel Adams believed that Salem would respond quickly to Boston's initiative by organizing its own Committee of Correspondence. But prospects there steadily dimmed until at last he gave up hope. The governor, he thought, had successfully interfered there.[39] Hutchinson's role notwithstanding,

Pickering and Salem's other leaders had their own reasons for holding back, for they did not altogether approve of the tendency of recent events. The passionate rhetoric of Whig authors whose pieces appeared regularly in the *Essex Gazette* was not entirely distressing. Even Pickering used words such as *slavery* and *tyranny* in describing British policy. But too many radicals were calling for organization and resistance. This went far beyond anything Pickering and his friends had in mind. Naturally, then, they were reluctant to follow where Boston led, fearing that the movement to organize Committees of Correspondence represented a serious step down the road to open rebellion.

For six months Salem's leaders held firm, refusing to give even passing consideration to the organization of a Committee of Correspondence. In time, however, as town after town fell into line behind Boston, the growing pressure could no longer be resisted. Still Pickering and the other members of Salem's conservative Whig elite had no intention of going too far. A carefully managed town meeting appointed a special committee to draft a response to Boston's now months-old initiative. Pickering, a prominent member of this committee, played a major role in articulating town policy.

The committee's letter to Boston, which was quickly adopted without amendment by the full meeting, reflects the continuing skepticism that Pickering and evidently others in town felt about the course being charted by Boston's radical Whig leadership. Salem was in a difficult situation, for her reluctance to support the popular movement had, by May 1773, caused many to question openly her commitment to Whig principles. Thus, a good portion of the letter to Boston was written in justification of the town's earlier inactivity. More fundamentally, the bulk of this long letter was an enthusiastic endorsement of those Whig ideals earlier articulated by Boston and other towns. Europeans had once been as free as Englishmen, the Salem letter remarked, but having failed to defend their liberties, they had been enslaved. The same fate awaited America if she did not make a firm defense of her rights. It was of the greatest importance, Salem affirmed, that all Americans be continually informed "of every measure of Administration whereby our just rights are infringed, or that has the remotest tendency to destroy or alter our happy Constitution."[40]

Considering the passion with which Salem now publicly, though belatedly, embraced the principle of continuing correspondence, Pickering and the other members of the drafting committee might reasonably have been expected to conclude this letter with a series of ringing resolutions, reminiscent of those passed by other towns, including one organizing a Committee of Correspondence. In the only really substantive aspect of the letter, however, they did nothing of the kind. Salem informed Boston that she was not going to organize a committee because there was "no immediate necessity for one." Instead, the selectmen would be empowered to act as "such a committee, till the town shall chuse one for that purpose."[41]

Pickering's drafting committee thus managed a neat ploy. Endorsing Whig principles cost nothing. Appointing the conservative selectmen a Committee of Correspondence, moreover, changed nothing. Most important, the town avoided the danger implicit in organizing a separate committee authorized to speak for the town on provincial affairs. But if maximum flexibility was thus preserved, time was nevertheless running out for Pickering and for Salem. Soon events beyond local control would require a genuine commitment to the revolution.

TWO

The Revolution Closes In

THE TEA ACT and the crisis it spawned, culminating in the Boston Tea Party of December 1773, at last moved Pickering down the road toward active resistance to ministerial authority. But it was the Boston Port Act, labeled by Samuel Hall "one of the most CRUEL ARBIT-RARY ACTS that ever disgraced the reign of a tyrant," that fully aroused his nationalist consciousness.[1] By the middle of 1774 he was actually romanticizing about a unique American future. Writing to his nephew, the Boston minister John Clarke, he became enthusiastic over the "growing empire" he saw opening and urged Clarke to play a more active role in Whig affairs. "America now demands the genius, learning, and virtue of all her sons," he wrote. "Either slavery will make one universal blot; or heroes and patriots of this western world will grace the annals of the present age."[2] Yet Pickering continued to shrink from confrontation. How he hoped to achieve America's future while settling issues with England short of independence we do not know; nor did he.

Boston's Whig leaders were quick to respond to the closing of their city's port. A town meeting urged Americans everywhere to end all trade with Great Britain and with the British West Indies. Economic sanctions might yet force England to alter her policy. But the Bostonians realized that organizing the economic power of the colonies was going to be difficult, for the merchants of Philadelphia, New York, and other seaboard towns had to be convinced to stop their trade voluntarily at a time when Boston was to be bottled up by law. Their first object, then, was unity within the province. Thus, the same town meeting that passed the resolution on nonintercourse dispatched a special committee to seek the collaboration of towns closer to home, including Salem and Marblehead.[3] Within a few days Boston's representatives were in

Salem conferring with Pickering, Derby, and other town leaders. In short order the agenda of a conveniently timed upcoming town meeting had been altered to include the question of the Boston Port Bill.[4]

On the day of the meeting itself, the *Essex Gazette* appeared with news that emphasized the importance of this particular meeting. It was rumored that the newly appointed governor, Thomas Gage, had orders to move the capital from Boston to Salem, and that he was to bring a large military force with him. It now became imperative to unite in support of Boston. The entire future, Samuel Hall wrote, depended upon how Americans responded to Parliament's challenge at this critical juncture. "The proceedings of the Colonies on this most alarming occasion must necessarily be of the highest importance—they will determine whether we shall be SLAVES or FREEMEN—there is no alternative."[5]

The Salem town meeting needed no prodding from the *Gazette*. First, two conservative Whigs, Richard Derby and John Pickering, were elected to represent the town at the forthcoming session of the General Court. Then the town finally elected a Committee of Safety and Correspondence with Timothy Pickering (who had earlier opposed the creation of such a committee) as its chairman. Finally, Salem voted its solidarity with Boston, urging the other colonies to join with Massachusetts in a complete program of nonintercourse with Britain and the British West Indies until the Port Act had been repealed.[6]

The speculation that the capital was to be moved to Salem proved accurate. On June 2, 1774, General and Mrs. Gage, in company with many of the ministry's friends in Boston, made the twenty-mile journey to Salem. As the procession neared the town, it was met by a swelling stream of horsemen, carriages, chairs, and wagons that had come out from Salem and nearby Marblehead to join the governor. By the time he arrived, Gage headed a parade, a minor spectacle that trailed through the streets of Salem to the home of William Browne, colonel of the Essex County militia and a leading Tory. There Gage was publicly welcomed, and there he began his short-lived career as the civil governor of Massachusetts.[7]

The ministry had many sound reasons for moving the capital to Salem.[8] There was one advantage to the move, however, that London had not considered but that nevertheless served its purposes well. Salem stood to gain financially, first because Boston was closed to shipping, and further by becoming the provincial capital. If a number of her merchants could be induced to cooperate with the ministry, this would undermine provincial solidarity. Resistance to the Port Act might then more easily be crushed. This thought was on more than a few minds at the time. John Adams, for example, recalled that often during his administration Thomas Hutchinson had dangled the prospect of becoming the capital before Salem. In the past the town had resisted, largely because it was clear that the army would move with the governor, and Salem did not want that.[9] In June 1774, however, the government and the army were already in Salem whether the people there liked it or not. Why not, then, accept the advantages offered as long as the disadvantages were already to be endured?

This, evidently, was the thinking of a number of loyalists in town who early in June spoke out in a petition to the governor. Earlier these "freeholders and merchants" had not felt secure enough to oppose the resolution of solidarity with Boston. Now, however, with British bayonets to protect them, they promised that if their rights were guaranteed Salem's trade would flourish.[10] Gage, delighted at this early manifestation of disunity, responded enthusiastically.[11]

Pickering and the rest of the town's Whig leadership were as nonplused as Gage was pleased by this development. The loyalist petition raised questions about Salem's support for Boston throughout the colony. To quiet these fears they sent their own message to Gage, one signed by almost three times as many merchants and freeholders as the earlier one. It was politely phrased, but nevertheless to the point. Though a "happy union with Great Britain" was "anxiously" hoped for, the Whig petition made it clear that the price currently being asked by the ministry was too high. The town would not acquiesce in the Port Act.[12]

Gage, who was having his difficulties with Salem's Whigs, found the transplanted assembly which convened on June 7 in Salem's court house no more cooperative. At first some pretense was made that the legislators might be willing to seek accommodation with London. But then on June 17, while the assembly was in session, the doors to the legislative chambers were locked. Samuel Adams "misplaced" the key. The majority then voted Massachusetts' adherence to a Continental Congress shortly to be convened in Philadelphia, and elected representatives. At the last moment, Gage was informed of what was afoot by a loyalist representative who slipped from the hall just before the doors were locked. Too late, the governor sent his secretary scurrying over to the court house to dissolve the legislature before it could act. The doors remained locked, and the assembly concluded the business at hand while George Flucker stood outside in the hall, reading the governor's proclamation.[13]

After the dissolution of the legislature, Massachusetts seethed. Boston remained obdurate, refusing to pay for the tea, the port remained closed, and Governor Gage gave every indication that he was content to remain permanently in Salem. As the summer progressed, there was much talk of insurrection throughout the province, and though he said he did not credit it, Gage took precautions. Before the second week in July, he had five regiments at his disposal, with two more on the way.[14]

No incidents were reported between the troops stationed in Salem and the townspeople, but tensions were increasing, and for those in town who continued to support the ministry, it was apparent that only the king's troops stood between them and popular retribution. A few shopkeepers, for example, insisted on selling tea despite the general feeling against it. Whig displeasure was made clear one evening in the middle of July when one store was broken into and eighty pounds of tea were dumped in the street and destroyed. The cask itself was then tied to the public whipping post, a warning for all to see the next morning.[15]

The situation then was already volatile when on August 6 news of the Massachusetts Government Act was received. It was a sensation, dwarfing in significance even the Port Act. An overt assault on the charter and the long-established system of provincial government, it first stunned Salem's leadership and then propelled them into action. Quickly, in collaboration with other leaders in Essex County, they laid plans for a county convention to be held at Ipswich. Next, in spite of the fact that the new law forbade town meetings (other than the regular annual election meeting), a special meeting was scheduled to elect delegates to the county convention. Gage, incensed at the threatened violation of the new law, called the selectmen together and lectured them on its meaning. But Pickering and the others stood firm, charging that Parliament had acted unconstitutionally in annulling the charter. The governor then warned that he had come to enforce Parliament's law and that he would hold the selectmen responsible "for any bad consequences." It took little imagination to comprehend the full meaning of Gage's words. Only the day before this angry meeting, transports had disembarked His Majesty's Fifty-ninth Regiment to reinforce the governor in Salem.[16]

The governor and Salem's selectmen were on a collision course. Yet acquiescence in Gage's demands seemed out of the question, both because it would have been an admission of the validity of the Massachusetts Government Act and because popular opinion would have rebelled against it. Pickering and his colleagues met in a desperate last-minute effort to find an alternative. The solution they struck upon, which offered only the slightest hope that a confrontation might be avoided, was to have the town's Committee of Correspondence call the meeting. It would not then be an official town meeting, although it would serve the same purpose.[17] The next move was up to Gage.

Though angry, the governor restrained himself until the last possible moment. He remained determined to enforce the law and was by no means willing to wink at this subterfuge. The town and the entire countryside were so aroused, however, that it probably seemed to him the wisest course to give Salem's leaders as much time as possible to reconsider. It was 8:00 A.M. on August 24, the morning that the town was scheduled to assemble, before Gage acted. He sent his secretary to inform Pickering and the other members of the Committee of Correspondence that he wished to confer with them in one hour, precisely the time the meeting was scheduled to convene.[18] His house was in Danvers, but he had risen early that morning and was waiting at Colonel Browne's house on Essex Street only a short distance from the court house when the committee arrived. Gage, Pickering later wrote, was in an "indecent passion." Well he might have been, for he had no alternative but to enforce the law; yet he realized that if he acted to break up the meeting, it could be the beginning of a massive armed revolt. He stormed and raged, demanding that the committeemen disperse the meeting.[19]

Never, as he took political advantage of the revolutionary situation, had Pickering imagined that one day he would find himself in confrontation with imperial authority. Nor was he really prepared for it. In fact he seems to have been intimidated, even paralyzed, at the sight of Governor Gage in an abusive fury. Therefore, although he was the chairman of Salem's Committee of Correspondence, it was the more aggressive Captain Richard Derby, Jr., who spoke. He told Gage that the people would decide for themselves when to disperse. Irritated, the governor charged that the meeting was a violation of law and was being held for seditious purposes. When Derby retorted that it was neither his nor the people's intention to violate any laws, Gage exploded, warning that he was in Massachusetts to enforce the law, not to "quibble" about it. He then gave the committee notice that if the meeting was not called off, he would send the high sheriff to break it up and would use troops if the need arose. Ultimately the Fifty-ninth Regiment was called out. However, before the troops could be marched into town from their encampment, the meeting, which had begun during this frenzied argument, quickly completed its business by electing a number of delegates, including both John and Timothy Pickering, Derby, and Jonathan Gardner, to the Ipswich County Convention. It then dispersed before the troops arrived. It had been a hairs breadth escape from violence.[20]

Gage had been totally humiliated, and now, acting irrationally and without regard for the possible consequences, he insisted that warrants be issued for the arrest of Salem's entire Committee of Correspondence. Peter Frye, the justice of the peace who issued these warrants, had been one of those who had voted to rescind the Massachusetts Circular Letter in 1768. Over the years, as a result of his persistent support of ministerial policy, he had become even less popular. Now he found himself in an impossible situation. He could not bring himself to disobey the governor. Yet he had to be careful about whom he offended, especially at a moment when the town was on the verge of a popular explosion. Certainly arresting the entire Committee of Correspondence would mean the end of him in Salem.[21]

Whether as a result of fortuitous circumstance or careful calculation, Frye arrested Timothy Pickering before proceeding against the rest of the committee. Pickering, anxious to avoid violence, went voluntarily to Frye's office. There he posted a bond of one hundred pounds and was released.[22] No one will ever know exactly what took place between Frye and Pickering as the two men confronted each other on that fine August day. However, after their talk, Frye temporarily gave up his search for the other members of the committee. It is likely that he and Pickering agreed that violence should be avoided and that Pickering, not Frye, might best accomplish this. Certainly if the other committeemen resisted arrest or insisted on going to jail, the town, indeed the entire region, might explode.

On leaving Frye's office, Pickering sought out his friends on the committee and urged them to submit to arrest and pay bond. Some of his arguments, as when he suggested that resistance was illegal, must have sounded a little foolish. But he was desperately searching for anything that might convince the angry and resentful committeemen to cooperate. "If we opposed now, & the governor should persist in his attempts to execute the laws," he told his friends, "a tumult & carnage must ensue; for the people are exasperated to a high degree."[23]

Pickering had reason to be concerned, for armed men were already assembling in Salem intent upon blocking any move by the governor to arrest the committee. By the evening of August 26, Boston had reports that three thousand were in readiness and that the Marblehead militia was prepared to march to Salem's support.[24]

Despite the explosive situation, Pickering was unable to influence his friends. Richard Derby and four other members of the committee, including Pickering's own brother-in-law, Captain George Williams, were prepared as a group to go to jail. When they were brought before Frye, they all refused to give bond, literally daring him to lock them up.[25] The terrified justice of the peace, who knew that he was sitting on a powder keg, rushed off to confer with the governor.[26]

Gage, however, was not yet ready to accept his humiliation without playing one last, though weak, card. The committee, he announced, had until four that afternoon to surrender themselves, post bail, and agree to appear at the next superior court to answer charges of "high crimes and misdemeanors." If they did not comply, the responsibility for what might take place would rest squarely on their shoulders.[27] Four o'clock came and went, and the other members of the committee did not give bond. Gage nevertheless took no action. He could not, for he had no more than twelve hundred men with him in Salem and another eight hundred in Boston. He was certain that, if fighting actually broke out, as yet unorganized militia units in the region would be sure to swell the already impressive ranks of the opposition.

Hostility toward General Gage had been running high on the North Shore since he had marched the troops into Salem to break up the meeting on August 24. By the twenty-sixth the atmosphere was so highly charged that Captain John Montresor, a member of his staff, felt compelled to warn the general that his life was in danger as long as he remained in the area.[28] There is no solid evidence to suggest exactly how Gage reacted to this personal threat. He may well have taken it seriously, however, for on the very day that Montresor issued his warning, he decided to return to Boston.[29] Once there he began the fortification of Boston Neck.

Timothy Pickering had faltered badly during those anxious days of August 1774. He revealed himself as weak and indecisive, caught between his Whig rhetoric and his fear of confrontation. At a time when the community was in no mood to give ground, his decision to pay bond rather than go to jail might well have cost him dearly. Fortunately the newspaper account of the affair that reached Boston and other nearby towns, an account that was in all likelihood written by Pickering himself, mentioned nothing of his behavior. As far as the general public knew, the Salem Committee of Correspondence had been united, ready to accept imprisonment rather than bow to the dictates of the governor.[30] But private sources told another story, that the committee had been divided and that two members had actually posted bond.[31]

Sensing his vulnerability, Pickering rushed to reaffirm his commitment to the Whig cause, publishing a strident essay in the *Essex Gazette*. Neither he nor other "moderate men" wanted civil war, he wrote. Yet as he perceived it, England and America were on a collision course. Only a last-minute change of heart in London could reverse the tendency of events and forestall what seemed to him, under existing circumstances, the inevitable. The English Constitution, Pickering claimed, had been undermined and corrupted. An all-powerful ministry working with a debased majority in Parliament seemed determined to impose tyranny in America. The passage of the Port Act and the Massachusetts Government Act was proof enough of that, for such measures could never have passed unless "through the boundless means of bribery in the hands of a corrupt ministry." The attempt to establish tyranny in Massachusetts was nothing new. James II and his minion Edmund Andros had tried much the same thing toward the end of the last century. However, Pickering wrote, the current situation was more sinister. King James had attempted to rule without Parliament, but now Parliament was attempting to rule without "the consent of the governed." Worse, while the forms of constitutionalism were cleverly preserved, its very meaning had been corrupted and destroyed. How, Pickering wondered, could any sane man believe that liberty survived "while Boston and Salem were occupied by two thousand British soldiers?" [32]

What is particularly striking about this essay is that even under intense political pressure Pickering remained reluctant to pursue his reasoning to its logical conclusion: he could not bring himself to advocate either violence or independence. Instead he ended the essay on an inconclusive note. "May God preserve us from the calamities of a civil war," he wrote. "Let us conduct with manly firmness but with courteous prudence and then we need not fear the utmost efforts of our unprincipled oppressors." [33]

Pickering was suffering the deepest kind of intellectual agony, the result of a dilemma he could neither resolve nor ignore. He insisted that the Massachusetts Government Act was a nullity. Yet, in the face of British intransigence, how long could violence and civil war be avoided? Other delegates to the Ipswich County Convention shared Pickering's dilemma. It was easy enough to agree that the new law should not be allowed to go into effect.[34] The more critical question, however, one that evidently stimulated heated debate, was whether or not the colony should confine itself to nonviolent measures in its opposition to the law. On this issue Pickering and other so-called moderates won a victory of sorts, for the first in a series of resolutions produced by the convention went no further than to advise the people to "pursue all reasonable measures by which any attempts to enforce an immediate obedience to that act may be defeated." How the people were to accomplish this was left unstated.[35]

The convention also resolved that judges, justices, and all other civil officials holding appointments under the old charter were to be considered the legitimate officers of the colony, and that other men appointed to various positions under the new law should be neither acknowledged nor obeyed. Moreover, those who insisted on supporting the new legislation as well as those who accepted royal appointments under the act were to be considered "malignant enemies" of the province. In an obvious reference to recent events in Salem, the convention further reasserted the right of towns under the charter to hold meetings, and concluded by calling for a provincial congress to organize some kind of colonywide response to the new law.[36]

Pickering hoped to abide by these and other resolutions passed at Ipswich but was simultaneously anxious to avoid violence or anything tending toward a final break with England. Paradoxically, however, as the chairman of the town's Committee of Safety and Correspondence, he frequently found himself with no alternative other than to use force in support of Whig policy. Nothing more clearly reflects this than his management of the question of the importation and sale of tea in Salem.

Only a few days after Gage left town, a merchantman carrying more than thirty casks of tea arrived in the harbor. Pickering, made aware of its arrival by the Marblehead Committee of Correspondence, quickly ordered a guard placed on the ship, thus ensuring that none of the contraband would find its way ashore.[37] Simultaneously, he dispatched an express rider to Boston requesting both information and advice from the Committee of Correspondence there. The tea, it seemed, was consigned to Smith and Atkinson, merchants of Boston.

The Boston committee explained to Pickering that these men denied any knowledge of the shipment. They promised, however, to do what they could to have the tea reshipped to England.[38] This was of little help to Pickering, for the presence of that ship in Salem harbor over any extended period was an invitation to violence. Nor did the Boston committee provide any guidance. It had long since adopted a careful "hands-off" policy regarding the activities of other committees of correspondence and safety.[39] Boston offered nothing more than a reminder of how other towns facing the same situation had reacted. The ultimate decision would have to come from Salem's committee itself.

So for three days the ship remained under guard in the harbor. Finally Pickering's committee ordered it to sail for Halifax.[40] Some might brand this decision radical. The committee had after all used force to prohibit the landing of tea and in a few days' time sent the ship carrying the unwanted cargo packing. In context, however, the committee's response was really rather moderate. First, by placing a guard on the ship Pickering not only enforced the popular ban on the importation of tea, but protected that tea from marauding "Indians" as well.

Second, in view of the excited state of public opinion at this time, there was no possibility that the tea could have been landed without its having been destroyed. Sending it to Halifax, then, was a method of avoiding more extreme violence.

But even after the departure of this most recent shipment, the tea issue persisted. During General Gage's presence in Salem, some merchants had been selling tea on the open market. After Gage and the troops left, Pickering's committee agreed to allow these merchants to sell their remaining stocks before enforcing a ban on future sales. It was an effort on the committee's part to respect the rights of property, at least to the degree public opinion made that possible. Early in October, however, two incidents forced a reversal of this policy. At the beginning of the month, a free Negro who had heard that there might be a market in Salem for tea appeared there with a cask and foolishly offered it for sale. A crowd quickly assembled, the tea was destroyed, and, as the *Gazette* politely put it, the man was "obliged to leave town immediately."[41] Scarcely a week later someone else attempted to smuggle a small quantity of tea into town on a wagon coming from Boston. The wagon was apparently searched, for the tea was discovered. This time a crowd of "several hundred persons" swiftly formed and the tea was publicly burned.[42] The crowd, convinced that such incidents would continue as long as merchants were allowed to sell tea, was prepared to take matters into its own hands. At this point, the Committee of Correspondence belatedly stepped in, forcing those storekeepers who held supplies of tea to turn them in "to be stored," once again using force to avert more serious violence.[43]

In dealing with the tea issue, Pickering had acted against his own inclinations in support of radical policy. He was discovering that the political circumstances of 1774 were choking off options. He faced the same quandary in other sensitive areas where he also found himself acting inconsistently. At Ipswich he had endorsed the principle of political intimidation. Those who refused to resign their commissions under the Massachusetts Government Act were to be branded "malignant enemies" of the people.[44] However, as British authority evaporated and the revolutionary mentality in Massachusetts grew more pronounced, Pickering developed serious second thoughts about the growing popular demand for political conformity. By the autumn of 1774 the public recantation of past sins had become a requirement for those who in the recent past had shown their sympathy for the ministry in its quarrel with Massachusetts.[45] In Salem it even became dangerous to maintain a membership in the Library Society, which had for so long been the gathering place of the Tory element in town.[46] Pickering watched with something less than enthusiasm as dozens of his fellow townsmen, including some personal friends, were coerced into making public apologies in the *Essex Gazette* for their political errors.

All men are, of course, a bundle of contradictions, and some may suggest that it is pointless to remark on Pickering's inconsistencies over a long lifetime. Nonetheless there is something fascinating about this man, who later vigorously enforced conformity through the instrumentality of the Sedition Law in 1798, but who was in 1774 so genuinely concerned about the preservation of the rights of Salem's Tories.[47] He believed that as a group these people represented the backbone of Salem society. Worthy citizens, they would under other circumstances have been considered the town's most responsible element. He despaired for the future if the town should stoop to driving out or destroying these industrious, hard-working people. It was morally wrong, and from the depths of his soul Pickering ached to cry out against it. Again, however, the revolutionary situation forbade this, and Pickering found himself urging those who had offended Whig opinion in the past to apologize publicly. It was the only way they would be allowed to stay, and he truly wanted them to remain, bulwarks of stability in town life. Early in September he actually drafted one such recantation for the hated Peter Frye, who signed and published the document.[48]

In some cases such recantations staved off popular retribution, but for Frye it was not nearly enough. A few weeks after his published statement appeared in the press, a fire mysteriously broke out in his woodhouse.[49] It spread rapidly to his home and store and then jumped to Nathaniel Whitaker's meetinghouse. With leather buckets and primitive fire engines, hundreds rushed into the streets to fight the flames. Muscles ached and strained to keep water from the harbor coming, but it was never enough. It must have been a dry October, for the flames leaped from building to building, and smoke billowed hundreds of feet into the air. For a time the fire seemed unstoppable as first one and then another of the town's vulnerable frame structures fell victim to it. Then, as though cued by some master playwright with a sense for melodrama, more than a hundred volunteers from Marblehead hauling their fire engines and carrying their buckets arrived, if not in the nick of time then at least in time to save Salem from complete disaster. The morning was well on toward noon before the fire had been quenched.

When it was over, one large meetinghouse, the customs house, eight dwellings, and fourteen other buildings had been burned out. Amidst the charred and smoking ruins the firefighters ate a hearty breakfast at Goodale's Tavern.[50] There was an expensive irony in all of this which, provided he had strength enough left to appreciate it, Pickering may have enjoyed. Frye had been burned out, it is true, but so too had his personal and political enemy, the Radical Whig minister Nathaniel Whitaker, whose meetinghouse was completely destroyed. The flames had been no respecter of politics; even the building housing Samuel Hall's *Essex Gazette* was gutted.[51]

In the wake of the Massachusetts Government Act, and concurrent with the growing popular demand for political conformity, a grassroots movement to arm developed throughout New England. Massachusetts was ready to fight, a point it made early on the morning of September 1, 1774, after General Gage's troops seized a powder supply stored near Cambridge. Within a few hours of the event, between three and four thousand men assembled at Cambridge and, had it not been for the efforts of Dr. Joseph Warren and other radical leaders, this might have marked the beginning of the war.[52]

In Essex County the circumstances were not much different, although Marblehead seems to have been more aggressive about arming than Salem or the other towns. Early in October the Marblehead militia decreed that training days would be held four times each week instead of four times each year. At the end of the month the *Gazette* reported that the Marbleheaders were going through their maneuvers in deadly earnest but wasting neither powder nor shot. Samuel Hall was exultant, for "the military spirit prevails greatly, and must lay such a foundation for American liberty, as cannot be shaken by savage despots."[53] Though he did not mention Salem by name, Hall noted that some towns seemed less active. He urged these to follow Marblehead's example, for America's future literally depended upon it. Only "a general Attention to the Art Military" would make Americans "secure, notwithstanding the Designs of oppressive Tyranny."[54]

Pickering, still anxious to avoid civil war, understood that the movement to arm brought conflict one step closer. Nevertheless, when the Massachusetts Provincial Congress passed resolutions calling on local militia companies to organize and prepare for action on short notice, he went right along.[55] This was by no means an easy decision. Many, including his brother-in-law, Paine Wingate, advised against it. This lukewarm New Hampshire Whig thought "the situation of our affairs too precarious to willingly stand in any responsible stations." He intended to remain neutral for as long as possible and advised Pickering to quit the militia and do the same. Nor was Pickering safe from criticism at his office in the Registry of Deeds. There his old friend Mehetibel Higginson and he often became embroiled in heated arguments as she attempted to dissuade him from the course he had charted. Sometimes her acid tongue got the better of her, as when she accused her young friend of being motivated by personal political ambition.[56]

Despite the pleadings of friends and members of his family, Pickering clung to the provincial militia and the Whig coalition. Mrs. Higginson was unquestionably correct in assigning him political motives. It was after all as a Whig that he had risen in Essex County. But Pickering was not so simple a character as that. If in the first place political and social aspirations led him to assume the role of a Whig leader, characteristically he explained his decision in moral terms, soon convincing even himself that righteousness had more to do with his political choices than ambition. If the Whig cause was tainted by the opportunism of some of its more cynical leaders, he wrote, it was nevertheless "founded in justice."[57] He would stand on principle.

Pickering's *Easy Plan of Discipline for a Militia,* a manual of arms that he published early in 1775, serves as a superb example of how he mixed utopian Whig ideas with personal self-interest. The fundamental premise of this pamphlet, carefully articulated, was that America had produced a society different from and superior to Europe's, and that training for the men who would fill the militia's ranks had to reflect a new and enlightened policy. Continental military establishments, Pickering maintained, had lost their keen fighting edge, having been corrupted over generations past. Luxury, that bane of society, found its counterpart in military affairs on the parade ground, where a bewildering array of pointless drills and maneuvers had been developed simply "for show." Why, Pickering wondered, "should we waste our time in strenuous idleness?" Nor did he have any enthusiasm for the flamboyance of European military dress:

> Will a long tail and powdered hair obstruct the passage of the keen edg'd sword? Or a rich garment prevent the entrance of the pointed steel? . . . Away then with the trappings (as well as tricks) of the parade: *Americans* need them not: *their* eyes are not to be dazzled, nor their hearts awed into servility, by the splendor of equipage and dress: *their* minds are too much enlightened to be duped by a glittering outside.[58]

The pamphlet was designed to get back to first principles, for in unaffected simplicity there was strength.

Marshal Saxe, the great French strategist, held that soldiers should be blindly obedient, "mere machines only animated by the voice of their officers." In the European context, Pickering thought, this was inevitable. Armies there were composed of professionals who fought only for pay. But in America, Pickering reasoned, it was essential that "the men be clearly informed of the REASON of every action and movement or the USES to which they can be applied." The militia, after all, was an army of equals, and in such a force orders had first to be explained before they would or should be obeyed. He had no fear that a republican army would be ungovernable, for he was convinced that there could "be a just and necessary subordination and obedience without servility." "There are motives," he explained, "sufficiently powerful to produce submission among a people who are trained and disciplined only to *defend* their *laws, liberties* and *country;* without the terrors of ignominious barbarous scourgings, which disgrace humanity." The point could not be too frequently made:

> As the Militia of America is composed of men of property, and will be engaged not to make conquests for Ambition, but merely in their own defense, so they will need only an information of their duty to dispose them to do it. As they are reasonable beings as such they are to be treated. When men see the reason and use of any action or movement they will learn it with much more alacrity and pleasure.[59]

Pickering did not publish his manual of arms simply out of public spirit or because he was unable to contain his patriotic zeal. His military ambitions dated back at least to 1768 when, as a young lieutenant, he had begun a movement for the reform of Essex County's then wholly undisciplined militia regiment. He wanted a military command and published his *Easy Plan* in part at least to bring his abilities to the attention of the public. Nor was he disappointed. On February 13, 1775, a meeting of regimental officers at Danvers deposed the obdurate Tory William Browne and chose Pickering to replace him as the colonel of the Essex County militia.[60]

Pickering never would have attained this prestigious post had it not been for the revolutionary crisis. He basked in the knowledge that he held an appointment until then reserved for the most powerful gentleman in the community. But as the events of early 1775 were to demonstrate, there existed an unresolved tension between the young colonel's ambition for status and his continuing reluctance to become too deeply embroiled in what was developing into an actual resistance movement. Like so many other "moderate men" of his generation he was not yet prepared to take the last irretrievable step into open rebellion. Exposed as he was, embarrassments inevitably came thick and fast.

Not two weeks after Pickering had been elected to lead the Essex County militia regiment, a British force attempted a surprise landing on the North Shore. Colonel Alexander Leslie's mission was to seize a cache of artillery reportedly being mounted on carriages in North Salem. Pickering should have been able to raise some seventy-five minutemen almost immediately. To be sure, this small band was insufficient to oppose Leslie's three hundred regulars. But the rest of Essex County was organizing. Pickering might have led his men to some convenient location outside Salem and there put together a respectable force. Instead he remained out of sight during most of the day that Leslie raided Salem.[61]

In order to get to the shop where, intelligence had it, the artillery pieces were being kept, Colonel Leslie and his men had to cross the drawbridge over the North River that divided Salem from North Salem. But Captain David Mason and his patriot friends, having first hidden the cannon, drew the bridge, leaving Leslie and his men on the other side with no way to cross. What happened next was pure *opéra bouffe*, for there on that cold February afternoon His Majesty's Sixty-fourth Regiment, surrounded by curious, gawking townspeople, stood and shivered while, on the other side of the stream, Mason and his friends jeered. It was a standoff.[62]

Capturing the artillery was clearly no longer possible, but Leslie had been humiliated and was determined to regain at least some of his dignity by crossing that bridge. He therefore remained at the river throughout the afternoon. It was at this juncture that Pickering finally emerged to play a role in the day's events, not to fight but to mediate a compromise. Leslie was allowed to march his troops across the lowered drawbridge, but only on the condition that he would go no farther than fifty rods beyond the end of the bridge and search for nothing. This he did and, with his dignity sadly ruffled, returned to Boston.[63]

"The affair at the North Bridge," as it came to be known, provided Salem with amused conversation for many weeks. In taverns of an evening or after dinner before their fires, the people told and retold the tale with appropriate dramatic embellishments. Colonel Leslie's adventure, however, might have turned out far differently had he fired on the men who held the bridge. What brought uproarious laughter in retrospect might well have become the bloody beginning of the war for independence. This thought was by no means lost on Timothy Pickering, who anguished over the unknown future. On April 19, 1775, his anguish turned to despair at the news that fighting had broken out between British regulars and a party of militiamen at Lexington.

It was Daniel Epes, the captain of a Danvers militia company, who brought news of the battle to Pickering at the Registry of Deeds.[64] Having delivered this message, Epes returned to his men and caught up with the British rear guard during the retreat from Concord. His company was part of the American force that harassed Earl Percy's retreat from somewhere near Menotomy (Arlington) until finally, exhausted, his men gained the relative security of Boston.[65]

Pickering could have organized his men, been little more than an hour's march behind the Danvers companies, and played a role in the battle that day. Still unwilling to accept the inevitability of war, however, he delayed. Instead of sounding a call to arms, he left his office and hurried to Webb's Tavern, where he called an emergency meeting of the selectmen and other "leading gentlemen." There a debate ensued, with Pickering opposed to taking any action. He confidently predicted that after the engagement at Lexington the British would immediately withdraw to fortified Boston. At any moment, he argued, news was bound to arrive that the engagement had been concluded and peace restored. Salem was too far from the scene for her militia to be of any use. Marching would be a waste of time.[66]

Pickering found himself on the losing side of this debate. Elias and Richard Derby, both very ardent, gave him a difficult time. Someone finally delivered a crunching argument in favor of mobilizing the militia by pointing out that it was actually beside the point whether Salem's men fought in the battle or not. What was important was that at this critical juncture the town demonstrate its willingness to fight. At last Pickering gave in, organized his force, and began the march toward Boston.[67]

But he continued to procrastinate even while on the march. At Danvers, just past the Bell Tavern, though the men had progressed only a short way, he called a halt to "refresh" his troops and to begin the debate anew. He recommended that they wait near Danvers for news "of a British withdrawal." Others in the ranks, particularly the Derby brothers, objected. After about a twenty-minute pause during which the argument seesawed back and forth, the Salem militia once more moved hesitantly on its way. At Medford the column received intelligence that Earl Percy was still on the march for Boston and that he had taken the road via Charlestown. Pickering now had positive information that the British column was still in motion and, moreover, that a change in direction had placed it closer to his force. There was no longer any excuse for delay, and the column moved quickly along the road from Medford to Charlestown.[68]

Major General William Heath, a Massachusetts militia officer, had been busy all that day attempting to organize the dispersed American forces into some semblance of military order. Together with Dr. Joseph Warren, he had been in the thick of the battle for many hours when Pickering, a little ahead of his men, rode briskly up. The two men looked out from Winter Hill at the line of red uniforms receding in the distance and conferred together. Many years later Heath recalled that conversation, asserting that Pickering told him that he had "about 700 men" with him. In his *Memoirs,* Heath went on to suggest that Pickering's delays had cost the province a great victory. "Had these troops arrived a few minutes sooner, the left flank of the British must have been greatly exposed and suffered considerably; perhaps their retreat would have been cut off." [69]

Pickering's recollection of this aspect of that trying day, written in 1807, is far different. Pointing out that he had only about three hundred troops with him, he claimed that he and his men arrived in time to attack the British column on its flank. From the top of a rise they could see "the British force marching from Cambridge to Charlestown . . . and the smoke of musketry." He ordered his men to prime and load and prepared to advance when a message arrived from Heath warning him not to move "for the British now had artillery and could not be approached by muskets alone." It was only later, according to Pickering, that he and Heath conferred, after which he returned to his troops, who were guarding a bridge at Medford. [70]

Neither Heath's nor Pickering's recollections bear much scrutiny. Certainly Heath's charge that Salem's delay cost Massachusetts a complete triumph is open to serious question. But Pickering's writings seem even more fanciful. There is absolutely no evidence that Heath advised Pickering not to attack. Moreover, the reason given by Pickering for Heath's supposed order to hold off makes no sense, for the British had been using field pieces against the American militia all afternoon. Finally, if Pickering had been so instructed, he certainly would have made this known much sooner than he ultimately did, for he was sharply criticized in the immediate aftermath of the Battle of Lexington for his failure to engage the enemy. If Pickering did again hesitate, and he himself testified that he did, it was because he could not yet bring himself to take that last irrevocable step.

Nor was he any more willing to accept war on the day after the battle. On April 26, Joseph Warren, the radical Whig leader, held a council of war at his headquarters in Cambridge. Pickering came in from Medford where his men were encamped. As he rode, evidence that the fighting would continue was all about him, for he came as part of a stream of angry, resolute farmers pouring into Cambridge. Every hour brought more. They came not only from Massachusetts, but from Rhode Island, Connecticut, and New Hampshire as well. In a few days they would be arriving from even more distant parts. Pickering believed that these "zealous & determined" men would not return to their homes before the British in the city had been either driven out or obliterated. Moreover, though he clung still to the hope of reconciliation, he sympathized with them.[71]

Warren arranged the meeting at Cambridge to propose the organization of a regular army for Massachusetts and the beginning of siege operations around Boston.[72] He was determined that Lexington and Concord would not go down in history as one more in the long series of incidents that had in recent years marred Anglo-American relations. This was to be the beginning of civil war. Of the officers who attended, Pickering was the only one to oppose Warren. He argued that such an operation would be militarily foolhardy, that it would lead to great loss of life among the civilian population of the city. Moreover, even if a siege were successful and the British were driven to evacuate, Britain's control of the seas would spell Boston's doom. The town could easily be destroyed by naval gunfire, and there was nothing anyone on the American side could do about that. These military arguments against the beginning of offensive operations were, strictly speaking, not to the point. Admitting that the people, having taken up arms, could not now "tamely" lay them down again, he nonetheless believed that "pacification upon honourable terms" was still attainable. He hoped the militia would take a strictly defensive position around Boston while negotiations were begun with General Gage. A "compromise," he thought, might yet be reached.[73]

With nothing more substantial than this to offer as an alternative to war, Pickering stood alone. On the day following, the Provincial Committee of Safety, acting on its own authority since the Provincial Congress was not in session, established a regular army of eight thousand men to be enlisted for seven months.[74] General officers were requested to compile lists of those militiamen who would be willing to enlist in the new regular force. Pickering refused to serve, after the meeting, returning to his troops. With the exception of those who remained to enlist, he returned with them to Salem.

THREE

A Taste of Battle

ONCE BACK IN SALEM, Pickering quickly concluded that there was little choice but to support the war. The middle ground that he had held since 1770 had at last given way beneath him. In the emotionally charged atmosphere following the battle there was a great deal to be lost by further delay. His career, his prestige in the community, his status as a leader, all these had been built on Whig foundations. Others, less prominent, had the option of maintaining a kind of personal neutrality by remaining quietly at home. But that was not a possibility for a previously outspoken Whig political leader who was also the colonel of Essex County's militia regiment.

The decision to aid the rebellion was costly to Pickering in a number of personal ways. Most important, it permanently shattered his relationship with his father, who remained a Tory to the end of his life. It strained friendships too, sometimes to the breaking point. One of the earliest casualties was Pickering's long and close relationship with John Higginson's widow, Mehetibel. After hostilities began their arguments grew heated as she prepared to emigrate to Halifax and tried to convince him to do the same. Angrily Pickering defended himself. He had not intended the imperial crisis to end in civil war, yet war had come. What then were his alternatives? He was by no means convinced that the so-called friends of government had a monopoly on virtue. On the contrary, with his political ambitions and ideological convictions at last in harmony, he vehemently defended the Whig position.[1] The issue had come down to a choice between freedom and slavery, he exclaimed. Then, more in sadness than in anger, he added, "I do not feel an inclination to survive the liberties of my country."[2]

If Pickering experienced certain personal difficulties in the aftermath of the Battle of Lexington, these were partially mitigated by new opportunities. High-ranking Tories had fled their homes to sanctuary in Boston, Halifax, or England, leaving behind offices to be filled. Pickering, having already become town clerk and register of deeds for the county as well as colonel of the militia, hoped to replace the exiled Peter Frye as justice of the Court of Common Pleas. His nomination, however, ran into stiff opposition in the legislature where some recalled his recent objections to Joseph Warren's plan for a provincial army and the beginning of siege operations around Boston.[3]

Informed of these difficulties, Pickering scrambled to exonerate himself. His stand against Warren, he wrote, had been founded not upon political but upon military considerations. He had never, he claimed, opposed a break with England on political grounds. It was simply that Massachusetts was unprepared for war. At Cambridge, Pickering went on, the majority had ruled, and he was ready to support the war fully and without reservation.[4] This was an altogether unconvincing performance. Nevertheless, with what amounted to a loyalty oath in hand, Pickering's friends in the legislature were able to win him the new appointment.[5] Shortly before the end of the year he was also appointed the Admiralty Court judge for the counties of Suffolk, Middlesex, and Essex.

Politics was finally beginning to pay. The fees Pickering collected from his various offices amounted to a substantial living. And it was just in time, too, for he had recently met and was paying court to Rebecca White, from the nearby town of Bradshaw. During the first thirty years of his life Pickering had very little to do with members of the opposite sex. He was shy and insecure around women. Tall but physically awkward, bald and so nearsighted that he was virtually blind without his spectacles, Pickering was painfully aware of his own unattractiveness. What a misfortune, especially for one grown up in a generation that expected a certain degree of gallantry from its gentlemen.

Finally, however, at the age of thirty, he fell in love. Pickering did not think Beckey White beautiful. But then he was by no means certain that physical beauty was much of an asset. Far more important in his scheme of things (as he frequently though perhaps undiplomatically reminded his *nearest friend*) were an honest heart and a cultivated mind. In young Rebecca's tenderness, Pickering discovered something else of great worth. He found a warmth that stimulated a kind of inner self-confidence he had never known before. Beckey's youth, for she was nine years younger than he, contributed to still another dimension of their relationship. Timothy was not only her lover but, in his own mind at least, her protector and teacher as well.[6]

During the time that the two young people courted, Pickering revealed romantic inclinations he had never shown before. He frequently traveled the twenty miles to Bradshaw to spend the day with Beckey. When he couldn't be there, he wrote love letters to her for the sheer pleasure of the images and feelings they raised in his mind. Poetry flowed from his pen: "Night never shuts the busy scenes of day / nor dawns the morning, but I think of you." In December 1775, after one of his visits with Beckey, he was so exuberant that, though the snow was thick upon the ground, he walked all the way home. It took him eight hours "through a crusty, trackless snow, on paths ill trodden" but it seemed worth it, an expression of his unbounded happiness.[7] He was a schoolboy on holiday and in love with the world. When, on April 8, 1776, the two young people were married, Pickering thought himself a completely happy man. He was devoted to his new wife, and his political career was going very well.

Before the end of the year, however, the war intruded directly into the New Englander's personal life. A serious military crisis developed in New York, where General Washington had been outmaneuvered and his army defeated in the Battle of Long Island. Only a miraculous nighttime retreat to the mainland saved the Americans on the island from annihilation or capture. Forced into a retreat across New Jersey that did not come to a halt until he had put the Delaware River between himself and the pursuing British, Washington found himself in an extremely dangerous situation. General Howe seemed to be waiting upon but two developments before crushing him and taking Philadelphia. The first was solid ice upon which to cross the river. The second was the evaporation of his little force. By the middle of the month, the army's paper strength had shrunk to fewer than eight thousand men, and no more than five thousand of these were fit for duty. On January 1 the situation would become even worse, for the enlistment period of a large number of militiamen would then be over. When these men left, as surely they would, for they were dispirited from defeat, retreat, and inadequate transport and supplies, his "army" would number no more than fifteen hundred men.[8] Desperate, Washington put out a call for volunteers to fill his thinning ranks. His appeal was relayed to militia units throughout New England.

Pickering faced a difficult choice. As the colonel of the regiment he was required to recruit men, and he knew that he himself should volunteer. But Beckey, who was more than six months pregnant, made a powerful argument against this. Torn by conflicting loyalties, he at last decided that he could not reject Washington's appeal. Assembling the militia, Pickering made an impassioned plea for three-month volunteers, concluding with the dramatic announcement that he would be the first to go. With the harvest season behind them, the men responded enthusiastically.[9] On Christmas Eve, 1776, while far away on the Delaware Washington prepared for his dramatic raid against the Hessian forces at Trenton, Pickering led his regiment toward Providence, Rhode Island. There it became part of a larger force commanded by General Benjamin Lincoln. The ultimate destination of this small army was New Jersey, where it was to reinforce Washington's dwindling command.

The march of the Essex County militia regiment was, in its own way, symbolic of Pickering's personal convictions about the meaning of the war. Those who happened to be abroad on that wintry day as the regiment paraded were treated to a truly republican spectacle. There were no resplendent uniforms. And the colonel, instead of riding horseback at the head of the column, marched with a pack and blanket strapped to his back like any other soldier. Throughout the war, it remained a conviction of his that in a republican army the officers should suffer along with their men and that the best, indeed, the only way to lead American soldiers was to do as they did, and outdo them at it.[10]

During his long lifetime Timothy Pickering enjoyed thinking of himself as a man of moderation and control. He placed great emphasis on personal simplicity. He dressed plainly, eschewed powder or a wig for his bald head—in short, worked painstakingly to create the outward image of a simple republican. His ostentatious lack of ostentation, however, offers a clue to the inner man. He was, by his very nature, incapable of doing anything in a moderate way. Whether in his dress, his eating habits (which were quite simple), or his politics, he was a man of seething passion and unparalleled determination, forever in search of righteousness or, as he preferred to call it, truth. Once he had satisfied himself as to the nature of truth, once he had committed himself to a purpose, he normally struggled with all his ability to see it accomplished. In this way he became passionately committed to the war effort. Though slow at first, once he was involved, few surpassed him in zeal, expected more of their countrymen, or were so easily embittered when the movement failed to live up to his conception of its promise. Pickering was in short an extremely vulnerable ideologue, and the war for independence was to prove a long, disillusioning experience for him.

At Providence, Pickering joined General Lincoln's force which then marched to Danbury, Connecticut, a staging area for troops operating in the New York–New Jersey region. It was on this leg of the journey that Pickering first learned of Washington's important victory at Trenton. This success, followed by another triumph at Princeton a few days later, altered the military situation entirely. The enemy, seemingly dominant only days before, was now on the defensive, and the commander in chief saw the opportunity to drive him entirely out of New Jersey. Moreover, these two victories had revived the flagging spirits of cautious Pennsylvania and New Jersey Whigs. Militiamen who had hung back when they were needed now began to flow into Washington's temporary headquarters at Newton. The manpower so urgently called for as late as December 18 was, only ten days later, of little immediate importance.[11]

There were other uses for the men from New England, however. Washington believed that Howe had overextended himself by pushing into New Jersey. If, after having suffered successive defeats at Trenton and Princeton, he were to be threatened from the rear, he might be enticed into any one of a number of tactical errors, the most likely of which was a retreat to New York City that would put him in serious supply difficulties. Soon orders were on their way. General William Heath, the senior Massachusetts officer in the area, was instructed to take command of the New England militia and make a feint in the direction of New York City.[12] A week later in Danbury, Pickering received his new orders, and after detaching two companies to reinforce the Americans holding the Highlands, a strategic mountain pass on the North River, he paraded his regiment and marched for North Castle and a rendezvous with Heath. The day was cold and the ground was covered with ice and snow. Nevertheless, the Essex County militia covered twenty-six miles before finding quarters for the night at Bedford, about six miles from North Castle. On the morning of the fourteenth, Pickering rested his men, wearied by the exertions of the preceding day, and took the opportunity to write a short letter to his wife. Soon, he wrote, he would get his first taste of action. "God grant us success and restore me with honor to my beloved." Later in the day, he paraded his regiment and moved out.[13]

Pickering's emotional letter to his wife must in retrospect have seemed a bit foolish. He was about to participate not in some heroic military encounter, but in a comedy of errors with Heath playing the leading role while he, Lincoln, and the rest of the officers stood by in frustrated humiliation. General Heath had decided to use his approximately thirty-five hundred militiamen in an assault on Fort Independence near Kingsbridge, just north of New York City. His plan was simplicity itself. At sunrise on the morning of January 18 the American force, divided into three columns, was to storm the fort. There was, Pickering later noted, only one difficulty. The enemy's little stronghold was too well constructed to be taken in this way, a fact Heath might easily have discovered had he bothered to reconnoiter his target beforehand.

In the initial attack Pickering's regiment drove in a few pickets who occupied barracks outside the fort, and captured some houses in the surrounding area. There followed some idle cannonading, with Heath's six-pound cannon balls bouncing harmlessly off the walls of the well-built fortification. The Hessians and New Yorkers within replied with eighteen-pounders. Then, while Pickering cringed in embarrassment, Heath, "with ridiculous parade and groundless vain expectation," delivered an ultimatum to the enemy threatening to put the garrison to the sword if it did not surrender. Pickering and the other officers could hardly believe their ears. The fort was "ditched, fraised and surrounded by an *abatis.*" In Pickering's view the New Englanders had neither the discipline to storm it nor the artillery to destroy it. The enemy would have had to "be fools and arrant cowards to have regarded" Heath's demands. That they weren't and didn't was no surprise to him.[14]

For almost two weeks Heath held his position. Nothing Pickering or the other officers could do or say would budge him, even though some of the men were suffering from exposure and rations were short. Then, on January 30, a British man-of-war and thirteen troop transports were sighted in Long Island Sound. Suddenly Heath panicked. Fearful that this new British force would land in his rear, he ordered an immediate retreat that did not come to a halt until he had raced all the way to White Plains. This headlong flight from fantasy (the British were not at all concerned with Heath's doings) proved the capstone to two weeks of incredible and exhausting foolishness, a fitting end to the siege of Fort Independence.[15] Heath had been sent on this expedition to frighten the British, but he succeeded only in amusing them. Indeed, General Howe was so unimpressed that he actually weakened his force in New York City at this time to strengthen the garrison at New Brunswick.[16]

If Timothy Pickering's first experience as a soldier of the Revolution was disappointing, his second was inspiring. Shortly after the end of the unsuccessful siege of Fort Independence, orders arrived assigning the Essex militia to the Main Army. Nine laborious days later, he and his men arrived in Morristown.[17] There Pickering discovered in Washington and among the youthful and dedicated men who served on his staff the kind of self-sacrificing resolve he truly admired. It is curious, considering Pickering's studied efforts in later years to reduce Washington's prestige, but this earliest contact between the two men was very positive. The New

Englander served happily in Washington's command, and the general was pleased to have him.

The remaining weeks of Pickering's enlistment passed uneventfully at Morristown. In late March, with mixed memories of his service, he set out for home. To the delight of family and friends, he arrived in Salem on April 1, 1777, and saw for the first time his little son John, already six weeks old. For three months he had endured miserable cold, snow, and all the discomforts of a winter campaign. He had been the victim of Heath's ineptitude and a witness to Washington's unhappy plight. But now he was home. Together with Beckey and the baby he prepared to take up once again a life of happy domesticity.

Shortly after his return to Salem, Pickering was offered an appointment as adjutant general in the Continental Army. He was loath to reject this opportunity to leap from the circumscribed existence he had originally projected for himself in Essex County into the grand arena of national political and military affairs. But there were conflicting responsibilities at home. John was just a baby, and Beckey again objected to her husband's going off to the army. Reluctantly, therefore, he at first turned Washington down.[18] But in the days that followed he found that he could not let the matter rest. Before long he had persuaded himself that it was his duty to join Washington's staff. Rebecca was in all likelihood somewhat more difficult to convince, but in the end he may even have won her approval. It made no sense, he pointed out, for Whigs to remain at home and deny the army their support. Its failure would be a "general calamity," a disaster for all Whigs, himself included. Quite characteristically, Pickering had translated his own driving ambitions into a moral imperative.[19]

As the adjutant general of the army, Pickering quickly came to define the revolutionary struggle as a moral crusade; he set unrealistic goals, expecting a kind of uncompromising national commitment that in more rational moments even he might have admitted was delusionary. His assessment of America's military situation was overly optimistic as well. He estimated that there were five hundred thousand men in the United States able to bear arms. British forces numbered perhaps twenty thousand. How could America lose? And indeed, before leaving Salem, Pickering prophesied an end to the war by the winter of 1778. Once in the heady atmosphere around headquarters, however, he altered his estimate, and wrote expansively of final victory within a year.[20]

If Pickering expected a united American people to react to the challenge of war with virtue and sacrifice, he also had some rather clear-cut opinions about what sort of moral character the army of the American republic ought to display. Among some he found a deep moral commitment. But too many officers, he thought, whiled away the long weeks and months in camp by gambling, drinking too much, and avoiding the dreary but important business of drilling and disciplining the soldiers. Whenever such abuses came to his attention, Pickering was quick to seek a remedy. Even the army's chaplains were not exempt from his studious concern. On learning that divine services might or might not be held, depending on the whereabouts and sometimes the sobriety of these men of God, he quickly took them to task. One of his first orders as adjutant general was a warning to the chaplains that absence from their brigades would not be tolerated. Officers and men too were warned to attend religious observances, and to do so regularly. "The Commander-in-Chief expects an exact compliance with this order, and directs it to be observed in future as an invariable rule of practice." Failure to attend church services, Pickering threatened, "will be considered not only a breach of orders but a disregard of decency, virtue, & religion."[21]

On the whole, however, the level of corruption Pickering found in the army was by no means so troublesome to him as the growing concern he felt for the moral rot he thought he saw developing throughout society as a whole. The campaign of 1777 was a jarring experience for him, not only because it did not result in that decisive victory he had so confidently predicted, but also because it revealed all too clearly to him that his earliest assumptions about the innate virtue of the American people had been misguided. From the Battle of Brandywine to the desperation of Valley Forge was one long grueling and depressing lesson for Pickering.

Summer on the eastern seaboard is normally warm, but July and August 1777 were the warmest months in a generation. In Philadelphia, John Adams complained that he and his colleagues in Congress had been "sweltering for a great number of days together under the scalding wrath of the Dog Star."[22] It was much worse for poorly shod American soldiers tramping the scorching roads. Adding to the army's difficulties, both the Quartermaster General's Office and the Commissariat had nearly broken down. The army was, therefore, forced to bargain for provisions with the people in the countryside. Although food was plentiful, the farmers, almost without exception, charged extortionate prices. This embittered many, but few more than Pickering. "Pennsylvania, for enhancing the price of commodities," he wrote, "is the vilest place on the continent."[23]

Nor did his irritation abate as General Howe advanced on Philadelphia, for of the state's sixty-five thousand militiamen, fewer than two thousand actually joined the army. Those who did were frequently unreliable, often deserting in great numbers. Indignantly the adjutant general poured out his wrath to his brother. Before he arrived in camp, he had often been told that many who lived farther south were in the habit of ridiculing New England's militia. He "had expected something better" in the middle states. But no militia could be more despicable than Pennsylvania's.[24]

On the eve of the Battle of Brandywine, as Pickering contemplated the dangers to come, his emotions fluctuated in a sort of passionate confusion. He wondered whether Americans really deserved to win their liberty. Though he concluded that they did, it was not because they were really so virtuous as he had once believed. On the contrary, he was ready to admit that his was "doubtless a wicked generation" and that even the army, which he still insisted was the central repository of virtue in the country, "too much abounds in profaneness and debauchery." No, America would not ultimately triumph because of her unquestioned moral worth. Rather her victory would be the result of the unhappy fact that the enemy was even more degenerate. Too, the cause of liberty was just and transcended the interests of America alone. All of Western civilization was involved. As he sat in his quarters at night, writing by lamplight to his wife far away in Salem, he knew that what happened in Pennsylvania in the next few weeks would be of great consequence to all "the poor oppressed people in every kingdom in Europe."[25]

Now convinced that because of a lack of popular support the war would be a long and grueling contest, Pickering concluded that this was necessary, for purification could only come to America through the fire of affliction and war. His conversion to this Old Testament view by no means marked him out as singular. It was an attitude characteristic at this time of many among the most passionate American republicans. John Adams, for example, contemplated the loss of Philadelphia to the British with equanimity. The British occupation would, he believed, "purify this City of its Dross. Either the Furnace of Affliction would refine it of its impurities, or it would be purged yet so as by fire." Adams's friend Benjamin Rush agreed. "Liberty without virtue," he thought, was no blessing, and virtue could only be earned through trial. As Rush waited in Philadelphia for news of battles yet to take place, he prayed that victory would not come too quickly or easily. "A peace at this time would be the greatest curse that could befall us. I hope the war will last until it introduces among us the same temperance in pleasure, the same modesty in dress, the same justice in business, and the same veneration for the name of the Deity which distinguished our ancestors."[26]

Although Pickering had served with the army during the preceding winter, the campaign of 1777 was his first taste of real combat. It was a confusing and depressing experience for him, and he found it extremely difficult to maintain his emotional equilibrium in the face of a kaleidoscopically changing military situation. During this time he revealed that fundamentally, though he had once written enthusiastically about an army of citizen soldiers, like so many other officers, he was predisposed to favor a large, regular army for America. Such a force would probably have been much more effective than the confusion of Continental troops and militia that Washington commanded. To say this much, however, is to miss an important point that neither Pickering nor most other officers seemed to appreciate. The kind of fluid force that Washington led actually had some advantages, the most significant of which was its truly remarkable capacity for self-regeneration in the aftermath of a tactical defeat. At critical moments some militia and volunteers nearly always appeared, just as Pickering and his men had in December 1776. This is not to say that Pickering was any less observant than others attached to Washington's staff, or even that he was wrong in believing a regular army would have been better for America. It is, however, useful in explaining both the extraordinary emotional gyrations he experienced that autumn and his persistent failure in judging the seriousness of the military situation.

In the aftermath of the Battle of Brandywine, for example, no one could have been more depressed than he. On the evening of the day of the battle, together with Washington and the rest of the staff, he lay exhausted in cramped quarters at Chester. Little was said. All were weary and emotionally spent. Robert Harrison, Washington's private secretary and Pickering's close friend, was so completely worn down that he could barely move, let alone write the letter Washington had ordered sent to the president of Congress informing him of the defeat. Though his body ached and his myopic eyes burned with strain and fatigue after a long day in the broiling sun, Pickering undertook the task himself. It was a despairing letter, so depressing in fact that Washington ordered a revision that included an optimistic prognosis for the future. At the general's insistence, then, Pickering managed, as he brought the unhappy narrative to a conclusion, to end it on something other than a note of hopelessness. "Notwithstanding the misfortune of the day," he wrote, "I am happy to find the troops in good spirits, and I hope another time we shall compensate for the losses now sustained."[27]

Pickering wrote as he had been instructed, but without conviction. Yet only a week later, rearmed and reinforced, the army was ready to try its luck once more. Again, however, the pattern of frustration was repeated. Just before the British main force engaged the Americans near the Warren Tavern on the Philadelphia Road, a drenching rain began to fall that quickly penetrated the cartridge boxes of the Americans and ruined their entire supply of ammunition. An army that had been prepared for battle was, only moments later, forced to march miles through a torrential downpour to keep clear of an enemy whose principal weapon was the bayonet and whose cartridges remained dry in watertight containers.[28]

As before, Pickering's optimism quickly waned, for in the aftermath of this second disappointment the desertion rate skyrocketed. Men left in such numbers that it was impossible to keep an accurate record of how many were actually present and fit for duty. Pickering wondered whether the entire army was on the verge of dissolution. In a fit of depression, he wrote to his brother John that the army had lost more men in a few days through "straggling and desertions" than had been killed or wounded in recent battles.[29]

Yet, once again, the situation rapidly improved. Reinforcements soon arrived from Peekskill, New York. Others came from Connecticut and New Jersey. Militia from Maryland arrived in some numbers, too. By early October Pickering was no longer despairing. Less than a month after the last aborted battle, Washington had more men under his direct command than did General Howe. Preparations began for still another encounter.

This series of setbacks suffered by the Main Army in 1777 not only kept Pickering in a regular state of emotional exhaustion, it also gave him reason to question Washington's abilities as a general officer. A harsh judge of others, Pickering believed that in each of the three major engagements of the campaign, the Virginian had made costly mistakes. At Brandywine, for example, he thought poor staff work was largely responsible for the defeat. The creek had not been reconnoitered carefully. Washington was unaware of a fording place to the north of Chad's Ford that allowed Howe to outflank him. Nor did he take sufficient steps to keep himself informed of Howe's movements prior to the battle. With more careful preparations and better intelligence, Pickering felt confident that the Americans might have won the Battle of Brandywine.[30]

A week after this, at the abortive battle that almost took place near the Warren Tavern, Pickering thought he discerned in Washington's conduct a dangerous indecisiveness. Skirmishing between advance elements of the two armies had already taken place and the British main force was advancing when it began to rain. As the rain increased, the American artillery began sinking into the mud. Together, Pickering and Nathanael Greene urged the general to withdraw to a higher, more defensible position in the rear, and to pull back the artillery. Otherwise, if it became necessary to retreat, the guns would be lost. With the enemy already moving toward his lines, however, Washington proved hesitant. There ensued a frustrating, time-wasting debate among all of the high-ranking officers before the decision to withdraw to a high ridge behind was finally made.[31]

On another occasion, at Germantown, Pickering was convinced that Washington's indecision actually cost him the victory. The attack, though well planned, had not begun well. Almost two-thirds of the entire American force, the column under Greene's command, was more than an hour late getting to the battlefield. Nevertheless, in the early fighting the Americans had much the better of it and managed to drive the British before them. It was a foggy, windless day, made more obscure by the smoke and haze created by the firing. In the confusion and mist the British managed to station about two hundred men in a large, well-built stone house, the former residence of Judge Benjamin Chew. This building was directly in the line of the American advance. From their little fortress these men poured a deadly fire into the advancing Americans. They "annoyed us prodigiously," Pickering testified, "and absolutely stopped our pursuit."[32]

Pickering wanted to bypass the house and urged Washington to station a small contingent of men there to keep the garrison within penned up. In the meantime, he proposed that the advance be pressed to keep the initiative. The general, however, was dubious, and again a frustrating debate ensued. Henry Knox warned that it was tactically wrong to leave "a castle" in one's rear, and in the midst of the battle actually produced a book on military strategy to support his contention. Washington was won over to the artilleryman's point of view while Pickering fumed. In his estimation Knox and Washington had frittered away more than an hour and the opportunity for a smashing victory in a fruitless attempt to drive the defenders from Judge Chew's house.[33] Then suddenly the tide of the battle turned. As Pickering noted in his journal, "our troops gave way on all sides, and retired with precipitation." This was, if anything, an understatement, for it seems clear that at that critical moment in the battle, panic gripped the American forces and they fled in something akin to uncontrolled terror. Certainly nothing their officers could do managed to slow down what turned into a rout.[34]

As far as Pickering was concerned the fog and smoke which many relied upon to explain the defeat at Germantown actually explained very little. The enemy, also blinded, won. Though he was willing to admit that the haze probably hurt the Americans more than it did the British, this was no satisfactory explanation for what occurred that day. With victory in his grasp, Pickering charged, Washington had thrown his opportunities away. Although ungenerous, Pickering probably did not miss the mark by much. Even Washington agreed. Had he not delayed at the Chew house, the general later told Pennsylvania's Joseph Reed, the outcome would have been much different.[35]

By the end of the campaign of 1777, Pickering was not, then, among Washington's greatest admirers. But he was no mindless critic either. He thought that those in Congress who were then making invidious comparisons between Washington and Horatio Gates, the victor at Saratoga, were being ridiculous. Gates could not have accomplished more in Pennsylvania than had Washington. On the contrary, in spite of the indecisiveness he deplored, he still considered Washington the best general officer in the American army. "In point of solid judgment," he wrote to his Salem friend William Pickman, "I do not, among all the general officers I have met with know his superior, and for attention to business perhaps he has no equal."[36]

The critical element in the mosaic of defeat patterned in Pennsylvania, Pickering thought, was not Washington's leadership, but the hostility of the people there. He tried but could not imagine Howe winning such a series of victories in New England. There, the militia would have turned out in force to resist his advance. In Pennsylvania, Pickering counted himself lucky that they did not turn out in greater numbers against America. It would have been bad enough had the Pennsylvanians only refused to help fight the British. But it was worse even than this, for as the army slogged along Pennsylvania's muddy roads, the people along the way would sell nothing to the army save at extortionate prices paid in specie. In helpless indignation Pickering wrote that the farmers "refuse even to supply our poor wounded men... with necessary provisions, without the *solid coin*." He took solace in one thing only: the war was going to continue on their ground and it was they who would suffer its "calamities." It was what they deserved. Washington was by no means to blame for the failure of the unfortunate campaign of 1777; Pennsylvania was.[37]

FOUR

The Board of War

IN NOVEMBER 1777, Pickering learned that he had been appointed to the recently reorganized Board of War. Reassignment, however, did not spare him from all of that dreadful winter at Valley Forge, for it took General Washington three months to find a replacement. Though Pickering did not suffer personally during this interval, what he witnessed would not quickly be forgotten. The army, lacking food, tools, shelter, and clothing, was melting away. Its official strength was 21,788 men. But as early as December Pickering calculated that only 9,976 were present, and fully 10 percent of these were unfit for duty because they lacked adequate shoes and clothing.[1]

Desperate as things were in camp, a visit to the military hospital at Reading proved even more shocking. There the wounded, lingering in pain and filth, experienced critical shortages. Without blankets, bandages, or even fresh clothing, they lay as they had been brought in from the battlefield in their torn and bloody garments.[2] Doctor James Craik, who worked in the hospital at Reading, wrote despairingly to Pickering of the situation there. What was to be done only "God of Heaven knows," he exclaimed. Unless dramatic changes took place quickly he expected the men there would "die with putrid disorders." He begged Pickering to aid in the search for supplies.[3]

Pickering did what he could, urging friends and relatives in New England to locate clothing and other supplies for the army. What he discovered both astonished and appalled him. There was no shortage of cloth in New England. On the contrary, privateersmen had captured so much woolen cloth in the last few months that there was a glut on the New England market. The army in fact might have been well clothed and the hospital well supplied had either the Clothier General's Department or Congress bothered to make the necessary purchases.

John Pickering found the entire situation terribly ironic. Once he had opposed independence because he was convinced that the colonies did not have the resources to sustain a war effort. Now he discovered that the resources were available but not utilized. He did not know whose fault it was that the army was "naked & starved." But, he argued, "if no remedies can be applied we had better contend no longer. The disgrace of a submission to Britain cannot equal that of having an army so treated." [4]

It was only toward the end of November that Pickering received the cheering news that Congress had instructed the prominent merchant Samuel Otis to purchase available woolens and see to their manufacture. Though Otis acted quickly, it was too late, for as winter approached the roads became impassable. Little would reach the stranded men at Valley Forge before spring. Surrounded by miserable suffering soldiers, Pickering was left to reflect bitterly on a letter from his friend William Pickman, who wrote that New England had hardly ever been so prosperous. Some privateersmen, it was true, had run into bad luck, but by and large privateering was immensely profitable and "many emerging fortunes" were the result of it. [5]

In January 1778, Pickering left Valley Forge for the provisional American capital in the village of York, Pennsylvania. It was an unattractive town, wholly unsuited to the task of accommodating even the rump Congress that made its home there. Housing and provisions were scarce, primitive, and expensive. Yet Pickering was glad to be there. He had always loved politics, showing both a disposition to be in the middle of public affairs and a craving for power. Now he was at the center of national politics. This is not to say that Pickering found the view from the political summit entirely exhilarating. On the contrary, once at York, he discovered that the abuses he had tried to curb in the army were only the tip of the iceberg. For years Americans had flaunted their "virtue" to the rest of the world. Pickering only wished that "there was more reason to boast of it." Too many officeholders, he soon concluded, were outlandishly dishonest. Methods "of defrauding the public" had been developed which he had imagined "flourished only in the most corrupt corners of the old world." But Pickering, like some Old Testament prophet, thrived in such situations. Convinced of his own righteousness and the ultimate justice of the American cause, he persevered. [6]

Accommodations were almost impossible to find in York, for the little town had been overrun by an influx of congressmen, administrators, and an assortment of hangers-on. At length, however, Pickering found a room for himself and his servant, Joseph Millet, with an aged widow, Mrs. Mihmin. A "neat, clever, obliging old woman," she reminded him very much of his mother. Her house was modest by any standards. Still, there was a "decent lower room, warmed by a stove after the German fashion, and a small kitchen, furnished with every necessary utensil." Besides these, there was "a warm chamber" where Pickering lodged. In one corner Millet had fixed what the New Englander described as "a little cabin." There he had placed a straw bed and upon that a mattress. With a bag of straw for a pillow, he found himself perfectly comfortable. "I have not felt myself so much at home," he wrote, "since I left Salem." [7]

In Congress it was taken for granted that Pickering would be overshadowed by at least three of the other members of the Board of War: the former commissary general, Joseph Trumbull; Thomas Mifflin, until recently the quartermaster general; and the president-designate of the board, General Horatio Gates. None of these men, however, played any consistent role at the War Office. Trumbull, ill and in any event piqued because he believed Congress had given preference to Pickering in making the appointments, never attended a board meeting. [8] Mifflin and Gates became victims of the political storm that arose over the so-called Conway Cabal. Though each served for a time, neither participated in the attempts of the War Office to bring order out of chaos. [9] In effect, then, the only reliable appointees to the board were Pickering and Richard Peters, a Pennsylvanian who had served on the original board since 1776. Pickering, the more aggressive of the two, soon became the paramount figure in the War Department.

At times during that terrible winter of 1777 Pickering wondered whether it would be possible to carry on. But in the spring the newly appointed quartermaster general, Nathanael Greene, proved his abilities by providing the army with substantial quantities of supplies. Before the end of April the situation at Valley Forge was much improved. Although shoes remained scarce, Samuel Carlton reported to Pickering that the soldiers were reasonably well clothed and that food was plentiful. Almost as miraculously, men and boys began to trickle into camp. Well before summer Washington again commanded a respectable force. Moreover, morale was high while discipline flourished under the able ministrations of Baron Steuben. [10]

Encouraging news from abroad complemented that coming from Valley Forge. In April it was learned that the French had formed an alliance with the United States. Shortly thereafter Pickering conferred with a French representative in York who was there to assess America's military needs. At the conclusion of these talks he wrote exultantly to his brother John that the French were going to provide unlimited military aid. It was a bit late to expect much help to arrive for the campaign that year, but in 1779, if the war continued, the United States would be exceedingly strong. He confidently predicted that in the future American forces would "want nothing."[11]

With France as an ally, Pickering was convinced that America's independence was no longer at issue. For the first time, in that heady atmosphere of 1778, he began to look beyond independence. The United States now had the upper hand and would not make peace until Canada, Nova Scotia, and both the Floridas were "also recovered to freedom and independence; and a free fishery secured to New England." Nor would Britain "for too much longer be the tyrant of the seas. We will contend for and win its freedom for ourselves."[12]

Yet spring brought its disappointments, too. For some time Pickering had been anxious to return for a visit to Salem. His father had long been in declining health, and although he continued to go to meetings, tenaciously presevered in his Tory views, and remained mentally alert, it seemed evident that his life was ebbing away. Pickering wanted the opportunity to reconcile their disagreements before it was too late. Other things troubled him as well. He had not seen Beckey or young Jack in many months, and letters from home were few and far between.[13]

Moreover, in the time he had been away, the New Englander had been shaping new ideas about his and his family's future. He had just about made up his mind to move at war's end to Philadelphia and begin life as a merchant. He had mentioned this to nobody, not even Beckey. But he wanted to talk to her, to have a chance to describe the comfortable city and the life he envisioned. In Massachusetts, there was little to look forward to save appointment to some poorly paid local office. In Pennsylvania he sensed opportunity. A continent was opening, and as a merchant located on the Chesapeake, he would be able to take advantage of that. But Pickering could not get away that spring. The Board of War was overwhelmed with work. The projected visit home would have to wait.[14]

Fires have consumed large portions of the records of the War Office. Those that remain, however, when complemented by the personal papers of Pickering, Richard Peters, Washington, and Quartermaster General Nathanael Greene, provide a reasonably clear guide to Pickering's performance as the ad hoc president of the Board of War. Not surprisingly, the hallmark of his years in the War Office was a commitment to reform. In collaboration with General Gates, who served as president of the board during the early months of its operation, he convinced Congress to stop the almost wholesale issuance of army commissions to Europeans, a practice that had long irritated American officers. He had a hand too in some important administrative changes, helping with the reorganization of the Quartermaster General's Department and using his influence to see to it that Jeremiah Wadsworth replaced the ineffective William Buchanan as commissary general.[15]

Though Pickering never lost any of his enthusiasm for reform, he sometimes ran into obstacles too well entrenched to be overcome. He was, for example, frustrated in his attempts to deal with the corrupt, virtually unregulated systems of distribution employed by Quartermaster General Greene and by the Office of the Clothier General. Double-entry bookkeeping was a centuries-old idea by the time of the American Revolution. Yet among the thousands of deputies and agents in these departments it was too frequently an unknown art. Neither department so much resembled an efficient bureaucracy as it did a loose confederation of thousands of semiautonomous agents spread out all over the country and accountable to practically nobody. There were, of course, regulations that were supposed to govern the activities of these men. Such rules, however, were honored only in the breach. Under these circumstances where was almost unlimited opportunity for theft and fraud at all levels.

Of the two departments, the Clothier General's Office was by far the worse. "If the officers of the army were to compose a jury for the tryal of the Clothier General," Adjutant General Alexander Scammell wrote from Valley Forge, "his term of existence would shortly expire."[16] Pickering complained to Washington that the department was such a tangle of inefficiency and corruption that it was impossible to guess what proportion of the clothing purchased for the army was being stolen. It was obvious that until someone found a way to punish malefactors, the army would always be in danger, not so much from the enemy as from those posing as its friends.[17] But no amount of complaining did much good. There were repeated investigations, but Congress never solved the puzzle of the Clothier General's Office.

The quartermaster general's domain posed another problem entirely. Nathanael Greene's department was no model of bureaucratic efficiency, to be sure, but it functioned. Greene's object was to keep the army supplied and mobile, and though he denied it, he was unconcerned with corruption. Indeed, there is evidence to suggest that he believed the department could function successfully only if his employees were allowed to steal. Serving for inadequate fixed salaries in a period of runaway inflation, they could not support themselves in any other way. "Some impositions and many neglects," he wrote, were part of the price the country would have to pay for keeping the army supplied.[18] This was not because his employees were more dishonest than others. It was simply that corruption, which neither began nor ended with the quartermaster's office, was pervasive in America. The "great evil" that the nation faced did not in his view originate in the want of honesty or economy in managing government operations "but in the depreciation of the money and the growing extravagance of the people." America suffered first from a moral rot that spawned rampant inflation. This in turn caught all in its grip, forcing even the honest into corrupt paths if only to survive.[19]

Timothy Pickering agreed that the spread of moral decay and avarice had gone so far in America that it engulfed even honest men. Not until the war was over and more normal circumstances restored, he once wrote, would there be any chance for the restoration of public virtue.[20] But in spite of these feelings he was constitutionally incapable of coming to terms with corruption, let alone accepting it as necessary to the operations of a government agency. It probably never crossed his mind that the elimination of corruption from the Quartermaster Corps might lead to its collapse. Honesty in his staunchly moralistic frame of reference was an absolute good, a worthwhile end in itself. He and Peters therefore pressed Greene to enforce regulations that would reduce corruption in the department.[21] But the War Office got no cooperation from the quartermaster general, who refused to abide by rules that he was convinced would lead to the breakdown of his department and disaster for the army. It was clearly a case in his mind of honesty not being the best policy.

Pickering's interference in the affairs of other departments might perhaps have been better received had the War Office itself been run as a model of efficiency. Although there is no question but that Pickering was honest, his record as an administrator was inconsistent. In some areas he proved both energetic and imaginative. He superintended the development of large-scale weapons production and organized factories owned and operated by the government where shoes were manufactured for the army.[22] Aware of the critical relationship between the iron industry and the war effort, he was unusually responsive to ironmakers' needs. He sought military exemptions for their workers and convinced Congress to underwrite the operations of certain ironmakers faced with bankruptcy.[23] When runaway inflation threatened to make purchasing impossible, he found at least a short-term solution for that problem, too. At his urging Congress authorized him to pay his suppliers in specie certificates, interest-bearing notes that were redeemable at face value in specie at a designated future time.

It is to Pickering's credit that he responded so creatively to all of these difficult challenges. Unhappily, however, his performance as the ad hoc president of the Board of War was by no means uniformly impressive. Too frequently he proved politically inept and administratively maladroit. His mishandling of the appointment of special agents to purchase emergency provisions for the army during the terrible winter of 1777 was an early example.

When Congress authorized the board to purchase flour in Pennsylvania for shipment to the army at Valley Forge, Pickering acted speedily. But with no appreciation for the delicate political situation in that state, he appointed as his purchasing agents outspoken enemies of the Pennsylvania Constitution of 1776. The Pennsylvania legislature, offended by these appointments, chose agents of its own to do the purchasing. There then ensued a ridiculous competition between the board's agents and those of the state. This rivalry not only drove the price of flour up, but fueled political bitterness in Pennsylvania. In the end Congress intervened at the behest of Pennsylvania's delegates. Just as the board's appointees were getting ready to ship their flour to the army, they were relieved of their duties. Before all of the political maneuvering was over, a full month had been lost in the battle against starvation at Valley Forge.[24]

Pickering, who never understood that the board's political ineptitude was in part responsible for the frustrating delay, responded with characteristic self-righteousness. He and Peters had, he believed, acted nonpolitically, choosing able men to handle a difficult administrative task. It was evident to him that others, motivated by narrow political prejudices, had interceded to frustrate the board's efforts. Bitter at what he considered the inability of some to focus their attentions upon the crucial business of war, Pickering's mind began to move in authoritarian patterns. "The present situation of public affairs," he wrote to Adjutant General Alexander Scammell, "reminds me of the distracted state of Britain in the first years of the last war." America, like Britain then, needed a great leader who would create national unity and find a way to eliminate petty political squabbling. "Would to God we had some great Patriot Pitt, to rescue us from impending danger and conduct us to victory and glory, by a wise arrangement & vigorous execution of public measures!" But there was no Pitt, and America seemed condemned to die squalidly in a sea of political corruption. These dark thoughts moved Pickering to redouble his own efforts. "Every good man will endeavor to restrain the vicious, and defeat their pernicious designs," he wrote. Perhaps in the end the effort would fall short. Yet if this did prove the unhappy outcome, then at least each good man would still be able to "console himself with this reflection,—*that he has done his duty.*" [25]

Even when he should have had a situation under control, Pickering sometimes mishandled it. Because the Clothier General's Department no longer functioned by early 1778, Congress delegated the responsibility for purchasing winter clothing for the army to the War Office. Though the frugal Pickering went right to work, he failed to order clothing in sufficient quantities. Quite by chance Washington himself discovered the mistake, intervening personally to make sure that serious shortages did not recur. [26] Later in the same year Washington was again forced to prod the War Office when it became apparent that Pickering was doing nothing to ensure that the clothing would be transported to winter quarters before bad weather set in. On still another occasion in the summer of 1779 Pickering neglected to arrange for the transportation of a large quantity of lead from Boston, where it had been purchased, to Philadelphia, where the factories that would convert it into shot were located. When at last it dawned on him that the army might run out of ammunition as a result of this oversight, he sent a panic-stricken letter to Nathanael Greene begging him to have the lead moved. The annoyed quartermaster general came immediately to the rescue. [27] Privately he fumed to Charles Pettit, his deputy in Philadelphia, that the men who ran the War Office "never apprehend evil until such is at their door. They will always be in distress until they can learn to do business regularly." [28]

Pickering's frequent administrative lapses beg for an explanation. Of course he faced serious financial problems. Yet his blunders seldom had anything to do with money. A better answer seems to be that, with only one clerk in the office, he and Peters found themselves overburdened. Yet to leave the explanation at that misrepresents the situation. If Pickering had wanted a larger staff he probably could have had one. Congress generally gave him whatever he requested. The truth is that although he was an extraordinarily energetic man, Pickering hadn't the least notion of how to administer an office that was beyond the capabilities of one individual. Almost constitutionally incapable of delegating authority to others, he was easily distracted from important concerns and could usually be found buried under a mountain of paperwork. To make matters worse, though sharply critical of others who failed to attend to their official responsibilities, he was not devoting his full energies to his job. Instead, he spent a good portion of his time working as a commercial agent for several New England merchants whose privateers—one was named the *General Pickering*—sent prizes up the Chesapeake for sale.[29]

After General Henry Clinton evacuated Philadelphia in June 1778, Congress lost no time in returning to the city. Of course the Board of War moved too. At first Pickering was delighted, for Philadelphia seemed the same fine place that he remembered from his visit there prior to the occupation.[30] It wasn't long, however, before he began to develop certain sanctimonious second thoughts. If the Quaker City remained physically the same, he sensed a kind of moral degeneracy among its inhabitants. It was as though they had in some way been contaminated by their British conquerors. He was particularly appalled by women's hairstyles, some of which, indescribably ornate, towered a foot or more overhead. To Pickering, who affected the garb of a plain republican and who refused to wear even a wig to cover his baldness, it was all rather disturbing. He took solace, however, in the fact that "a few men (members of Congress as well as others) liked plainness & simplicity in dress as well as" he did. He wondered whether an infusion of republican virtue might have a good effect upon the city.[31]

Pickering had little time, however, to dwell on either the moral or the aesthetic failings of Philadelphia's wayward people. The supply problem was a constant drain on his attentions. There was, moreover, a new military danger opening in the West, where the great Mohawk chieftain, Joseph Brant, together with Walter Butler led a band of Indians and irregulars against American settlements. Information had to be gathered and plans made for a counteroffensive. It all took time and a great deal of energy.[32] For the most part Pickering was too busy to be lonely, to think about Beckey or the little son he had not seen in over a year. Inevitably, however, there were moments of peace, opportunities for remembering. And just as inevitably loneliness overcame him as his mind wandered "to the Eastward." Desperate for his family, he wrote frequently to Beckey of the misery of separation:

> When shut into my chamber or taking my solitary walk along the banks of the Codorus (a charming scene) I am discontented. Your presence only can relieve me. I think too of your situation. I see you, fixed in recollection, counting the long tedious months of absence—I hear your tender sighs—your impatient wishes for my return. Yet: I am obliged to tell you, the time *when* is still uncertain.[33]

Quiet moments also gave him time to dwell on the fact that he had not yet seen his ailing father. He had received not one word from him since joining the army. Occasional letters from others in Salem, however, made it clear that the old man was dying.[34] In a last effort to reconcile their disagreements before it was too late, Pickering wrote to his father, but his words were stilted and stubborn. He would not ask forgiveness, he explained, for he had done nothing wrong in taking the Whig side in the war. He hoped, though, that despite their differences they could agree to forget the past.[35]

But Pickering's letter to his father went unanswered. The year progressed and he remained engrossed in his job and busy with his work as a commercial agent. In July letters from Salem brought news that his father was dead.[36] To some, he knew, the deacon had seemed an irascible, contentious old man. Yet he was certain this was not so. His combativeness and irascibility, denounced by so many, deserved instead "respect because they were dictated by an upright heart; and were deemed erroneous, only because they did not coincide with the *practices* or *fashions* of the world which ever was and is too corrupt to be governed by principles founded solely on *Love to God & Love to Man.*"[37]

Only in the autumn did the pace of events slow sufficiently to allow Pickering the opportunity for a leave. Long before, however, he had made his plans. He rented a house on Front Street in the city and wrote urging Beckey to prepare to come.[38] He kept his financial plans to himself, but he was certain that after the war he would try a merchant's life in Philadelphia.

In October Pickering set out for Salem and a happy reunion with Beckey, John, and the rest of his family. Two months later he was back in Philadelphia happier than he could ever remember being. Even the miserable trip by wagon down from Salem hadn't troubled him. Beckey was a delight. She rode uncomplainingly by his side, singing and looking wide-eyed at the countryside. Little John, lulled by the movement of the wagon, spent half the time asleep. And the teamster hired for the trip, Isaac Perkins, couldn't have been more able. Pickering was so pleased with his work and so happy to have his family with him that he paid Perkins more than the two had first agreed upon, throwing in a pair of "woolen overalls" that Perkins had admired in the bargain.[39]

When at last the family was settled and comfortable, Pickering calculated that the move had cost more than twice what he had expected. Part of the overage was the result of inevitable extras, the plague of travelers the world over. But the New Englander was also paying the price of the runaway inflation. Pickering had tried to defend against inflation before leaving for Salem when negotiating a salary agreement with Congress for the coming year. He was not rich, hardly any better

off, in fact, for the modest inheritance his father had left him. With a
family to support and his future to consider, he had no intention of
seeing himself ruined. He warned Congress that unless they doubled
his pay he would not return to the Board of War. It seemed a reasonable moment to retire, and privately he hoped that Congress would
refuse. The army was well clothed and would in a few more weeks be
comfortable in winter quarters. No one could accuse him of having
failed in his duty. Still, he decided that if Congress agreed to his terms
he would stay on. And he did, for Congress accepted his conditions
without quibbling.[40]

But Pickering was not so shrewd a bargainer as he had imagined. In
doubling his salary Congress guaranteed him a living at the inflationary
rate prevalent in October 1778. The ratio between specie and Continental paper then stood at somewhere between 4 and 6 to 1. By the
time he returned to Philadelphia the rate had risen to 9 to 1. It hit 12 to
1 in April and was heavenbent at 45 to 1 that November.[41]

Pickering's annual salary of four thousand dollars was totally insufficient to meet his family's ordinary expenses. By the end of the year he
had dipped into his thin personal resources to the tune of ten thousand
dollars simply to keep body and soul together. He could no longer
entertain friends or, for that matter, accept invitations, since he hadn't
the money to reciprocate. His landlord had raised his rent to four
thousand dollars for the coming year, and he could not afford new
clothing for the children. The price of a man's pair of shoes, he complained to his brother, was a hundred dollars; a simple suit now cost
more than a year's supply of clothing for his entire family had not long
before. As things stood at the end of 1779, his government salary would
not even cover food costs.[42]

The inflation which proved such a personal trial for Pickering in
1779 was a worse disaster for the War Department. Employees working
for fixed and increasingly inadequate salaries that were in any case
months in arrears grew restive, threatening to leave unless something
was done to meet the rampaging cost of living. Munitions factories run
by the department were threatened by paralysis, the result of financial
stringencies as well as friction between civilian workers and enlisted
men who worked side by side but for grossly unequal salaries. Needless
to say, military operations were seriously hindered as well.

With the inflation completely out of hand and Congress seemingly
unable to do anything about it, Pickering became convinced that it
would soon be impossible to carry on even the normal functions of the
War Department. What troubled him most was that he had been saddled with the task of purchasing clothing for the army, though strictly

speaking this was the clothier general's responsibility. Since Congress required its purchasing agents to insist that the face value of Continental currency was its real value, he found himself in the position of either violating the law in order to acquire desperately needed supplies with depreciated currency, or adhering to the law and seeing the army go naked. It was an uninviting pair of alternatives to one who saw himself as a potential scapegoat when things went wrong. Desperately, he sought a way out. Arguing that he was much too busy with other things, he urged Congress to divest him of these unwanted responsibilities.

Early in 1779 Congress agreed to take the War Office out of the purchasing business. The legislators, however, neglected to vest responsibility elsewhere. Still, freed from the worrisome business himself, Pickering at first said nothing. At length, however, he was forced to speak out. Supplies of clothing were being bought up by speculators, he warned. If something was not done quickly, Congress would be faced with a choice of purchasing clothing at extortionate prices from these men or seeing the army go without.[43] Despite the seriousness of the situation Pickering remained unwilling to assume purchasing responsibilities himself. Instead he recommended that Congress vest a committee of its own with that dubious honor.[44]

When Congress instructed the Secret Committee of Commerce to take up the burden, Pickering believed that his problem had at last been solved.[45] He conferred with the committee's members, explained what had been accomplished during the preceding year, turned over the records, and wished them well. This committee, however, no more anxious to undertake responsibility for purchasing than the Board of War had been, returned the records within two weeks, claiming that it had no constitutional authority to make purchases within the territorial confines of the United States.[46]

The Secret Committee of Commerce and the board were at an impasse. But given the circumstances it was Pickering and Richard Peters who suffered, for they were in the middle, plagued by angry military commanders who were convinced that shortages were the result of the board's failure. Pickering might protest that he had other burdensome duties and that purchasing was not his responsibility, but as long as Congress failed to take effective action there was little he or Peters could do save try and fill the vacuum. During the summer they therefore attempted to purchase clothing, though they refused to pay the extortionate prices demanded by speculators. Inevitably these efforts ended in failure.

By September 1779, the inflation had almost totally destroyed the value of Continental currency. Congress, Pickering insisted, would have to face the facts; it no longer had the means of financing the war effort.[47] The only alternative, he argued, was to turn responsibility for supplying the military over to the states. To smooth the transition to a system of state provisioning, he suggested that Congress continue its own efforts, using what credit remained to it and expending the last of its meager resources. Whatever the lawmakers decided to do, however, Pickering at last made one thing clear; he was through with the purchasing business.[48]

By the end of 1779 the Board of War was, to all intents and purposes, nonfunctional. Its failure, and the near paralysis of the Quartermaster General's Office as well, had a direct and negative effect on the conduct of all military operations. In no area was the situation more critical than in the South, where Benjamin Lincoln commanded a ragged, undersupplied force of six thousand men. Facing an assault by a combined army of eighty-five hundred British, Hessian, and Tory troops under the command of Sir Henry Clinton, Lincoln pressed the Board of War for reinforcements.[49] At Pickering's urging Washington agreed to detach eight hundred Virginians and North Carolinians from the Main Army to reinforce Lincoln. It was up to the quartermaster general and the Board of War to find a way to move them. This, however, was more easily said than done, for there was no money in the Treasury.

Pickering worked on this problem with Charles Pettit, one of Nathanael Greene's top deputies and a man quite familiar with the inner workings of Congress and the Treasury Board. Pettit had been in Philadelphia only a few weeks before, pleading the case for the quartermaster's service. At that time Greene's department was somewhere between ten and fifteen million dollars in debt—Pettit wasn't sure of the exact figure—and would be unable to function for the rest of the campaign if it was not granted more funds. These scare tactics produced a small supply of money, not enough to finance the rest of the year's operations but enough to limp along for a while.[50]

By the time Pickering brought the critical South Carolina situation to his attention, Pettit had used up all available money and the Treasury had no more to offer. The government was in fact bankrupt and without any regular source of revenue. Even under these circumstances it might have been possible to move the men by sea had not the British blockade been so effective. Moving them overland, however, seemed out of the question. Early in December Pickering informed Congress that there was little if any forage for horses between Philadelphia and South Carolina and that food supplies were inadequate too. There was some hope that the reinforcements might be able to get as far as Williamsburg. It might be as long as three months, however, before the supply problem could be solved and the men transported the rest of the way. But Pickering believed that even if this force did get through it would be "much reduced by desertions and other casualties" before it arrived in South Carolina.[51]

Timothy Pickering has not generally been faulted for overoptimism. In this case, however, he was incorrigible. By March 1780, the situation around Charleston had deteriorated badly. Lincoln urgently needed large-scale reinforcements. Pickering however, advised Congress that the Main Army could spare no more than the eight hundred men already allocated. He suggested instead that Congress appeal to Virginia and North Carolina for five thousand militiamen to help defend Charleston. It proved impossible to raise the militia, however, and Pickering continued unable to move the troops that were available. Four and one-half months after they had begun to consider ways of transporting these men southward, both Pickering and Pettit gave up. They had done their best but could not purchase the forage and other essentials they needed on credit: the government had no credit. Even the teamsters Pettit had hired to move the men grew restive after a time, demanding their back pay, already several months in arrears. "Not a board nor wagon can be put in motion without money to pay their wages," Pettit reported to Pickering, "nor can the necessary forage be procured from the state purchasers, or by our purchasers where we are yet allowed to purchase, without money to pay for it." It would take a minimum of 2,640 million dollars to move Lincoln's eight hundred reinforcements.[52]

Not long after Pickering gave up hope of transporting these men, Lincoln surrendered Charleston and his army to the British. It was one of the most disastrous defeats suffered by American arms during the war. When Pickering first heard the news he simply would not believe it. When there was no longer any room to doubt the extent of the disaster, he became angry and exasperated. There was in the first place the ridiculous and completely unnecessary financial crisis to blame. Then too he wondered what kind of people they were in Virginia and North Carolina who would not lift a finger but instead allowed Charleston, along with over six thousand American soldiers, to be surrendered to the enemy.[53]

The question of reinforcements for the Southern Army, serious in itself, was only symptomatic of the generally critical situation. Without funds, supply officers and purchasing agents all over the country found it impossible to do business. Like Pettit they soon discovered their credit was exhausted. The board, meanwhile, was bombarded with letters urging it to do something. The governor of Virginia wrote of the "starving condition" of British prisoners being held at Charlottesville. Supplies were available but not without cash. Washington, too, complained because the state provisioning system recently established by Congress was not working. Supply magazines were almost empty. Yet there was little Pickering could do. Without money it appeared his prophecy of a few months before that the army might dissolve was on the verge of coming true.[54]

Pickering was reduced to pleading with the governors of Pennsylvania, Maryland, and Delaware for food in order to keep the army eating. He noted in a message to Congress that while the few hundred barrels of provisions thus raised saved the Main Army from immediate dissolution, difficulties were bound to continue. The state provisioning system was not functioning and Congress ought to understand that. At the same time, the commissary general of purchases, Colonel Ephraim Blaine, had no staff and no money. Everywhere prisoners and soldiers alike were on the brink of starvation. Unless Congress found a way to raise a real revenue, restore public confidence in its currency, and end inflation, Pickering warned, there was little hope of carrying on.[55]

FIVE

Quartermaster General

PICKERING ISSUED HIS BLEAK PROGNOSIS on March 23, 1780. By that time Congress had already begun to act. On the eighteenth it reversed an earlier decision to distribute no more paper currency and began issuing bills of a "new emission." This was part of an attempt to fund the government's operations, finance the war, and simultaneously curb inflation. Provisions of the new financial policy stipulated that the value of old Continental bills of credit be established at a ratio of 40 to 1 to the new bills. Simultaneously, the legal value of the new currency was set at par with specie. In theory this would reduce inflation by taking great quantities of old currency out of circulation.[1] The decision to issue a "new" currency was complemented by a drive for retrenchment in the operations of the government and cutbacks in the size of the army.

Little of this made much sense to Pickering, who believed that the government's fundamental problem, inflation, could only be solved if Congress won the taxing power and then funded its debt. To call for reductions in the size of a none-too-large army in the midst of a war seemed utterly mad. What infuriated him most, however, was a congressional scheme for the enforced retirement of an extraordinarily large number of veteran officers. For years these men had sacrificed their interests in the service of the Revolution; and now they were to be dismissed. Why? The answer was obvious. If they served for the duration they would qualify for pensions already promised by Congress.

If Pickering railed at congressional attempts to reduce the size of the army, he was of an altogether different opinion when legislative ax wielders turned their gaze in the direction of Quartermaster General Nathanael Greene. He had hoped for some time, in the interest of both efficiency and economy, to require Greene to enforce existing regulations, but he had failed. Now, with rumors of large-scale corruption in the quartermaster's service circulating widely, Congress became a formidable ally.

Quite naturally Nathanael Greene and his principal aides, Pettit and Colonel John Cox, were not inclined to support reform. They knew very well that the department was a honeycomb of corrupt practices but thought this of little immediate consequence. Even if a general house cleaning should cut costs, Pettit wrote, where was the money needed to fund operations to come from? He had little faith in more paper currency! If Congress had really been interested in saving the situation, he thought, it would have addressed the more basic problem of establishing a revenue for itself while restoring the national government's credit by funding the debt. But instead, he predicted, the legislators would waste their time debating measures of economy, efficiency, and public morality. Meanwhile the army would starve.[2]

Greene, who shared Pettit's anger and frustration, at least thought he understood congressional motivations. Unable to deal with its real problems, Congress was about to use his department as a scapegoat. More than a year before, when criticism of the department had been particularly sharp, he had predicted both that Congress would investigate his operation and that once begun such an inquiry would quickly gain momentum. "A charge against a Quartermaster-General," he observed, "is most like a cry of a mad dog in England. Everyone joins in the cry and lends their assistance to pelt him to death."[3]

A well-known advocate of reform, Pickering was appointed along with General Philip Schuyler to a committee organized by Congress to reorganize the Quartermaster General's Office. When Nathanael Greene's old enemy Thomas Mifflin was added to the committee Schuyler resigned, convinced that a conspiracy against Greene was afoot. During the next several weeks this charge repeatedly surfaced as friends of Greene's sought to discredit the committee. But there seems to have been no conspiracy. Undoubtedly Mifflin, who despised Greene, relished the idea of initiating reforms that he knew would irritate and perhaps even hamstring the quartermaster general. But he was operating within guidelines carefully laid out beforehand by Congress. In any event Pickering was no conspirator. He was only an honest, if misguided and overly zealous, reformer anxious to clean up a corrupt corner of government that had long troubled him.

Late in March 1780, after some two months of deliberations, the Pickering-Mifflin committee produced a series of proposed congressional resolutions designed either to correct abuses that had developed in the Quartermaster General's Department, or to conform to a congressional demand for cost-cutting through departmental reorganization. Thus the committee urged that the department adopt a regular accounting system, that all departmental deputies and agents be required to make regular monthly returns detailing purchases, disbursements, and materials on hand, that employees be prohibited from owning means of conveyance or draft animals that were contracted in the government's service, and that precautions be taken to eliminate payroll fraud.[4] Pickering and Mifflin also included among their proposals one for departmentwide reorganization. Purchasing was to be eliminated as a function of the quartermaster's service and handed over to the states, while staff was to be reduced wherever feasible.

Two of the committee's recommendations were especially galling to Nathanael Greene. The first was the projected elimination of the positions held by his principal aides, Pettit and Cox. The second was a plan that would have cut his income drastically by ending the commission system for paying the quartermaster general, putting him on a regular salary instead.[5]

Hardly had these proposals been sent to Congress before Greene attempted to enlist Washington's support in opposition. He complained that purchasing was an integral part of his operation. If it was separated from the department and left to the states, chaos would result. In fact it seemed that all of the essential powers of his office were being stripped from him and vested in either state authorities or the Board of War. He would be no more than a figurehead, a convenient scapegoat when the system failed. But Greene went further. In an obvious attempt to excite the general's old antagonism for Mifflin, he warned that with Pickering's aid the Pennsylvanian had set out to destroy Washington's reputation as well. He pointed out that under the new plan all payments made by the army were to be approved personally by the commander in chief. It would be impossible, Greene insisted, for Washington's staff to scrutinize such a volume of disbursements. There would be some wrongdoing, and when this was discovered Washington would be held responsible.[6]

A few days later Greene wrote again expressing even greater discontent. "The more I view it the less I like it, and the stronger my conviction is that it is calculated not less to embarrass your excellency than to disgrace & injure me." Mifflin was behind the plan and Pickering and the members of the Massachusetts congressional delegation were his dupes. "Depend upon it," Greene wrote to Washington, "he has a scheme in concert with others."[7]

Though Washington was unconvinced that a conspiracy existed, he nevertheless agreed that the Pickering-Mifflin project would not do. He forwarded his own objections to Congress and sent Greene to

Philadelphia to explain the army's point of view.[8] While in the capital Greene had the good sense not to mention his fear of political conspiracy. Instead he took plausible ground, warning Congress that although the plan was theoretically sound it was not practical. "Speculative projections in matters of business," he explained, "are like . . . metaphysical reasonings in matters of religion. Experience is the great school of human life; and the only sure guide."[9]

Greene's conspiratorial fantasies were quickly if only temporarily dispelled when, to his amazement he won an easy victory. On April 14, Congress voted to ignore the Pickering-Mifflin recommendations. Instead a special congressional committee would meet with representatives of the army to work out a plan agreeable to both.[10]

Though Greene won a tactical victory, he ultimately lost the larger political contest. The system proposed by the special committee, a plan he endorsed, did not satisfy an economy-minded Congress. Through the spring and the early part of that summer the membership wrangled over details. Finally, in mid-July, Congress passed resolutions calling for the complete reorganization of the quartermaster's service. Included was a plan for state provisioning of the army, the stipulation that the quartermaster general be paid a regular salary, as well as a number of other changes previously suggested by Pickering and Mifflin. Greene thought the congressional scheme so unworkable that although a major military campaign was in the offing he quit on the spot. Jealous of its prerogatives and insulted by Greene's intemperate behavior, Congress promptly accepted his resignation and began the search for a new quartermaster general.[11]

After Charles Pettit refused to replace his former superior, Congress turned to Pickering. The New Englander, however, was no more interested in taking over the quartermaster's service than Pettit had been. It was evidently one thing to stand on principle and loudly denounce corruption while advocating reform, but something else again to attempt to make a "reformed" system work. Nevertheless, as the coauthor of a plan for reorganization not unlike the one soon to be implemented, Pickering was vulnerable. Congress subjected him to intense pressure until at length, caught in a trap of his own making, he was forced to accept the appointment. Sadly Pickering explained to his brother that though all of his personal interests would be better served by remaining in Philadelphia with the Board of War, "a kind of political necessity" made it impossible for him to refuse.[12]

Few, even among Pickering's friends, thought he could succeed in his new assignment.[13] Others, particularly those close to Nathanael Greene, were absolutely certain he would not. Pickering, wrote Colonel

John Cox, was a mediocrity, "by no means equal to the task."[14] Colonel Nathaniel Peabody and Richard Claiborne, also former Greene aides, were equally skeptical. Peabody thought the new quartermaster general arrogant and self-righteous without being particularly bright or efficient. Pickering, he noted, was quick to make moral judgments and snap decisions based too frequently on inadequate information. As the head of the quartermaster's service he would come to grief, because it took more than ordinary ability to make a complex bureaucracy plagued by difficulties operate.[15] Claiborne, perhaps less hostile to Pickering than Peabody or Cox, nevertheless agreed, observing rather shrewdly that the New Englander was too much the bureaucrat bound by rules and regulations, and not enough the imaginative administrator.[16]

There is no doubt about it; Pickering was in many ways a maladroit administrator. Thus, although the war effort would have been better served had he not tampered with the complex organization he inherited, early in his tenure as quartermaster general he conducted an extensive purge, firing many of Greene's former deputies simply because they had been connected with the old regime. The foremost requirement for those who would serve in his department, he observed in a characteristically self-righteous letter to his brother, was "honesty."[17]

An even more serious flaw in Pickering's performance was his inability to settle down to routine work. A day in the life of the quartermaster general was filled with a myriad of small but nevertheless important decisions. He hired the wagons and teamsters to move supplies, and the workmen to keep equipment in repair and the roads clear. He was also responsible for selecting and maintaining campsites, which meant that he had to be certain that there was a plentiful supply of fresh water, that latrines were dug, and that fuel and forage for the animals were always available. It was a backbreaking job requiring constant attention. Naturally, then, General Washington expected Pickering to spend most of his time with the army, delegating to others responsibility for handling the political side of his office. But as usual it was the political aspect of the job that intrigued Pickering. As a result he spent far too much of his time in Philadelphia to suit Washington, who complained constantly about his absence. The upshot was a conflict between the general's expectations and Pickering's predilections that strained their relationship to the breaking point.[18]

It would be tempting to use Pickering's many administrative failings to explain the paralysis that gripped the quartermaster's department soon after he took over. But the plain truth is that, his personal weaknesses notwithstanding, the quartermaster's service collapsed as a result of difficulties beyond his or anybody else's control. In the first place the system of state requisitions so heavily relied upon under the new plan of organization did not work. State legislatures, given more to debate than to decisive action, too frequently failed to provide the supplies required of them.[19] At first Pickering reacted by authorizing his men to requisition the essentials. Many states, however, resentful of this invasion of their sovereignty, passed legislation specifically forbidding requisitioning by Continental officers. Pickering was blocked at every turn. As he saw it, the states wouldn't provide for the army and he couldn't. Bitterly he complained to Charles Pettit (who may have smiled as he read this letter) that his position was completely untenable. If he acted to save the army through a system of direct requisitions he was accused of "arbitrary, unreasonable, or illegal conduct." If, however, he left matters to the states, the army would starve and he would be subjecting himself "to the charge of neglecting duty."[20]

Continuous financial difficulties added immeasurably to Pickering's problems. At the time of his appointment the department was without funds. Nor could the Treasury provide the cash necessary for day-to-day operations. In order to compensate for this Congress authorized Pickering to issue specie certificates, interest-bearing notes of indebtedness that Congress guaranteed would at some time in the future be redeemed in specie "or other current money equivalent." In spite of this Pickering found it next to impossible to do business.

Public confidence in the ability of Congress to redeem its debt simply did not exist.[21] From Trenton, Colonel John Neilson informed the harried quartermaster that he would be unable to rent teams and wagons or even purchase forage unless he had cash. At Fishkill on the Hudson in upstate New York, Colonel Udney Hay wrote requesting an immediate supply of cash for the purchase of forage for horses and oxen used in supplying the post at West Point. From Boston, Pickering received the same bad news. The deputy quartermaster there reported that tent cloth needed by the army as cold weather approached could not be provided by the Navy Board. If, however, Pickering could forward cash, there was plenty to be purchased from private sources.[22]

Toward the end of September, prompted by his purchasing difficulties and a growing suspicion that Congress might be tempted to renege on its promise to redeem the certificates at par with specie, Pickering pressed Samuel Huntington, the president of Congress, for a reaffirmation of their agreement. He was especially anxious to pin Congress down on the definition of "other current money equivalents." If Congress gave way to the temptation to declare bills of the "new emission," then circulating at a ratio of about 40 to 1 to gold, to be the real equivalent of specie, Pickering warned that he would have no choice save to resign.[23]

Pickering's threats seem extreme, but if they were it was because he sniffed betrayal in the wind. The whole concept of reform rested on his ability to do what he called "substantial justice" to his employees and those who did business with him. In his mind that meant paying salaries and expenses in a medium that had a genuine value. If Congress refused to grant this premise, it had no right to expect him or his subordinates to continue in the service.

A month passed and Pickering received no answer from President Huntington. Then, while he was preparing the army for winter quarters, a letter arrived from his friend Paul Fooks, a congressional translator. Congress had betrayed him, "explaining away" earlier resolutions "and making hard specie as an equivalent" to bills of the "new emission." Quickly Pickering scanned the *Journals of Congress* for the preceding weeks and discovered the offending congressional resolution. It declared "that the salaries & contracts fixed & promised to be paid in specie, should be paid in bills of the new emission as equivalent to specie." Moreover, he soon learned that salaries of officers "on the civil list" which had earlier "been fixed & made payable in specie or other current money equivalent" were now ordered to be paid in bills of the new emission.[24]

Though Congress had clearly gone back on its commitment Pickering did not resign. With the slim resources at his command he did what he could to keep supplies moving. At the end of October he warned President Huntington, however, that unless something was done before bad weather set in the army would either starve or be forced to disband.[25]

But Congress was unresponsive to Pickering's pleas. Even before the winter of 1780–1781 the Quartermaster General's Department had all but ceased to function. As a result, by early December the Main Army quartered at New Windsor was already experiencing serious shortages. Food and clothing were scarce, and as winter came on the soldiers were forced to build their huts without tools. General Henry Knox was astonished at the situation, blaming Pickering for the breakdown: "the people whose business according to the common course of things, it was to provide the materials necessary have either been unable or neglected to do it." Despite their privations, Knox observed, the men persevered. He thought the nation must "be grateful to these brave fellows—it is impossible to admit of the idea of an alternative."[26]

Bad as things were with the Main Army, they were worse at outlying military posts. At strategic West Point, then under the command of General William Heath, the situation was grim. Early in December Heath reported to Washington that there was no forage for the animals and only eight barrels of flour left in the magazine. Fresh meat had long since disappeared. The post was being maintained hand to mouth and survived only because a trickle of supplies reached it by small craft coming down the river. Heath warned that if "a severe storm should happen, and the river be impassible but three or four days, the troops must inevitably suffer."[27] During all of that winter the garrison at West Point never had more than a two-day provision of flour on hand, while salted meat remained in even shorter supply. For all of this Heath blamed the quartermaster general.[28]

Washington was well aware that there was an ample supply of flour in the vicinity of West Point ready to be shipped. But he was at a loss to understand why Pickering had not moved it. In truth, by this time the commander in chief had lost patience with his quartermaster general. In the first place, Pickering had a record of almost unremitting failure. Moreover, although it had been clear from the beginning that Washington wanted Pickering to remain with the army under all but the most extreme circumstances, over the preceding several months the quartermaster general had spent much of his time in Philadelphia. During these absences he left the army without his vital services. Now the strategic base at West Point was in jeopardy and Washington's patience was exhausted. He wasn't interested in excuses. He wanted the kind of performance from his supply service that Nathanael Greene had once provided.

Washington informed Pickering of Heath's charges and a few days later arranged to meet with the two men at West Point. At this meeting Pickering undoubtedly explained his financial difficulties. But Washington refused to accept excuses. West Point was too important strategically to allow its garrison to be starved out for lack of a few dollars. Throughout January he kept up the pressure, buffeting the unhappy quartermaster with demands that he find a way to keep the post supplied. Quantities of salted meat and flour were ready to move, he wrote. It was up to Pickering to see that they arrived promptly. Washington was so annoyed that his well-known emotional reserve gave way. Vastly irritated, he went so far as to issue a blunt warning to the quartermaster general:

The time is come when these things must be done and the execution rests only with you. For whenever it shall be known that there were provisions in the neighborhood & that the troops have suffered for want of them, all the ill consequences & the whole blame arising therefrom you must be sensible will be attributed by the army and the country to your department.[29]

Such threats served only to make Pickering angry and resentful. To be sure, there were supplies of flour at Ringwood and Warwick, towns nearby and on the river. The problem was that as winter set in and the river began to choke with ice, the ship owners who had previously carried supplies to the beleaguered outpost grew reluctant to risk their boats. Pickering did everything he could think of to entice them to continue the trade, but to no avail. He even considered buying some small river boats himself, only to discover that there were few serviceable craft available and no oak, timber, or iron to make repairs on them. And, of course, there was no money for the purchase of either boats or materials.[30]

Finally Pickering gave up his efforts to use the ice-clogged North River and turned his attention to finding means for overland transportation to supply both West Point and the Main Army at New Windsor. Yet despite the fact that the distances between state magazines and the military posts were often insignificant, he commanded so few wagons and draft animals that it was impossible to maintain a regular flow of supplies to either place during the remainder of the winter. He suggested impressing the teams and wagons that he required from the civilian population, but Washington would not hear of it. Only an occasional heavy snowfall which provided good sledding and allowed for the movement of considerable quantities of goods with relative ease gave Pickering means of continuing even in a sporadic way to supply Heath's forces at West Point or the Main Army itself.

In March Congress relieved some of the pressure by reversing its earlier decision declaring bills of the new emission to be the real equivalent of specie. In spite of this the spring, which had in previous years provided relief for the army from the rigors of winter, this time brought no change in its pitiful condition. Congressional credit was at low ebb, currency was of little value and difficult to accumulate, and specie was unavailable. Also, Pickering found his specie certificates little more attractive than they had been during the preceding winter. It continued therefore to be next to impossible for him to move supplies.[31]

By early April not only West Point but Fort Schuyler at Albany and the Main Army itself were all experiencing critical food shortages, the result of a complete breakdown in the Quartermaster General's Department. Washington continued to bombard Pickering with demands that supplies begin to move again. What was at issue, he insisted, was not only the "safety of our important posts on the river, but the very existence of the army." [32] He demanded "vigorous and energetic measures to relieve the garrison and the army from the horrors of impending famine, & me from the incessant complaints & perplexities which are occasioned by our present disagreeable circumstances." [33]

Increasingly bitter at Washington's unwillingness to credit the efforts he had made, Pickering again assured the general that he was doing everything humanly possible to get supplies moving. Simultaneously he appealed to Governor Trumbull of Connecticut for aid.[34] He also wrote to the justice of the peace at Warwick urging him to issue warrants for the impressment of civilian teams and wagons to move desperately needed supplies. Pickering had little hope, however, that Trumbull could act quickly enough to save West Point, Fort Schuyler, or even the Main Army at New Windsor from disaster. He had even less confidence in the Warwick justice of the peace, for on previous occasions when he had tried this approach he found local officials unwilling to impress the teams and wagons of their constituents.[35]

What Pickering needed most was money, and he needed it in a hurry. For three days following his latest appeals for help he grappled with the problem, finally striking on a solution, which, though it ran counter to every instinct, seemed to offer a partial way out. He ordered Hugh Hughes, his deputy quartermaster for New York who was then in Connecticut, to sell a portion of the supplies collected there and earmarked for the army. The revenue thus raised Pickering intended to use to pay teamsters to move the remaining supplies. It was a desperate proposal, since even the supplies available would not have filled the ordinary needs of the army.[36]

Distressed over this "wretched" business practice and disturbed too because he knew that he was proposing the sale of supplies that the army genuinely needed, Pickering wrote Congress, hoping to apply pressure where it would do the most good. If Congress disapproved of his plan it might countermand the order. But then it would be up to Congress to provide an alternative. Bitterly he commented on his inability to run the department without funds. When all supplies "absolutely stop," he wrote, he hoped nobody would blame him. "If any other man, can, without money, carry on the extensive business of this department, I wish most sincerely he would take my place. I confess Myself incapable of doing it." [37]

Before Congress could respond, Washington forbade the sale of any portion of the supplies needed by the army.[38] With no other way of forwarding materials, Pickering again began to urge what many others considered unthinkable: the use of military force to impress horses, oxen, and wagons from the civilian population. But as before Washington refused to consider the proposition. He was "utterly opposed" to the use of force against the people in the countryside. Such action would undermine the Revolution. Even those ordinarily predisposed to support the cause would be alienated if the army oppressed the people.[39]

Though he agreed in principle, Pickering was by no means sure that the people he had in mind were very enthusiastic for the Revolution in the first place. Early in spring, as it became more feasible to move goods over greater distances, he had turned his attention to the country west of the Connecticut River where large supplies of food were available and draft animals and wagons were plentiful among the farming population. He appealed to the patriotism of the farmers in the area, urging them to volunteer their teams and wagons to get supplies through to the half-starved American forces at New Windsor, Fort Schuyler, and West Point. But appeals to patriotism had no effect. Next he offered to hire teams and wagons. But few farmers would willingly risk either horses or wagons in return for the rapidly depreciating specie certificates Pickering had to "spend." At this point, had he been free to exercise his own judgment, Pickering would in all likelihood have resorted to force to gain his point. "With people so utterly regardless of the most essential interests of their country," Pickering was convinced "that nothing save military force would have any operation."[40]

This was the nub of a fundamental difference between Washington and Pickering. The Virginian feared the effect on the people if the army oppressed them. Pickering, however, was convinced that the people were in reality oppressing the army. Americans, though prosperous, refused to support a military establishment that existed to protect them from British tyranny. Under the circumstances Pickering viewed the use of force to impress teams and requisition supplies as little more than a necessary act of self-defense on the part of the military.

Pickering very nearly won the argument as Washington bent under the almost irresistible pressure of military necessity.[41] The news that Fort Schuyler near Albany would have to be adandoned if meat and flour were not provided left him with no choice but to instruct Pickering to impress transport for the army if civil authorities refused to do so. Pickering responded to those new orders quickly, informing Washington that he had only recently sought civil cooperation but without success. The supply situation was so critical, he warned, that no more time should be wasted.[42]

The ferocious enthusiasm with which the long-frustrated Pickering responded to his orders startled Washington, who approved his plan but urged that the job be done as tactfully as possible.[43] At that Washington was not satisfied that he had acted wisely. Therefore, when three days later the Massachusetts legislature forwarded him nine thousand dollars in bills of the new emission earmarked as pay for the men of the Massachusetts line he diverted it instead to Pickering for use in hiring transportation. Realizing that he ran a serious risk in withholding the money and that if news of his decision leaked it could bring on a crisis in the Massachusetts line, Washington cautioned the quartermaster general against revealing the source of the money.[44] A few days later he reinforced his decision, offering to procure money of the new or old emission on his personal credit in order to avoid using force against civilians. Simultaneously he dispatched General Heath on a tour of northeastern state capitals literally to beg state authorities to help move the supplies so desperately needed by the army.[45]

At this critical juncture in early 1781, the army was saved not by Pickering or Washington but by the intervention of the recently appointed superintendent of finance, Robert Morris. Originally Morris had no intention of getting involved in the thorny question of supplying the army. But he was impelled to act by the critical situation, the inability of either Washington or Pickering to solve it, and the growing tendency both in the army and in Congress to rely upon coercion as a means of forcing reluctant farmers to provide supplies, draft animals, and wagons. When, late in May, Congress passed a resolution authorizing Washington to impress supplies, Morris decided to intervene.

The most prestigious and perhaps the most powerful merchant in America, Morris immediately arranged for a shipment of one thousand barrels of flour to the Main Army, pledging his personal credit in hard money to arrange the transaction. This was only the beginning, for during the spring and summer, working through a network of merchants closely connected with him in his mercantile endeavors, Morris directed his energies toward keeping the army supplied and mobile. Before the end of 1781 the financier had reorganized the entire supply system. The unwieldy state requisitioning program was scrapped, replaced by a network of private contracting agreements with merchants who not only provided supplies for the various army posts but took over responsibility for transportation in the bargain.[46]

Quartermaster General Pickering was of course delighted to give up the onerous task of trying to arrange transportation and to confine himself to managing the distribution of goods provided as if by magic through the manipulations of the financier. Some may have doubted Morris's integrity, but few questioned his ability. As for the quartermaster general, he thought the Pennsylvanian a miracle worker. He had saved the army from starvation or dissolution and Pickering from bearing the onus of responsibility for that disaster. Moreover, it seemed clear that without him there could have been no Yorktown campaign, for it was he who provided supplies and mobility for the army at that critical juncture.

SIX

Peace and Disillusion

WHATEVER PLEASURE Pickering felt on being extricated from his financial difficulties by Robert Morris was tempered by a deep yet growing bitterness. Not even the victory at Yorktown tasted so sweet as he had once imagined it would. He was sick of the war and the constant demands that it made upon him, tired of wearing threadbare clothes while others reaped golden harvests, and above all utterly wearied by Washington's carping criticism. The ideologue was fatigued and emotionally incapable of carrying on.

As much a victim of the delusion that a peace treaty would soon put an end to the war as the most optimistic of his countrymen, Pickering used the many months following the Virginia campaign to plan his and his family's future in postwar America. Old Salem friends urged him to return home, promising political patronage. But there was little money in any of the offices Massachusetts had to offer, and Pickering was certain that he wanted to make no more "sacrifices" in the public service. He saw opportunities opening in two directions. The West seemed an area of great potential. He was convinced that the war had only temporarily stopped the natural tendency of Americans to move into new, unoccupied lands. At war's end, he believed, the migrations would begin again and with new vigor, even to the point of draining large elements of the population from the East.[1] This of course was the preoccupation of most land speculators of the Revolutionary period. But Pickering was not cut of precisely the same mold. He speculated in unoccupied lands, to be sure, but his personal impulse went beyond buying and selling to actual settlement. He envisioned himself acquiring large tracts of land ahead of the migratory swarm, then selling off portions as population growth forced land prices up. With the profits he would clear a large estate for himself and his family, build a comfortable house, and settle down, a landed aristocrat.

At intervals during the next twenty years this vision recurred, and on two occasions Pickering actually pursued it. But in 1782 there seemed a more civilized way to grow rich. During the period before the revolutionary war there had been a burgeoning commerce between New England and Philadelphia. Relying upon his excellent connections among northeastern merchants, Pickering now proposed to revive that trade as a commission merchant in the Quaker City.[2]

In March 1782 he took the first step in that direction, renting a farm just five miles from Philadelphia. It was a lovely place, the home during the preceding year of the French minister to the United States, the Chevalier La Luzerne. The farm would provide all the fuel, grains, dairy products, and other staples that the family needed. There was good fishing too in the Schuylkill River that ran by just at the foot of the hill on which the house was situated. Nearby lived General and Mrs. Mifflin, by this time old acquaintances. And hardly two miles away was Belmont, the seat of his closest friend, Richard Peters. It seemed a near perfect setting.[3]

Long before the war was officially over, Pickering thus indulged his fantasies. But like some inescapable nightmare, a state of war persisted. He talked of quitting "an office so burdensome and a service so ungrateful." But in truth he had no intention of resigning. Though he explained it as a matter of honor to see the war through to its final conclusion, financial considerations were more significant. He would have been the last to admit it, but his salary and allowances were substantial. Moreover, in 1780 Congress had agreed in principle to pay those officers who served for the duration a pension of half-pay for life. As he himself explained, with peace seemingly close at hand it would have been foolish to quit and perhaps miss out on "the fruit of so much toil."[4]

Caught in an agony of conflicting impulses, Pickering refused to resign but could not bring himself to return to the drudgery of army life either. Instead, during most of 1782 he used every conceivable excuse to absent himself from camp while waiting in vain for news of the peace treaty that was to unchain him. Finally, after absences that totaled more than eight months, he returned to camp to serve for the duration.[5]

Any other military commander would have either court-martialed or dismissed Pickering for this gross negligence. But Washington, who shunned such confrontations, never found it in himself to do this. Instead, he vented his anger in his correspondence, remarking bitterly to Secretary of War Benjamin Lincoln that "for any good or even knowledge I derive from this gentleman . . . I might as well be without a Quartermaster General." Washington complained that he had been "left totally in the dark with respect to every matter and thing in his department." Pickering's irresponsibility had been so damaging, he continued, that it was impossible to tell "when the army will be able to take the field or whether it can be done at all."[6]

If on returning to camp Pickering suffered under Washington's steely gaze, his distress was only intensified by an unsettling fear that in the end there might be no special reward for those who had remained in service for the duration. Many in Congress were agitating against the pension promised in 1780. And while the people seemed able to "indulge in a luxury to which before the war they were strangers," the army was all but ignored. Pickering complained that even the sick and disabled were "left to perish for want of a wholesome diet, or with cold for want of proper clothing!"[7] He wrote in broad strokes of a nation's lack of appreciation for an army that had won its liberty. But the feeling was deeply personal. It was Pickering lashing out in pen and ink against an unappreciative people, demanding recognition and reward, and then lapsing more deeply into bitter reflections.

A more merciful Providence might at least have allowed Pickering to serve out the remainder of the war uneventfully. But it was as though some malevolent yet impish spirit was tracking and tormenting him, driving him deeper into forever lowering regions of pain and frustration. Thus, throughout most of 1782 he was forced to function with the threat of a new congressional plan for the reorganization of his department hanging over his head. There was of course a good deal of irony in this. That the army's most passionate cost cutter should himself be threatened by congressional ax wielders probably amused a number of those who in the past had been victims of Pickering's economizing. Certainly they would have found justice in it. Not surprisingly, however, Pickering didn't see it that way. During the spring he fought off moves to cut staff and salaries. That autumn, however, Congress returned to the attack.[8]

The quartermaster general's sense of persecution was fully aroused. If Congress should cut his salary, he raged to his obsequious friend and subordinate, Commissary General Sam Hodgdon, he would quit. "I have served my *country* under circumstances and emergencies peculiar & extraordinary; and am now to be treated with *ingratitude*."[9] It was of a piece with everything else that had happened to him since volunteering. The public, having first used and abused him, now seemed intent on taking still further advantage of him. Some in Congress evidently thought of him as a dependent with no alternative save to accept their decisions or starve. But he assured Hodgdon that he was too proud to acquiesce in such treatment. If Congress insisted on pursuing its visions of retrenchment at his expense, he vowed, he would leave.[10]

Of course when the blow actually fell Pickering did not resign. Rhetoric was one thing, but his salary was all that stood between him and poverty. After rushing to Philadelphia to enter a vain protest, he returned to camp with his pride a ruin and his salary cut nearly in two.[11]

Nor was fate through punishing the embattled quartermaster general. On the evening of January 18, 1783, after a small dinner party that he gave for Generals Washington and Hand and their ladies, Pickering was suddenly placed under arrest. A local speculator by the unlikely name of Melancthon Woolsey had bought up some three thousand dollars in specie certificates issued in Pickering's name and was demanding payment. Under New York State law, agents of the Continental Congress could be held personally liable for debts they incurred in the name of Congress.[12] Pickering gave bond, hired an attorney, and vowed to resist to the last extremity.[13] He was spared a court appearance, however, when the New York legislature, bowing to congressional pressure, stayed Woolsey's suit and prohibited similar ones.

Though alienated from Washington, victimized by Woolsey's legal harassment, and depressed as a result of a long series of other disillusioning experiences, Pickering nevertheless clung to his commission. Not only did he need his salary, but he still hoped that officers who served for the duration might receive either a pension or a substantial bonus. He was evidently not, however, among those officers who worked with Robert and Gouverneur Morris, Alexander Hamilton, and certain other nationalist politicians during 1782 and early 1783 to win a pension for the army as well as greater power for the central government. Not until March 1783, when he played an active role during the debates that followed the appearance of the famous Newburgh Addresses, can his involvement be documented.[14]

Pickering was preparing for an inspection trip to state supply magazines in Albany and points north when the Newburgh Addresses, anonymously written by Major John Armstrong, began circulating in camp. Only days before the appearance of the first of the addresses, Colonel Walter Stewart returned to Newburgh fresh from Philadelphia carrying the news that with peace all but assured Congress was laying plans to disband the army, but that no thought had been given either to providing back pay for the officers and men, then far in arrears, or to legislating the long-promised pension. Armstrong's addresses were essential ingredients in a plan drawn up by Stewart and a few others to organize a coherent, militant resistance to this congressional scheme.[15]

Some officers (Washington and Knox were the most prominent) condemned the addresses because they seemed thinly disguised appeals to violence. Pickering, however, steeped in bitterness, found in them a clear expression of his own feelings of betrayal.[16] Convinced that if the army were dissolved Congress would ignore the officers' claims to back pay and a pension, he hoped that the addresses would elicit a series of strong resolutions from the army to Congress and forestall demobilization and the consequent destruction of the army's effectiveness as a political force. With this in mind, he postponed his trip north in order to attend a meeting of the officers that was held on March 15. There he listened attentively, taking careful notes as Washington first spoke. It was in many ways, he thought, "a handsome speech," very complimentary to the army and the reputation it had gained. But when the general turned his attention to the Newburgh Addresses, Pickering found himself in total disagreement. Where he saw only an honest expression of justifiable bitterness, Washington discovered "insidious designs." He even suggested that the author might be in the pay of the British.[17]

After his talk Washington left the meeting to the officers, who then began their own deliberations. Pickering, completely at home in the town meeting atmosphere of the assembly, played an important role during the day's debates. He was particularly proud of his part in winning passage of the officers' second resolution calling on Congress to maintain the army intact until all accounts had been liquidated, balances due collected, and regular sources of revenue for the national government established.[18] Certainly if the officers were ever to collect pensions or a bonus, it was essential that Congress have the power to tax and thus fund its debts. He thought that the army's feelings could not be ignored and did not mind in the least that political leaders at both the national and state levels believed there was the possibility that the military might take matters into its own hands.[19]

But Pickering's pleasure turned to chagrin late in the debates when, in response to Washington's earlier remarks, a resolution was introduced denouncing the author of the Newburgh Addresses and his "insidious" attempts to subvert "all order and discipline" in the army.[20] The foundation of the army's political influence was the implied threat that it might use force to accomplish its ends. Pickering didn't want violence, but neither did he want Congress or the states to be overconfident on that score. He therefore thought the fifth resolution, which passed without opposition, made it a good deal less likely that the army would realize any return for all its efforts or that Congress would gain the taxing power. "By the last resolution," he thought, the army would "suffer in its reputation, & consequently in its present views."[21]

Pickering's gloom was by no means matched in the quarters of Henry Knox, who could not have been more delighted by the results of the meeting. Washington had blunted the potential for violence with an address that he characterized as "a masterly performance." In reporting on the meeting to his friend Secretary of War Benjamin Lincoln, he judged that "though intended for opposite purposes," it had turned out to be "one of the happiest circumstances of the war." It would "set the military character of America in a high point of view." With the crisis past, he suggested that Lincoln urge Congress to authorize at least a substantial bonus for the officers.[22]

Less than a week later Lincoln replied. He too was pleased at the way the meeting of the officers had turned out. He was even happier to report that Congress had just commuted the proposal that the officers be pensioned at half-pay for life to a plan to pay each man a bonus amounting to five years' full pay. Compensation was to be made in the form of 6 percent interest-bearing federal certificates.[23]

The pleasure that Lincoln felt at being able to report that the army had at last wrung from Congress this commutation resolution did not obscure the fact that the central issue, funding, had not yet been resolved. He hoped that the army's debt would be made distinct from the general national debt and paid in cash. Too often in the past, he thought, the army had been the victim of speculators. He did not want that to happen again. Speedy payment therefore was essential, for most of the officers were penurious and if their congressional certificates were not soon redeemed they would be forced to sell them to speculators at a fraction of their face value.[24] But since the states were an unlikely resource and Congress did not have the taxing power, redemption seemed only a faint possibility. Lincoln was forced to admit that insofar as the army was concerned, it was at least possible that everything had been lost save honor.[25]

General Horatio Gates, something more than a casual friend of Pickering's at the time, and one of those who endorsed the Newburgh Addresses, was very bitter over these developments. In a long note sent to Pickering in mid-May 1783, he inquired as to how the officers were reacting to the commutation plan and whether, since Congress had no revenues, there was any probability that the states would actually fund these debts. "If not," he thought, "how basely, & ungratefully are we treated." Gates denied any concern over his own losses. He had enough to live on exclusive of the commutation. "But I feel as poignantly for the distresses of the poor fellows who have been our faithful companions through the war, as if those distresses were all my own. . . . Perdition take the catifs who have deceived them."[26] Pickering, who shared Gates's sentiments, put at the head of his list of villains the name of George Washington, who he believed had undermined the political influence of the army at Newburgh.[27]

On the evening of March 25, as the quartermaster general sat in his quarters writing to Beckey about plans to move from the farm on the Schuylkill into Philadelphia, news arrived in camp of a preliminary peace treaty between the United States and Britain. To all intents and purposes the war was over and the process of demobilization could at last officially begin. On April 11, having been informed by Sir Guy Carleton, the British commander at New York, that Great Britain had declared a cease-fire, Congress reciprocated. Four days later it quickly ratified the preliminary treaty.[28]

With the war at an end, the officers and men of the army grew eager to shed their uniforms. Congress, of course, frightened by its recent brush with the army, was no less eager to demobilize. As usual, however, things were not so easy as they seemed. Some back pay would have to be provided, for most of the men heading home were totally destitute. Yet where was the money to come from? Here was irony, thought Pickering's old friend Richard Peters. For years, the problem was to find the money to keep an army. Now the problem was to find the money to disband it.[29] After considerable wrangling Congress agreed that the financier should issue $750,000 in treasury notes, the sum needed to cover three months' salary for the officers and men. Then, on May 26, a resolution was passed furloughing most of the men of the Continental Army.[30]

Early in June demobilization began in earnest, and Pickering was in the thick of it. To a busy quartermaster general, ending the war was almost as troublesome as running it had been. There were public buildings and war surplus materials to be sold. Livestock had to be disposed of as well, and Pickering did a thriving business in surplus dragoon horses, selling them to infantry officers who otherwise would have been forced to trudge long miles to their homes. Scythes and sickles as well as cannon, shot, and shell, not to mention the great chain that had guarded the passage up the Hudson at West Point, were converted into bar iron and sold to the highest bidder.

Most poignantly, there was the human side of demobilization. Prisoners of war had to be moved to nearby seaports and transportation found for them. And of course there was the problem of the returning veterans. The exodus began early in June, but it was the end of the month before Robert Morris could forward funds for demobilization authorized by Congress. By that time all but a few thousand enlistees had been furloughed. They left to return to their homes penniless, some in rags and, as Washington bitterly pointed out, "without the settlement of their Accounts or a farthing of money in their pockets." It was a national disgrace.[31]

During those chaotic days in early June, Pickering did what he could to aid the departing troops. But thousands of men were on the move, and he had practically no resources.[32] In no more than three weeks it was over. The last ragged soldier of the Continental Army had begun the long walk home, leaving behind Washington, some of the officers (including an irate quartermaster general), and a small force of Continentals who would remain in service until General Sir Guy Carleton actually surrendered New York.

From first to last, thought Pickering, the army had been treated shabbily. "Their sufferings & services seem already to be forgotten by multitudes," he wrote. The country had now surely lost its "reputation for justice and good faith."[33] Pickering felt a good deal of animosity too for George Washington, who in his estimation was largely responsible for the disaster. For he had undermined the influence of the Newburgh Addresses. Next, he allowed the demobilization of the army and the destruction of its political influence without so much as a protest.

The commander in chief was so popular, his charisma so compelling at this time, that even Pickering seldom chanced setting his honest feelings on paper. On this occasion, however, as thousands left camp with not even a word of thanks from the general, he could not resist commenting to Samuel Hodgdon on the "general disgust" that Washington's silence had aroused. He noted with evident delight that the officers of the New York line had presented "a manly, elegant & affectionate address to the Baron S[teuben]" but that they had not even taken leave of the commander in chief. Among Washington's "idolators," Pickering knew, this would be keenly felt. "Sea and land will be compassed," he predicted, "to procure addresses in the wonted stile of adulation" from those who remained. Pickering assured his friend, however, that he would not sign any such address.[34]

Washington was probably guilty of an oversight in not issuing some sort of informal statement of thanks and farewell at this time. But the demobilization was confusing and swift; moreover, the men being mustered out were not actually being discharged. They were being furloughed on the chance that something might go amiss and the war continue. In this event they would have been recalled. Washington was simply waiting for the appropriate moment to take his farewell, and Pickering was being waspish in attacking him for this. Few could have been more sympathetic to the troops than their commander in chief. Indeed, he was one of those most critical of the manner in which Congress had mishandled the demobilization, noting at the time that "ingratitude" such as this was common throughout all ages of history and that "Republics in particular have been famed for the exercise of that unnatural and Sordid Vice." "From my Soul," he wrote, "I pity the Army."[35]

A few days before leading a remnant of the victorious American Army into New York City, General Washington issued his Farewell Orders. A member of the committee selected to draft a reply, Pickering remained determined not to put his name to any statement that did not express his feelings.[36] He was almost as good as his word and surprisingly successful in winning the other members of the committee, Henry Knox and Alexander McDougall, to his point of view. When they met at West Point, these officers knew that New York had refused to endorse a new congressional plan of finance, the latest scheme to win the taxing power for Congress. It seemed an end to all hope that the officers' federal certificates of indebtedness might be redeemed in real money. Under these circumstances Pickering, McDougall, and Knox agreed that their reply to Washington offered a last chance for the officers to speak collectively. It was a judgment that combined poor taste with pointless politics, for as Pickering and the others knew, the battle had been lost when the army was demobilized. Nevertheless, with Pickering to help guide them, the three men formulated a reply to Washington that was as much an exercise in public self-pity as it was a note of farewell.

Absolving Washington of responsibility for the fact that the officers had not been rewarded for their service became a way of indicting the country. "If your attempts to insure to the army the just, the promised rewards of their long, severe, and dangerous services have failed of success, we believe it has arisen from causes not in your excellency's power to control."[37] For two pages more the officers' address dwelt not on Washington's role as a leader but on the injustices done to the army:

> To that merit in the Revolution, which, under the auspices of Heaven, the armies have displayed, posterity will do justice; and the sons will blush whose fathers were their foes. Most gladly would we cast a veil on every act which sullies the reputation of our country. Never should the page of history be stained with its dishonor: even from our memories should the idea be erased.[38]

The address attacked those states that opposed the plan of finance, lamenting "opposition" to "measures which alone can recover and fix on a permanent basis the credit of the States: measures which are essential to the justice, the honor, and interest of the nation." In the long run, the address continued, justice would surely triumph. Therefore, although the army had been treated shabbily:

> Still we hope that the prejudices of the misinformed will be removed, and the arts of false and selfish popularity, addressed to the feelings of avarice, defeated. . . . We trust, the disingenuousness of a few will not sully the reputation, the honor, and dignity of the great and respectable of the States.[39]

Finally, indeed almost anticlimactically, the address got down to the business of congratulating Washington on the great victory. A few modest but well-chosen words of praise followed, concluding with what was at least for Knox and McDougall an earnest wish.

> We sincerely pray God that happiness may long be yours, and that when you quit the stage of human life, you may receive from the Unerring Judge the rewards of valor exerted to save the oppressed,—of patriotism and disinterested virtue.[40]

In this way, with what was in some measure a snarl of self-pity and defiant outrage, Timothy Pickering bade farewell not only to George Washington but to the American Revolution as well. Bitter because he felt that he had been cheated by his countrymen and damning himself for his stupidity in wasting so much of his life, he turned now with a vengeance to making up for lost time. For those with ambition and vision, fortunes remained to be made; Pickering was determined that in the future he would neither "piddle in trade" nor "starve in public office."

SEVEN

The Allure of Western Lands

ON MAY 10, 1783, at what seemed an ideal moment, the firm of Pickering and Hodgdon, commission merchants, opened its doors in Philadelphia. For eight long years the war had denied Americans regular access to European and English goods. Now the fighting was over and an economic boom was in the making. Unhappily, however, Pickering and his partner were only two among a myriad of new merchants who, as Alexander Hamilton noted some time later, "without capital and in many instances without information . . . rushed into trade" in this period.[1]

Competition was ferocious, and even though Pickering's friends and relatives in Massachusetts patronized the fledgling company, there was never enough business. Worse, the boom was short-lived, and by the following year the country was in the grip of economic crisis. The national market was quickly glutted with European manufactured goods and surplus domestic agricultural products. Adding to the nation's distress, an unfavorable balance of trade drained America of specie, causing stagnation everywhere. From Boston, Pickering's friend and sometime business associate, Congressman Elbridge Gerry, complained that the "Scarcity of money in consequence of our excessive and extravagant importations of British frippery" had been responsible for economic disaster.[2]

By 1785 the situation was grave, with merchants everywhere failing. The prominent Baltimore merchant Clement Biddle was forced out of business, and in Boston no less a figure than Samuel A. Otis went into bankruptcy. Even the powerful Robert Morris found himself in serious difficulties.[3]

Pickering and Hodgdon managed to avoid bankruptcy, not because they showed greater business acumen than many others who failed, but because they remained on the government payroll, Pickering as the quartermaster general of a virtually nonexistent army, and Hodgdon as the equally unimportant commissary general of military stores.[4] During the war Pickering had frequently expressed bitterness over the personal sacrifices he claimed to be making by remaining in public service. Now the public was paying him back and he was not complaining. His salary allowed him to live comfortably in Philadelphia with Beckey and his family, now grown to three sons, in spite of worsening business conditions. There was even enough left over to dabble in some potentially profitable land speculations.

For Pickering, who had previously been opposed to all kinds of speculation, "land jobbing" was something new. But in late 1783 he began to divert the greater part of his energies to the purchase of undeveloped lands.[5] That fortunes might be made by buying and selling land fascinated many at this time, and Pickering was but one of a galaxy of businessmen who caught the fever. In 1784 he and Hodgdon purchased Virginia land warrants for some twenty-five thousand acres.[6] Later that same year, when the Philadelphia speculator Tench Francis approached him with another proposition, Pickering plunged once again. Together with Francis, Hodgdon, and Tench Coxe, he bought up twenty-thousand acres in what is now northeastern Pennsylvania along the Great Bend of the Susquehanna River. These richly forested holdings, located in the "Old Purchase," an area acquired from the Indians in 1768, were within 150 miles of Philadelphia. Pickering believed they would become the basis of his personal fortune.[7]

As long as the speculative enthusiasm persisted, Pickering remained actively involved. Early in 1785 he began to take an interest in lands in the so-called New Purchase, five million acres in the northern and western reaches of Pennsylvania.[8] On April 6, shortly before New Purchase lands went on the market, Pickering, together with Hodgdon, Coxe, Duncan Ingraham, and Miers Fisher, formed the Potter Land Company. Named for General James Potter, the company's surveyor, the firm was organized to acquire holdings in the New Purchase. Pickering wanted Elbridge Gerry to take a share in the company but his friend refused, arguing that the Pennsylvania legislature, taking advantage of the recent speculative surge, had set the price of the land too high. Old Purchase lands had sold for one hundred pounds per thousand acres, approximately one-third the price of the more distant New Purchase offerings. Moreover, under the pressure of speculation, the market price of depreciated Pennsylvania soldier's notes as well as old state-issued certificates of indebtedness which might be used to purchase state lands had gone up by about 50 percent. Gerry plainly did not believe that the market could long sustain these price levels. They would hold for a time, he thought, but when the continental land office began selling federal lands, the glut would be so bad that there would be few buyers at any price.[9]

Gerry had nothing against speculation per se and advised his friend to buy Pennsylvania soldier's notes which, in the spring of 1785, were selling at about one-tenth of their face value. These notes were bound to increase in value as land speculators bought them up, thus guaranteeing substantial profits. In the long run, Gerry believed, they would appreciate at least as fast as land. At the end of several years, he predicted, a careful investor might, if he were so inclined, use the certificates to purchase as much land—"improved in a considerable degree" at that—as he could under present circumstances.[10]

But Pickering wouldn't listen, for he was not interested in substantial profits. Anxious to make up for lost time, he was in search of instant wealth. That was the allure of land speculation. He remained a captive of these optimistic imaginings throughout his lifetime. At least in this respect the reputedly frugal Pickering was no different from a compulsive gambler.

During the weeks preceding the official opening of sales in the New Purchase, Pickering and Hodgdon bought up depreciated soldiers' notes and certificates of indebtedness which, when exchanged for "new loan" certificates, could be used to purchase lands at the Pennsylvania land office. The market was tight and, as Gerry had predicted, the price they had to pay was high, more than 20 cents on the dollar. They managed nonetheless to raise the necessary $25,200 in certificates. Later in the month, without even the benefit of a preliminary land survey, the Potter Company bought up ninety-six land warrants. Pickering's share amounted to approximately 11,500 acres.[11]

Regrettably, Pickering's ambitions bore no relationship to reality. Four years later not one acre of Potter Company land had been sold or leased, nor had any settlements grown up in the vicinity. As General Potter explained, not only had there been no increase in the number of settlers in Pennsylvania, there had been an actual decrease.[12] Gerry had been right; Pickering was saddled with over 11,000 unsaleable acres.

Many of those closest to him tried to convince Pickering to abandon his land speculations and accept a political appointment in Massachusetts.[13] But he refused. It would have been the same as swearing an oath of poverty, for none of the offices Massachusetts had to offer paid particularly well, and Pickering had no means of making a supplemental income. Instead he clung to his job as quartermaster general and pinned his hopes on making a fortune in the land market.

Pickering's uncontrollable urge to speculate in undeveloped lands was curious behavior for a man who regularly extolled the virtues of frugality. More than that, it was dangerous, for his resources were slim and his position as quartermaster general of the army was insecure. Sooner or later Congress would fill the vacancy in the War Department created when Benjamin Lincoln resigned in November 1783. When that happened, Pickering knew, his own job would in all likelihood be eliminated. His major hope was that he would be made the new secretary of war. Failing that, he could only aspire to some other position in the bureaucracy. Embittered though he was over his years of public service, Pickering had no place else to turn.

In February 1784, Pickering was informed by the politically alert Sam Hodgdon, who spent a great deal of time gossiping on the outskirts of power, that Congress would probably soon fill the vacancy in the War Department. He lost no time making his friends in Congress aware of his interest.[14] Unhappily, however, Pickering found little encouragement, largely because Henry Knox, who had Washington's endorsement, had preempted him with many of New England's delegates. Even Elbridge Gerry, who seemed genuinely sympathetic to his candidacy, warned Pickering that in all likelihood he would not be able to support him.[15] As for Thomas Mifflin, president of Congress at the time, Pickering badly misjudged him. In attempting to convince the Pennsylvanian to endorse him, Pickering guilefully insinuated that if he were appointed he would be able to combine the quartermaster general's office with the War Department job, thus saving Congress one salary. Mifflin never replied to Pickering's note but was probably the source of an embarrassing rumor that Pickering had offered to combine the two offices and to serve for a meager $1,400 a year at that.[16]

An entire year passed before Congress finally filled the vacancy in the War Office. In the interim Pickering's congressional contacts attempted to steer him into some other position. In December, Samuel Holten asked him about the possibility of taking a place on the newly created Treasury Board.[17] At first Pickering was interested, but when he learned that Congress required members of the Treasury Board to give up their speculative activities in Continental paper, he took himself out of the running, reminding his friend as he did so of his continued interest in the War Department. It was a futile hope. He had no firm support in Congress.[18]

When in March 1785 Knox was appointed secretary of war, Pickering reacted indignantly. In a letter to Horatio Gates, a tirade against Washington, he charged that the only reason Knox had been chosen was that he had the support of the "Great Man" who "interested himself warmly" in his behalf. For Pickering, losing out to Knox was more than a humiliating political disappointment; it was an economic disaster. His business was a failure and his federal appointment would probably soon be terminated. In any event, he wrote proudly to Gates, he still had his lands, "and while God gives me health I can raise bread for myself, my wife & our little ones." [19]

But again, as on so many earlier occasions, Pickering's words stood in marked contrast to his behavior, for he refused to give up his job as quartermaster general, administratively redundant though it was, without one last effort to save it. Through his business partner, Hodgdon, he appealed first to Secretary Knox and then directly to Congress.[20] But it was to no avail. Not long after this, Congress voted to eliminate the Quartermaster General's Department entirely.

Denied his government sinecure, Pickering managed to limp along until the summer of 1786, but his economic prospects were at low ebb. Supported by Gerry, Holten, and Congressman Rufus King, he made one last attempt to gain a federal appointment but was again thwarted.[21] With business in the doldrums he had only two choices. He could return to Salem, a failure, or move to the frontier in a serious effort at developing his Pennsylvania lands in the Old Purchase. He decided in favor of the frontier.

In August 1786, Pickering set out to survey his holdings on the north branch of the Susquehanna River near the New York state line.[22] He was depressed by his business failures and humiliated by his inability to win any of a number of federal or state appointments. Yet it was exhilarating to be out in the woods, back on the land, and Pickering was amazed at the potential he discovered. Shawnee Plains he described as "the most beautiful tract of land my eyes ever beheld!" The soil seemed "inexhaustibly fertile" and the crops "luxurious." Only the settlers, most of whom had come originally from Connecticut, proved a disappointment. He expected more from New Englanders, but their agriculture was "ordinary" and their homes, "the hovels they dwell in," were "wretched beyond description," no more than "poorly constructed log houses, some without chimneys, but only a hole in the roof to let the smoke out." He had never before imagined that such "wretchedness could be found in the United States." Nothing, Pickering felt, could excuse "such general negligence."[23]

Pickering knew that prospects for developing the entire region, including his holdings, hinged on ending the violence that had wracked the Wyoming Valley for the past seventeen years. The war, of course, was partially responsible for the continuing stagnation of the area. But both before and after the conflict local civil war had flared intermittently, the result of a rivalry between settlers who had come from Connecticut and who based their land claims on titles granted them by the Connecticut-chartered Susquehannah Land Company, and other so-called Pennamite land claimants who held titles to 110,000 acres in the same area granted them by the Penn family.[24]

In December 1782, a federal court in Trenton had laid the foundation for a settlement to this quarrel when it recognized Pennsylvania's sovereignty in the area and ruled against the Susquehannah Company's claims. Simultaneously, members of the court suggested that while the claims of the company to millions of acres were invalid, it would be sound policy for Pennsylvania to recognize the legitimacy of land titles issued by the company and held by settlers actually living in the area, and to compensate Pennamite claimants for any lands they would be forced to give up as a result.[25] Pennsylvania, however, ignored the court's advice. Both sides continued to insist on the legitimacy of their claims, until by 1785 relations between the Connecticut settlers and the commonwealth had completely deteriorated.

Pickering thought the court's recommendation excellent. It seemed only fair to confirm the claims of people who had lived on the land, improved it, and defended it during the war. Moreover, such a move was clearly in Pennsylvania's interest. It would effectively divide the original Connecticut freeholders (he estimated they numbered some three hundred families) from the company, destroy the most important element of the company's power in the region, and allow the immediate economic development of millions of acres.

Pickering's calculations were the result of a comfortable one-to-one relationship between morality and self-interest. He held only about 450 acres in the area actually in dispute, but all of his holdings were included in the larger region that stood to increase in value once the fighting had stopped. Pacifying those settlers who held titles granted them by the Susquehannah Company and thus eliminating the company as a factor in the area were therefore objects of considerable interest to him, as well as to a number of other speculators who held Pennsylvania land titles in the Old Purchase.[26]

Pickering returned to Philadelphia hopeful of convincing the state's Republican leaders that peace could be achieved in the valley and the Susquehannah Company eliminated as a political factor there, if certain conditions were met. First, the Wyoming district would have to be set off as a separate county, thus guaranteeing the Connecticut people local autonomy and control of their own courts of justice. Next the Pennsylvania assembly would have to pass special legislation legitimizing the titles of those Connecticut claimants who had actually settled land prior to the Trenton decision of December 30, 1782.[27] Pickering understood that such an arrangement would not satisfy all of the people in the area who held claims granted by the Susquehannah Company. Since 1785 the company, seeking to strengthen its position in the region, had been granting between one and two hundred acres of land to settlers who would agree to defend the company's claims by force if necessary. A small private army of perhaps as many as three hundred half-share men was already in the region, and more were being recruited all the time. Pickering gave no thought to confirming their land titles, for these people had migrated to the area after the Trenton decision and as part of a large-scale effort to render it inoperative. Then, too, Pickering felt confident that they did not constitute a force sufficient to maintain company power in the region. Finally, the half-share men were encroaching in areas that Pickering and his friends and business associates claimed for themselves in the township of Athens near Tioga.

In the seesaw struggle for power that characterized Pennsylvania's politics during the Confederation Period, the Republicans had just regained the upper hand. Many of their leaders were determined to set the Wyoming controversy to rest once and for all. James Wilson, Benjamin Rush, and Robert Morris, the acknowledged leader of the Republicans, were only three of the important legislators and speculators with whom Pickering conferred. What he had to say conformed perfectly with their own thinking and reinforced a move already begun to settle the Wyoming dispute.[28]

This was the beginning of a major new political undertaking for Timothy Pickering. Rush and Wilson both suggested that he was the perfect choice to bring peace to the troubled valley by establishing government and the rule of Pennsylvania law there. A New Englander by birth, he would create confidence among the suspicious Connecticut claimants. A Pennsylvanian by choice and well connected in the legislature, he would inspire trust in that quarter as well.[29]

The flattering attention paid to him by Morris and others among the Republican elite in Philadelphia was too much for Pickering to resist. In return for a commitment from the Pennsylvania Assembly to establish a new county and a guarantee that the claims of the settlers from Connecticut (excluding the half-share men) would be confirmed, he agreed to move to the Wyoming Valley and undertake the difficult task of making peace. But he also insisted upon being appointed to a number of local offices that he believed would produce a substantial income in fees as the population grew. Moreover, he arranged to become the land agent for several of his friends who also held lands in the area.[30] Once peace and the rule of law were firmly established and the Susquehannah Company driven out, land prices would surely rise as settlers moved into the region. When they did, Pickering would be on hand to manage his own interests as well as those of his business associates.

During the earliest stages of this new venture, events moved with remarkable smoothness. On September 23, 1786, Luzerne County was created by the legislature. Within three weeks the Pennsylvania Council had appointed Pickering to virtually every important county office that was within its power to dispense. Opposition got nowhere. When Charles Pettit, a Constitutionalist leader and at the time a delegate to the Continental Congress from Pennsylvania, recommended another man for the office of prothonotary in Luzerne, the nomination was quashed. Benjamin Franklin, president of the Council, informed Pettit that Pickering was "a nearly unanimous choice."[31]

To the delight of Pickering and Pennsylvania's Republicans, the prospect of driving the Susquehannah Company out of state was given a significant boost by a gentleman's agreement arranged between Connecticut and Pennsylvania. Connecticut had been urging Congress to accept her western land cession, but insisted simultaneously on retaining rights of soil to a strip of land 120 miles wide beyond the western boundary of Pennsylvania. There was great resistance to this proposal on the part of other states. However, when Pennsylvania agreed to acquiesce in Connecticut's reserve, if in return the latter would withdraw all support from the Susquehannah Company and other dissidents in the Wyoming Valley, the other states went along. The company, facing a determined effort by Pennsylvania to eradicate its influence in Wyoming, had in effect been isolated and now faced an attack upon its power from within.[32]

In the battle shaping up between Pennsylvania, soon to be represented in Luzerne County by Pickering, and the Susquehannah Company, the company was at a serious disadvantage. While it could count on the support of the half-share men, who were totally dependent upon the company for their lands, it had few other allies. It could not rely on support from the government of Connecticut. Nor could the original settlers in the area any longer be considered completely trustworthy, for Pennsylvania was attempting to lure them away. Not even the company's commissioners resident in the Wyoming region could be totally relied upon. Of the six, only John Franklin and John Jenkins were completely loyal. The others, Colonel Zebulon Butler, Captain John Paul Schott, Nathan Denison, and Obadiah Gore, were all question marks.

Early in January 1787, Timothy Pickering returned to the Wyoming

Valley, this time as a settler and public official empowered to organize county government and arrange local elections. It seemed certain that the company would try to block the elections, possible that it might even resort to violence.[33] That, however, was a problem that would have to be faced if and when it arose. A more important question was whether John Franklin and Zebulon Butler, appointed to help him organize and supervise the elections, would cooperate. Pickering suspected that Butler would probably go along, but Franklin, a fiery defender of the most extreme claims of the company, would in all likelihood refuse. It was a troublesome way to begin. Had there been any possibility of proceeding without depending on these men, Pickering would doubtless have preferred that option. But Franklin and Butler were the two foremost leaders in the area. To have ignored them at so critical a point in the county's political development would have been to alienate the settlers, who trusted only their own leaders.

Pickering's earliest political efforts in the valley were aided by the fact that when he arrived, Franklin was in Connecticut at a meeting of the directors of the Susquehannah Company. With Franklin out of the way he had little difficulty convincing Butler to cooperate in supervising elections scheduled for February 1.[34] Once Butler had been brought into the fold it was not difficult to convince Schott and Gore to go along.

Whether peaceful elections could actually be held in Wyoming was another question, one that occupied Pickering during the next few weeks. On the day after news of the upcoming balloting was announced, he was deluged with visitors anxious to ascertain how the elections would affect their economic interests. Among the callers was John Jenkins, a Sequehannah Company commissioner and a colleague of Franklin's. Jenkins arrived in the afternoon and spent two hours debating the issues with Pickering in the presence of a large and interested gathering. Debating is perhaps the wrong description; it was a shouting match, with Jenkins charging that the elections were a trap. Once the people voted, thus admitting Pennsylvania's sovereignty, they would, he alleged, be "stripped of their lands." If the legislators really intended to do the settlers justice, he enquired, why did they not confirm land claims prior to the elections?

Pickering, who could hardly admit that the legislature distrusted the settlers and viewed the elections as a test of their good faith, avoided a direct answer while insisting that important men in state government realized mistakes had been made in the past and wanted to correct them. Once elections had been held and county government actually began to function, he assured Jenkins, the settlers' land claims would be confirmed.[35] But the settlers should not misunderstand. The state had no intention of confirming the entire Susquehannah Company claim. It was only those settlers who had moved into the region before the Trenton decision who could hope for confirmation. If the settlers insisted on standing with the company, everyone would lose, for Pennsylvania would never surrender on that point. Jenkins left the debate unconvinced, but Pickering may have had more success with others who had been listening as the two men argued.[36]

Against a background of political instability and potential violence, Pickering barnstormed the huge county trying to convince the settlers to hold peaceful elections. It was a frustrating business, for rumors of Philadelphia's deceitful intentions circulated freely and were not easily quashed. At one public meeting Pickering faced the charge that as soon as county government began operating the state would demand twelve years in back taxes. Frequently he was forced to respond to Jenkins's earlier allegation that the projected elections were a trap, that once the people had accepted Pennsylvania law they would be evicted from their lands. And always there was the problem of convincing the settlers that contrary to what Jenkins and others might say, Congress was not going to intercede in support of the Susquehannah Company's claims.[37]

When not responding to one or another of the false allegations hurled from all directions by Jenkins and his friends, Pickering promised that if the people would show their good faith by holding peaceful elections, the state would in turn confirm the land titles of those who had been in the valley prior to the Trenton decision. After eighteen years of violence and insecurity, Pickering's appeal held out the promise of peace on attractive terms. But promises had been made before. Pickering understood that it was difficult for people who felt that they had been consistently mistreated and deceived by Pennsylvania to ignore the past, and sensed the need for some more substantial commitment. When one of his listeners remarked that the settlers would have greater trust in him if he would buy land under a Connecticut title, he agreed on the spot. It was an inspired move that did as much as anything else to disarm his opponents.[38]

Opposition errors helped Pickering too. One of the best indications of a general lack of coordination among the company's forces was the fact that leaders in Connecticut and New York did not know that Butler, Schott, and Gore were cooperating with Pickering. As a result these men continued to receive confidential correspondence from other company leaders that they frequently turned over to him. He could hardly have been better informed had he been on the company's governing board. One letter to Butler from William Judd, a New

Yorker who was among the most militant of the company's leaders, proved particularly useful.[39] At Pickering's suggestion, Butler read this damaging piece of correspondence before a large meeting in Wilkes-Barre. Its impact was very great, for it demonstrated that, far from being concerned with the interests of the settlers, Judd was in fact willing to sacrifice them in the service of his own adventurous economic vision.[40]

Of course Pickering experienced some setbacks. At Nanticoke he was nearly mobbed by a group of half-share men sent by John Jenkins to disrupt the meeting. And he never was able to convince Wilkes-Barre's minister, Parson Jacob Johnson, to come over to his side. The parson swore that he would *"never change till the day that Christ comes to judgment."* Even to Pickering that seemed a definitive stand. Reflecting on his run-in with the "wild boys" of Nanticoke and his failure with Johnson, Pickering grew philosophical. "Perhaps the most difficult characters to reason with are the young & the old," he wrote, "the former are too sanguine and rash—the latter think that 'years teach wisdom' & having long entertained their prejudices, it is next to impossible to eradicate them."[41]

Pickering played his political role at this time with patience and skill. Impressive in his appearances before meetings of the settlers, he remained cool and emotionally collected throughout most of the preelection period. Significantly he refused to be upset by persistent reports that the opposition planned to disrupt the election. As early as January 11 he heard reports that Franklin had instructed Jenkins to do whatever was necessary to stop the elections from taking place. On the thirteenth Butler and Schott, whose sources were unimpeachable, reiterated the danger of violence when they reported that Franklin and the notorious Ethan Allen were said to be returning to the valley.[42] Eight days later Pickering received yet another warning that the elections were in trouble. An anonymous correspondent from Tioga, where the company was strongest, wrote to inform Pennsylvania's increasingly worried representative that "there is about 30 persons intends to act desperate on the election day to disturb it if possible."[43] These omens of potential trouble led Pickering's supporters to suggest that he prepare for an attack, but realizing that arming would be widely misconstrued, he resisted this temptation. Instead he publicly dismissed rumored violence as not worth his notice and continued to urge the Connecticut people to hold the elections and trust Pennsylvania to confirm their titles.[44]

Cautiously optimistic, Pickering waited out the last days before the voting. Election day itself was peaceful; some 140 freeholders even took the oath of allegiance to Pennsylvania. Participation in the various electoral contests was nothing short of impressive. There were 222 votes cast in the race for the assembly and 218 in the election for councilor. Contests for some of the local offices attracted even greater interest. It would have been a complete triumph for Pickering except that to his chagrin John Franklin was elected to the Pennsylvania Assembly.[45]

Franklin's election was by no means the result of mere chance. Failing in their effort to discourage settlers from voting, his friends quietly organized support for him hoping that his election would provoke the Pennsylvania Assembly into reneging on its promise to confirm titles. Shortly after his election, in a move certainly designed to add insult to injury, Franklin informed the speaker of the assembly that he would be unable to attend the current session.[46]

Long before the elections took place, Pickering had begun to consider the problem of petitioning Pennsylvania's Assembly for a confirming law. His month-long stay in the area and his conferences with Butler, Obadiah Gore, newly elected Councilor Nathan Denison, and other settlers had taught him a good deal about the complexities of the land tenure situation in the valley. When he first arrived, he thought that all the settlers who would be affected lived in seventeen townships that straggled along the river. He soon learned, however, that about one hundred freeholders owned land in "pitches" not encompassed by any township. These claims would also have to be confirmed.

He also discovered that the definition of a settler in common use in Philadelphia was inadequate. The legislature had intended to confirm the holdings of those who had come to the valley, settled, and improved their lands prior to the Trenton decision. Many of the claimants, however, though they had come to the region before that landmark decision, had not been able to settle their own lands. During the war the menace of the British and the Indians made it too dangerous to live in unpopulated regions, so they had squatted in relatively safe places until after the war. In this category there were about a hundred freeholders whose claims would also have to be confirmed. To disallow them, Pickering thought, would be not only unjust but foolish, for it would lead to the breakdown of the fragile peace he was working so hard to solidify.

In sum, by the time he began drafting the petition to the assembly, Pickering realized that his earlier estimate of the number of settlers who qualified for confirmation was low by a factor of two and that much more land was involved than he had earlier supposed. Pennsylvania would have to cede something in the neighborhood of 180,000 acres to satisfy the settlers while compensating Pennamite claimants for 110,000 acres that would be lost as a result.[47]

Months before, the legislators had made it plain that they would pass no confirming law that could be broadly construed. Anxious to avoid ceding one more acre than was necessary, they expected individual settlers to petition for confirmation, providing as they did an exact description of the land they claimed. Yet Pickering drafted a petition calling for a statute that would establish the state's blanket commitment to confirmation immediately.[48] There are a number of possible explanations for this. It may even be that he did not want to give the legislature time to become provoked by John Franklin's recent election. However, it is difficult to avoid the conclusion that he was anxious to win a commitment to confirmation because he realized that the legislators did not yet know exactly how much land was actually involved and he feared that when they found out they would balk.

Early in February 1787, when Pickering left Wilkes-Barre for Philadelphia, carrying with him one copy of the carefully drawn petition, he was in a rather optimistic frame of mind. To that point things had gone well. The political situation in Wyoming, however, was still extremely fluid and far more unpredictable than he imagined. A key factor in his early successes had been the absence of John Franklin, the most dynamic opposition leader in the region. But shortly after Pickering left Wilkes-Barre, Franklin returned. Old political patterns quickly reemerged as he rallied to his support those who continued to distrust Pennsylvania and intimidated those who favored compromise. It is indicative of how rapidly change could occur in the area that when Franklin's partisans seized and publicly burned a second copy of the petition for a confirming law that was then still circulating, no one objected.[49]

In this changed political atmosphere many of those who had formerly cooperated with Pickering began drifting back into Franklin's orbit, among them Zebulon Butler and John Paul Schott. When Franklin called a Susquehannah Company Court of Commissioners to order for the purpose of making new land grants and deciding land disputes among claimants holding titles already issued by the company, Butler sat as a member of the court and his son served as the secretary. Schott, whose house was used as a hearing room, also participated.[50] The political situation was soon so far out of hand that Dr. Joseph Sprague, one of Pickering's friends in Wilkes-Barre, wrote warning him that all that had been accomplished might quickly be undone. "To make a long story a Short one the Divel is to pay and the Sucomstance of this place is goeing wose and wost and I am afraid twil Ind in the Totol Dessilation of this Setelment."[51]

Though distressed by this news, Pickering, who believed that his success or failure ultimately hinged on passage of a confirming law, remained in Philadelphia where he would be in a position to influence the legislature. On March 5, Nathan Denison, Luzerne's councilor, presented Pickering's carefully drawn petition to the assembly. On the day following it was sent to a special subcommittee. One of the committee members was George Clymer, a friend and business associate of Pickering's, but the committee was not dominated by men so sympathetic. To most of its members the petition was a disappointment because, as their report stated, it "advances claims collectively, and is made for entire and extensive districts." The committee wanted to know exactly how much land the legislature was being asked to give away and where it was located.[52]

There was more to the committee's discontent than simple disappointment over the form of the petition. Renewed violence in the valley, John Franklin's election, and his refusal to attend the assembly's session were all grist for Pennamite mills. Nathan Denison was so troubled by the tide of hostility running against the people of Wyoming in Philadelphia that he wrote hurriedly to Zeb Butler naively urging him to get Franklin to attend the assembly. The Pennamites, he wrote, are saying openly that he will not attend. If he did not, Denison wrote, it would make "us appear like a faithles People as Some . . . hear have us to be." Denison was sure that the assembly was prepared to do the right thing. But accomplishing this would be much simpler if Franklin would only appear. Even if he came only long enough to answer one roll call, it would "stop the mouths of those who wish to have him not Come."[53]

For the next several days Pickering was a very busy man. Both he and Denison were among those called to testify before the committee. He also spent a good deal of time with friends in the legislature lobbying in favor of the petition. Denison was impressed. He informed Butler that Pickering, who was "very active," had used "Every reasonable argument in favor of our title and Spares no Pains to bring the matter to a reasonable settlement."[54]

Unhappiness over the nature of the petition persisted on the committee in spite of everything Pickering and Denison could do. Had it not been for the fact that the preservation of peace seemed to hinge on passage, the committee would probably have rejected it. Instead, with a good bit of reluctance, it recommended that the legislature pass a general law confirming the land claims of the old Connecticut settlers. It further proposed the appointment of three special commissioners to implement the law. Finally it suggested that Pennsylvania (Pennamite) land claimants whose titles would be invalidated by this statute be compensated with an equivalent value in public lands elsewhere.[55]

On March 27, 1787, only a few days after the bill was reported out of committee, it was rushed to a vote and passed. Blitzkrieg political tactics worked where a more judicious approach to the legislative process would in all likelihood have failed, for although a majority of the legislators supported the principle of confirmation, few from either party actually had any idea of just how much land they were ceding. When the question arose during the short debate, advocates of confirmation answered with vague references to about 20,000 acres of "first quality" land as well as other acreage elsewhere, whereas in fact at the very least the legislature was committing itself to grant 180,000 acres to the Connecticut settlers. Nor had the question of compensation for the Pennamite claimants to be dispossessed by the law been carefully considered. One irate legislator later testified that he had voted for confirmation only because he had been assured that the Pennamites were willing to accept an equivalent in undeveloped lands elsewhere in payment. When this turned out to be untrue, he as well as others in the assembly charged outright deception.[56]

All of this would come back to haunt Pickering. At the time the law was enacted, however, it seemed everything he hoped for. It was broad enough to include all Connecticut settlers who had come to the valley before the Trenton decision. It established a commission (Pickering was chosen as one of the members) that was authorized to investigate individual claims, to survey, and legally to certify them. Finally, the commission was given ample time, eight months, to complete the entire confirming process.[57]

Pickering was elated, for he believed that the Confirming Act marked the end of his contest with the Susquehannah Company. On the day it was enacted he wrote excitedly to his brother that after nearly eighteen years of continuing strife, "peace and good government" were soon to be introduced to Luzerne County. It seemed the beginning of important personal economic and political opportunities, too. Pickering instructed his brother to sell his remaining land in Salem. "I . . . consider myself as fixed for the remainder of my life in this state; and here I should wish to concenter my interest."[58]

Pickering now prepared to crush the opposition in the valley once and for all. His first move was to advertise the coming of the commissioners to implement the new law.[59] His second was to bring Zebulon Butler and John Paul Schott back into line. Sensing his strength, Pickering sent a sharp rebuke to Butler for his willingness to participate as a Susquehannah Company commissioner on Franklin's tribunal. He found it "extraordinary that some people at Wyoming should not have patience enough to wait for the result of the assembly's deliberations" before they began putting into effect "the unwarrantable resolves of the Susquehannah Company." In a less than oblique warning he remarked that such actions served to convince many in Pennsylvania that though some in Wyoming talked peace they had other intentions. Having given Butler this firm warning he then informed him that the Confirming Act was more generous than anyone could have expected, for the land was to be granted to the settlers free and the surveying costs would be slight.[60] To make it perfectly evident to Butler that he would be wise to get back on the right side, Pickering further remarked that representatives of Connecticut then in Philadelphia were absolutely delighted with the Confirming Act. In other words, rebels in the valley could count on no support from that quarter.[61]

Pickering also took care to inform Butler that Daniel Shays' uprising in Massachusetts had been crushed. Rumors of separatist conspiracies regularly surfaced in the Wyoming Valley and Pickering believed them to be accurate. He knew from correspondence between company leaders earlier turned over to him that some of them hoped for the fragmentation of the union. They viewed Shays' Rebellion as the beginning of a chain reaction that could destroy not only the federal authority but state governments as well, creating an entirely new political situation.[62] While it is difficult to be precise about the extent of Pickering's fears, he was clearly delighted to hear that the Shaysites had been routed. He was also very pleased that a constitutional convention was soon to convene in Philadelphia.

Early in the second week in April, Pickering was back in Wilkes-Barre, determined to bring Butler and Schott back into the fold and to hold elections for justice of the peace in the three districts that composed Luzerne County. On both counts he had one very powerful argument in his favor: the Confirming Act was law. Once back he was pleasantly surprised to discover that Butler could be counted upon to support elections. The old gentleman was not so easily convinced, however, to stop sitting as a Susquehannah Company commissioner. Gradually, though, Pickering's blandishments had their effect. By the end of April, John Franklin was near despair. Only one of his fellow commissioners, John Jenkins, could be relied upon. Butler was a serious question mark. Schott, though somewhat more reliable, was too opportunistic to be considered secure. Denison was supporting the Confirming Act, and Obadiah Gore, always ready to sacrifice the company's interest for his own, could not be trusted at all. Recently he had even refused to survey two new townships for the company. "Ingratitude blacker than Hell!" raged Franklin.[63]

The political advantage that the Confirming Act gave to Pickering was further revealed during the elections for justices of the peace held that April. Pickering viewed these elections as a test of strength and expected Franklin to attempt to stop the voting. If violence occurred anywhere, observers expected that it would come in the county's third district, to the north near Tioga, for it was there that most of the half-share men lived. As soon as plans for voting were announced John Jenkins traveled to Tioga to organize the opposition. But he had little success. When the polls opened only six men would stand with him. James Smith, son of William Hooker Smith, who supported the elections, managed to raise a force of thirty-two men who went to the polls in a group determined to vote. Sensing that the elections would be held on schedule, Obadiah Gore, who was superintending the voting at Tioga, even gave in to Jenkins's demand that he be allowed to read publicly an inflammatory address from William Judd to the freeholders urging them to resist Pennsylvania's rule. As Gore suspected, none of the prospective voters were impressed, and the opposition quickly crumbled. To Jenkins's chagrin, many of those whom he had brought with him actually voted.[64] In the other two districts, delays and some violence did occur. But by May 4, 1787, elections in all three districts had been held. Franklin's career, Pickering rejoiced, was "at an end."[65]

EIGHT

Kidnaped

PICKERING'S CONFIDENCE that passage of the Confirming Act marked the end of his struggle was in fact misplaced, for resistance to the implementation of the law soon developed. In Philadelphia the Pennamites raised a furious outcry. Claiming that their property rights had been invaded by the legislature, some even threatened armed resistance. Before long, rumors that the Confirming Act would be repealed were circulating openly. Hodgdon, who served as Pickering's eyes and ears in the capital, wrote that "every art is trying to embroil affresh this happily terminated dispute."[1]

John Franklin, meanwhile, had not given up the fight either. His first instinct was to seek outside help. He petitioned the Connecticut General Assembly for aid but was rebuffed.[2] Another promising approach soon occurred to him, however. If the commissioners appointed to implement the law could be stopped from confirming titles until the end of November, their powers would expire. It would then be up to the legislature to extend them, and it was not at all clear that this was possible. In the first place the Pennamites, whose clamorous objections to the law could be heard all the way to Wilkes-Barre, had their friends in Philadelphia. Moreover, the assembly had been none too enthusiastic about passage in the first place. Here was Franklin's best hope, for if the assembly refused to extend the law, it would throw the situation in the valley back into chaos and restore the company's influence there. A curious alliance was in the making between Franklin and the Pennamites. Both had the same immediate object: to see to it that the Confirming Act was never implemented.

Franklin had one enormous advantage. The hostility and distrust characteristic of relations between the settlers and the common wealth of Pennsylvania had grown so great that mutual confidence was largely impossible. Pickering offered peace on fair terms, which the settlers wanted, but Franklin mirrored their darker side. It was this shared sense of distrust between Franklin and the settlers that gave him much of his influence and power in the community. If Pickering represented the people's hopes, Franklin reflected their underlying fear that in the end they would be betrayed.

In fact the Confirming Act had made little more than a dent in the established pattern in the valley. After its enactment many settlers professed optimism and indicated their willingness to go along with Pickering, yet a deep skepticism persisted. It was as though they were waiting for Pennsylvania to drop its friendly masquerade. Thus, as May 28—the day appointed for the opening session of the claims commission—approached, rumor swept through the region that Pickering and the other commissioners would not appear. The assembly, it was said, intended to repeal the law. When the commissioners did not arrive by the morning of the twenty-eighth, gloom and anger settled over the valley. Though they appeared late that afternoon, the mood of the people hardly changed. One set of rumors simply gave way before another. Pennsylvania remained the enemy.[3]

Working in this atmosphere, Franklin had little difficulty executing his obstructionist plans. One of the commissioners, Joseph Montgomery, had a long-standing reputation for enmity toward the Connecticut claimants. Franklin easily convinced a large number of settlers to support a petition calling for his removal from the commission. When he learned of this Montgomery promptly resigned, hamstringing the commission until a replacement could arrive. Stephen Balliet was quickly appointed, but he delayed his departure from Philadelphia and did not reach Wilkes-Barre until early in August. In the meantime General Daniel Heister, the other commissioner, resigned. His replacement, William Montgomery (whose reputation was no better than Joseph Montgomery's), was also slow in coming to Wilkes-Barre.[4] In this way precious months that might have been used to confirm land claims and ease tensions were wasted. It was almost as though the settlers' distrust worked as a self-fulfilling prophecy. Their objections to the first Montgomery triggered a series of delays that, taken together, tended to confirm fears and feed suspicions.

The settlers were not the only ones discouraged by the strange turn events had taken. Those who realized that the Confirming Act had passed largely because many legislators had not understood how much land was at stake became anxious, too. Sam Hodgdon, viewing the situation from Philadelphia, grew increasingly suspicious as weeks passed and the commission, plagued by delays, failed to meet. Though he had no solid evidence, he nevertheless wondered whether some in high places were not having second thoughts about the Confirming Act. Were they trying to stall until the assembly reconvened in September? By the end of July, Hodgdon's doubts had taken substantial form. He was certain, he explained to Pickering, that Balliet was deliberately delaying his departure for Wilkes-Barre. Nor was it clear that William Montgomery would agree to accept his commission. If he didn't, rumor had it that Balliet would quit. With things gone so badly awry, Hodgdon was convinced that a conspiracy existed to block implementation of the law.[5]

By the second week in August, Pickering too had grown suspicious. Heister's resignation was particularly troublesome. The people were becoming restive, their distrust of Pennsylvania growing more pronounced. And of course Franklin and his friends were taking full advantage of this.[6] The only way to counteract Franklin, Pickering knew, was to begin confirming titles. With this in mind, he wrote William Montgomery urging him to leave immediately for Wilkes-Barre. Montgomery's reply stunned him. Pickering's letter, he claimed, was the first indication he had received that he had been appointed to serve in any new official capacity. His suspicions now thoroughly aroused, Pickering wrote quickly to the council urging that Montgomery's commission be forwarded without further delay.[7] He also unburdened himself to Benjamin Rush concerning his own misgivings. Rush was not much consolation, however. Of course, he assured Pickering, he would have the "steady support" of his friends. He also implied, however, that strong opposition to implementation of the law did exist and suggested that a visit to Philadelphia during the coming session of the assembly might be in order. "Keep a *good heart,* and put a bold face upon things," the doctor advised, *"All will end well."* [8]

When by August 20 Montgomery had not arrived in Wilkes-Barre, Pickering decided to hold hearings without him. He and Balliet began receiving claims on the twenty-first. Soon threats of violence began to circulate. In public Pickering scoffed at the rumors, but privately he took them seriously for he realized that he had backed Franklin into a corner. Sleeping with a pistol in easy reach, he tried to prepare himself mentally and emotionally to kill the first man who made any move against him.[9]

Settlers once dubious about submitting to Pennsylvania's authority now trooped before Pickering and Balliet to have their holdings confirmed. Even some company leaders saw the handwriting on the wall.

Eliphalet Dyer, a staunch company man and one of the attorneys who had represented Connecticut at the trial in Trenton, now asked Pickering to confirm his son's title to lands he had occupied before 1782. Ebenezer Gray, another long-time Susquehannah Company supporter, was not far behind Dyer, urging Zebulon Butler to intercede on his behalf with the commissioners. Those company men who were not yet ready to give in began squabbling among themselves. John Franklin, who was getting a good deal of encouragement from men who lived outside the valley but little in the way of material support, felt betrayed. He wrote to Joseph Hamilton, a company commissioner who lived in Hudson, New York, accusing him of abandoning his friends in Wyoming. But Hamilton retorted that it was, after all, Franklin and not he who had allowed Pennsylvania law to take hold and the Confirming Act to go into operation.[10]

Such encouraging signs notwithstanding, Pickering soon came to believe that success had not yet been assured, for there were indications that a new problem had arisen.[11] The first clue that something was brewing came in a letter from Hodgdon, who disclosed that Philadelphia was buzzing with rumors of a separatist plot in the back country. Hodgdon had been advised that, in an off-the-record session, the council had heard testimony from an anonymous informant to the effect that the plans of Franklin, who was working in concert with William Livingston and Colonel John McKinstry of New York's Genesee Land Company, were already well advanced. Moreover, the council was also warned that the conspirators were seeking support from the British at Fort Niagara.[12]

Pickering, who had earlier been most exercised over Shays' Rebellion in Massachusetts, credited the story, having heard it from a separate source. According to Pickering's informant, Colonel John Butler, the British commander at Niagara, had refused to encourage the conspirators. Pickering nevertheless feared that, even without British involvement, he faced a serious threat. Franklin had been extraordinarily active that August granting half-share titles around Tioga. He had even surveyed and opened two new townships in the region to accommodate fresh immigrants. It seemed evident that he was building up his forces.[13]

Any doubts that Pickering had relative to Franklin's intentions were finally erased early in September when he received sworn depositions from two men who had until recently been close to Franklin. Tunes Dalson testified that between September 1 and 4 there had been a meeting in Tioga at which Franklin, Jenkins, and McKinstry had plotted the establishment of an independent state. But his deposition was based entirely on hearsay evidence.[14] Thomas Wigton, however, had been present at the meeting. He did not go so far as Dalson but did testify that the three men Dalson named, together with Zerah Beach and others unnamed, had conspired to oppose forcibly the laws of Pennsylvania in the Wyoming region.[15] Despite Wigton's unwillingness to testify to the existence of a separatist movement, Pickering was certain that this was the conspirators' real object. Hoping the authorities would take some action, he sent Wigton's and Dalson's depositions to Philadelphia.[16]

The council reacted swiftly. An agreement was reached with New York to cooperate in the effort to crush the separatists. Next, a warrant was issued for the arrest of Franklin, Zerah Beach, John McKinstry, and John Jenkins, ringleaders in the alleged conspiracy. A small group of militiamen under the command of Colonel John Craig was then ordered to Wilkes-Barre to make the arrests. If Franklin was the first to be taken, Craig was instructed to return him to Philadelphia immediately without attempting to capture the rest. He was to take no chances on losing the central figure in the conspiracy to an aroused mob.[7]

The decision to arrest Franklin came none too soon for Pickering. He had just learned that his fiery opponent had sent out a call to the half-share men ordering them to assemble under arms on October 9. Though it is by no means certain that Franklin was about to begin hostilities, there was no doubt in Pickering's mind. He wanted Franklin stopped before he could act.[18]

On October 2, 1787, unaware that the authorities were searching for him, Franklin rode into Wilkes-Barre. When Colonel Craig and five others tried to arrest him, a furious fight broke out. Finally, but not before he had blackened the eyes of all six arresting officers, the battered Franklin was bound, placed upon his horse, and led off in the direction of Philadelphia. A short while later some of Franklin's partisans, learning of his arrest, organized a band of men to ride to his rescue. Hearing of this, Pickering sped ahead to warn Craig. After helping the militiamen tie Franklin to his horse so that the arresting party could make good their escape, he returned home.[19]

On that same day one of Pickering's staunchest allies in the valley, William Hooker Smith, heading another body of men, intercepted Asa Starkweather, secretary to the Susquehannah Company Commission in Luzerne County, and took him prisoner. Starkweather was returning from Hudson, New York, where he had been conferring with Joseph Hamilton. Although there was no warrant out for Starkweather, Smith brought him to Pickering's house, where he was illegally searched and confined. Pickering found correspondence from Hamilton to Franklin that lent further support to the theory that a secessionist conspiracy was hatching. He took copies of these letters and sent the originals to the council. Other copies were sent to Governor Clinton in New York. This led to Hamilton's arrest and the capture of still more incriminating papers.[20]

Operating on the sound theory that one political hostage might best be ransomed with another, a number of Franklin's adherents made an assault on Pickering's home on the same day that Franklin was arrested. Fearing just such a threat, Pickering had stationed a few loyal supporters at some distance from the house. While at dinner, he was warned of the mob's approach. He grabbed a little food and a loaded pistol, and he fled. Together with Griffith Evans, secretary to the Board of Commissioners, who lived with him, he hid near the house. Beckey, their five children (little Edward Pickering was only a few weeks old), and his sister-in-law Betsey White, all under the protection of his clerk, Ebenezer Bowman, were left behind. Lying noiselessly in a nearby field, Pickering watched as the rioters came shouting out of the darkness. They searched the house and released Starkweather but left disappointed on discovering that Pickering was not at home. The Luzerne County authorities could do nothing to stop the rioting that night.[21]

All evening Pickering and Evans lay in hiding, watching the house but afraid to return. Just before dawn they began the long trip to Philadelphia, trudging a full forty miles before they came upon a farmhouse where they were able to hire horses to complete the rest of the trip. At Savage's, a tavern on Sullivan's Road, Pickering heard that Beckey had been taken prisoner and was to be sent as a hostage to Tioga. In frustrated impotence he wrote a long, passionate letter to John Swift, a friend of Franklin's who reportedly commanded the rioters. He appealed to Swift's humanity, urging him to let Beckey go. Any injury done to her, he warned, would never be forgiven. Helpless, he hurried on toward Philadelphia where he quickly learned that Beckey was safe after all.[22] That was one piece of good news on an otherwise bleak horizon.

In one wild day much of what Pickering had accomplished in the Wyoming Valley was undone. The Connecticut settlers had been conditioned for a generation to view Pennsylvania as their deadly enemy. Then Pickering appeared promising peace and justice. Most of the settlers, though they cooperated with him, continued to question the state's sincerity. Every event, every move or action by the authorities, was automatically tested against a set of preconceived and extremely negative notions about the state. Positive experiences meant little in this context. But negative ones reinforced already well-established views.

For this reason Franklin's arrest had an extremely deleterious effect on relations between the people of the valley and the state. Outside prison walls Franklin had been an increasingly ineffective political leader, but behind those walls he became a symbol to many in the valley. His imprisonment was a continuing reaffirmation of the image of Pennsylvania as the enemy. Removing Franklin from the jurisdiction of the Luzerne County courts, where he might have been tried by his neighbors, only made matters worse.

The situation was equally grim in Philadelphia. It was a certainty that the powers of the claims commission, soon to expire, would have to be renewed by the legislature before the Confirming Act could be implemented. But that would not be easy, for the Pennamites were demanding repeal, and an increasing number of legislators in both parties, at last aware of the enormous quantity of land at issue and aroused by the recent violence, were inclined to support them.

The first order of business, Pickering realized, was to restore order in Luzerne County without being forced to call out the militia. Any new outbreak was certain to damage what hope remained that the powers of the commission would be extended. He appealed for leniency toward the rioters, and the council responded by promising that no one who agreed to lay down his arms and abide by Pennsylvania law in the future would be prosecuted. Nathan Denison, Luzerne County's councilor and a former Susquehannah Company Commissioner who was well liked in the valley, was sent west to convey that message.[23]

Meanwhile Pickering, who had been warned that his return to Wilkes-Barre would probably provoke a new outbreak, tried to prevail upon John Swift, the leader of the dissidents, to end the violence.[24] He did not count upon his persuasiveness alone to convince Swift and his followers to come back to the right side of the law. If anything would keep them in line, he believed, it was the fact that John Franklin was a political prisoner in Philadelphia. Nor was he above using this kind of leverage, remarking archly in a letter to Swift that Franklin's treatment, *"for better or worse"* would depend upon how soon "order and tranquility" were restored in Wyoming.[25]

While detained in Philadelphia, Pickering worked tenaciously to influence the state assembly, then deliberating the future of the Confirming Act.[26] But his frantic efforts had little effect. When his friend George Clymer introduced a bill to extend the powers of the claims commission, it ran into stiff opposition from members of both parties.[27] The legislators were clearly of a mind either to repeal the law or at least to reduce sharply Pennsylvania's obligations under it. Though that session ended in deadlock, Pickering was left with the sinking feeling that repeal was inevitable. A wave of self-pity overwhelmed him as he complained to his old friend Richard Peters, the speaker of the assembly, that he would never have accepted responsibility for establishing order in the valley under the conditions the assembly now seemed likely to impose.[28]

Pickering was by no means mistaken. From the opening of the second session of the Twelfth General Assembly it was clear that the Confirming Act was in jeopardy. The Republicans had a majority in the assembly, but they were badly divided on the question. As for the Constitutionalists, George Clymer remarked that they seemed anxious to foster any measure that would encourage "insurgency and civil war" but refused to support ideas that might bring permanent peace to Wyoming.[29] Translated, that meant they could not be counted upon to support an extension of the Confirming Act. In fact, Clymer had few nice words to say about either party. "One I detest," he wrote, "the other I despise."[30]

On March 20, 1788, by an overwhelming vote of 42 to 21, the assembly suspended the operation of the Confirming Act. James McLene, the Constitutionalist leader who introduced the bill, supported it first as a punitive measure, a response to the violence that had forced the state's commissioners to flee Luzerne County. Second, and really more to the point, he argued that the meaning of the original law was ambiguous and that the legislature needed more time to consider its implications. McLene would have spoken with greater candor had he noted directly that when the law was first enacted few assemblymen understood exactly how much land they were giving away.[31]

By the time the blow fell, Pickering was no longer in Philadelphia, having returned to Wilkes-Barre in January. He was quickly informed of this latest development, however, by an angry Sam Hodgdon, who believed the Confirming Act was as good as dead. In the face of this latest bit of adversity. Hodgdon nevertheless hoped the people in Luzerne would remain calm and do nothing that would play into the hands of their enemies. "Steady boys steady should be their motto," he wrote.[32]

Pickering may be forgiven if he felt just a little less steady on receiving the unhappy news. He had returned to the valley against the advice of close friends who feared for his safety. The Suspending Act of course added to his insecurity. The only remaining guarantee that peace might be maintained or that he and his family would not be molested was the fact that John Franklin was still safely behind bars. Now state authorities seemed about to remove even that hedge against renewed trouble. Franklin had been attempting to arrange bail since

January, when it became evident that he would not be given a speedy trial. Until late April, however, the courts had proven uncooperative. But finally, just after the assembly passed the Suspending Act, the State Supreme Court set bail at two thousand pounds.[33]

On May 27, Pickering, who had been instructed to collect the sureties from among Franklin's supporters, sent the bail commitments to Philadelphia. Simultaneously, however, he warned the council that bail or no bail, once Franklin was freed civil war would break out in Luzerne County.[34] On receiving Pickering's message the council went immediately into executive session and did not emerge for a full three weeks. A delighted Sam Hodgdon was then able to report that the council judged the bail offered to be insufficient. Franklin would "remain confined."[35]

Pickering opposed releasing Franklin on bail because he believed that would be dangerous. As events proved, however, keeping him locked up had its drawbacks, too. For some time John and Stephen Jenkins, Jonathan Swift, and a few other militants had been discussing the possibility of kidnaping Pickering and exchanging him for Franklin. There is no evidence to suggest an organized conspiracy. On the contrary, there seems to have been very little planning of any sort, just a lot of frustrated talk. The news that the council had refused to allow bail for Franklin nevertheless provided the spark for a kidnap attempt. A group of younger half-share men ("wild boys," some called them), encouraged by the Jenkins brothers as well as their militant fathers, took matters into their own hands. Late on the night of June 26, fifteen of them, all but two disguised as Indians, broke into the Pickering house. They surprised the sleepy-eyed Pickering, dragged him from his bed, and carried him off into the woods where they were joined by five others.[36]

When the time came for action the Jenkins brothers proved unreliable. At the last minute they both tried to call the kidnaping off. When they found themselves unable to dissuade their enthusiastic followers, they stated their final opinion most eloquently with their feet, heading north for New York as fast as they could to join forces with William Livingston, Colonel John McKinstry, and the New York Genesee Land Company.[37] They left behind twenty bewildered kidnapers and their victim. Ignorant and leaderless, these men tramped the woods for nearly three weeks, moving constantly in order to avoid bands of militia sent against them by Luzerne County officials. Only later did Pickering learn that the men who did the actual kidnaping were convinced that it was to be the signal for a general uprising. They had the vague idea that Jenkins and McKinstry would follow up their initial action by raising a force that they, in company with their prisoner, would then join.[38]

No sooner had the kidnapers left with Pickering than Beckey rushed a message to Andrew Ellicott, a Philadelphia friend who was visiting the valley. Ellicott immediately contacted Zebulon Butler and John Paul Schott, who hurriedly called a council of war. Ellicott wanted to ride out after the abductors that night. But Christopher Hurlbut and others more sympathetic to Franklin than to Pickering objected. Ellicott later complained that "they threw a damp on all our measures, and prevented the spirited execution of any one plan." It was not until ten the next morning that Captain Schott and a party of eighteen men went in pursuit. On the following day, twenty-eight more men took up the hunt and on July 1 they were joined by another fifty.[39]

Ellicott was highly critical of Luzerne County's authorities, charging that they had been slow to react and that, had they given chase immediately, Pickering could have been rescued in a matter of hours. But he was a stranger in the valley. The fact that within four days nearly a hundred men had been mobilized to rescue an agent of the Commonwealth of Pennsylvania was most remarkable. Stephen Balliet and William Armstrong, who were better acquainted with the atmosphere in Luzerne County, certainly saw it in this light. These men, who arrived in Wilkes-Barre on another political errand on July 1, were delighted to be able to report that although violence had again broken out, this time county authorities had the situation under control. The militia had been organized, and law and order were being upheld.[40] Zebulon Butler proudly forwarded the same message to Philadelphia. He knew the identities of most of the kidnapers, and the local militia was out hunting for them. Meanwhile the fathers of the young dissidents had all been arrested and were being kept in custody. Butler took pains to publicize this information, confident that it would soon reach the wandering band. The season for taking hostages, it seems, was not yet over.[41]

For nineteen days Pickering and his captors tramped through the woods, constantly moving to avoid detection. Though the July temperatures were warm it rained frequently, and the men were sometimes forced to lie in brush shelters to keep from being drenched. Except for two days when they dined on venison, their diet was a monotony of fried salt pork, bread, water, and "coffee"—"a crust of wheat bread" burnt and "then boiled in water" and sweetened. Sometimes it was worse even than this. "Milk for supper. No meat to-day," ran one line in Pickering's journal. On July 3 he was placed in irons and when at rest sometimes chained to a tree. His captors, though friendly and polite, explained that they had orders to treat him just as Franklin was being treated in Philadelphia. They provided him with pen, ink, and paper. He could write to his wife and to the authorities in Philadelphia if he wished. He was not forced to write to anyone, however, nor was he ever in any serious danger.[42]

Throughout the ordeal, though he seethed inwardly, Pickering was sensible enough not to let this show. He refused to write to Philadelphia but did correspond with Beckey. Realizing that whatever he wrote would be read by his kidnapers, he was careful to give no hint of impatience. Anxious to make his captors understand that he was prepared to wait them out, he explained in a note to Beckey that he expected to be gone for a very long while. The "dignity and safety of the state," he wrote, could not "be sacrificed to the interests of an individual family." Philadelphia would surely not give in to this blackmail, and he would be the last man in the world to ask that. Reinforcing the impression that he was determined not to give in, he concluded this rather long letter with carefully detailed instructions for running the farm in case of his prolonged absence.[43]

Pickering showed the same patient front in conversation with his abductors. He talked with them of their common experiences as farmers and tried to learn what he could of their agricultural techniques. From a former Vermonter in the band he learned how land was cleared and wheat sown during the first year of farming in that region. Daniel Taylor and he discussed the care and feeding of sows and how best to use oxen for plowing. When he noticed ginseng growing wild near one campsite in the deep shade of a hemlock forest, he made a note to try growing it in the shade of trees in an orchard or garden. He might have been a gentleman farmer on an agricultural tour. He certainly gave no indication that he was prepared to write Philadelphia asking for an exchange with Franklin.[44]

By mid-July Pickering's captors were ready to quit. It was clear that neither the Jenkins brothers nor anybody else was about to join them. The militia was after them, and they couldn't cart Pickering through the woods indefinitely, amiable companion though he seemed. They tried to make a deal with him. If he would agree to ask the council to be lenient with them, they would set him free. But Pickering, realizing that he now had the advantage, proposed a bargain of his own. If they would reveal the names of those who had planned the kidnaping, he would ask the council for leniency. After giving this some thought, the boys decided simply to let him go. After that it was every men for himself.[45]

On July 17, 1788, his forty-third birthday, Pickering appeared like some bedraggled apparition on his own front doorstep. His anger, so carefully restrained for so long, now at last came out into the open. He organized a posse and set furiously about the business of capturing his abductors. But the obstacles were many, as they had friends in the region and the forests were deep. Nonetheless, by the end of July two had been taken and were being held in Easton jail, and three others had turned themselves in. One of the kidnapers, Joseph Dudley, was mortally wounded in an exchange of fire with the militia. The rest fled in all directions, some through the great swamp, some toward Tioga, and still others in the direction of the lakes.[46]

Pickering found it impossible to restrain his annoyance with the people of Luzerne County any longer. Considering what he had been through over the preceding sixteen months, this is perhaps understandable. In letters to Benjamin Franklin and Peter Muhlenburg, the president of the Pennsylvania Council, he argued that genuine pacification was utterly impossible because of the vast reservoir of distrust prevalent among the population. At bottom the people felt they could only be secure in their lands "by use of the rifle and tomahawk," he wrote. Thus they could easily be manipulated by men such as John Franklin and John Jenkins. His kidnaping had shocked the people, bringing them temporarily to their senses. But he predicted more violence in the future unless troops were stationed near Tioga, the center of the opposition's strength.[47]

In contrast to Pickering's glum view, Zebulon Butler literally glowed with pride as he explained in a letter to the council that the kidnap plot had been foiled and that "an attachment to government very universally prevails among the people." Even around Tioga the settlers had armed themselves and gone out to hunt down the kidnapers or at least drive them from the area. The great majority were firmly behind the government, he reported. Advising against the introduction of troops, he remarked that the area "never shall again be disturbed with such tumults and dissentions as we have seen in times past."[48]

The Pennsylvania Council, out of touch with events in Luzerne County during the last two weeks in July, received these conflicting messages from Pickering and Butler almost simultaneously. Wisely, its members took Butler's advice against sending in the militia. They followed this up with a decision to prosecute the captured kidnapers only for rioting, not for treason. William Bradford, the state attorney general, explained to Pickering that the kidnapers were going to be indicted on the lesser charge in order to find out once and for all whether an honest and impartial grand jury could be impaneled and the judicial system made to function in Luzerne County. It was unlikely that the people there would stand for a mass treason trial; but indictments and convictions on charges of rioting were well within the limits of reasonable expectation.[49]

At first Pickering objected to this lenient approach. But as the county grand jury did its work, indicting fourteen of the fifteen original kidnapers for rioting he changed his mind. He was even more pleased when shortly before the court convened the grand jurors indicted John Franklin, along with Zerah Beach and John McKinstry, for treason in plotting the establishment of an independent state.[50]

As his anger gradually eroded, Pickering became aware that he had won a good deal of sympathy as a result of his recent ordeal. He tried to turn this to political advantage in Philadelphia, urging passage of a new confirming act.[51] But he misjudged the situation. When a new confirming bill was brought to the floor of the assembly that November, the opposition succeeded with a motion for postponement. The struggle continued for the next seventeen months, with the Pennamites gaining strength all the while. Finally, on April 25, 1790, the assembly voted by an overwhelming majority to repeal the original Confirming Act.[52]

Had repeal come earlier it might have led to some sort of outburst in the Wyoming Valley, but the moment for violence had passed. John Franklin, though by this time out on bail, had been chastened by sixteen months in a Philadelphia prison. With a charge of treason still pending he was unwilling to take any further risks. Even if Franklin had proven more adventuresome it is still doubtful that he could have aroused many of the settlers. Circumstances had changed. Pennsylvania's sovereignty in the region seemed assured, an irreversible fact. Certainly the Susquehannah Company had demonstrated its impotence. Nor was Connecticut any longer a factor in the complicated politics of the region. Finally, the hopes of some that Congress would reverse the Trenton decision or hold a new trial to decide private rights to the soil had expired along with the Confederation Government itself.

Instead of further appeals to violence, the settlers, including Pickering (who owned over seven hundred acres under a Connecticut title), hired the Philadelphia attorney William Lewis and prepared to defend themselves against any legal maneuvers the Pennamites might make to eject them. In this way a long court battle was joined. Even as this new aspect of the struggle got under way Pickering guessed, and correctly as it turned out, that the Connecticut settlers were so firmly entrenched that in the long run Pennsylvania would be forced to admit the legitimacy of their claims. Right or wrong, however, this made little difference to him. His dream had been to settle the dispute in the region and begin the development of his lands in the immediate vicinity. Those hopes were dashed by the repeal of the Confirming Act. Land titles in the valley continued in dispute. As long as that was the case, his dream of making a fortune in Pennsylvania lands remained only a fantasy.

NINE

"Civilizing" the Iroquois

THE MORE THAN TWO YEARS that Pickering spent in the Wyoming Valley left him on the brink of financial ruin. During all of that time he had earned next to nothing while using his slim resources to purchase farm land, build a house and barn, add to his already large landholdings, and clear ground for planting. The expense was overburdening. He tried to sell some of his treasured Luzerne County land, but there were no buyers.[1] He borrowed, first from his brother John, and then from his brother-in-law, George Williams. He also appealed for funds from outside sources. By the spring of 1789 some of his creditors were demanding their money, and Pickering was forced to go back once again to the family for help. On several occasions he wrote imploringly to Williams for more money, admitting that he was close to bankruptcy.[2] Each time a few hundred dollars came to tide him over. But life was a continuing misery. He complained that even the food the family ate was "plain and frugal—such as we had never known before."[3] With Beckey, her sister Betsey, and now six young sons to support, he became increasingly distracted by his financial problems.

Given these desperate circumstances and the unpromising state of affairs in the valley, Pickering began to scramble for some sort of political appointment. Late in 1789 he sought the lucrative office of state surveyor general. But the political tide was shifting in Pennsylvania, and in spite of the fact that Robert Morris, Tench Coxe, James Wilson, and other powerful Republican leaders endorsed his candidacy, the job went instead to Daniel Brodhead, a Constitutionalist.[4] Pickering had no better luck at the national level, where President Washington, recalling his insubordination during the revolutionary war, wanted nothing more to do with him.

116

But Pickering's influential friends continued to work on his behalf until, in September 1790, fortune at last smiled upon him. He was in Philadelphia, serving as Luzerne County's delegate to the state constitutional convention, when Washington, acting in defiance of his own better judgment, appointed him a special emissary to an aroused group of Seneca Indians living along the west branch of the Susquehanna River. Simultaneously, the president assured Pickering that a permanent position would soon be found for him in the federal bureaucracy.[5]

Although inexperienced in Indian relations Pickering jumped at Washington's offer, for he desperately needed the salary that he would earn while serving as an envoy to the Senecas. His principal interest, of course, was in the promised bureaucratic appointment that would mean status, a return to solvency, and a comfortable life in Philadelphia. Though he had no idea at the time, the appointment that eventually materialized was to prove far less significant than his developing involvement in Indian affairs. Indeed, his mission to the Senecas in October 1790 launched him on a career in Indian diplomacy that lasted for more than five years and transformed him into a staunch and influential advocate of the rights of native Americans.

The particular group of Senecas with whom Pickering was to treat that autumn were greatly aroused over the recent murder of two of their tribe by white frontiersmen. Considered in isolation, Pickering's mission to pacify them may seem relatively insignificant. However, the importance of what he was about to undertake can better be appreciated when integrated into a more generalized picture of the administration's overall Indian policy.

The United States was officially at peace with the Senecas as well as with the other tribes of the Six Nations in 1790. Further west, however, along the Ohio frontier, there was open war with the Shawnee, Chippeway, Wyandot, Wabash, Miami, and several other western tribes.[6] In spite of the fact that the Senecas and other Iroquois tribes refused to join in the war, their sympathies were with the western Indians. Knowing this, the Washington administration feared that the continuing murders of these peacefully inclined Indians by whites might provoke them into full participation in the war. Pickering's embassy was designed to forestall this. He was to try to make amends for the recent murders, distribute gifts, and generally do what he could to keep the Senecas pacified.[7] Meanwhile the War Department would finish preparations for a military expedition under the command of General Josiah Harmar that was calculated to force the western Indians to accept American claims to a boundary north of the Ohio.

Pickering arrived at Tioga Point, the site selected for the treaty, a few days before it was scheduled to begin.[8] He was nervous and ill at ease for he hadn't the least notion of what to expect. A three-week delay in the opening of the negotiations did nothing for his nerves but gave him ample opportunity to ruminate on the possibility that he might fail. When talks finally did begin, however, aside from an occasional minor breach of Indian etiquette, he did very well indeed.[9] He handled himself capably during the ceremony of "burying the hatchet," placated the principal mourners of the two murdered Indians with gifts, and distributed presents to all who attended the treaty. In a moment that revealed both his generous intentions and his naïveté, Pickering also announced that the murder of Indians by whites would no longer be tolerated. There would be equal justice for red and white men alike from that time forward.[10]

Early in the negotiations Pickering came to realize that the murders, though deeply felt, were not the only reasons for the meeting. The Indians wanted to discuss the recent sale of a large portion of their lands to Oliver Phelps, a New York land speculator. In 1788 at a treaty held at Fort Stanwix, Phelps had bought a full third of the Senecas' remaining lands in New York State for five thousand dollars and an annuity of five hundred dollars. Farmer's Brother, an important Seneca chief, complained to Pickering that since these lands had been lost there had been hard times among his people. He claimed that the agreement was invalid since only a few unauthorized chiefs had arranged the sale and charged that the written agreement used by Phelps to prove his purchase did not comport with the verbal explanation given to the Indians by an interpreter at the time it was signed.[11] The great Seneca orator Red Jacket elaborated on what Farmer's Brother had said, avowing that Phelps had promised to pay ten thousand dollars for the land but had only paid half the stipulated price. Alleging that he and his tribe had been defrauded, Red Jacket demanded the return of the land.[12]

Taken by surprise and, moreover, completely ignorant of the details of Phelps's purchase, Pickering reiterated a point he had made at the very opening of discussions when explaining recent federal legislation designed to guarantee that Indians would not in the future be defrauded by speculators. According to this 1790 law, Indian land sales would be considered legal only if a federal representative was on hand to sanction them. Pickering made it clear, however, that lands already sold could not in all likelihood be restored. As far as the Phelps purchase was concerned, he promised nothing but agreed to investigate the possibility of fraud. He made it a point to emphasize, however, that only if fraud was actually proven could the land be restored.[13]

At one time Pickering had been able to write with a kind of detached objectivity of the inevitable growth of the American empire and of the extinction of the Indians.[14] But after meeting the Senecas at Tioga, his attitude changed. His experience at the treaty added a dimension of humanity to his understanding of the Indians' condition. He was touched by the honesty and simplicity of these people and simultaneously angered by the injustices heaped upon them. Quite by accident Pickering had stumbled upon a moral issue that he could not ignore. From that moment on, in the conflict between the rights of Indians and the pressures of expansion, he took his stand with the native people.

Pickering returned to Philadelphia convinced that land jobbers like Phelps and the "white savages" who inhabited the New York and Pennsylvania frontier were primarily responsible for the unsettled conditions there. When white men weren't busy stealing the Indians' land, they were killing them. On the average, one Seneca had been murdered each sixty days since the "chain of friendship" had last been "brightened" between the United States and the Senecas at Fort Harmar in January 1789. Yet not one white man had been convicted of these murders. Nor did it seem likely that a jury of white frontiersmen would ever convict another white man of murdering an Indian.[15]

The problem of land-jobbing was extremely serious as well, for many Indians were easily manipulated into alienating their precious holdings. After some investigation Pickering was forced to admit, for example, that Oliver Phelps had done nothing that was strictly illegal. He was equally sure, however, that the Indians had been misled by duplicitous advisors. In arranging for the sale the Senecas had relied on Joseph Brant, the Mohawk chief, several British advisors including Colonel William Butler of Niagara, and the Reverend Samuel Kirkland, an American missionary living among the Oneida. Pickering's inquiry convinced him that Phelps had bribed Brant to endorse his proposal. Moreover, Butler and others from Niagara upon whom the Indians relied for advice were actually in partnership with Phelps. It was a shoddy, but perfectly legal, undertaking.[16]

In a letter to Washington written shortly after his return from Tioga, Pickering expressed his outrage at the way in which Indians were being treated by whites. Honest men, he wrote, would have no difficulty in dealing with the Six Nations. Moreover, only the most insensitive of men would not sympathize with them in their recital of the injuries they had experienced from "white men."[17] Later he would go even further in expressing opposition to federal policy. Directly contradicting administration explanations, he alleged that the war against the western Indians was the product of white injustice, and in February 1791 he refused an appointment as Arthur St. Clair's quartermaster general. Questioning the need for war, he wrote that the western tribes were only "taking their revenge" for wrongs done by whites. The important thing was to send an honest and sympathetic negotiator to deal with them.[18]

Like many another well-meaning American, Pickering wanted to help the Indians. The problem was how to go about it, and there was no simple answer to that question.[19] Consider the case in point. Red Jacket maintained that Phelps had defrauded the Senecas at the treaty of Fort Stanwix by promising to pay ten thousand dollars for the land he purchased and then delivering only half that amount. Now five thousand dollars one way or another was of very little consequence. The question that puzzled Pickering was why any of the leaders of the Six Nations would agree in the first place to sell land that they knew was essential to the survival of their people. On some occasions, he realized, the Indians were browbeaten until they agreed to sell. Frequently, however, they sold their lands willingly. This was the case in the Phelps purchase. Even Red Jacket admitted as much, claiming only that Phelps had not lived up to the original bargain.

Complicating matters even further, Pickering realized that if lands could be restored to the Indians after once having been sold, they might well be sold again to some other speculator with the few thousand dollars and rum enough to send a thousand red men on a week-long drunk. Indians, even the most prestigious leaders, he believed, had a passion for liquor and would do anything for it. Farmer's Brother, Red Jacket, even Joseph Brant, Pickering thought, would sell their people's birthright for the privilege of drinking themselves into a stupor. Moreover, as Red Jacket rather pathetically pointed out to him at Tioga, they would do this realizing what they were doing but would nonetheless be unable to resist the temptation. Drinking, with all of its manifest implications, was a pathological problem for the Iroquois people.[20]

If Pickering had no immediate solution for the problem of alcoholism among Indians, he nevertheless believed that certain things could be done to protect the Six Nations from land jobbers. Though a great deal of land had already been sold, he believed that regaining what had been lost was of less consequence than maintaining the territory that remained. He therefore endorsed the appointment of a federal superintendent of the Six Nations with the responsibility of representing the interests of the Indians, defending them not only against speculators but also against their own simplicity.[21] But preserving the Six Nations' remaining land was only a partial step. If in the long run they were to survive (and this became one of Pickering's ruling passions), they would have to modify their way of life by giving up hunting and turning to agriculture. There was not enough land left for the Iroquois to survive as hunters, but as farmers they might prosper. Pickering therefore urged Washington to undertake a program designed to "civilize" these Indians. From modest beginnings he hoped his plan for acculturation might grow into a concrete national commitment.[22]

Pickering had little appreciation for the more subtle implications of what he was suggesting. Like most reformers who were concerned for the future of the Indians, he failed to see that they lived within a complex culture of their own. What the Iroquois called the "old ways," Pickering defined as mere savagery. He thought that by a simple process of education and example not only the Six Nations but ultimately all Indian peoples could be brought to adopt white ways. He recognized that the Indians were in a state of decline. But it was beyond his capacity to understand that the movement to "civilize" them by forcing their adaptation to agriculture might actually hasten disintegration.[23]

Pickering's advocacy of a program designed to transform the Six Nations through acculturation hardly marks him out as intellectually unique. Within the administration both Knox and Jefferson had long been enthusiastic about the idea. In fact, Pickering only joined a movement that had already grown to prominence.[24] One aspect of his perception was unusual, however. He sensed that acculturation not only offered the Indians an alternative to extinction but also provided the government with a possible solution to a dilemma that it had been unable to face. There was a conflict between the assumption that the nation would inevitably expand and the notion that the Indians enjoyed legal rights to the lands they occupied. Pickering believed that as farmers the Indians would need far less land than they did as huntsmen. Moreover, once the Indians had turned to agriculture they could be expected to sell part of their remaining lands to purchase tools, seed, and all the other things farmers needed. In short, as agriculturalists the Indians would be no obstacle to the advance of the frontier, whereas in their "savage state" they were a formidable one.[25]

Within the cabinet Pickering found his philanthropic views enthusiastically seconded by Secretary of War Henry Knox. On the subject of Indian rights and government policy, perhaps no one at the cabinet level was more sympathetic to the Indians than he. America's international reputation, in a sense the very meaning of the American Revolution, would in part be determined, he thought, by how the government managed its relations with the Indians. If they were exterminated—a distinct possibility—world opinion would condemn the United States. Knox thought "the honor and future reputation of the country more intimately blended" with the question of Indian policy "than is generally supposed."[26]

Knox deeply appreciated Pickering's success at the Tioga conference. In the first place, and considering only the practical side of the question, Seneca neutrality became even more important in the wake of Josiah Harmar's defeat at the hands of the western tribes. But just as significantly he applauded the manner in which Pickering had conducted himself. The talks had been handled with "an ability and judgment," he wrote, that had unquestionably helped preserve Seneca neutrality. Moreover, Pickering had shown "the candour and humanity which ought to characterize all the treaties of the General Government with the unenlightened natives of the country."[27]

The war secretary urged Washington to offer firm guarantees to the Iroquois that they would be allowed to hold the remainder of their lands in perpetuity. He recommended, too, a small annual pension for Cornplanter, an important Seneca leader, in order to secure his aid in arranging a treaty with the warring tribes. Finally he sent to the president, who was then at Mount Vernon, a proposal drawn up by Cornplanter himself for the acculturation of his people.[28]

Cornplanter's project went beyond anything Pickering had proposed, but it was very much in keeping with his views on acculturation. The Indian leader urged that his people be taught to farm, to build and operate sawmills, and to work in metal. "Above all," he wanted teachers to instruct the children in reading and writing and the women in spinning and weaving. It was an ambitious scheme calling for a large investment and could have served as a pilot project for the eventual acculturation of all Indians.[29]

Washington was willing to make some concessions to the Senecas, not out of enthusiasm for "civilizing" schemes, but because he valued their neutrality and needed their help in dealing with the western tribes. He therefore assured Cornplanter that the United States would protect his people against land fraud and also approved a pension for the Seneca leader. The president even endorsed the idea of acculturation, although he would not adopt Cornplanter's expensive scheme. The United States would spend something on the project, he promised, but privately he told Knox that spending was to be kept to a minimum. He sent along to Knox a copy of Pickering's more modest proposals with the notation that these sound recommendations ought to be pursued.[30] In this way Pickering's early thoughts on acculturation gained official sanction and became the foundation for more elaborate programs that developed later.

After making his report in the capital, Pickering returned to Wilkes-Barre with the president's praise still ringing in his ears and absolutely confident that an important federal appointment was on the way.[31] But before a suitable opening developed he was again pressed into service as an Indian diplomat. In mid-March 1791, not four months after the conclusion of the treaty of Tioga Point, four Senecas were viciously murdered by a body of Westmoreland County militia on the Pennsylvania frontier near Fort Pitt. Cornplanter, even then carrying a message of peace to the western Indians, was devastated. He wrote despairingly of these latest killings, warning that though he had promised to do what he could to help make peace, success was now further away than ever. " You struck the innocent men first," he wrote. If peace did not come it would not be his responsibility, "as your people has broke good rules."[32]

Although Cornplanter assured Washington that he and his people would remain at peace, Knox, who realized that other leaders of the Six Nations might not react so passively, feared "pernicious consequences" from the murders. They were not long in coming. Early in April he had news that a body of Delawares and Wyandots accompanied by some Senecas had murdered nine men, women, and children about twenty miles from Fort Pitt. The presence of the Delawares and Wyandots that far east was bad news in itself. The fact that some Seneca warriors were collaborating with them was even more disturbing, for it suggested that at least some elements of the Six Nations were actively involved in the fighting.[33]

By the beginning of the second week in April, the situation had further deteriorated. Local white residents, having seen Cornplanter in the vicinity of the second set of killings, concluded that the raid was his doing and set out to murder him. They failed, but they did capture and plunder a boat carrying gifts that he had been given during his stay in Philadelphia. Realizing that the settlements of the Cornplanter Seneca along the Allegheny River were in serious danger, Knox reinforced the army post at French Creek to protect them. He expected that at any moment full-scale war might break out across the entire region.[34]

In spite of everything the administration had done to keep the Six Nations divided from the western tribes, Knox believed that a new Indian confederacy might soon form, loosing at least a thousand warriors on the Pennsylvania and New York frontiers at a time when the government had all it could handle in the West.[35] He therefore con-

vinced the president to send Pickering on an extraordinary mission to
the Six Nations once again to "brighten the chain of friendship."[36]

Pickering quickly accepted the new appointment. It was an important
assignment, an opportunity to demonstrate that even in a period of
grave crisis dealing fairly with the Indians could produce sound results.
In truth, however, he was motivated by more mundane considerations
as well. He explained to his brother that the "profits of the former
treaty" had been very substantial. He expected those from the one
approaching to come close to getting him out of debt.[37]

Neither Knox nor Washington expected that Pickering would be able
to accomplish much at his meeting with the Six Nations, for they believed a wider war inevitable. Indeed, they viewed the treaty more as
part of the administration's overall military strategy for 1791 than as
diplomacy. The date for the meeting was carefully scheduled for mid-
June, by which time it was hoped that Arthur St. Clair's army would be
ready to strike in the West. Painted Post, a little settlement just to the
north of Tioga on the Susquehanna, the site for the meeting, was also
carefully chosen. Most of the Indians would have to travel long distances to meet with Pickering on this spot. Knox knew that it took large
numbers of Indians long periods to gather for a treaty. It might be
months between the time the more western groups living at Buffalo
Creek started for the treaty and their return home. This too was calculated to give St. Clair time to act. Knox was candid about it. While
Pickering kept the Six Nations busy at Painted Post, he awaited St.
Clair's victory in the West.[38]

On April 20, after having sent express riders to the Indians and
summoned his interpreters, Jasper Parrish and Joseph Smith,
Pickering journeyed to Philadelphia for conferences with Secretary
Knox. Unlike administration leaders, he was optimistic about what
might be accomplished. He did not view the projected treaty as a
stratagem but rather as an opportunity to ensure the continued neutrality of the Six Nations while simultaneously furthering his plan for
"civilizing" them.

Of all the figures involved in diplomacy with the Iroquois at this time,
Pickering showed not only the best motives but also the soundest conception of policy. The questions he prepared for Knox's consideration
clearly reveal what he intended to make of this meeting. If the Indians
wanted some of their children brought to eastern schools for education,
should he agree? If they wished their children to be taught the art of
farming, what then? If they should desire teachers to come among
them to instruct in reading, writing, arithmetic, and farming, or if they
asked for tools to farm their lands, how should he reply? What prom-

ises could he make? Finally, if the Indians didn't bring these subjects up, should he?[39] The omissions on Pickering's list are as significant as what he included. There was no reference to politics or the war in the West. The best way to preserve the neutrality of these Indians, he believed, was to ask for nothing but to emphasize the benevolent aspects of American policy by using the treaty to advance the program of planned acculturation.[40] Genuine philanthropy and sound policy, he seemed to be saying, implied giving, not trading or taking.

Understandably, then, Pickering was utterly baffled by a set of instructions that required him to recruit warriors from among the Six Nations to aid in the war against the western Indians.[41] What could have possessed Washington and Knox to include such a provision, he wondered, especially since they both thought it very possible that the Six Nations might actually join in the war against the United States? Pickering was absolutely certain that any attempt at recruitment would only irritate the Iroquois, jeopardizing chances to secure their neutrality. He urged Knox to redraft the instructions. But with the president out of town and time pressing, the secretary of war was unprepared to make any changes on his own responsibility.[42]

The interests of a powerful land speculator also threatened Pickering's hopes to structure the treaty along purely philanthropic lines. Robert Morris had acquired the preemption rights to a vast portion of the land of the Six Nations lying between the Genesee River and Lake Erie. On learning of the treaty he planned to send his sons Tom and William to purchase some of these lands. Morris was a friend of Pickering's, and it was difficult for him to turn the Pennsylvania land baron away. Yet he was absolutely certain that any move to purchase land at the treaty would arouse Indian suspicions and undermine his fundamental objectives. Before Pickering could act, Knox did. He and Alexander Hamilton warned Morris against making any attempt to purchase land at the treaty. Morris acquiesced, informing Pickering that although his sons would attend they would only be there to make contacts for future negotiations.[43]

In mid-June Pickering rode toward Painted Post. With him went a few clerks and servants, his interpreters Parrish and Smith, some Quaker missionaries, and his little boy Tim, thrilled at the prospect of seeing real Indians. As the caravan traveled north, the river grew shallow. The boats, loaded with supplies, went aground near Newtown Point, about twenty miles south of Painted Post. There, early in July, Pickering finally met the Iroquois.

By the time he arrived at Newtown Point, Pickering was genuinely optimistic about the prospects for the meeting. Reports from his former clerk, now Captain Ebenezer Bowman, as well as others who carried news of the treaty to the Indians, suggested that fears that the Six Nations were preparing for war were highly exaggerated.[44] As the Indians trickled into his encampment he saw nothing to contradict that view. With nearly a thousand Indians present, he wrote Beckey, those who had thus far assembled seemed "well disposed."

Pickering anticipated no trouble, although he would have been more pleased had there been less rum available. White traders were doing their best, which was very good indeed, to keep the Indians supplied. For their part the Indians were doing what they could to maintain their reputation for prolonged drunkenness.[45] It depressed Pickering, for where there was rum, it seemed, there was always pathos. Farmer's Brother, the prominent Seneca chieftain, even gave his only coat as security for a pint of whiskey. "He told me about it," wrote Pickering, "and I gave him a shilling to redeem it."[46] The threat of violence was ever present too. At the Ceremony of the Full Moon, which took place during the course of the treaty, blood nearly flowed as boastful Seneca and Oneida warriors confronted each other. Only the intercession of Fish Carrier, a Cayuga chief, prevented a full-scale battle.[47]

By the time the Iroquois were at last prepared to talk, Pickering had concluded that, contrary to what was believed in Philadelphia, there was a good chance of confirming their neutrality. This led him to fret all the more over his instructions to recruit warriors for service with Arthur St. Clair's army. Not only was he confident that the attempt would fail, he feared it would backfire by undermining the philanthropic reputation he was so carefully cultivating among the Indians and by encouraging an atmosphere of distrust.

Pickering was a willful man and, as Washington had cause to know, was not above violating even the most specific instructions. He had done it frequently enough during the revolutionary war. He now did it again, but with results that turned out to be most beneficial. Later there would be some lame explanations, but they were really beside the point. Convinced that he was doing the right thing, Pickering never raised the subject of recruitment among the Iroquois. Instead he concentrated on his basic purpose, which was to secure their neutrality.[48]

After two days of speech-making, the Indians, ready for a little relaxation, spent the next five in a state of general drunkenness.[49] Though very agitated, there was nothing Pickering could do except bide his time, waiting for the rum barrels to run dry. When the talks finally resumed, he was rewarded for his patience by Chief Good Peter's assurance that the Six Nations would remain neutral in the war.[50]

With political success quickly assured, Pickering used the remainder of the treaty to make the case for the planned acculturation of the Six Nations. He soon ran into powerful opposition, however, from Red Jacket, the great orator of the Senecas. Red Jacket's object was to preserve the cultural heritage of his people. His tactic at the treaty was to contribute to this by undermining Pickering's already established reputation for honesty and fair dealing among the Iroquois. It was an unfair match, for Pickering never fully appreciated Red Jacket's purposes nor could he match his sophistication.

The first clash between the two men occurred only a few days after the treaty had begun, when Pickering suggested that the Iroquois were too dependent upon British advisors. He warned that frequently English advice had not been the best, as when they urged the Indians to make war upon the United States during the Revolution. It was a serious *faux pas* to bring up the memory of past defeats at a treaty, and Red Jacket seized upon it. When Indians met to discuss peace, he remarked, they spoke only of peace. Neither he nor his brothers wished to be reminded of "little birds who lead them astray." It was a long and extraordinary outburst after which Red Jacket suddenly sank in his place, announcing his weariness. The council, he said, had been meeting all day, "the tobacco does not smoke well, and as you have always used to wash our mouths," he said, looking meaningfully toward Pickering, "we expect you will do it again." [51] For one of the few times in his life Pickering had no response. There was plenty of rum for the Indians that night.

A few days later Red Jacket and Pickering collided once again, this time over the idea of acculturation itself. In an attempt to demonstrate by example the great advantages of an agricultural existence, Pickering invited some of the principal Indian leaders to join him and some of his white friends at dinner. The luxury of a groaning board and the promise that the Indians might enjoy the same every day of their lives if they adopted a sedentary agricultural existence, he thought, would help convince them to give up their culture. At dinner he spoke eloquently and at length of the prospect of future peace and amity between Indians and whites, living together as one people under the benevolent umbrella of a single national government. [52] After he had finished Red Jacket responded in a way that changed the whole mood of the dinner. He had noticed with increasing rage during the course of the treaty that various young white men at the conference were in the habit of slipping off into the woods with some of the more attractive Indian girls. In responding to Pickering he thanked him for the dinner, the good advice, and the promise of real peace and friendship between Indians and whites. Then, his voice dripping irony, and looking pointedly at some of those who had been fraternizing with the young girls of his tribe, he expressed his hope that these young men would "feel that patriotism which your oratory is calculated to inspire . . . by intermarrying with our women."[53]

Red Jacket precipitated yet another flare-up, again in an attempt to undermine Pickering's "civilizing" schemes. Basic to Pickering's plan was the idea that craftsmen and instructors should be sent among the Six Nations to teach skills ranging from reading and writing to agriculture and ironworking. A few days after Pickering laid out his proposals, Red Jacket rather casually announced at the council that in keeping with Pickering's "promise" that there should be a gunsmith appointed to live among the Indians and mend their weapons, he had appointed a Mr. Thomas Harris who was then at the treaty site. Red Jacket knew his man. Even before he had finished, Pickering was on his feet shouting that he had made no such promise. At that, Red Jacket sat quietly down and said that he thought it would be of little use "to talk much more— for perhaps we have been deceived in the whole!"[54]

By July 17, Pickering's forty-sixth birthday, a treaty that had begun on a promising note seemed in near disarray. The philanthropist was frustrated, the diplomat was growing uneasy. Then, at the final session, a last little crisis arose that revealed the difficulty even a well-intentioned man like Timothy Pickering could encounter in protecting the Indians against their own naïveté. A group of Seneca chiefs asked him to act as an official government representative under the law of 1790 to certify the legitimacy of two land cessions they wished to make, one to a John Richardson and another to the two daughters of Ebenezer Allen, a white man who had married a Seneca woman and who lived among the Indians.[55] Though Pickering did not wish to allow the Indians to cede any of their lands, he was reluctant to refuse. The Senecas had the right to divide their holdings if they wished. Since the line of descent in the tribe was through the female line, the deed to the Allen girls was perfectly in keeping with traditional Indian custom. Moreover, at the very beginning of the conference Pickering had been at pains to assure the Indians that under federal law they had the right to sell or to refuse to sell their lands as they saw fit. A denial, he feared, "would lead them to think that the solemn assurances of the President were made but to amuse & deceive."[56]

Pickering agreed to certify the Richardson grant without the least hesitation. He objected, however, to the size of the Allen grant, for it was a huge tract. He felt sure that Allen would sell the land and that the girls would see none of it. After some difficulty, including heated words with Allen, the deed was withdrawn. But another one, granting the girls a smaller tract, a mere four square miles, quickly replaced it. Again Pickering objected, claiming that thirty-two farming families could live comfortably on the land. This time, however, Red Jacket intervened in Allen's behalf and the chiefs overruled Pickering, who was honestly but unsuccessfully attempting to protect them.[57]

The treaty at Newtown Point proved to be something of a disappointment to Pickering. He made little outward progress in his attempts at convincing the Six Nations to adopt the life of sedentary agriculturalists and had been roughly handled by Red Jacket in the bargain. When attempting to convince the Senecas not to alienate their lands, he was forced by circumstances to acquiesce in, and even officially sanction, cessions he would under other circumstances have forbidden. The life of a philanthropist, he was discovering, was not all that it was cracked up to be.

From a political standpoint, however, the treaty had some positive results. Indeed, the perservation of the Six Nations' neutrality was the only success in Indian affairs that the administration could claim in 1791. This proved especially significant because General St. Clair had been sluggish in organizing his army. Originally it had been hoped that he could move against the western tribes in July while Pickering met with the Iroquois well outside the theater of operations. As things turned out, he was not ready to move until well into the autumn. As a tactic the treaty had been meaningless; as diplomacy, it yielded important results. The administration was properly impressed. Secretary Knox thought Pickering had conducted himself "with great ability and judgment," and that was the way it went down in the record. Washington was even more pleased, rewarding Pickering with the long hoped for federal appointment. He was to become the postmaster general of the United States. That night he wrote joyfully to Beckey, "I pray God to preserve you and my dear family, that you may see good, after so many evil days."[58]

TEN

A Diplomat
Among the Indians

DURING THE NEXT FEW MONTHS Pickering's memories of poverty and frustration in Wilkes-Barre receded before the prospect of a comfortable life in Philadelphia. Once again he found himself an actor on the national stage, close to power and secure in political office. Becoming acquainted with his new responsibilities was not at all difficult. One trip to New York for a briefing by the former postmaster general, Samuel Osgood, a few days familiarizing himself with the routine of the tiny office, and he had things in hand. Learning the political realities of life under the Constitution was only a little more trying. Pickering suffered an initial embarrassment when he jumped heedlessly into a patronage squabble over Boston's lucrative deputy postmastership. He was brought up short, however, when it became apparent that his views on the appointment clashed with those of influential Massachusetts merchants and congressmen.[1] He soon came to listen when legislators or cabinet officers spoke, however, and had little trouble thereafter, presiding efficiently over the postal service until he left to become secretary of war in 1795.

Pickering's personal correspondence as well as the records of the Post Office Department reveal a man adrift in a sea of bureaucratic detail yet characteristically unwilling to delegate authority. Local postmasters issued quarterly accounts that he personally evaluated. He decided whether existing post roads would be extended or new ones added, tracked down mail thieves, prepared postal legislation for congressional consideration, appointed new postmasters in growing towns, and replaced those in more established regions when that seemed necessary. Simultaneously he carried on continuing negotiations with stage companies and post riders, bargaining relentlessly in the interest of government economy.[2]

Long hours and hard work were nothing new to Pickering. As to life in Philadelphia, it was a dream, albeit an expensive one, after his long exile. The most troublesome aspect of those early months was finding a house that he could afford to rent and that would accommodate his large family. While he searched, Beckey, his sister-in-law Betsey, and seven of his by now eight sons (the oldest, John, was attending school in Salem) remained in Wilkes-Barre. Finally, in March 1792 he took a house at 117 North Second Street. It had a yard paved in brick where the children might play, a pump, some fruit trees, a "large garden," and a barn. Before summer the family was again happily reunited.[3]

Though Pickering spent an enormous amount of time and energy in the Post Office, he nevertheless continued to work as an advisor to the president on Indian relations. In 1791 administration hopes for an early end to the Indian war rested with the army of General Arthur St. Clair. These hopes were dashed, however, when the western tribes decimated St. Clair's force late in the autumn.[4] This defeat dimmed chances for an end to the war on the Ohio frontier and shattered the administration's confidence in earlier pledges of Iroquois neutrality. Not only would the government have to find the wherewithal to rebuild the army, but it would have to do so while facing the electrifying prospect that the Six Nations might widen the war.

Responding to this crisis, Washington called Pickering to a hurriedly scheduled council of war in mid-December 1791. Earlier, while at Newtown Point, Pickering had invited several leaders of the Six Nations living at Buffalo Creek to visit Philadelphia. His purpose then had been to implement his "civilizing" plan. Washington, who shared none of Pickering's enthusiasm for the project, had originally been prepared to allow the idea to die. But the bleak military outlook that December forced him to reconsider. He asked Pickering to reissue the invitation, intending not only to implement the plan for acculturation but to reaffirm Iroquois neutrality. Because of this political consideration it seemed especially important to the president that the influential Mohawk chieftain, Joseph Brant, also be invited to the conference.[5]

In the months between the time that Pickering tendered the invitations and the arrival of an Indian delegation in Philadelphia, administration objectives underwent a subtle transformation. Perhaps without fully appreciating what they themselves were doing, Washington and Knox decided by degrees to alter the principal purpose of the conference. Though failing to inform either Pickering or the Indians, they concluded that at the conference neither acculturation nor even neutrality should be of paramount importance. Instead they set themselves the far more demanding task of enticing certain leaders of the Six Nations into acting as intermediaries to arrange negotiations with the western tribes.

Had either Washington or Knox apprised Pickering of their changed intentions, he would surely have objected. His experience at Newtown Point had given him firsthand knowledge of how extremely reluctant the Iroquois were to be drawn into the war in any capacity, even as mediators.[6] Moreover, he would undoubtedly have protested on the ground that his invitation made no reference to the administration's new ideas. Not only the government's but his own personal credibility was at stake. But nobody informed Pickering of the government's changed intentions. He remained blissfully ignorant, indeed gratified, that the war which had been so harmful to so many nevertheless was to provide the impetus for putting his civilizing venture into operation.

The administration's anxiety to open talks with the western Indians did not reflect any new hope that negotiations would succeed. Neither the president nor the War Department actually believed that the victorious Indians would prove tractable.[7] Domestic political pressures, however, required a new diplomatic offensive. St. Clair's costly defeat was followed by an outburst of public opposition to the war. Newspaper essayists, especially in New England and the Middle States, demanded an end to the fighting, charging that administration policy toward the western tribes was both immoral and unjustifiable. Secretary Knox was even accused of practicing genocide. The war's real purpose, one pseudonymous writer alleged, was to "extirpate" the Indians in order to take their lands.[8] A North Carolina senator, Benjamin Hawkins, deeply aroused by the injustice of the war, saw other dangerous tendencies emerging from its continuation. The prolonged fighting on the frontier, he claimed, was part of a War Department conspiracy designed to create a large standing army and to make excessive profits for government contractors.[9]

It is interesting to note that Timothy Pickering was among those largely out of sympathy with administration Indian policy in the West. He thought the war unjustified and believed that diplomacy had not been given a fair chance. Twice in the recent past he had been sent to negotiate with the Six Nations in what seemed desperate circumstances; yet each time he had convinced the Iroquois to remain neutral. Pickering was certain that these successes might be duplicated in the West.

The postmaster general's naïve confidence rested in part upon the shallow premise that all difficulties between Indians and whites were the result of white injustice and manipulation. Too frequently in the past, he thought, land jobbers and other "unprincipled men" had been sent to negotiate with the Indians and had instead provoked them. But a carefully selected commission composed of well-intentioned individuals might succeed in arranging a settlement. Then too, he was unconvinced by administration claims that negotiations with the western tribes had been attempted but had failed. "How or by whom the overtures were made," he remarked to his wife, "I am not informed."[10] Finally, Pickering believed that the basis for a settlement existed. The western Indians were in fact fighting for the Ohio River boundary established by the treaty of Fort Stanwix of 1768. But in common with Washington and Knox, Pickering shared the misconception that the boundary line drawn at the treaty of Fort Harmar in January 1789, establishing the American claim to some territory north and west of the Ohio, was acceptable to the western tribes. Since, as Knox frequently alleged, the United States wanted "not one extra foot" of Indian land, Pickering assumed negotiations would succeed, provided they could be arranged.[11]

That was both the rub and the point at which Pickering developed a certain empathy with Washington and Knox, for he presumed that they would have made more serious attempts to negotiate had it not been for the British, who not only encouraged the Indians to continue the war but posed a major obstacle to holding talks. From strategically located posts at Niagara, Detroit, and five lesser locations in the American Northwest, they exerted enormous influence over the western tribes. Pickering was satisfied that agents of the British Indian Department as well as merchants and traders living in and around these posts worked ceaselessly to mislead and deceive the Indians into continuing the war. He knew that only the year before they had frustrated the War Department's efforts to contact the western tribes. He was equally convinced that "the arts of the British" would be used "to frustrate or impede" future attempts to negotiate.[12]

On March 14, 1792, three months after Pickering reissued his invitation to Iroquois leaders for a conference in Philadelphia, Indian delegates from distant Buffalo Creek (among them Pickering's old nemesis Red Jacket) arrived in the capital city. Much to the unhappiness of Washington and Knox, however, the influential Joseph Brant was not among them. In part this was due to the emphasis Pickering had placed upon acculturation in his original invitation. The Dartmouth-educated Mohawk chieftain resented the postmaster general's condescending tone, not to mention the announced purpose of the meeting. He knew all that he cared to know about farming and the other so-called civilized arts; he had no need of further instruction.[13] Brant also suspected that Washington had more on his mind than philanthropy. That Philadel-

phia should want to discuss "civilizing" projects in the wake of a disastrous military setback didn't add up. The stated purpose of the talks, he
therefore concluded, was a ruse designed to get the delegates to
Philadelphia. Once they were there the real political motives of the
government would be revealed. To make the point that he did not
appreciate what he took to be transparent chicanery, he told the
Stockbridge chief, Captain Hendrick Aupaumat, a man he knew to be
in the employ of the War Department, that he was not interested in
"civilizing" schemes. However, he remarked, had he been invited to
work as an intermediary in arranging a treaty between the western
Indians and the United States, he would gladly have come.[14]

Brant was not being altogether candid with Captain Hendrick. It is
doubtful that he would have come to Philadelphia as part of any large
Indian delegation. He had no intention of parading through the city's
streets along with a few dozen other Indian leaders, a sort of freak for
children to gawk at. Brant was keenly aware of his standing both among
Indian peoples and in the white United States. If Washington wished to
discuss the possibilities for a settlement in the West, he would willingly
do so, but only on terms of personal equality.[15]

Naturally, since he had issued the invitations that brought the Buffalo Creek leaders to Philadelphia, Pickering assumed that he was to
play an important role during the talks. The "civilizing" plan was, after
all, his creation and as yet he had no idea that Washington and Knox
had other things on their minds. During the first several days of the
Indians' stay, however, no one in the administration showed any inclination to consult him. Pickering began to fret, not only because he was
being ignored but also because he felt Knox was mismanaging the visit.

Pickering had expected serious discussions to begin soon after the
Indians arrived. Instead, the first week of their stay went by without
any official contact. The visit was turning into a circus with the Indians
continually drunk. Adding to the comic-opera atmosphere, the entire
tailoring establishment of Philadelphia was put to work making American military uniforms complete with gold braid for each of the visiting
leaders. Even the death of one of the chiefs became the occasion for
more of what Pickering considered pointless spectacle. At the inter-
ment of French Peter in the Arch Street burying ground, an "innumer-
able multitude," perhaps a full third of the adult population of the city,
turned out.[16]

Although the carnival atmosphere distressed the sober Pickering, he
did nothing to interfere until he learned through a private channel the
details of the address Washington was to deliver at the opening session
of the conference. It made no mention of acculturation but instead

probed the possibility of using leaders of the Six Nations as inter-mediaries with the western tribes. Only then did Pickering break his silence, reminding Washington of the original purpose of the visit. He urged the president not to press political questions at least until after agreement had been reached on acculturation.[17] According to Samuel Kirkland, a missionary who accompanied the Indians to the city, Brant had already warned the Buffalo Creek leaders that the administration was attempting to deceive them about the real reason for the visit.[18] If the government proposed using them as intermediaries prior to dis-cussion of the "civilizing" plan, it would confirm these charges and jeopardize the government's credibility. However, Pickering argued, if acculturation were considered first, the administration might then be able to go on to other issues. Even at that it would require great caution and circumspection if the Indians were to be convinced to act as inter-mediaries.[19]

Impressed by Pickering's logic, Washington instructed Knox to bring him into the negotiations. Knox in turn invited the postmaster general to the War Department, and together they drafted the address that Washington delivered when the conference officially began.[20]

The president's speech focused first on the question of Iroquois acculturation. He promised that the plan for "civilizing" the people of the Six Nations would be quickly implemented. He next moved on to the subject he obviously viewed as of far greater importance, the war with the western Indians. Reiterating his long-standing contention that the war was the product of a misunderstanding, that his government wanted no land from these Indians, Washington expressed his hope that the problem might be cleared up without recourse to further com-bat.[21] Significantly, the president made no mention of any plan to use representatives from the Six Nations as intermediaries. That aspect of administration policy remained obscured, to be brought out cautiously by Pickering as the talks proceeded. Three days later, as though to affirm once again that the primary purpose of the conference was the implementation of Pickering's plan for Indian acculturation, Washington asked Congress to grant an annuity for the introduction of the "civilized arts" among the Iroquois.[22]

For two solid months Pickering carried on talks with the Buffalo Creek leaders. He had to be patient, for there were constant delays because of drunkenness. Moreover, getting the Indians to discuss the possibility of accepting the role of intermediaries in the war was a touchy business. They much preferred to go back over old injustices suffered at the hands of white land speculators. Thus, Pickering lis-tened at length and not without sympathy to the long, distressing, even pathetic narrative of the Oneida Chief Good Peter, who explained how his people had lost their holdings, how they had been thrust onto small reservations and impoverished as a result of land deals with Governor George Clinton and other representatives of the State of New York. As before, Pickering became incensed. But there was nothing to be done for the Oneidas or for any of the other tribes. Clinton and other state agents had acted within their legal rights. Pickering calculated, nevertheless, that the Oneidas, Onandagas, and Cayugas had surrendered an empire for a total cost to New York, including "benevolences," of $22,362.50[23]

At last Pickering managed to wrestle the Indians around to discussing their possible role as intermediaries between the United States and the western tribes. They were reluctant even to consider the idea, for they feared that if they succumbed to American blandishments they would lose their credibility in the West and open themselves to attack from that direction. Nevertheless, Pickering somehow managed to convince several of the Buffalo Creek leaders to make up a delegation. These Indians were provided with a map on which Pickering carefully marked the extent of the American territorial claims above the Ohio. They were instructed to assure the western Indians of the friendly intentions of the United States. The delegation was also empowered to propose a treaty to be held at "Fort Washington [Cincinnati] on the Ohio, near the mouth of the Little Miami, where provisions in abundance will be ready for their support."[24]

From the moment that he was brought into the negotiations in Philadelphia, Pickering remained continuously involved in the formulation and implementation of policy relating to the war with the western tribes. He not only convinced the chiefs of the Six Nations to send a delegation to the West but also worked closely with Captain Hendrick Aupaumat, who went on a similar mission that spring. Joseph Brant and two American army officers, Captain Alexander Trueman and Colonel John Hardin, were sent on identical embassies.

During the next several months, while waiting for the results of this impressive diplomatic offensive, Pickering kept in close touch with developments in the West. The signs were ominous. The *Philadelphia Aurora* reported that a new Indian confederacy seemed on the verge of forming. According to the *Aurora*, the western tribes had attracted support from the Seven Nations of Canada as well as the Six Nations. If this was true, the war would spread quickly to the New York and Pennsylvania frontiers. It was feared that anywhere from four to five thousand warriors, four times the number that had decimated St. Clair's army, were preparing for renewed war.[25] At about the same time the *Aurora* reported that British forces around Niagara had been substantially increased. Lieutenant Governor John Graves Simcoe of Upper Canada, it was said, now commanded at least sixteen hundred regulars.[26]

Dispatches received by the War Department were no more encouraging. An early report from Brant and the chiefs of the Six Nations indicated that there was little likelihood that a treaty could be arranged. The western tribes, supported by the British, were holding out for a boundary line that was completely unacceptable to the administration. It even appeared for a time that none of the various envoys sent to make contact with the warring Indians would get through. Toward the end of the year, however, the situation suddenly changed. Delegates from the Six Nations did attend the Grand Indian Council held at Au Glaize in September and early October 1792 and reported that the western tribes were prepared to meet with representatives of the United States at Sandusky on Lake Erie in May 1793. Joseph Brant, who conferred with the Buffalo Creek leaders after the council, confirmed this in letters to the War Department and to New York's Governor George Clinton.[27]

These assurances were in fact deliberately deceptive. The record of the Grand Council shows that while the militant western tribes did indeed consent to a meeting, they did so only on two preconditions. First, the United States would have to accept an Ohio River boundary. Second, the government would be required to abandon the line of military posts recently established north of Fort Washington.[28]

Brant and the other Iroquois leaders knew that these terms were unacceptable to the United States and that to reveal them would preclude any chance for a treaty. They resorted to misrepresentation because the alternative was unthinkable. Prolonged warfare against the United States could only end in disaster. Under the circumstances their best hope was to convince both sides to make peace. Though it was certain that the Washington administration would never accept the Ohio River boundary, Brant and the other leaders of the Six Nations nevertheless thought that St. Clair's defeat provided an opening for the achievement of a binding compromise. The hope was to bring the two sides together and then convince each to surrender something in the interest of peace. Assuming the possibility of a settlement, Brant's next step would have been to attempt the organization of a powerful Indian confederacy under his personal leadership to defend it.[29]

Philadelphia was caught off guard by the unexpected prospect of negotiations. Nor were administration leaders altogether pleased, for the projected talks threatened to interfere with already well-developed plans for a military offensive in 1793. Washington responded promptly, however, agreeing to meet. At the suggestion of the Iroquois, he nominated Pickering to be one of three envoys and then chose Benjamin Lincoln and Beverley Randolph, the former governor of Virginia, as the other two American delegates. Simultaneously, he ordered a halt to all offensive military operations north of the Ohio River.[30]

Historians are usually reluctant to write in terms of inevitability, yet it seems reasonable to suggest that this, Timothy Pickering's most important foray yet into the field of Indian diplomacy, was destined to fail from the outset. The warring tribes were demanding an Ohio River boundary and the demolition of all American military posts northwest of the river as the price of peace. The United States was just as insistent on the line established in 1789 at Fort Harmar. In the middle were Joseph Brant and a few other Iroquois leaders hoping to arrange a compromise at a conference that had been based upon a deception.

The administration's military policy made it even more unlikely that the American negotiators could succeed. Washington's orders to General Wayne were to act strictly on the defensive until the results of the Sandusky conference were known. Nevertheless, the army continued to hold posts north of Fort Washington in unknowing violation of one of the preconditions to a treaty laid down earlier by the warring tribes. Moreover, in March 1793, in a move that was guaranteed to arouse the Indians' suspicions, Secretary Knox ordered Wayne to transfer his main force from Pittsburgh to Fort Washington on the Ohio where it was within easy striking distance of the towns of the western Indians. George Morgan, a former Indian agent who had been helpful to Pickering as he prepared to meet the western tribes, warned that this not only undermined possibilities for a successful treaty, but placed the commissioners themselves in physical danger.[31]

As though there weren't enough obstacles to a successful negotiation, Pickering, Lincoln, and Randolph had also to cope with the British, who would be in an excellent position to influence the course of the talks. Because England controlled the lakes, Lieutenant Governor Simcoe was first able to put himself in position to exert leverage by insisting that he and not the Washington administration would supply the liquor and provisions for the conference.[32] Next, by working through Alexander McKee of the British Indian Department, who had superb connections with the Shawnees, Simcoe was able to elicit a "spontaneous" request from the Indians for British mediation.[33]

The impact of these developments in Philadelphia can hardly be overestimated. It was an article of faith there that the western tribes would long since have agreed to a compromise had it not been for the English who controlled them. Blind to the fact that native peoples were actually capable of defining their own interests, American decision makers confused efforts by the British Indian Department to influence the tribes with a capacity for domination. It never occurred to Pickering or anyone else involved in policy formulation that the British might have lost their influence had they not shared a consensus of interests with the militant western Indians.

Given this fundamental misperception, the fact that the English were carving out a significant place for themselves at the talks was terribly distressing to the administration. Washington even gave some thought to canceling the conference. On considering how the public and Congress would respond to this, however, he decided to go ahead. The British would be allowed to supply the Indians. And while he balked at the prospect of mediation, the president did agree that British representatives might be present at the treaty to advise the Indians as to their rights and interests.[34]

The Sandusky conference was scheduled to begin on May 20, 1793. On April 30 the three envoys, heading a party of twenty-five, set out. It was a diverse group including the secretary to the commission, Charles Storer; an unnamed but evidently absent-minded physician who managed somehow to leave his medicine chest behind in Philadelphia; the federal commissioner to the Six Nations, General Israel Chapin; four interpreters; a cook; an assortment of servants and laborers; and six missionaries from the Society of Friends, one of whom was the well-known John Heckewelder.[35] Pickering and Beverley Randolph did not travel with the main body, setting out instead overland on horseback for Niagara. Lincoln and the rest of the entourage went by ship to Albany. Then, transferring baggage and supplies to a number of small boats, they traveled by river and lake to a rendezvous with Pickering and Randolph at the British post.

The envoys joined forces at Niagara a few days after the treaty had originally been scheduled to begin. Instead of sailing immediately for Sandusky, however, they were forced to endure weeks of inactivity at Navy Hall, Lieutenant Governor Simcoe's residence near Fort Niagara. The most militant of the western tribes, the Shawnees, Delawares, and Wyandots, had called a general Indian Council at the rapids of the Miami River near Detroit prior to the opening of talks. They hoped to discover from Brant and the other leaders of the Six Nations whether the American envoys were prepared to admit the preconditions for a treaty established at the recent Grand Council at Au Glaize. Their suspicions were already aroused, both because in accepting the invitation to treat Secretary of War Knox had made no reference to the required concessions, and because of General Wayne's recent move from Pittsburgh to Fort Washington. The militants also hoped to establish a united Indian front to include the Six Nations, the Lake Indians, and other less warlike tribes before going to Sandusky.

From the moment of their arrival at Niagara, Pickering and the other envoys realized that they would not be free to carry on independent negotiations with the Indians. The British seemed to have anticipated every possibility. While they were kept at a distance, forbidden by the Indians from participating in the council at the rapids, Colonel John Butler and Alexander McKee of the British Indian Department attended that gathering.[36] Nor was it long before the envoys discovered that if they were not precisely Governor Simcoe's prisoners, they were not exactly free men either. Thus, when they attempted to move out of Navy Hall to an encampment at nearby Queenston, Simcoe objected, "and in such terms," Pickering wrote, "that we could not, without rudeness avoid a compliance with his request."[37] Simcoe was even more explicit in demanding that the envoys accept a British escort if and when they should journey to the treaty site. He was, in fact, so insistent on this point that in order to avoid having British officers thrust upon them, the commissioners actually invited some along.[38]

The envoys' suspicions of British intentions were by no means allayed by more intimate contact with Simcoe. Though he treated them courteously during their weeks of inactivity at Niagara, his strong anti-Americanism too often got the better of him, as when he exclaimed to Bierce Duffy, one of Pickering's servants, that President Washington was a "damned stupid blockhead."[39] His animosity—especially toward Pickering, whom he considered "a violent, low, philosophic, cunning New Englander"—was altogether too obvious.[40]

The three envoys, Pickering, Lincoln, and Randolph, came rapidly to the conclusion that while they remained immobilized at Niagara, McKee and Butler, meeting with the Indians at the rapids, were probably attempting to undercut the possibility of an agreement. These men, together with Simcoe and other British officials in Canada, seemed to be playing a duplicitous game. Officially, they endorsed peace between the Indians and the United States. Simultaneously, however, the Americans believed they were in all likelihood urging the Indians to make no territorial concessions, knowing full well that the administration could not accept an Ohio River boundary. This "as perfectly hedges up the way to a peace," Benjamin Lincoln wrote, "as if the British should advise the Indians to a war." Lincoln and the others feared the warring tribes would do nothing "contrary to the opinion of the commanding officer in Canada, whom they consider as the true representative of *the King their father.*"[41]

Though there was little the frustrated trio of Americans could do to counteract what seemed to be taking place, they did send one of their interpreters, William Wilson, along with Captain Hendrick and four other Indians, to the rapids of the Miami. They were to gather information on what was taking place at the council and to sound out the western tribes on possibilities for a settlement.[42] Pickering, who drew up Hendrick's instructions, interpreted the commission's powers as liberally as possible in order to entice the Indians into a negotiation. Hendrick was to inform the hostile tribes that although it would be difficult for the United States to cede lands that had already been sold and settled, the envoys did have the power to make some concessions regarding the boundary. But Hendrick's fundamental purpose was to undo, if he could, the damage done by McKee and Butler. He was to urge the Indians to keep their minds open for a free exchange of views with the American envoys.[43]

For weeks the envoys remained at Niagara until finally John Heckewelder and other Quaker missionaries urged them to come to Detroit. There was some danger in this, they admitted, for rumors were rife among the Indians that in violation of the truce General Wayne had moved his army from Fort Washington to the Miami plains. The missionaries nevertheless believed that as long as the envoys remained at Niagara nothing could be accomplished. At Detroit they would at least be in a position to gather information and to treat if the opportunity should arise.[44]

Plans were immediately made. But before the envoys could sail for Detroit a delegation of some fifty Indians led by Brant arrived at Niagara from the council at the rapids. Brant raised two issues. First, he objected to the provocative activities of General Wayne, who appeared to be strengthening his posts northwest of the Ohio. Second, he asked whether the commissioners had the authority to establish a permanent boundary in the Northwest.[45]

For the first time since undertaking their mission Pickering and the other commissioners suddenly felt the warm glow of optimism. These were reasonable questions rather than the uncompromising demands they had feared. Pickering assured Brant that the truce remained in force, that Wayne would be restrained, and that the commissioners did indeed have the authority to establish a boundary. This, he hoped, would be the major topic of the upcoming treaty. On the following day Brant assured the American envoys that their answers had been satisfactory and that the treaty would soon commence.[46]

As with almost everything else relating to these negotiations, confusion surrounds the real purpose of the Brant mission. According to Brant himself he lived up to the precise meaning of his instructions from the Indian council.[47] Alexander McKee, however, evidently believed that the Mohawk chieftain had been sent on a more demanding errand. He informed Simcoe just prior to Brant's departure for Niagara that he had been instructed to find out whether the commissioners were empowered to arrange an Ohio River boundary and whether they could agree to the demolition of all army posts on the northwestern side of the river as well. Unless they had these powers, McKee wrote, it seemed clear from "the general union of sentiment throughout all the nations" that the Indians would not make peace. Moreover, considering the agitated state of mind of some of the tribes, unless the envoys had such powers they would be placing themselves in extreme jeopardy by even attending a treaty.[48] The writings of John Heckewelder, observing the situation from Detroit, tend to confirm at least part of McKee's story. On July 2, Heckewelder confided in his journal that unless the commissioners conceded an Ohio River boundary he had it on good authority that the war would continue and "they & all with them may be knocked in the head."[49] Nothing that Heckewelder heard in Detroit reflected the conciliatory attitude Brant displayed at Niagara.

Governor Simcoe was utterly dumbfounded by the meeting with Brant. On the one hand, McKee had written him of extreme demands by a united Indian confederacy. This suggested the inevitability of continued war. On the other hand, Brant seemed to be opening the door to a negotiated settlement on terms far less stringent. The Mohawk leader even left Simcoe with the impression that the Shawnees, long one of the most militant tribes, would agree to a compromise. If nothing else was clear to Simcoe it was at least evident that the Indians were by no means united. Indian disunity could spell disaster, not only for their cause but for London's lingering hopes for an Indian barrier state in the Northwest. He wrote McKee at the rapids on the importance of Indian unity and found a moment in private to deliver the same message to Brant.[50]

If the conference with Brant confused the depressed Simcoe, it delighted Pickering, Lincoln, and Randolph, who sensed a breakthrough coming.[51] In good spirits for the first time since arriving at Niagara, they sailed for Detroit aboard the British schooner *Dunmore*. On July 21 the little ship dropped anchor in the mouth of the Detroit River and the commissioners went ashore, finding quarters at the nearby farm of Matthew Elliott, McKee's deputy in the British Indian Department. There they awaited an invitation to meet from the Indians.

A week after the arrival of the *Dunmore,* a second Indian delegation came down from the council and encamped on Bois Blank Island, across from Elliott's farm. This group was accompanied by three British officers: Elliott, whose hospitality the envoys were then enjoying; Thomas Smith, Alexander McKee's assistant; and James McKee, his son. Insisting that the earlier delegation led by Brant had misrepresented the Indian position, a Wyandot war chief handed Pickering and his colleagues a written request for the answer to one question: Would they accept an Ohio River boundary and undertake to remove American settlers from the northwestern side of the river?[52]

The commissioners' optimism, now all but shattered, had been based on a false hope that Brant, who had spoken so moderately at the Niagara conference, reflected the feelings of the western tribes. But after his return from Niagara to the council, the Mohawk chieftain was denounced by the militants at a series of meetings held in late July. As a result the council fragmented, with Brant and his Mohawks, the rest of the Six Nations, and the Lake Indians insisting on negotiations. The militant westerners were opposed unless the Americans first ceded an Ohio River boundary. It was the militants who now confronted Pickering and his friends at Elliott's farm.

At last faced with the demand for an Ohio River boundary, the American envoys made a final attempt to save the situation. In their carefully phrased response they emphasized the substantial financial remuneration they were prepared to make in return for a boundary acceptable to the United States, and urged face-to-face negotiations to work out such a line. They were forced to admit, however, that they were not empowered to surrender an Ohio boundary.[53] On August 1, speaking through Simon Girty, an interpreter, the Indians explained that there was no basis for an agreement and that the envoys might just as well return to Philadelphia. At this juncture, something peculiar happened. Matthew Elliott broke into the translation, saying, according to John Heckewelder, "No, No, they was not to have said [the last words]." There then followed a short conference between the British officers and the Indians after which the speech was amended to read: "We will take your speech to the great Council, from whence you shall receive an answer; we desire you not to go but to wait for our answer."[54]

Contemporaries then and historians since have debated the significance of Elliott's interruption of the translation, but to Pickering and his colleagues the meaning was clear.[55] It signified, once again, something they had believed from the time they arrived at Niagara two months before. The English were the real enemy; they controlled the

Indians and had been busy undermining chances for a settlement all along.[56]

For eleven days after the meeting between the commissioners and the Indians on Bois Blank Island, the *Dunmore* lay at anchor in the Detroit River. Finally, on August 12, the envoys decided to chance a confrontation with the Indians at their council and asked Captain Ford of the *Dunmore* to set sail as soon as possible. Ford, however, refused, informing the astonished Americans that he took orders only from Captain Bunbury, their British escort. There followed an angry exchange between the commissioners and Bunbury, who made it clear that without instructions from McKee he was not prepared to allow them anywhere near the council. During the next few days tempers periodically flared. Then on August 16 the long overdue message from the Indians insisting on an Ohio River boundary arrived. This left the envoys with no choice but to return empty-handed to Philadelphia.[57]

It is clear that chances for a negotiated settlement disappeared because Joseph Brant and those other Iroquois leaders who were present at the council at the rapids could not convince the western tribes to accept a compromise. But Pickering and the other American delegates never came close to understanding this. They vastly underrated the capacity of the Indians to make independent decisions, confusing an attempt by agents of the British Indian Department to exert influence with actual control. Thus they were unable to appreciate the fact that the Indians themselves were demanding an Ohio River boundary. Instead they left for home infuriated, blaming British interference alone for the setback. It had been "the craft of the *man* or *men* who control the Indians," Pickering explained, "to keep us at a distance lest by free and daily communications and friendly intercourse we should make some impression.[58] This judgment reinforced a fundamental misconception about the nature of the Indian war that would long prevail in Philadelphia.

ELEVEN

The War Department, Securing the Peace

IN MID-SEPTEMBER 1793, after an uneventful trip, Pickering arrived in New York City where he first learned that Philadelphia was experiencing an epidemic of yellow fever. He hurried southward against a current of humanity fleeing the dread plague. Germantown, Reading, and other villages in the vicinity were jammed with exiles. The capital, by contrast, stood as if besieged. "The streets are lonely to a melancholy degree," wrote Henry Knox. "Hundreds are dying and the merchants have fled." [1] It was as though some phantom army occupied the city while the terrified inhabitants remained indoors behind shuttered windows. Commerce ground to a near standstill. Ships arrived with cargoes that went unclaimed. The banks were virtually deserted while the coffee houses, where businessmen once met to discuss the state of the economy, closed their doors.

Life did not, of course, come to a complete halt. Those businesses that continued to operate, however, were in most instances related to the problems of a plague-ridden city. Chemists, apothecaries, and coffin makers were kept very busy. And those who traversed the city's streets that sultry September were primarily physicians, nurses, or bleeders attending patients, carters bearing the dead to obscure burials in the town's overflowing cemeteries, or the sick seeking help where there was little to be found. When the epidemic first developed, the bells of the city's churches rang constantly in deadly alarm. After a time the depressing effect caused the city to still the bells, but the silence proved no less disheartening. [2]

Pickering found Philadelphia in the grip of a hysterical controversy over the methods of treating the pestilence. Even in the beginning, when the argument was largely confined to the city's physicians, it had political overtones, as some Federalist and some Republican doctors squared off against one another.[3] One group, spearheaded by the volatile democrat Dr. Benjamin Rush, advocated a rigorous treatment involving extensive bleeding as well as repeated purges of calomel and jalap. But Dr. Adam Kuhn, like Rush a member of the city's prestigious College of Physicians, pronounced his "cure" a "murderous dose."[4] Kuhn, Edward Stevens, and other Federalist practitioners advocated instead the more traditional "bark and wine" treatment long employed by European physicians who dealt routinely with the disease in the West Indies.[5]

After Alexander Hamilton publicly endorsed his friend Stevens's treatment, the political aspect of the controversy escalated sharply. Though a serious oversimplification, it was soon generally understood throughout Philadelphia that two cures, one "Federalist" and the other "Republican," were being practiced by rival physicians.[6] Benjamin Rush certainly did nothing to dispel that impression when he "declared his cure the only truly egalitarian form of medicine and published instructions on how to bleed and purge in the newspapers" as though to prove that medicine, too, could be made democratic.[7]

Hardly had the disputatious Pickering returned to the city when he leaped with unrestrained enthusiasm into the dispute. The beleaguered Rush was a friend. Moreover, as the Pickering family's physician he had treated young Henry Pickering, who subsequently recovered from the fever. Finally, Rush was on the right side ideologically, for Pickering was still two years from converting to Federalism. Denouncing as "fatally erroneous" the views of those who disagreed with his friend, Pickering collected every story, even mere rumor or hearsay, that tended to support Rush's claims, while ignoring all evidence to the contrary. According to Pickering, no one who adopted Rush's treatment need die. The fact that each week hundreds more were buried was, he insisted, the result of the work of Rush's opponents, who had "consigned multitudes to their graves from sheer stubbornness and bad judgment."[8]

Taking a leaf from the doctor's book, Pickering became a democratic healer, practicing Rush's treatment on members of his own household. When a maid became ill, he immediately sent for a bleeder who took a full ten ounces of the girl's blood. She was then given the doctor's purge, after which Pickering believed her symptoms abated. When two servant women from the adjoining house fell ill, he prescribed for them, too, and they also seemed to improve. Then when he felt himself coming down with something, he followed what by that time had become standard practice. "I lost some blood, and lived abstemiously, and several times rode moderately a few miles to breathe the pure air of the country." Soon he felt fully recovered.[9]

The epidemic persisted, and though other members of Pickering's family fell ill, on being treated they too quickly recovered. Of course, with each new success Pickering's confidence in Rush was strengthened. Then, late in September, six-year-old Edward, the youngest of his eight sons, caught the fever. As soon as the symptoms developed, Pickering hurried to Dr. Rush's house on Third Street for a consultation, returning to nurse the stricken child personally through the terrible days that followed. He bled and purged according to Rush's instructions but with no noticeable positive effect. He wrote frequently to Rush describing the boy's condition and asking advice. Nothing seemed to do any good. Finally the child refused all nourishment, complaining that his throat was stopped. Hands trembling as he wrote, Pickering had one last pathetic question for Rush. Would it do any good to forcefeed the lad?[10]

On October 10, the little boy died. It was a numbing experience, watching the child's coffin as it was lowered into the grave. At least outwardly, Pickering responded with the fortitude he characteristically displayed at times of personal sorrow. He tried to comfort Rebecca while consoling himself with the thought that, somehow, this was God's judgment.[11] One thing he did not do, however, was question his own beliefs. Rush's cure, he continued to insist, was effective.

October of 1793 was warmer than usual. The female mosquito *Aedes aegyptie,* carrier of the deadly fever, thrived, and the city maintained the aspect of a charnel house. From faraway Mount Vernon President Washington, concerned for the future of his government, wrote to Pickering, the ranking federal official left in Philadelphia, inquiring about the chances that the fever would dissipate before December, when Congress was scheduled to convene. Could Germantown or perhaps Reading provide accommodations if Philadelphia remained under siege?[12]

Pickering sought Rush's advice, consulted with civic leaders, and then journeyed to Germantown to look into the situation there. Earlier the little town had been crowded with exiles. Some, however, had since scattered to other parts of the country. There would be room if Congress decided to meet there. But Pickering's real hope was that the fever would disappear before December. In 1762 the city had experienced a similar outbreak of yellow fever but it had gone with the first frost. If this pattern repeated itself, Pickering wrote, November would bring an end to the plague.[13]

On the night of October 27 Philadelphia experienced the first frost of the season. The next morning, Pickering measured ice one-fifth of an inch thick in his back garden. This, combined with the rapidly declining death rate, gave cause for real optimism. Many of those who had earlier fled returned to the city. "Shops are opening, business increasing, and the countenances of the citizens" for the first time in weeks looked "cheerful," he wrote. The plague had not yet completely abated, however, and he warned the president against coming back just yet. He felt increasingly confident, however, that by December the city would be safe.[14]

The disease disappeared almost as quickly and mysteriously as it had come. When Congress convened that December, life in Philadelphia had almost returned to normal. It was a modest blessing that the government was able to confront its many problems without having to grapple with an epidemic. There were difficulties enough. Serious tensions had developed in Franco-American relations. There were worse difficulties with the English, whose entry into the Wars of the French Revolution added a trying new dimension to the nation's many foreign policy problems. Finally, of course, there remained the confused Indian situation. Far to the west, supply difficulties, an outbreak of influenza in the army, and the delay caused by the abortive negotiations of 1793 had combined to thwart Anthony Wayne's plans for an offensive. Closer to home there was the now perpetual problem of securing once again the neutrality of the Six Nations.

The possibility that the Iroquois might decide to widen the war was substantially increased during the first half of 1794 as a result of the developing crisis with England. In February Lord Dorchester, the governor general of Canada, gave a well-publicized speech to the Indians of the Seven Villages of Lower Canada, predicting a conflict between Britain and America and encouraging the Indians to join in the struggle. A week later he ordered the construction of a new British post on an old site some sixty miles south of Detroit at the rapids of the Maumee. Deep in American territory, this new fort was provocatively placed in the very heart of the area that General Wayne was even then preparing to attack.[15]

The politically sophisticated Iroquois quickly sensed the importance of the changed circumstances. Joesph Brant, who had earlier advocated a compromise on the western problem, now gave serious thought to the possibilities of an Anglo-Indian alliance against the United States.[16] And Cornplanter, long the foremost advocate of conciliation with America, seemed anxious for war.[17]

By July 1794, the situation in western Pennsylvania had become menacing. General Israel Chapin, the American commissioner to the Six Nations, strongly advised Knox to hold a treaty with the Buffalo Creek Iroquois to head off war. Administration leaders responded immediately, assigning Pickering the delicate task of conducting the talks. The point at issue was the recent establishment of an American settlement in the Erie Triangle about two hundred thousand acres of land in the extreme northwestern part of the state, land the Indians claimed never to have ceded. But behind that lay the growing threat that, encouraged by the prospect of British participation in the war against the United States, the Six Nations might at last be ready to abandon their neutrality.[18]

When he left for the treaty site, the situation seemed just as bleak to Pickering as it did to others in the administration. On September 19, however, while at Canandaigua, he learned that General Wayne had won an important victory over the western tribes at Fallen Timbers. Moreover, though the battle took place within sight of the recently reestablished British fort at the rapids of the Maumee, the English had done nothing to aid the Indians.[19] The American envoy did not miss the significance of what had occurred. Not only had the long-hoped-for military victory in the West at last materialized, but the threat of British intervention had nearly evaporated. The Six Nations were now isolated.

Pickering moved quickly to assert his newfound strength. The Indians had originally demanded that the treaty be held at Buffalo Creek. Because of the site's proximity to Niagara, administration leaders had been uneasy, fearing further British interference. But since the alternative seemed an open break, they reluctantly acquiesced. In the light of Wayne's victory, however, Pickering thought it an unnecessary act of weakness to give in on this point and informed the Iroquois that the treaty would be held at Canandaigua or nowhere at all. The Indians, revealing that they too understood the significance of changed circumstances, agreed. Joseph Brant, so militant a few weeks earlier, did not even bother to attend.[20]

By the time the Indians assembled at Canandaigua late in October, Pickering found himself in an even stronger bargaining position. A reliable source just arrived from Niagara informed him that Simcoe had just received dispatches from George Hammond, the British minister in Philadelphia, indicating "that the complexion of the British with respect to a war with the United States had totally changed."[21] This was confirmed shortly thereafter by a message from Henry Knox, who enclosed extracts of a letter from John Jay, then in London working on a treaty of amity and commerce. The British, so menacing in the early part of the year, now wanted peace. Moreover, Jay and Foreign Secretary Grenville had already agreed to the establishment of a *status quo* arrangement in the West under which both sides agreed "that all encroachments on either side should be done away" with. Since this agreement had been made with particular reference to the new British post at the rapids of the Maumee, Knox fully expected that Governor Simcoe would soon withdraw that garrison.[22]

In mid-October, just after the main contingent of Indians from Buffalo Creek arrived, Pickering wrote to Beckey of the weariness he felt at undertaking yet another negotiation. He was sick to death of the drunkenness and the inevitable delays but nevertheless confident of success. Twelve hundred Indians were already present, with about three hundred more soon to arrive. As usual it would be a long and arduous business. One thing he had noticed, however: the Indians seemed as "friendly as I ever knew them."[23]

At the very beginning of the negotiations Pickering made it evident that he was not prepared to participate in talks as long as British representatives were present. When William Johnson, an interpreter sent by Joseph Brant, took a seat at the council at Canandaigua, Pickering threatened to leave. He denounced Johnson as a "British Spy" and went on to charge that the English had been responsible for the failure of peace efforts during the preceding year. Rehearsing England's past injustices, dating back to her retention of the northwest posts in 1783, he charged that George III meant to "reinslave" the people of the United States and hoped to do it while "the French, our only potential ally, were struggling for their own freedom" in a great European war. Pickering concluded by noting that recently President Washington had sent John Jay, "a wise counsellor," to London to make peace, and it appeared that he would succeed. This was not, however, because the British crown had experienced a change of heart. On the contrary, it was because the once beleaguered French had won the upper hand in Europe and were "overrunning the countries of the tyrants who attacked them."[24] All things considered, it was a remarkable performance for a man soon to be known as the nation's leading Francophobe. It certainly had the desired effect on the Indians, who agreed with very little opposition that Johnson should leave.

Pickering's angry outburst notwithstanding, he did not forget his deep commitment to the well-being of the Indians. Since 1790, he had helped bring about important improvements in Indian policy. At Canandaigua in 1794 he continued his work, aided by a growing realization on the part of many leaders of the Six Nations that cultural change was inevitable. There were, of course, some like Red Jacket who fought against it. But with their hunting grounds diminishing and game in the Northeast dwindling, the Iroquois were coming increasingly to realize that what Pickering and so many others had been preaching was true. Their survival depended on the adoption of an agricultural existence.[25]

Pickering was particularly distressed at the plight of the Oneidas, a tribe that had already lost most of its land and was living on a small reservation in New York. The land still controlled by these Indians would have been enough for them if no more was lost and if they became agriculturalists. He feared, however, that the State of New York, owner of the preemption rights to their land, would someday press the Oneidas to sell what was left. He therefore cautioned them against holding any more treaties with state land agents. These "bad men," he predicted, would attempt to frighten them into selling their remaining holdings. Should this happen, he urged the Oneidas not to be intimidated, but to rely for protection on the federal government.[26]

The New Englander did more than give good advice, for he believed that in order to adapt successfully, the Iroqouis needed not only technical aid but absolute assurances that the lands they still held would not be taken from them. At Canandaigua and in a separate treaty negotiated a month later with the Oneida, Stockbridge, and Tuscarora tribes, he moved forward on both fronts. His handling of the land question showed boldness and a determination to establish a fair and lasting peace.

The Senecas had long claimed that the land cessions extracted from them at Fort Stanwix in 1784 and reaffirmed under the terms of the treaty of Fort Harmar were invalid.[27] This issue had been raised at every treaty Pickering had attended. At Canandaigua he redrew the boundary, retroceding more than a million acres to the Senecas and wiping out at the stroke of a pen a long-standing grievance that had soured relations between the Six Nations and the United States.[28] This massive retrocession was complemented by an agreement that not only clearly defined the boundaries of lands held by the various tribes comprising the Six Nations but guaranteed that they would own these in perpetuity. In return the Indians agreed to give up all claims to lands beyond these boundaries.[29]

Pickering also committed the United States to a new program of technical assistance for the Six Nations. The inadequate annuity of fifteen hundred dollars established in 1792 was tripled, the funds to be used to purchase clothing and farm implements, and to pay "useful artificers" who would live in the Indian towns and teach the people basic skills. The Oneidas, who had been allies of the United States during the revolutionary war, were also granted a gristmill and sawmill to be built at government expense. Experts would be employed to operate the mills for three years during which time they would teach the Indians how to run and repair the mills themselves.[30]

The agreements that Pickering signed in 1794 were extraordinarily generous, considering the great political advantages the Washington administration enjoyed at the time. However, they were not wholly without territorial advantage to the United States. The Indians, too, made some concessions. All Iroquois claims to the Erie Triangle were extinguished and, after some hard bargaining, the United States gained the roadway from Fort Schlosser to Niagara, the strategic link between Lakes Erie and Ontario.[31]

The Indian treaties of 1794 represent the consummation of the creative aspect of Timothy Pickering's career as an Indian diplomat. He in fact viewed them as epoch-making. On November 20, after the council fire at Canandaigua had been extinguished, he wrote to Joseph Brant, detailing the land cessions and economic aid he had promised, and predicting that a "new era" in Indian-white relations was about to begin.[32]

At the end of 1794, following Henry Knox's resignation, Washington rewarded Pickering for his latest successes in Indian diplomacy by appointing him secretary of war. At one time such an appointment would have been unthinkable to the president. However, the primary responsibilities of the War Department lay in the area of Indian affairs; and no one was better prepared to take over these duties than Pickering. Also, the president, who had experienced difficulties when attempting to interest better-known candidates in the job, was certain that Pickering would accept. With no independent income and no alternative means of support, he was one of the few public figures of his time who was totally dependent upon the federal bureaucracy for his livelihood. He had become, of necessity, a sort of early career man with the national government.

Cabinet status meant a great many things to Pickering, not the least of which was a substantial salary increase. It involved him in a whole host of new activities as well. He was called upon the select sites for new federal arsenals, to report to Congress on the requirements of America's tiny military establishment, and to superintend naval construction. But most significant, as the secretary of war he had primary responsibility for overseeing the negotiations at Greenville that followed General Wayne's victory at Fallen Timbers.

On learning that early reports of the outcome of the battle had been highly exaggerated, Pickering realized that diplomatic success at Greenville was by no means a foregone conclusion. Casualties on both sides had been so slight, in fact, that he at first wondered whether the

Indians were sufficiently chastened to agree to talk.[33] Even after it became certain that they were prepared to treat, Pickering believed the outcome of the negotiations would hinge on two considerations. First, he feared that if General Wayne did not command a visibly impressive force when talks began, the Indians would refuse to come to terms. Second, Pickering thought American control over the northwestern posts central to long-term possibilities for peace. If the English should publicly announce their intention to withdraw from the posts before the talks got under way, the Indians would be left with no choice but to seek an accommodation regardless of the size of Wayne's force.

Since the enlistment period for most of Wayne's troops would expire in June, maintaining the army's strength in the West was a serious problem. As a stopgap measure, Pickering transferred a small body of militia from Fort Pitt to Greenville.[34] Meanwhile he shepherded through Congress an administration bill calling for the expansion of Wayne's Legion, pay increases for the officers, and larger bounties for enlistment or reenlistment.[35] But improved benefits attracted few recruits, and manpower problems continued to plague the War Department. By April 15 Pickering was nearly desperate. He urged Wayne to try to convince men already in the legion to reenlist, hoping that the increased bounty would convince some to stay. He even approved a special bonus to any veteran who would agree to continue in the service until autumn, by which time the forthcoming treaty should have been concluded.[36]

Pickering's inability to do much for Wayne, whose army seemed to be melting away, led him to place increased emphasis upon the importance of the diplomatic side of the equation. He waited anxiously for some news of the results of John Jay's mission to England. On March 7 an authenticated copy of the Jay Treaty reached the office of Secretary of State Edmund Randolph, but for three months the treaty remained in the exclusive care of the president and the secretary of state.[37] No one else was allowed access, not even Pickering, who knew that Jay had been instructed to seek the cession of the northwest posts and who considered the issue critical to the outcome of the pending negotiations at Greenville.[38]

The Senate began its debate on the treaty on June 8. Though the upper house voted to maintain secrecy until a decision had been reached, the cloak of confidentiality began unraveling. The anxious Pickering, for one, learned the details of the agreement at least twelve days before Senator Stevens Thomson Mason of Virginia leaked its contents to Benjamin F. Bache, printer of the *Philadelphia Aurora*.[39]

When Pickering at last saw the treaty, he was in the main unenthusiastic. On most questions it seemed to be more advantageous to the English than to the United States. Yet in the end, he supported ratification.[40] Pickering's endorsement was not the result of any strong Federalist predispositions. In fact it cannot truly be demonstrated that at this time he revealed many of those foreign policy views commonly associated with Federalism. For example, he showed no symptoms of hostility to France. On the contrary, he continued sympathetic to the French Revolution long after many others had turned their backs on it. He even defended the executions of Louis XVI and his queen as necessary in view of the threats the revolution faced from "tyrants" and "despots" anxious to destroy liberty.[41] There is no reason whatever to doubt that Pickering meant exactly what he said when he explained to Anthony Wayne in August 1795 that "prudent thinking men, the real patriots, the truly independent spirits" could "rejoice in the successes of the French against the combined tyrants who would have overwhelmed them" yet simultaneously "desire to be on good terms with the British."[42]

Nor can it truly be said that Pickering was particularly friendly to the English at this time. His various contacts with British officialdom in his capacity as an Indian diplomat had been uniformly unfriendly. His hot-tempered refusal to treat with the Iroquois at Canandaigua as long as a British interpreter was present stands as further evidence of his opinion of the English. No less a figure than George Hammond, the British minister to the United States, described Pickering in 1795 as a man characterized by a "most blind and undistinguishing hatred of Great Britain."[43]

Pickering endorsed the Jay Treaty because he came at the problem from the perspective of the War Department. Whatever its other failings might be, the agreement offered one all-important advantage: it stipulated the withdrawal of the British from the seven strategically located northwestern posts.[44] If ratified it would seal the fate of the English in the Old Northwest, destroy the influence of the British Indian Department as well as British traders in the area who had done so much to keep the Indian war going, and lay the foundation for a lasting peace with the western tribes. It would, in short, provide the capstone to Pickering's extended career in Indian affairs, paving the way for that "new era" in Indian relations he had earlier predicted. If the treaty was rejected, it would mean renewed British machinations among the Indians and even perhaps the continuation of the Indian war.[45]

June 1795 was a month of anxious waiting in the War Department—waiting for the Senate and then the president to approve the Jay Treaty, waiting for the treaty that was scheduled to open at Greenville on the fifteenth of the month to get under way. News from General Wayne was not at all encouraging. Representatives of the British Indian Department continued to do everything possible to convince the western tribes not to attend. Meanwhile, other British agents were encouraging Indian raids into Kentucky. They were being aided by Kentucky secessionists, who sponsored retaliatory raids into Indian country in order to keep the war going and their own chances for secession alive. Wayne thought he would have to stop both the Indian raiders and the separatists if he was to succeed at Greenville. A worse problem was the state of the legion. Its numbers were rapidly dwindling as enlistment periods ended. Unless large numbers of reinforcements were provided immediately, he warned, the army would soon dissolve and with it any chance for peace.[46]

From personal experience Pickering knew that the treaty at Greenville would probably be delayed several weeks. He hoped that by that time a copy of the ratified Jay Treaty calling for the withdrawal of the British from the northwest posts would be on its way to Wayne. Unable to reveal the exact stipulations of the agreement during the Senate debate, he nevertheless informed the general that the treaty, which he predicted would soon be ratified, would greatly strengthen his negotiating position.[47] When the Senate approved the treaty, excepting its twelfth article, an exultant Pickering informed Wayne that the president's signature was only a formality and that before long a copy of the treaty would be in a dispatch bag heading west.[48] War Department hopes for quick ratification, however, were soon shattered. President Washington was perplexed over what to do with the treaty that had not been endorsed in its totality by the Senate. He and Randolph soon decided to revise Article 12 to make it more acceptable. Constitutional questions then arose that he put to the cabinet. Would the Senate expect to debate the projected revision of Article 12 before he went ahead with ratification? Would it be constitutional to revise the article and ratify the treaty without further Senate debate?

Pickering wanted no further delays. Success or failure at Greenville might hinge on swift ratification. His advice to the president, certainly unconstitutional, reveals the extent of his anxiety. The president, he wrote, could revise Article 12, include it in the treaty, and ratify the whole package without again consulting the Senate. Oliver Wolcott, Jr., the secretary of the treasury, joined Pickering in this opinion. Even Randolph tentatively agreed.[49]

While the cabinet's virtually unanimous opinion satisfied Washington as to the technicalities he had raised, he was left with nagging doubts about the wisdom of ratification. Therefore, instead of going ahead with the redrafting of Article 12 and conditional ratification, he sought a point-by-point evaluation of the treaty from Alexander Hamilton.[50] Before the New Yorker could reply, however, Philadelphia learned that the Royal Navy had begun a vigorous new offensive against American provision ships bound for French ports.[51] Washington was stunned, as was Randolph, who considered these depredations totally "irreconcilable" with the Jay Treaty. The secretary of state insisted, and Washington agreed, that the treaty could not be ratified until the attacks had stopped.[52]

With diplomacy at a standstill, Randolph observed that the crisis created by the new provisions order offered a useful opportunity to reopen talks with His Majesty's Government regarding several of the more objectionable aspects of the treaty. He suggested that a memorial be sent to the Foreign Office proposing renewed negotiations on four points: impressment, compensation for slaves taken from the South during the Revolution, payment to American merchants who had lost ships or cargoes under the Orders in Council of 1793, and the control of British privateers then preying on American commerce. Washington agreed and ordered Randolph to draw up the memorial.[53] A few days later the president left for Mount Vernon, not expecting to return for many weeks.

Aside from the secretary of state, no one in the cabinet had been kept informed of the fast-moving developments of early July. Randolph's proposal calling for a reopening of negotiations, then, landed like a bombshell on men still waiting expectantly for ratification of the treaty. Pickering was especially distressed, for he feared that the British would reject further negotiations, that the treaty would prove abortive, and that the war in the West would be prolonged.[54] When Randolph came to his office to discuss the issue, there was an angry scene. More than thirty years later Pickering still recalled that moment. He rose from his seat and, clutching Randolph's memorial in one hand and flailing the air with his other fist, he exclaimed, "Why, this is throwing all up in the wind!"[55]

Pickering's recollection of that encounter may or may not be accurate. At the very least, however, he was remembering with great precision his feelings at the time. He was in fact on the verge of hysteria. Since he was never one to keep his emotions to himself, Pickering's extreme opposition to further delay soon became known all over Philadelphia.[56]

During July, much to the secretary of war's discomfiture, public meetings against the treaty erupted in towns up and down the seaboard. Boston was a focal point of protest. There the town meeting drafted twenty resolutions against the treaty and rushed them to Washington at Mount Vernon. Town after town followed suit. Soon Portsmouth, Trenton, New York, Philadelphia, Charleston, and Augusta all had sent the president resolutions opposing ratification.[57]

Shortly after Boston passed its antitreaty resolutions, Pickering received letters from his nephew Timothy Williams and from Stephen Higginson, an influential Boston merchant, insisting that the fifteen hundred people who crowded Faneuil Hall when the Boston resolutions were approved represented only an unimportant minority in the city. "Men of reputation," Higginson claimed, "would not attend the meeting, being opposed to the town's taking up the subject." The two merchants likened the popular fury over the treaty to a passing fever. In a few weeks, Higginson and Williams both predicted, passions would subside and those who endorsed the treaty "would be called patriots."[58] This amazing evaluation was in direct conflict with the assessment given not only by Republicans but by most Federalists as well.[59] Nevertheless, Pickering, now grasping at straws, quickly embraced it.[60]

A few days after news of Boston's meeting arrived in the capital, the secretary of war had the opportunity to witness a similar gathering firsthand when Philadelphia Republicans called their own mass meeting. Even by Pickering's conservative count, between twelve and fifteen hundred turned up. He came as a spectator, perhaps hoping for a chance to speak. If so, he was disappointed. The antitreaty forces were in no mood for a debate.

The meeting itself was a raucous affair, reminiscent in some ways of scenes in Massachusetts during the Stamp Act crisis. A series of resolutions was read to the crowd and voted on paragraph by paragraph. Each resolution was passed almost unanimously and without debate. Then Blair McClenachan, clutching a copy of the pact and waving it over his head, shouted, "What a damned treaty! I make a motion that every good citizen in this assembly kick this damned treaty to Hell!" The mob then marched by torchlight to the home of the British minister, where the treaty was burned.[61]

Fearing that public opposition to the treaty would influence Washington, Pickering forwarded to Mount Vernon a copy of Stephen Higginson's earlier letter describing the Boston meeting along with his own similarly distorted assessment of the Philadelphia gathering.[62] Washington's response was less than reassuring. He thanked Pickering for his attentiveness but admitted that he was more doubtful than ever about the treaty. If the opposition had failed to convince Washington not to ratify, they had nevertheless reinforced his indecision.[63]

At this point fate took a curious turn in favor of the treaty. Much earlier the Royal Navy had captured and turned over to the Foreign Office a packet of dispatches from Joseph Fauchet, the French minister in the United States. Lord Grenville forwarded several of these to George Hammond, the British envoy in Philadelphia, observing in a covering letter that "communicating" some of the information included in the documents "to well disposed persons in America" might "possibly be useful to the King's service."[64] Among these dispatches was one which seemed to indicate that Secretary of State Randolph, who pretended to be attached to neither party in the United States, was actually a democrat sympathetic to the French cause. The dispatch further demonstrated that he had been at least indiscreet in conferences with Fauchet and implied that on one occasion, during the Whiskey Rebellion in 1794, he had sought a bribe from the French envoy evidently for the purpose of encouraging civil war in America.[65]

Hammond, anxious for ratification, wondered what effect the disclosure of Randolph's earlier behavior would have on presidential decision-making. The secretary of state, after all, was the only cabinet officer opposed to immediate ratification of the treaty. Determined to find out, he first rendered an oral translation and then turned the incriminating dispatch over to Oliver Wolcott, Jr. Simultaneously he began to drop discreet hints in Pickering's direction that if the treaty was ratified his government might be inclined to speed up its evacuation of the northwestern posts. Pickering, still ignorant of developments at Greenville, was more than intrigued by that suggestion.[66]

Wolcott understood no French but, fearing a leak, was unwilling to trust a translator with the incriminating dispatch. He therefore turned it over to Pickering, who somehow produced a tortured translation. Next, he and Pickering paid a visit to Attorney General William Bradford at his country home outside Philadelphia. The three men agreed to keep the Fauchet dispatch a secret while prevailing on Randolph to call Washington back to the city. The secretary of state, as disturbed as anyone by the virulence of the Republican protest, agreed.[67] Pickering, however, not trusting Randolph to send the letter, decided to write to the president himself. In a letter marked "for your eye alone" he urged Washington to return as quickly as possible to the capital. "On the subject of the treaty I confess that I feel extreme solicitude, and for a *special reason* which can be communicated to you only in person." He urged the president "to decide on no important political measure in whatever form it may be presented to you." Then came what for Washington may have been the most puzzling part of this letter. Pickering explained that he, Wolcott, and Bradford had asked Randolph to write requesting him to come back to the capital. "He wrote in our presence," he explained, "but we concluded that a letter from one of us" would also be "expedient." Pickering signed this strange and enigmatic note "Yours and my country's friend."[68]

A day later Pickering sent a long and revealing letter to General Wayne, bringing him up to date on recent developments in the capital. He explained the mass meetings held to denounce the Jay Treaty as the work of Francophiles who sought to undermine American neutrality. With Fauchet's dispatch in his possession, however, he felt confident that the pact would be ratified. Though the president had so far declined signing, he wrote, he had no further doubt it would be done "and that in a few days."[69]

Washington returned to Philadelphia early on the evening of August 11. Many years later Pickering recalled that during the dinner hour a servant arrived at his home informing him that the chief executive wanted him to come at once. Rushing to the presidential mansion, he found Washington and Randolph together at table. The president suspected nothing, of course, but it was a trying moment for Pickering. He must have made it evident that he did not wish to speak in Randolph's presence, for the president managed to maneuver the secretary of war into the next room. When the president asked him the reason for his strange letter, he accused Randolph of treason.[70] Briefly summarizing the contents of the Fauchet dispatch, he left a copy and translation with the president. Stunned, the chief executive nevertheless decided for the moment to do nothing and say nothing to Randolph. He returned to dinner and Pickering went home.

Though inconclusive in itself, the dispatch was enough to cause Washington to rethink the recent past. Randolph had counseled delay and the reopening of negotiations with the English. The rest of the cabinet had urged ratification of the treaty. Was the delay perhaps intended by Randolph to force a war with England? Could he have been so completely deceived by his Virginia friend? There was another consideration as well. The British had a copy of the Fauchet dispatch. If he continued to delay ratification, it might end up in print along with a statement that he had seen and ignored it.[71] What the effect of that would be, no one could tell. After some consideration, Washington decided that the best thing would be to ratify the treaty excepting Article 12.[72]

Washington told Randolph nothing of his decision. Nor did he mention the Fauchet dispatch, preferring to get ratification out of the way first. On August 12, the cabinet met for further discussion of the treaty. The secretary of state came to propose formal agreement on his memorial to Great Britain. There was a furious debate. Washington remained silent throughout, but Pickering charged that attempts to delay ratification constituted a *"detestable and nefarious conspiracy."* [73] The argument continued only a short while. Then, to Randolph's utter astonishment, Washington announced the decision to ratify the treaty save for Article 12.

On August 19 the final act in this strange political drama was played. With the treaty ratified, Washington decided to confront Randolph with Fauchet's dispatch and called another cabinet meeting for that purpose. The secretary of state arrived late to find Washington, Pickering, and Wolcott already there. After a few strained pleasantries, Washington handed Randolph the Fauchet dispatch and asked for an explanation. Randolph read it through. It must have taken some time, for it was a long dispatch. The secretary of state, who knew that he was innocent, saw clearly what had happened. He attempted to explain, going through the letter a paragraph at a time with Washington, Pickering, and Wolcott sitting before him in judgment. But as he proceeded his sense of humiliation and anger grew uncontrollably. At length he suggested that he put his explanation in writing and asked to retain the letter for that purpose. Washington agreed, at which point the cabinet meeting was delayed for a few minutes while the president met with an unexpected visitor. When Washington returned to the meeting, he asked Randolph to step out of the room while he consulted with Wolcott and Pickering. While Randolph agonized in an adjoining room, Washington, Wolcott, and Pickering debated his guilt or innocence, but could come to no conclusion. The secretary of state was then called back. Washington asked his old friend if he still wished to write out his explanation. Randolph said yes, though he wondered whether he could convince anyone he had not been involved in the Whiskey Rebellion without Fauchet's dispatches numbers 3 and 6, which explained critical references in number 10. When Washington made no reply to this, asking only when he could have his explanation completed, Randolph retorted, "as soon as possible." Then on an impulse he announced that he could no longer serve as Washington's secretary of state. His resignation was on the president's desk at noon the following day. [74]

There is no reason to question what other historians have already so persuasively documented, that Pickering used the translated dispatch in a deliberate attempt to ruin Randolph's political career and smear his reputation. His object was to induce an aging and increasingly indecisive president to ratify the Jay Treaty by convincing him that in refusing to do so he was relying on a traitor's advice. A strong body of circumstantial evidence even suggests that to accomplish this he withheld documents from the president that would have exonerated Randolph.[75]

If there is no doubt as to what he did and why, it is nevertheless worthwhile to speculate on the process by which Pickering brought himself to such a ruthless act. Throughout a long public career he had never been charitable toward those who stood in his way. His instinct when thwarted was to strike for the jugular with whatever weapon came to hand. In this instance the impulse to crush Randolph must have been very great, for Pickering viewed ratification of the Jay Treaty as essential to the national interest, the capstone to an Indian policy that he had helped develop over five long years.

Still, the question remains, how could a person who prided himself on his honesty and virtue stoop so? At least a portion of the answer may be uncovered by probing some of the complexities of Pickering's personality. Hardly had he identified Randolph as an opponent before thought processes came into play that elevated the secretary of state to the stature of a diabolical enemy, the head of a nationwide conspiracy committed to blocking ratification of the treaty. Once Pickering had convinced himself of this, he found it not at all difficult to use unethical means to ruin the evil genius of the opposition.

It is both fascinating and appalling to retrace the steps by which Pickering managed to arrive at this incredible conclusion. First was the fact that, alone among the members of the cabinet, Randolph opposed the immediate ratification of the treaty. Second, there was Fauchet's dispatch. In all likelihood Pickering knew that the charge of treason against Randolph was spurious. Nevertheless it was clear from what Fauchet had written that Randolph had at least been indiscreet in his relationship with the French envoy. Pickering, who culled every available source for material damaging to the secretary of state, and was when he chose a master at reading between the lines, thought him guilty of much more than indiscretion. Finally, when pressed to extremities, he actually manufactured evidence. He "recalled" that after the first antitreaty meeting had been held in Boston, Randolph remarked that other meetings would probably soon follow and that they would proceed in a southerly direction. On reflection Pickering read sinister meaning into what he alleged Randolph had said, charging that the "meetings as Mr. Randolph *predicted,* followed one another from North to South and soon we saw the proceedings at Charleston."[76] These mass meetings, he insisted, happened too rapidly and in too neat a pattern not to have been previously arranged. Randolph's "prediction" of these developments seemed to him proof that he had helped plan them. The secretary of state, he charged, "intended that the people should rise in numerous meetings close at the heels of one another beginning in Boston, where our revolution began, and by their apparent numbers, their extension from one extremity of the states to the other, and the zeal and vehemence of their opposition, overwhelm the President and prevent his ratification."[77]

Assuming for a moment that Randolph did suppose aloud that anti-treaty meetings were likely to progress in a southerly direction, what of it? This was a logical assumption based on the uncomplicated judgment that news of Boston's meeting would stimulate Republicans in cities close to Boston before it arrived in the more distant regions of the South. More to the point, however, though Pickering insisted that the geographical development "predicted" by Randolph actually took place, in fact it did not. Portsmouth, New Hampshire, to the north of Boston, acted two days after Boston, while Charleston's Republicans met on July 17, one day before a similar meeting in New York and six days before Philadelphia acted. Certainly Pickering must have known this. Or is it possible with such an ardent and determined man that, when the need to believe conflicts with fact, truth is simply lost from sight?[78]

TWELVE

Secretary of State

FOLLOWING EDMUND RANDOLPH'S resignation, the president stunned Pickering and a great many other political observers as well by appointing him ad interim secretary of state. Washington had no intention of keeping the volatile New Englander in that position, however, and immediately began to search for a more qualified replacement. In October, after five candidates had turned him down in rapid succession, he asked Alexander Hamilton to contact Rufus King about taking over the State Department. But it came as no surprise when, like the others, King proved uninterested. In fact, Hamilton explained, no "first rate" man was available. It was "a sad omen for the government." [1]

With literally no one else to turn to, the weary Washington approached Pickering only to be rejected for a seventh time. The State Department was a more prestigious post than the War Office, and though he denied it there can be little doubt that the New Englander coveted the promotion. But it had been mortifying to serve as the acting secretary while Washington searched frantically for someone, almost anyone, to accept the post on a regular appointment. For many weeks Pickering had taken psychological refuge by openly agreeing with critics who charged that he hadn't the background for the office and was, moreover, too emotional to serve in a diplomatic capacity. [2]

Though Pickering declined at first to accept the appointment to the State Department, he was careful not to phrase his rejection in terms of any unwillingness to serve, insisting simply that the president ought to seek a more qualified candidate. Washington, having already exhausted a long list of people whom he judged more competent, persevered, suggesting to Secretary of the Treasury Oliver Wolcott that he coax the reluctant Pickering into changing his mind. Pickering, however, persistently maintained that he was not suited to be a diplomat. This curious ballet lasted for some days before coming to its inevitable conclusion when, having been repeatedly importuned to accept the State Department, Pickering at last surrendered, his dignity intact.[3]

Pickering's appointment marked the beginning of a major cabinet reorganization. A few months later the Maryland Federalist James McHenry took over at the War Department and a Virginian, Charles Lee, became the new attorney general. To some, the changes were a depressing symbol. In the brave days of 1789 Washington had brought the best minds in the country together in one administration. Only six years later, he presided over a cabinet of mediocrities. "Happy is the country to be rid of Randolph," Vice President John Adams remarked to his wife, "but where shall be found good men and true to fill the offices of government?"[4]

Once he was established in the State Department, Pickering's confidence and self-esteem blossomed. How could it have been otherwise? He was the president's principal advisor, regularly consulted on matters ranging from the appointment of a new director for the mint to the choice of new cabinet officers. Powerful people became his intimates. His correspondence suddenly included the names of such luminaries as Fisher Ames, George Cabot, and John Lowell. William Bingham, the influential Pennsylvania senator, invited him to an occasional dinner at his mansion in Philadelphia and provided a substantial unsecured loan when Pickering needed it.[5] He began a confidential correspondence with Alexander Hamilton, exchanging views with the former treasury secretary on such sensitive questions as appointment policy and the future of the Federalists after Washington's retirement. Once, truthfully or not, Pickering had insisted that he did not think himself competent to fill the demanding office of secretary of state. In December 1795, however, he assured Stephen Higginson that there was nothing to worry about; the nation's foreign policy was secure in his hands.[6]

Unhappily, Pickering overestimated his capacity for handling the State Department job. In a period of extraordinary international instability he hadn't the emotional balance, intellectual breadth, or finesse required to be a successful diplomat. In the first place Pickering was extremely self-righteous, with a penchant for disputatiousness and a tendency to elevate the controversies in which he frequently became embroiled to a high moral plane. Second, his extreme moral self-image both robbed him of the capacity to understand those who disagreed with him and made the resolution of differences through compromise virtually impossible. Finally, though he had some of the instincts of a brawler and political gutter fighter, he hadn't the capacity to shrug off criticism. He was therefore inevitably drawn to seek personal vindication through the newspapers when his behavior was called into question. These emotional and intellectual deficiencies would seriously impair Pickering's performance in the State Department, for to practice diplomacy in the newspapers is demeaning, while to reject the principle of compromise is self-defeating.

Pickering's early months as secretary of state were characterized by an extreme anxiety to witness the final implementation of the Jay Treaty, for the long-coveted northwestern posts were still securely in British hands and would undoubtedly remain so until the controversial accord was actually put into effect. Ratification should have settled the issue, but the Republicans made it clear that they intended to claim for the House of Representatives the right to decide on the treaty's constitutionality. Thomas Jefferson assured James Monroe, then the American minister in Paris, that the treaty would never go into effect. "It must be believed," Jefferson wrote, "that the House of Representatives will oppose it as constitutionally void." And John Beckley, the clerk of the House as well as an important Republican Party manager, explained in another letter to Monroe that only "cabinet intrigue" had brought the treaty to its current "dangerous state." He had little doubt, however, that it would remain forever an "unexecuted document."[7]

News that House Republicans planned to block implementation of the treaty reached across the Atlantic, where both the French and the English understood that an important political test was soon to take place. On December 1, 1795, the British undersecretary of state remarked to young John Quincy Adams that the upcoming session of Congress would be an important one. If the House did "not pass such laws as will be necessary to give effect to the treaty," he explained, *"we shall all be at sea again."* He had heard, he continued, "that the Antifederalists threaten very high."[8]

Secretary of State Pickering believed that the issue might turn on the state of Anglo-American relations at the time the treaty came before the House. His diplomacy, therefore, was aimed at convincing the Foreign Office to act with restraint. He approached this task with some optimism, for early indications were that Foreign Secretary Grenville, too, recognized the problem. George Hammond's departure from Philadelphia in August 1795 was certainly a good omen. Disliked by Federalists and Republicans alike, Hammond had long since come to view Pickering as a hopelessly irrational Anglophobe.[9] Pickering thought no better of Hammond, who was closely identified in his mind with John Graves Simcoe and Britain's antagonistic policy in the Northwest. It would have been difficult for the two men to have developed a decent working relationship. Fortunately, they did not have to try. Grenville's choice of Sir Robert Liston to succeed Hammond was another promising sign. Until recently the British ambassador at Constantinople, Liston was a congenial, middle-aged Scotsman whose obvious personal commitment to a policy of conciliation with the United States encouraged Pickering enormously.

Good auguries notwithstanding, during the summer of 1795 relations between England and America were beset by a number of troublesome issues. In July and August Captain Rodham Home, commanding H.M.S. Africa on station off Rhode Island, openly violated America's neutrality as well as her national sensibilities in a variety of ways. By the time Pickering ordered him to leave American waters, Home counted among his various extravagances the illegal search of the American coasting sloop Peggy, the attempted kidnaping of the former French minister to the United States, Joseph Fauchet, an outrageous letter to Governor Arthur Fenner of Rhode Island threatening the bombardment of Newport, and the impressment of three American seamen from the ship Anne, searched while in American territorial waters.[10]

British privateers continued to prey upon American shipping as well, and in spite of the Jay Treaty American trading vessels in the Caribbean regularly fell victim to these Bermuda-based marauders. Worse, judicial condemnation of ships and cargoes was virtually assured, for the vice-admiralty court in Bermuda was notoriously oppressive.[11] Finally, there was the growing problem of impressment.[12] Though not so serious as it was to become a decade later, this issue was nevertheless irksome to Pickering, who quailed at newspaper reports of each new incident.[13]

Despite continuing indications that all was not well with Anglo-American relations, Pickering explained irritants away, concluding that London was not exerting itself sufficiently to curb the excesses of overzealous subordinates. He thought it made little difference, however, whether these irritations were planned in London or simply the result of individual acts of insubordination. The result, the same in either event, was to infuriate the American public and strengthen the hand of the enemies of the Jay Treaty in the House of Representatives.[14]

Attacked repeatedly in the opposition press for endorsing the treaty while doing nothing about other evidences of "British Amity" such as impressment, the rapacious Bermuda privateersmen, and the incredible Captain Home, Pickering longed to vindicate himself and the administration publicly. But it was one of the frustrations of holding cabinet rank, he learned, that he would have to remain above the rancorous public debate. Denied his usual outlet for stress, Pickering set energetically about the task of awakening the British Foreign Office to the need for an immediate reduction in tensions. He instructed the American Ministry in London to make representations regarding the vexatious actions of British naval officers, as well as the activities of the Bermuda privateers. In addition he sought to convince the Foreign Office to cede the coveted northwestern posts with no further delay. Such a sign of Britain's friendly intentions, he disingenuously observed, would certainly help overcome the treaty's last obstacle in the House.[15]

The American minister at the Court of St. James's, Thomas Pinckney, was in Spain concluding the treaty that bears his name when Pickering's instructions arrived. In his absence the United States was represented by young William Allen Deas, the chargé, and John Quincy Adams, who had come to London to exchange ratifications of the treaty of 1794 and to discuss a series of related matters with the Foreign Office.

The results of independent efforts by both Deas and Adams to carry out Pickering's instructions were disappointing. The chargé received no reply whatever to his note objecting to recent impressments as well as the continuing depredations of the Bermudans. Grenville chose to ignore the young American, whom he disliked personally. He sent a dispatch to Phineas Bond characterizing Deas's "accusations" (which were in reality Pickering's) as "indefinite and so entirely unsubstantiated by any sort of proof" that they could not be taken seriously.[16]

John Q. Adams had no better luck. The foreign secretary told the young envoy that he could take no action against Captain Home of the *Africa* without first seeing a report from him. This, of course, would take many months, since Home would have to be contacted at sea. Nor did Grenville make any satisfactory response to Adams's complaint about impressment. Most distressingly, when Adams brought up the question of ceding the northwestern posts, Grenville became vague, remarking only that *"he believed"* orders for their return *"had been sent out."* This response was in discouraging contrast to earlier, more positive statements from the Foreign Office.[17]

Depressed by British unresponsiveness, Pickering tried a variety of approaches in the attempt to awaken London to the dangers inherent in the situation. He sent frequent letters to Phineas Bond and even appealed directly to Governor James Crawford of Bermuda for a crackdown on the privateersmen. "The advocates of peace and good will" in the United States, he explained, had been "silenced by the daily repetition of outrages in the impressments of our seamen, the vexatious captures and many illegal condemnations of our vessels and their cargoes." Peace itself had been placed "at hazard from the keen resentments and indignant feelings of the citizens of the United States."[18]

Pickering's best efforts notwithstanding, Congress convened in December 1795 with Anglo-American relations still in a sad state of disarray. It was generally assumed that the major business of that congressional session would be the House debate on the Jay Treaty. But it could not begin until the agreement had officially been declared in force, and Washington was unwilling to do that until he had proof of British ratification. Weeks passed, but no ratified copy of the accord arrived from London.[19] Pickering, who did not view a short delay before the beginning of the debate as of any consequence, became concerned. The British were scheduled to withdraw from the northwest posts on June 30. However, it was certain they would make no such move until the agreement had passed its last obstacle in the House. Yet if the British did not withdraw on time there would be a public outcry in the United States, that much more reason for Republicans in the House to block implementation. The inexplicable failure of a ratified copy of the treaty to appear, Pickering grumbled, had "occasioned much chagrin as well as serious embarrassments."[20]

Late in February, with time slipping away, it was at last reported in Philadelphia that an authentic copy of the ratified treaty had somehow found its way to Charleston. Convinced that it would be dangerous to wait any longer, Washington at last declared the treaty to be in effect.[21] House Republicans moved immediately to the attack, winning the first round in their struggle with the executive when a resolution calling upon the president to turn over all documents and correspondence relevant to the negotiation of the Jay Treaty passed by a vote of 62 to 37.[32]

Pickering's long-standing fear that the Republicans would attempt to exploit evidence of British unfriendliness as part of their overall anti-treaty strategy materialized just twelve days after the introduction of this controversial resolution. On March 14, in an obvious attempt to draw national attention to the highly emotional issue of impressment, Congressman Edward Livingston of New York introduced a bill designed to protect American seamen from British press gangs through the issuance of official certificates of United States citizenship.[23] This strategem placed congressional Federalists in a quandary. They were reluctant to support the bill, for it was clear that the British would never accept the legitimacy of such certificates. However, to oppose the proposal would strengthen the Republicans' hand in their assault upon the treaty by seeming to confirm the charge that Federalists were pro-British.

The introduction of Livingston's bill and the virulent press criticism of the administration for its failure to do anything about impressment aroused Pickering who, after all, had a sound record on the issue. He longed for the opportunity to publish a rebuttal to charges leveled against him by his Republican detractors. That being out of the question, however, he stepped up his pressure on the British, once again warning Phineas Bond of "the indignant feelings" of the American people over impressment.[24] When Bond objected that he could do nothing on the basis of unsubstantiated newspaper reports, Pickering instructed the collectors of customs at all ports up and down the seaboard to procure sworn affidavits from witnesses to acts of impressment and forward these to his office. He in turn would forward the statements, together with the necessary proofs that the men taken were American citizens, to Bond. It would then be up to the British to prove that they were prepared to act in fairness by freeing American seamen who had been unjustly taken.[25] It was all very frustrating. Pickering felt unable to make the political dimensions of the situation clear to London.

As though things were not bad enough, new difficulties with Britain surfaced in the very midst of the House debate on the treaty. Grenville decided, regardless of the June 30 deadline, that he would not remove British forces from the northwestern posts until the accord had been implemented. He now found justification for such a delay in the seeming contradiction between Article 3 of the Jay Treaty, which guaranteed British fur traders the right to continue their operations in the Northwest, and Article 8 of the Treaty of Greenville, which stipulated that all Indian traders were to be licensed by the American government. Bond was instructed to inform the State Department that until a special explanatory article guaranteeing British fur-trading rights was appended to the treaty, the posts would not be surrendered.[26]

Pickering, alarmed at the thought that these latest British demands might become public while the treaty was still before the House of Representatives, refused even to discuss the issue with Bond. Alexander Hamilton, quickly informed of this latest development by Oliver Wolcott, was equally distressed. "The British ministry are as great fools or as great rascals as our Jacobins," he wrote, "else our commerce would not continue to be distressed as it is by their cruisers; Nor would the Executive be embarrassed as it now is by the new propositions."[27]

Difficulties with Britain notwithstanding, Pickering advised Washington not to comply with demands made by the House majority for documents relating to the negotiation of the Jay Treaty.[28] His views were endorsed not only by McHenry and Wolcott, but also by Alexander Hamilton who, writing from his New York law office, urged

the president to stand firm. Hamilton, in fact, forwarded a long, carefully reasoned statement on the question, hoping that Washington
would adopt it in rejecting House demands.[29] Though Hamilton's was
an elegant, carefully conceived state paper, the president surprised
many by choosing instead to confront the Republicans in the lower
house with the short, blunt, and undiplomatic pronouncement drafted
earlier by Pickering.[30]

Republicans were amazed at what some took to be Washington's
declaration of war against the House majority, many incorrectly assuming that the message was Hamilton's work. "The absolute refusal was as
unexpected as the tone and tenor of the message was unproper and
indelicate," wrote James Madison. The Virginia congressman had "no
doubt . . . that the message came from New York."[31] Benjamin F.
Bache, too, thought that Hamilton had drafted the president's statement and took Washington to task publicly for valuing the advice of a
former secretary of the treasury more than the collective wisdom of the
people.[32]

Whatever pleasure Pickering may have experienced on having his
handiwork mistaken for Hamilton's was mitigated by his fear that
House Republicans, who seemed to command a twenty-vote majority,
would kill the treaty by the simple expedient of refusing to vote the
funds required for its implementation.[33] Congressman Theodore
Sedgwick, his confidant in the House, was equally pessimistic, especially
because during the entire debate the press teemed with repeated reports of what even he characterized as "shameful" acts of British impressment.[34]

Later in April, however, Pickering sensed that chances for the implementation of the treaty had markedly improved. The proximate
cause was an economic panic that suddenly gripped the nation's seaports. In anticipation of a war with England, marine insurance companies had stopped protecting shippers against capture.[35] The overall
number of sailings dropped sharply as an "actual" though undeclared
"embargo" took hold. Commodity prices tumbled while powerful merchants who had large stocks of flour and other staples seemed suddenly
to be threatened with bankruptcy.[36]

Under the pressure of such economic constraints, attitudes toward
the treaty began to change. Supporters of the agreement, employing
tactics earlier used by the opposition, organized some popular demon-
strations of their own. Even Boston, the scene of the earliest antitreaty
meeting, now did an abrupt about-face. A mass meeting held there
endorsed the treaty and opposed House obstructionism by a vote of
2,400 to 100.[37]

The Boston meeting was particularly good news to Pickering, who at last concluded that the combined pressure of public opinion and growing economic distress would break the Republican majority in the House. And so it did. On April 30, following a last emotional appeal for implementation of the treaty by Congressman Fisher Ames, the House appropriated the $80,808 required to put the treaty into effect.[38]

Pickering was delighted. Not only had the treaty been saved and the northwestern posts finally secured, but a basic constitutional issue had been settled. The outcome, he felt certain, would "strengthen the legitimate powers of the executive branch of government, and increase the confidence of foreign nations in future negotiations."[39]

During the long, drawn-out struggle over the implementation of the Jay Treaty, Pickering had been sorely tested by the virulence of the Republican attack on administration foreign policy. He longed to participate in the rough and tumble of what was certainly the most extravagant newspaper war that he had ever witnessed. The constraints placed upon him by his position, of course, forbade that. Nevertheless, though the national interest required it, Pickering was incapable of keeping his emotions completely under control. It was one of the ironies of his career that although he consistently sought power, he really had no idea of how to exercise it, recognizing few limits and seldom acting with restraint.

Frustrated at his inability to respond to Republican criticism, Pickering found in Pierre Adet, the increasingly militant French minister to the United States, an outlet for his anger and stress. In spite of the fact that Washington's policy was one of conciliation toward France, Pickering interacted with the French envoy as though he were once again a Salem selectman involved in a petty squabble with some local nabob. To be sure, Adet's strong objections to the Jay Treaty, his frequent criticisms of other aspects of American foreign policy, and the obvious connections sometimes to be found between Adet's correspondence with the State Department and Republican strategy in the press and Congress provoked the secretary. But it is difficult to avoid the conclusion that Pickering's abusive handling of Adet owed something to pure emotion as well. It is almost as though in some curious way he thought it possible to persecute and discredit the French minister as he had John Franklin and later Edmund Randolph.

This is not to suggest that Adet was totally blameless for the swift deterioration of his relationship with Pickering. On the contrary, it is clear that after Washington ratified the Jay Treaty the French considered further negotiations with Philadelphia futile and pinned their hopes for a restoration of friendly relations on a Republican victory in the elections coming in 1796.[40] Moreover, it is equally certain that Adet sometimes deliberately manipulated Pickering with the intention of weakening Federalism's political strength in the United States.

The central question, however, is not whether or not Adet was provocative, but how Pickering handled this difficult problem and the broader issue of relations with France. The astonishing answer is that he frequently showed not the slightest concern for either the diplomatic repercussions or the domestic political implications of his French diplomacy. Thus he was indefatigable in his persistent efforts to deny the French even the slightest advantage not guaranteed under the agreements of 1778. In this vein he acted swiftly to instigate litigation against French privateers suspected of violating American neutrality.[41] He defended the right of citizens of the United States to trade in contraband, offering no apologies for the fact that American businessmen were helping British purchasing agents prepare an army for the invasion of France's West Indian holdings. And in like manner he pursued a months-long crusade for the removal of the Republican James Monroe from the ministry in Paris without once considering what the Virginian's recall might mean for either the future of Franco-American relations or the upcoming presidential elections.[42] Incredibly, without informing Washington of his actions, Pickering sometimes went to the extreme of ignoring official diplomatic correspondence from Adet. Thus at least one harshly worded protest from the French envoy charging that the Jay Treaty conflicted with certain of America's commitments under the Franco-American accords of 1778 and two subsequent notes demanding to know what the State Department was doing about the growing problem of impressment went unanswered.[43]

Pickering's determination to fulfill obligations to England created by the Jay Treaty added to the growing discord. The Franco-American Treaty of Commerce of 1778 authorized French privateers and ships of war to bring their prizes into American ports. Moreover, although nothing was stipulated in the treaty, the administration had allowed prize sales to take place since the beginning of the war. In 1796, however, a problem arose because Article 24 of the Jay Treaty specifically prohibited such sales. The issue became serious late in June when a French privateer accompanied by two British prizes dropped anchor in Boston harbor. As soon as the Philadelphia papers announced the impending sale of these ships, Robert Liston entered a protest at the State Department.[44] Pickering responded quickly, seeking a court injunction to prohibit the sale. When this did not materialize in time he issued a direct order blocking it.[45]

No sooner had Pickering acted than Adet and the Republican press, operating in close collaboration, were up in arms. The French minister insisted that Pickering was violating France's treaty rights. Insinuating State Department prejudice, he demanded to know whether the president had given the order to thwart these sales or if it had come from Pickering.[46] But it was the press that most harshly pilloried the secretary. "Anticipation," a pseudonymous author writing in the *Boston Independent Chronicle*, was outraged. Throughout the entire debate on the Jay Treaty, he fumed, the administration had repeatedly insisted that nothing in the agreement in any way violated earlier commitments to France. However, no sooner had the pact cleared its last obstacle in the House of Representatives than the truth became clear. *"The People have been deceived,"* he exclaimed. Otherwise, why had the secretary of state changed long-established policy?[47]

Although such attacks were no less infuriating, by this time Pickering more or less expected them, at least from the opposition. In this instance, however, the Republicans were joined by a number of Federalists, especially merchants who saw a profitable trade in captured British ships and cargoes going down the drain. Young John Pickering, then in his last year at Harvard, informed his father that many were displeased, while some openly questioned his ability to handle the State Department job.[48]

Now Pickering was thoroughly annoyed. "If angels were to administer the principal offices of government," he wrote, "they would not escape reproaches from the present unprincipled slanderers of public men and their measures." But it was the Federalist criticism of Pickering's abilities as a diplomat that cut deepest. He had not sought the office, he complained, and had taken it only out of necessity. Pickering seems to have been hurt all the more because of the man he had replaced. Edmund Randolph was a traitor whose "inaccurate language, turgid sentences and weak observations," he wrote, "rendered him the derision of correct scholars and even of men of plain common sense." If he "could not restore the reputation of the department by his *abilities*," Pickering exclaimed, he would "at least not injure that or my country by *treachery*"[49]

As the attacks against him mounted, Pickering came emotionally unstrung. His psychological make-up was a combination of weaknesses. He was a righteous, strident, and intolerant activist, ambitious to be at the center of affairs. Yet he used power unwisely and took criticism so badly that even his friends feared to offer any. Under the brutal pounding he was forced to endure at the hands of Adet, the Republican press, and even some Federalist critics, he lost all sense of proportion. During the summer and fall of that critical election year, he was in effect a political disaster waiting to occur and was easily manipulated by Adet who, acting on instructions from his government, interceded on behalf of the Republicans during the last stages of the presidential contest.[50]

It was evident that the election of 1796, fast approaching, would be decided by only a few electoral votes one way or the other. In the first real contest for the presidency, Thomas Jefferson, supported by a well-organized political party, was given an excellent chance to defeat John Adams. The race was too close to predict, but it was generally agreed that Pennsylvania's fifteen electoral votes would be decisive. There, as in many other areas, the Federalists were divided and politically ineffective. Pennsylvania's Republicans, however, ably led by John Beckley, proved a model of early party unity and purpose, outmaneuvering the Federalists at every turn.[51]

In the last weeks before the election, an important collaboration developed between Beckley and Pierre Adet. Unlike many other Republican leaders, who thought the idea too risky, Beckley believed that as a last fillip to the campaign, a public statement from Adet denouncing Federalist foreign policy as nonneutral could help Republican chances. There is no hard evidence to prove that Beckley and Adet actually coordinated their activities. However, the French minister did attempt to influence the outcome of the election in Pennsylvania and did so in a way that correlated closely with Beckley's hopes.[52]

A week before Pennsylvania's voters were scheduled to go to the polls, a letter from Adet to Pickering appeared in Bache's *Philadelphia Aurora*. In it the French minister denounced the administration's failure to defend its neutral rights against England, detailed the effect this had upon France, and for the first time publicly announced a French maritime decree under which American ships were already being taken by French privateers. Adet was especially critical of Pickering for having ignored several official diplomatic protests. On three occasions, he charged, he had objected to the failure of the American government to defend its neutral rights but had received no replies. France, Adet insisted, did not want to adopt this new and harsh policy. It had been forced to do so by a government that had allowed the British "to sport" with its neutrality "and turn it to their advantage." Surely, then, no one could complain if France moved to "restore the balance of neutrality to its equilibrium."[53]

President Washington, for one, was shocked on reading Adet's letter. Had Pickering actually ignored French protests? He interrogated the secretary of state only to discover to his chagrin that the envoy was telling the truth. Pickering squirmed as he attempted to explain Adet's charges away, claiming that they were only technically correct since, although he had refused to answer some protests that were characterized by "indecent charges" and "offensive expressions," he had replied to similar French objections on other occasions.[54]

The unhappy fact that Adet's charges were accurate was only a single element in the broader problem confronting the aging president. He had no idea of just how to respond to Adet's last-minute political maneuver. It was totally uncharacteristic of him to risk the dignity of his administration by engaging in a newspaper dispute with a foreign emissary. But Pickering viewed Adet's letter as a superb opportunity to vindicate himself of criticism coming not only from the French envoy but from the opposition press as well. He warned that Adet's note was having a significant political effect and that it ought to be answered before election day in Pennsylvania. Unable to decide what to do, Washington sought Alexander Hamilton's advice.[55] But with the elections only three days off and still no word from Hamilton, Washington authorized Pickering to publish a reply to Adet. Because time was short he did not read the secretary's letter before it appeared in print. These proved to be two costly mistakes, for Pickering's letter, which appeared on November 3, was from beginning to end a political disaster.[56]

In his original public letter to Pickering, Adet had made two major allegations. He charged first that, although the principle of freedom of the seas had been incorporated into the agreements between France and the United States in 1778, the Washington administration had failed to defend this precept against the British. Instead, it had allowed England to trample on its rights. The effect was to place France at a serious disadvantage in the competition for American trade. Second, he contended that the State Department had shown hostility toward France by refusing to respond to legitimate requests for information relating to the American government's efforts to put a stop to British impressment.[57]

Incredibly, Pickering's indignant response confirmed Adet's charges. In spite of the fact that a liberal interpretation of the rights of neutrals had roots in the American diplomatic tradition dating back to the foundations of the republic and the Model Treaty of 1776, the secretary of state actually denied that the principle of freedom of the seas had any standing in international law. The treaties between France and the United States which incorporated liberal maritime principles had, he insisted, only bilateral significance. Moreover, the United States had never made any commitment to defend the idea of a free sea against Great Britain or any other third party. Pickering went even further in this politically foolhardy direction when he remarked in summing up that "captures made by the British of American vessels are warranted by the law of nations."[58]

The Republican press had a field day with that remark. One writer in the *Boston Independent Chronicle* suggested that Pickering appeared "rather a defender of the conduct of the British than a vindicator of the privileges of the United States."[59] Another Republican author made unfavorable comparisons between Washington's well-known commitment to the principle of freedom of the seas and what Pickering meant by "the law of nations." With Washington almost gone from the scene, he charged, "Mr. Pickering now arrogantly comes forward and as peremptorily declares that the British are warranted by the law of nations to take American vessels having French property on board." It seemed clear, the author continued, that current difficulties with France had been the creation of Pickering and others "in the various public departments who have acted in direct contradiction to the President." What sense did it make, then, to keep the Federalists in power? It would be wiser, he wrote, to elect the Republicans who, like Washington, stood for a free sea.[60]

Pickering blundered as well in responding to the charge that he had ignored several notes from the French legation inquiring into the American government's policy on impressment. He might have finessed the issue by detailing his very strong record in this area. Instead, his emotions in full ascendancy, he told Adet that it was none of France's business what the United States chose to do. He also charged that Adet's notes had been "insulting," that they were filled with "unjustified insinuations," and that "for the sake of preserving harmony" he had judged it best not to reply. Even the most obtuse reader might have wondered on what ground Pickering had decided that an ally was not entitled to information so obviously relevant to her national security. Moreover, it was clear from the tone of Pickering's letter that if at one time he had been concerned with continued Franco-American "harmony," that moment was long gone.[61]

It is difficult, of course, to judge with any accuracy the effect of this exchange between Pickering and Adet on the political outcome in Pennsylvania. It is not unreasonable to suggest, however, that it helped the Republicans, who won fourteen of the state's fifteen electoral votes and came within two votes of defeating John Adams in the presidential contest. Adams himself, attempting to minimize the blow, suggested that Adet had influenced only a few Quakers who were terrified at the thought of war. Yet even if he was correct, the Pickering-Adet dispute could still explain the razor-thin victory that gave the Jeffersonians all but one of the state's electoral votes. Other Federalist leaders were more frank about the impact of the Adet-Pickering exchange. Senator Benjamin Goodhue thought Adet largely responsible for the Jeffersonian victory. William Bingham more or less agreed, remarking that "Mr. Adet's strokes of diplomatic finesse" had played an important role in the Federalist defeat.[62]

Amidst the storm of controversy touched off by Pickering's ill-considered reply to Adet, one pseudonymous author, publishing in the *Aurora*, alleged that Alexander Hamilton, "whom quiet people supposed departed from the political world," was behind it.[63] Actually, Hamilton was appalled on reading what Pickering had published. Not only was it a political mistake, but it further exacerbated tensions in Franco-American relations. Hamilton took special exception to Pickering's refusal to reply to Adet's queries on impressment. But it was the whole tone of the secretary's reply that most disturbed Hamilton, for his "manner" was "too epigrammatical and *sharp*." The New Yorker warned Washington that "nations, like individuals, sometimes get into squabbles" needlessly as a result of such harshly phrased communications. Pickering would have to be more carefully controlled in the future. "I make this remark freely," he wrote, "because the card now to be played is perhaps the most delicate that has occurred in our administration." The critical point was "to avoid a rupture with France." If, however, a break did come, it was imperative that the people should believe that the government had tried in every way possible to avoid it.[64]

Hamilton's advice was particularly well timed, for Adet had not yet finished his work. On November 15 he published a second letter, this time addressed to the "People of the United States." It was a long and passionate piece in which Adet again catalogued the sins of the Federalists, with special reference to the Jay Treaty. Announcing the suspension of his mission in America, he simultaneously reaffirmed France's friendship for the American people and made it clear that whenever the government was prepared to return to a truly neutral course, relations could be restored.[65]

On reading Adet's latest letter in the New York newspapers, Hamilton quickly contacted both Washington and Wolcott, charting the course he believed the administration ought to follow. Since Adet had suspended his mission, there could be no reply to him. Hamilton therefore recommended "a full reply" to be addressed to General Charles C. Pinckney, the recently appointed American minister accredited to

Paris. A copy of this letter should be sent to the House of Representatives, which would publish it. Above all, Hamilton cautioned against repeating the errors of Pickering's note of November 3. In tone it should be "an inoffensive remonstrance—the expression of a dignified seriousness—reluctant to quarrel, but resolved not to be humbled." [66]

Washington did not have to be cautioned. He set Pickering the task of reviewing in detail the history of Franco-American relations from the beginning of the war. This tedious job took weeks, during which the president acted the careful editor. In his search for a document that would be "full, fair, calm" and yet not too "argumentative," he returned draft after draft to the State Department for revision. [67] When at last the work had been completed, the president took one last precaution, sending a copy of the finished document to Hamilton for comment. With the former treasury secretary's blessings, Pickering's letter to General Pinckney was sent to the House of Representatives and published. [68]

This long and reasonably dispassionate narrative of the recent history of Franco-American relations, so uncharacteristic of Pickering, appeared toward the end of January 1797 and won the applause of most Federalists, who saw it as definitive and unanswerable. [69] But it also brought down upon him the full fury of the Republican press. During the last several weeks of Washington's term Pickering, who took an incredible pummeling, was repeatedly identified as the central figure in a Federalist conspiracy to provoke war with France. His letter to Pinckney, it was alleged, was in fact designed to "rouse the people of the United States to a declaration of war." [70] One writer, publishing pseudonymously in the *Philadelphia Aurora,* had a more personal warning for the secretary of state: "Timothy Beware!" he wrote. "Among all the appointments of the President which have invariably proceeded from party considerations, no one has disgusted the public more than your own." [71]

For those who wish to understand when and why Timothy Pickering became the Francophobic arch-Federalist of tradition, the answer is to be found here, woven into the long, arduous struggle over the Jay Treaty. Like many another Federalist, Pickering believed that the survival of the republic depended upon the preservation of stability and order. This in turn assumed a continued harmony among the various classes that constituted society. [72] His ordeal in the State Department, especially the vilification he was forced to endure at the hands of Adet and the Republicans during the debate over the treaty, not only outraged him personally, but convinced him that the French Revolution, more particularly the faction it had bred in the United States, threatened these sacred principles. There was no subtlety to Pickering; there never had been. Throughout his lifetime he had repeatedly shown a facility for moving swiftly from one extreme to its opposite with little concern for consistency. And so it was that the intense Anglophobe of the years before 1795 became, in the words of the delighted British Minister Robert Liston, "one of the most violent anti-Gallicans I have met with." [73]

THIRTEEN

Pickering and Adams

IF TIMOTHY PICKERING did not breathe a sigh of relief on learning that John Adams had won the presidential election of 1796, he must at any rate have felt a good deal more relaxed. Had Jefferson been victorious he surely would have been forced to resign.[1] Adams's slim margin of victory meant that he could think in terms of at least four and possibly eight more years of national service. It was a comforting thought to a man who, at fifty-five, remained completely dependent upon his government salary. Nor was Pickering disturbed at the prospect of working with the new chief executive. Quite to the contrary, he looked forward to John Adams's presidency. His relationship with Washington had always been distant and excessively formal, a reflection of the negative feelings he had developed during the revolutionary war and which had never disappeared. No matter that Washington had given him three major political appointments over the preceding six years. The secretary thought it more significant that both cabinet appointments had come only after others had turned them down. In Pickering's crabbed view, Washington remained a much overrated, semiliterate mediocrity whose aides had saved him during the Revolution and whose brilliant cabinet ministers had made his first administration a triumph.[2]

If there is little confusion as to why Pickering was willing, even anxious, to serve in the Adams cabinet, it remains something of a puzzle that the new president was content to retain him along with Oliver Wolcott and James McHenry. The charge generally leveled against these three is that they were loyal to Alexander Hamilton rather than to Adams and therefore ought to have been removed.[3] With regard to Pickering, this allegation, born of unsubstantiated Republican charges

made during the waning days of Washington's second term, ought to
be scrapped. The record reveals no obsequious subordination to
Hamilton's will. On the contrary, though Hamilton struck up a correspondence with Pickering after his appointment to the State
Department, he had no success when it came to controlling the New
Englander's behavior.[4] Indeed, Hamilton soon became so skeptical of
his ability to influence Pickering that on those occasions when he
thought it absolutely essential to intervene, he preferred to work
through Washington or Wolcott rather than confront the secretary of
state directly.[5] That is hardly the tactic he would have employed had he
been dealing with a subordinate.

None of this is to suggest that Adams did not have good reasons for
replacing Pickering. The secretary's prolonged and needlessly provocative public dispute with Pierre Adet left him, and therefore the new
administration, vulnerable to Republican attacks at home while simultaneously reducing chances for a peaceable settlement to the festering
dispute with France. Both Elbridge Gerry and Stephen Sayre pointed
out to Adams that he might improve chances for a reconciliation with
the Directory by disposing of Pickering. Either "change the language of
your Secretary," Sayre advised, "or change the Secretary."[6] Sayre's
logic was sound enough. Adams was an unknown quantity. By removing Pickering he might give the French reason to make a fresh and
more favorable evaluation of his administration.

There remain only a few clues to help explain why Adams retained a
secretary of state who was such an uncommon liability. In the first
place, he may have believed that Pickering's dismissal would be interpreted in Paris not as a conciliatory gesture but as a sign of weakness
that would place him at an extra disadvantage in future discussions.
Moreover, he undoubtedly wondered whether he could afford to force
members of the old cabinet to resign. There was no precedent in 1797
for the resignation of cabinet officers upon the inauguration of a new
president. Nor had there been any resignations. Had Adams wished to
make new appointments, he would have been required to dismiss men
who gave every evidence of wanting to remain in office and who had
powerful connections in the Federalist coalition. Aware that he led a
divided country and party, the president may well have believed
neither one could stand any extra divisiveness.[7]

Though Adams was prepared to keep Pickering in the cabinet, it is
clear that he did not intend to depend solely upon his advice in the
formulation of foreign policy. Within the first weeks of his administration the president saw to it that his son John Quincy Adams, scheduled
to go as minister to Portugal, remained instead in northern Europe.

Thus he might have access to diplomatic information from a reliable source in the field without being entirely dependent upon Pickering at the State Department.[8] Later, he added William Vans Murray, minister at the Hague, to his list of private correspondents in a further effort to develop independent sources of foreign diplomatic information.[9] Moreover, he frequently made key decisions relating especially to French relations without so much as informing the secretary of state or, for that matter, anyone else in the cabinet.

Unhappily for all concerned, Pickering, who failed to appreciate the significance of John Quincy Adams's assignment in northern Europe or the fact that the new president seemed to be keeping his distance from the cabinet, was neither emotionally nor intellectually prepared to accept the role of an administrative appendage. On the contrary, he assumed that because Adams lacked experience, he would play a more responsible role in the new administration than he had under Washington. In keeping with these expectations, he sought to take the initiative in policy formulation shortly after Adams was inaugurated. Envisioning a more aggressive approach toward France than Washington would have approved, he drafted "a sketch of the facts" surrounding recent developments in Franco-American relations and urged the president to have it published. A bombastic denunciation of French policy that focused on the Directory's recent decision to force Charles C. Pinckney, the accredited American minister, to leave France, it was designed to prepare the public for what the secretary viewed as an inevitable confrontation with the old ally. When the president refused to publish his essay, Pickering was of course very irritated. Perhaps he realized, too, that John Adams was going to be a difficult man to get along with.[10]

The president's unwillingness to adopt Pickering's policy recommendations had at least as much to do with the substance of those proposals as it did with the fact that he was determined to maintain the upper hand over an aggressive secretary of state. No doubt influenced by the narrowness of his recent election victory, Adams was convinced that Pickering's pamphlet, far from encouraging unity, would only enhance partisan differences. Unlike the secretary, who too frequently ignored or underestimated such considerations, Adams thought the nation so badly divided that the only option open to him was to attempt negotiations with France. Moreover, he viewed it as absolutely essential that these talks be conducted by a bipartisan commission carefully selected to include southern representatives.[11]

It was soon understood in Federalist circles that the new administration was badly divided over French policy, with Pickering leading a "war faction" in the cabinet.[12] Convinced that the government was in no position to adopt the aggressive course being pressed by Pickering, and unaware of the degree to which Adams might be influenced by cabinet recommendations, Alexander Hamilton labored to convince the secretary of state that further negotiations and the appointment of a bipartisan commission were both necessary at a time when public opinion could not be counted upon to support a more militant policy.[13] But the New Yorker was totally unable to influence Pickering, who was not only strongly opposed to further talks but made it plain that if for some reason negotiations were decided upon he would oppose the appointment of any Jeffersonian to the commission.[14] Hamilton was troubled by his inability to impress Pickering, for he believed that the United States stood at a critical juncture in its relations with France. He feared, however, "that sensibility" would "be an overmatch for policy." With the impulsive secretary of state very much on his mind he felt helpless save to invoke the Deity. "God grant that the public interest may not be sacrificed at the shrine of irritation & mistaken pride," he wrote.[15]

Though earlier he had seemed unyielding, in April Pickering modified his views regarding negotiations with France. He was, of course, being pressed by a number of Federalist leaders all of whom endorsed more or less enthusiastically a further attempt to open talks.[16] But it was the deteriorating European situation that encouraged caution. Dispatches from American representatives abroad, especially Rufus King in London and John Quincy Adams in Berlin, brought grim predictions. The European coalition was collapsing and France, at the apex of her power, would soon be the mistress of the Continent and perhaps of the oceans as well. It remained to be seen how long England could survive. The Bank of England had already suspended specie payments; national bankruptcy seemed inevitable. King especially urged extreme caution, advice that became compelling when it was learned that the British were attempting to arrange an armistice with France.[17]

Pickering's sudden willingness to acquiesce in further negotiations should not be taken to mean that he was in accord with the president, for they remained poles apart on the substantive issues. In the first place, the secretary of state continued to oppose the inclusion of a Jeffersonian representative on the negotiating commission.[18] Moreover, it is certain from the structure and tenor of his recommendations to Adams that he viewed the projected talks as a delaying tactic designed primarily to buy time in which to augment the armed forces and discover more about the pending negotiations between England and France.[19]

Although there were important differences between the president and the State Department regarding the future conduct of relations with France, Adams's maiden speech to Congress, delivered on May 16, 1797, left them temporarily obscured. Pickering in fact was very pleased with the president's remarks. The announcement of a further attempt to negotiate with France was, after all, in keeping with his own recommendations. Moreover, the unmistakably militant quality of the speech led him to believe that Adams shared his skepticism about the outcome of the projected talks and was looking beyond to what would come later. He listened with rapt attention as Adams reviewed the recent history of Franco-American relations, blaming the French for current difficulties but promising that he would do everything possible, consistent with the nation's honor, to arrive at a settlement. The president's strong language, his call for increased national defense expenditures, and most of all his denunciation of dissent and obstructionism at home were balm to a secretary of state who over long months had been repeatedly savaged in the Republican press.[20]

But it was not long before he and the president were at odds over the make-up of the delegation to be sent to France. The issue of a bipartisan commission had been a bone of contention for more than two months.[21] The controversy flared up again when Adams suggested that his friend Elbridge Gerry be appointed along with Charles C. Pinckney and John Marshall to the negotiating team. Gerry had earned a reputation among Federalists for unreliability as a result of his vacillation during the debate over the Constitution. In 1797 he was not clearly identified with either Federalism or the opposition, which was of course why Pickering and others in the cabinet sought to block his nomination. But that was also a large part of the reason that Adams wanted him on the commission. The Republican leadership and the nation as a whole surely would have increased confidence in a delegation that included someone who was not a Federalist.

Aware that Gerry sometimes acted quixotically, Adams nonetheless trusted him not only as a long-time friend but also because he had been loyal during the presidential election in 1796.[22] However, when cabinet opposition to Gerry first developed, Adams sought common ground, turning to another old friend, Francis Dana, chief justice of the Massachusetts Supreme Court. When Dana refused the appointment, Adams resorted once again to Gerry, this time nominating him over the objections of McHenry, Wolcott, and Pickering, who went to the astonishing length of lobbying against the Gerry nomination in the Senate.[23]

Pickering's disagreements with Adams, first over whether or not negotiations should be attempted and then over the composition of the American delegation, were only the first episodes in a larger contest for control of the formulation of America's policy toward France. Adams was insistent upon having the last word. Rather than acquiesce, Pickering fought back, sometimes playing the role of obstructionist to the point of overt disloyalty. Many years later he attempted to justify this, maintaining that cabinet officers were independent members of the government and had not only the right but the responsibility to oppose the policies of a "wrong-headed" president.[24] But there was no substance to such a contention. The fact that Pickering was frequently reduced to political backstabbing is proof enough of his real impotence. Cabinet officers served at the discretion of the president. He appointed them and, as Pickering later learned to his own discomfiture, he could dismiss them. They had no powers save those he chose to confer upon them.

For months after Gerry and Marshall sailed to join Pinckney on the Continent, the State Department remained completely in the dark regarding the progress of their negotiations. By December nerves were beginning to fray. Then in January Pickering received, via William Vans Murray at the Hague, a private letter from John Marshall dated October 21 indicating that the envoys did not even expect to be acknowledged by the Directory.[25] Satisfied that the United States now had no choice save war, Pickering leaked this story to Claypool's *American Daily Advertiser,* hoping to stimulate public indignation.

Marshall's letter eliminated one of the main differences between the president and the State Department. Unwilling to accept further humiliation at the hands of the Directory, Adams's mind, too, strayed in the direction of war. He went so far as to consult his cabinet with reference to the possibility of negotiating an alliance with Great Britain, though simultaneously making his own strong opposition to such an arrangement quite obvious.[26] A few days later he dined with Theodore Sedgwick, leaving the Federalist congressman with a sense of the inevitability of conflict. Adams was firm and determined, Sedgwick wrote. What he seemed to fear most was that the Directory might find ways of delaying the break.[27]

A month passed and Pickering's nerves remained on edge. On February 26, he complained to William Vans Murray that nothing official had yet been received from the envoys. "We cannot account for the lack of direct information from them, on any other principle than their letters are intercepted."[28] A few days later the break came. First, Major John Rutledge handed Pickering a private letter from Pinckney. A bit more recent than Marshall's note, it confirmed what the Virginian had written, adding that the French press teemed with anti-American propaganda.[29] Then, on the evening of March 5, the first packet of dispatches from the envoys finally arrived. The fifth dispatch, which was the only one not in code, announced that the mission had been a failure. Moreover, indications were that the Directory intended to step up its offensive against American shipping. A new French maritime decree declared neutral ships carrying any articles that were the products or manufactures of Great Britain to be legal prize. Since virtually every American ship afloat fell into that category, there would be no protection for American merchantmen against French raiders except by armed resistance. In concluding this message the envoys wrote: "We can only repeat that there exists no hope of our being officially received by this Government or that the objects of our mission will be in any way accomplished."[30] Pickering immediately forwarded this dispatch to Adams. He in turn sent it on to Congress, promising the others as they were decoded. According to Congressman Sedgwick the news convinced even some Jeffersonian members that war was inevitable.[31]

Clerks in the State Department worked tirelessly to decode the four remaining dispatches. As Pickering read them he was astonished by the arrogance of the French. The Directory's refusal to receive the envoys and Foreign Minister Talleyrand's unsubtle attempts at international blackmail reconfirmed all of Pickering's feelings about the impossibility of peace with revolutionary France. Simultaneously, he realized that the disclosure of the XYZ affair would at a stroke disarm political opposition at home.[32] He therefore urged Adams to forward the dispatches to Congress without delay. But the president proved ambivalent. In their final message the envoys had indicated that they would make one last attempt to negotiate before demanding their passports. Adams had no way of knowing whether or not they had succeeded. If by some miracle talks had actually begun, the French might well become angry enough to discontinue them on learning the contents of the dispatches. Should that happen, it was reasonable to assume that the Republicans would claim the administration had deliberately published the dispatches in order to cause a breakdown in the talks. There was another consideration as well. The dispatches were of such an astonishing nature, so demeaning to the French, that Adams feared the envoys might be imprisoned or even murdered if copies of the published dispatches reached Paris before they had a chance to leave. "It is a very painful thing to him," Abigail Adams explained to her sister, but lacking assurances that the envoys had left Paris the president was "unable to communicate to the public dispatches in which they are so much interested."[33]

President Adams's March 19 message to Congress revealed nothing beyond the fact that the negotiations had failed. He authorized American merchant ships to arm defensively and urged legislative action on proposals for the national defense, stalled in Congress since the preceding May.[34] But Adams did not intend to keep the XYZ affair from the public for long. Following his appearance before Congress he authorized Pickering to send new instructions to Marshall, Pinckney, and Gerry, ordering them to demand their passports and leave France immediately unless, and this was unlikely, real progress was being made. Anticipating passage of a congressional resolution calling for the dispatches, Pickering warned the envoys that the president would soon have to produce them. Since time was of the essence, the fast-sailing brig *Sophia* was assigned to Clement Humphreys, a special courier, whose duty was to reach the envoys and present them with their new instructions as quickly as possible.[35]

While awaiting the inevitable congressional demand for the documents, Pickering and Adams, now both convinced that the nation should fight, debated war plans. Predictably, they had very different policies in mind. For more than twenty years Adams had preached noninvolvement in European wars, warning of the snares and dangers that lay in that direction. His European diplomatic experience had only served to convince him of the depravity of all of the great powers, England not excepted. Almost inevitably, then, Adams approached the idea of war with France cautiously, conceiving of it largely in terms of independent naval action designed to protect American shipping. Nor did he think in terms of a long-term involvement. Forced to fight in defense of the nation's honor and her right to trade, Adams hoped to take the first opportunity that presented itself to make an acceptable peace and return America to her proper position of neutrality.[36]

Pickering was far more emotional in his response to the XYZ affair. It would perhaps be unfair to say that he did not understand the nature of eighteenth-century dynastic diplomacy, but it is not in the least unjust to suggest that he did not allow his understanding to influence his thinking. In highly emotional outbursts addressed to his friend, the Massachusetts merchant Stephen Higginson, and to John Quincy Adams, he wholeheartedly embraced the idea of total war. "Nothing," he thought, would "satisfy the ambitious and rapacious" Directory short of "universal dominion." The United States had for a time managed to maintain neutrality. But it was obvious that she had only been "reserved for future plunder and oppression." Neutrality was plainly not feasible either for the United States or for other nations that had not yet become embroiled in the war.[37]

Pickering's conception of the nature of the European war was equally simplistic. He reduced the issues to a choice between right and wrong, good and evil. In instructions to John Quincy Adams sent only days after receiving the first set of dispatches from the envoys in Paris, he maintained that Britain now stood as the last stronghold of civilization "against the universal domination of France." [38] Nor was he at all bashful about making these same feelings known to Robert Liston. The American cabinet ministers, Liston duly reported to his superiors in London, "consider us the last bulwark against the usurper of civilization." [39] In short, Pickering reacted typically to this new stage in the crisis with France. He elevated it to a moral plane, defined the European war in similar terms, repudiated principles of neutrality, and argued that the United States should engage in full-scale war against France until she had been finally defeated.

This very basic difference of opinion between the president and his secretary of state soon came to a boil over the pivotal issue of an alliance with Britain. Adams believed that as long as the United States remained a cobelligerent without any formal ties to England, she could in any event depend upon British support. An alliance, however, implied a commitment to stay in the war until a general peace could be arranged. Thinking opportunistically, Adams feared it would "impede us, in embracing the first favorable moment . . . to make a separate peace." The president saw other difficulties, too, in a formal commitment. Mindful that England faced the threat of a full-scale French invasion, he was aware that the Channel fleet was a serious question mark. The Great Mutiny of 1797 had been subdued, to be sure, but no one could predict with confidence whether or not British crews would fight. With England standing "on the brink of a dangerous precipice," Adams inquired, "will not shaking hands with her necessitate us, to fall with her if she falls?" [40]

Pickering, by contrast, favored an alliance. Thwarted by Adams, he was further discouraged by Alexander Hamilton's rejection of the idea. In fact, Hamilton's thinking was strikingly similar to the president's. "In my opinion," he wrote, "bold language and bold measures are indispensable. The attitude of *calm defiance* suits us." The choice, as he saw it, was "between a tame surrender of our rights or a state of *mitigated hostility.*" Full-scale war was from the point of view of domestic politics, unfeasible, thought Hamilton. Nor did he believe France would court such a break unless she was first successful in her planned invasion of England. In that case, of course, the entire diplomatic situation would be revolutionized. In the meantime, however, he urged a limited and undeclared war, nothing more. [41]

Baffled by Hamilton's seeming insensitivity to what he defined as an obvious need, Pickering wrote to him twice on March 25. In one of these letters he detailed the story of the humiliations heaped upon Marshall, Pinckney, and Gerry in Paris. No one outside the administration knew the exact details of the abortive negotiations, and Pickering was taking a serious chance in writing such a letter. Adams would have been furious had he known that his secretary of state was leaking secret information to Hamilton. But Pickering evidently felt the risk worth taking if it might bring Hamilton around to greater militancy.

In his second letter to Hamilton, Pickering asked plaintively, "What shall we say to the British govt.?" The opposition, he noted, had long since charged that a secret alliance existed between England and the administration. Rather sadly, however, he acknowledged that Rufus King had not yet been instructed to take what to Pickering seemed the next logical step. With a critical cabinet meeting scheduled in the immediate future, Pickering asked Hamilton to send his views at once.[42] But again Hamilton disappointed him. In a hurriedly written letter he specifically rejected the idea of an alliance. The government could count upon complete cooperation from Britain in any event. What, then, was to be gained by a more formal commitment? He noted that public opinion was not prepared for such a move and that the opposition would be sure to argue, if an alliance were actually arranged, that this was "the point to which our previous conduct was directed."[43]

Frustrated at every turn, Pickering was forced to set aside his plans for a formal alliance. His instructions to Rufus King, dated two days before Adams submitted the XYZ dispatches to Congress, detailed the Adams approach to Anglo-American relations. The United States would "from time to time enter into cooperative military efforts" with England while simultaneously preserving her political freedom of action. Though the policy statement was clear, it was obvious that Pickering wanted much more. The president, he explained, had not yet enough justification to propose a formal agreement with Britain. Pickering expressed confidence, however, that continued French aggression would produce the popular support necessary for an alliance. He urged King to investigate the possibilities.[44] He was equally overt in conversation with Liston, who relayed his impressions to the Foreign Office. "From the tenor of the Secretary of State's conversation," he wrote, "I can entertain no doubt that he himself is deterred from speaking frankly, in part on account of the numbers and strength" of the political opposition, "and partly because he has received no instructions on the subject from the President."[45]

As soon as Alexander Hamilton learned that the Paris talks had failed, he rushed legislative recommendations for strengthening

America's military establishment to Pickering. The secretary of state, though enthusiastic about the proposals, doubted that Congress would act until the envoy's dispatches had been published. He counted on the revelation of the XYZ affair to "detach" many members whose support for the opposition was founded primarily upon questions of economy.[46] Pickering was, of course, correct. Moderate, nonaligned congressmen who controlled the balance of power in the House of Representatives might not agree with Jefferson, who claimed that the diplomatic correspondence was being withheld because it would not support the militant policy that Adams had advocated in his "insane" March 19 message to Congress. But neither were they prepared to follow the president without more evidence than he had thus far produced.[47]

In Pickering's judgment everything depended upon the passage of a Republican-sponsored resolution calling upon the president to produce the envoys' dispatches. The danger was that puzzled congressional Federalists, unaware of the president's reasons for keeping the documents secret, might successfully oppose this resolution, as they had two earlier antiwar proposals.[48] To deal with this possibility the president and Pickering, as well as other members of the cabinet, informed various Federalist congressmen that the disclosure of the dispatches would do a world of good for the administration.[49] As early as March 11, Congressman Theodore Sedgwick had it from Adams himself that he was withholding the dispatches only because he did not wish to expose the envoys to "assassination"; that he sought only a little extra time to allow them to leave Paris before copies of their published dispatches reached France. Shortly after his conversation with the president, Sedgwick explained to a friend that there was no longer any doubt "that secrets which will soon be disclosed will disembarrass government by destroying the baleful influence of its adversaries."[50] Considering how well informed congressional Federalists were, it is not surprising that the House resolution calling for the diplomatic correspondence passed with strong bipartisan support.[51]

On April 4, President Adams sent the envoys' dispatches, along with their original instructions, to Congress. Anticipating a quick declaration of war, Secretary of State Pickering waited anxiously for the congressional reaction. As he had expected, congressmen who had earlier questioned the integrity of the administration were forced to admit, after reading the instructions to the envoys, that they had been drawn with care and should have led to a fair settlement. Some even admitted that the Directory had "given . . . abundant cause to declare war." Yet, they contended, it was "not expedient" to do so. To become involved in the great European war in defense of the nation's commerce, they argued, would be a mistake.[52]

Pickering never fully appreciated the importance of this point of view, passing it off as mere partisanship. Yet there was more to it than that, as a letter from James Tilton written two weeks after disclosure of the XYZ affair should have made clear. Tilton, a Delaware Federalist, informed the State Department that there was general agreement in the Wilmington area that the nation should prepare to defend itself. There was a sharp difference of opinion, however, over whether America's foreign trade should be protected if that meant war. Tilton believed that had a vote been taken "a very great majority would be in favor of relinquishing it." For many in and out of Congress, it seems, national defense did not necessarily imply protecting an expanding commercial interest that had come under attack because it insisted upon taking advantage of the unusual though dangerous trading opportunities created by the European war.[53]

Distressed at Congress's failure to respond appropriately to the XYZ affair, Pickering could only hope that an aroused public would convince the legislators to act. On April 9, as he prepared the envoys' dispatches, fresh from the printers, for national distribution, he meditated on the importance of the popular reaction to the indignities suffered by the American envoys in France. In a note accompanying a copy of the dispatches sent to John Jay, he outlined what he believed was at issue. "If we do not defend ourselves at this point," he wrote, "our independence is at an end."[54] Nor was Pickering disappointed by the public's response. An impressive volume of letters and addresses of support soon deluged the president. Political news from New England was also very encouraging. Federalists won the yearly elections in some of these states by overwhelming majorities. In Massachusetts, for example, the incumbent Federalist governor, Increase Sumner, was reelected by a margin of almost 6 to 1 over his Republican opponent. Connecticut Federalists also won important victories.[55]

Pickering was equally delighted with the energetic, combative spirit of the president. Privately Adams raged at the envoys for having allowed themselves to be drawn into conversations with Talleyrand's unofficial representatives before they had been acknowledged by the Directory.[56] He designated a day of fasting and prayer to dramatize the crisis and spent hours each day at his writing desk formulating militant replies to the addresses of support that showered in upon him. He worked such long hours, in fact, that Abigail Adams grew concerned over his health. He was quite worn down, she confided to her sister. "I never saw him so thin." Yet, though he frequently "sighed" for the quiet of Braintree and Quincy, she explained, "his spirits" were "good and his fortitude unshaken."[57]

Pickering had almost everything he wanted: a militant president, an outraged public, and an overall atmosphere conducive to a declaration of war. Nevertheless, to his utter dismay, Congress remained reluctant to take aggressive action. Bills to augment coastal defenses and to increase the number of engineers and artillerymen in the army were quickly passed. But when Secretary of War James McHenry produced a $1.2 million estimate for defense expenditures, Republicans and uncommitted congressmen, aghast at the potential costs of war, cut the request by a full third. A bill to establish a provisional army of twenty thousand men that had been endorsed by a staunchly Federalist Senate was also emasculated in the House. The congressional attitude toward the navy was particularly discouraging to Pickering. It was agreed that several frigates already under construction would be completed, but the House reduced from sixteen to twelve the number of small armed ships to be built for convoy duty. Though the United States had approximately three-quarters of a million tons of shipping subject to French harassment, Congress refused to protect this vast and important investment.[58]

Pickering was by no means the only Federalist to be disappointed by Congress's continued inability to act decisively. Congressman Uriah Tracy, for example, complained to Alexander Hamilton that the deadlock in the House of Representatives had turned the session into a nightmare.[59] Connecticut's Roger Griswold was, if anything, even more disgusted.[60] And in Dedham the voluble Fisher Ames was grief-stricken at the way in which Congress was behaving: "The members still talk too much of *peace* as if we had our choice and as if we ought to chuse it *now*." He urged firm and decisive action upon Pickering: "Everybody asks shall we have war. My answer is we have war & the man who now wished for peace holds his country's honor & safety too cheap."[61]

Toward the end of May, much to Pickering's satisfaction, the legislative logjam at last showed signs of giving way. After a long and querulous debate the House approved an act authorizing American naval vessels and privateers to seize French privateersmen hovering off the coast. President Adams signed the bill into law on May 28. It was *"not all it ought to be,"* Abigail Adams wrote, but it was a step in the right direction. She was certain that "much more decisive measures would be pursued" once the envoys had actually left France.[62] The first lady knew exactly what she was talking about. In June, on receiving authoritative news that the talks had failed and that Marshall and Pinckney had left Paris while Elbridge Gerry, for reasons that remained unclear, had elected to remain behind, the previously deadlocked Congress authorized armed retaliation against France. Pickering was deeply relieved. "Nothing will save us from the fatal grasp of France but open war, and a resistance becoming a people really free," he wrote, and "for this we are preparing."[63]

But nothing was to work out precisely as the secretary of state hoped. In this instance Elbridge Gerry's extraordinary decision to divide the commission by remaining in Paris was the fly in the ointment. Not just Pickering, but a broad spectrum of administration supporters feared that Gerry's action would be taken to mean that the Federalist members, Marshall and Pinckney, had decided to leave France even though chances for a settlement remained. Fearing new divisions at home, a thoroughly outraged George Cabot fumed that Gerry had provided "a false hope to the weak & a pretext to the wicked part of our society."[64] Thomas Pinckney, recently returned from a tour through Kentucky and Tennessee, where administration popularity was unprecedented, warned Secretary of State Pickering of the precisely the same problem.[65] And Abigail Adams, undoubtedly echoing the private thoughts of her husband, described Gerry's decision to remain in Paris as a serious embarrassment to the government. It was, she thought, "wrong, very wrong."[66]

Pickering's own attitude toward Gerry oscillated between mere disapproval and deepest anger. On first hearing of the unpredictable Gerry's latest aberration he assumed that the instructions he had sent on March 23 would soon reach Paris and that Gerry, too, would then withdraw. But on June 12 he received a dispatch from William Vans Murray informing him (incorrectly) that Gerry had undertaken negotiations with Talleyrand.[67] This Pickering characterized as an act of "unpardonable arrogance and folly." In fact the secretary confided to Rufus King that he hoped Gerry would still be in Paris when the published XYZ dispatches arrived there. Then the French might do both themselves and him a favor by guillotining the old fool.[68] Two days later, however, Pickering's anger moderated somewhat when new dispatches from the envoys arrived, including one letter from Gerry in which he assured his superiors that although he had decided to remain, it was only because Talleyrand had warned that if he left the Directory would immediately declare war. Gerry promised Adams and Pickering that he would not carry on any negotiations and would stay in Paris only to await further orders. If there was to be a war, Gerry insisted, it ought to be the product of decisions made in Philadelphia and not something that was simply thrust upon the country.[69]

Gratified to learn that Gerry would not be returning home with a

French treaty, Pickering was nevertheless distressed at the damage the envoy had already done on the domestic front. Adams, equally displeased, tried to undo some of it on June 21 when he forwarded the latest dispatches from the envoys to Congress together with the ringing announcement that he would "never send another minister to France without assurance that he will be received, respected, and honored as the representative of a great, free, powerful, and independent nation."[70] On June 25, Pickering followed Adams's lead with a reproachful letter recalling Gerry.[71]

But the political damage had been done. Jefferson quickly drew the logical conclusion. Gerry's decision to remain behind suggested that chances for a negotiated settlement still existed.[72] Benjamin F. Bache, also aware of the importance of Gerry's behavior, commented at length on the significance of a divided commission in the *Philadelphia Aurora*. He also published a letter from Talleyrand in which the French foreign minister revealed what some thought to be a serious interest in reconciling differences between France and the United States.[73] Republican printers in other parts of the country were no less impressed with the significance of Gerry's action. The publisher of the *New York Timepiece* wondered if Gerry, "on the spot," didn't have a better understanding of "how France is affected to this country . . . than a few gloomy bigots, who reason from their prejudices and their passions and are at a distance." A few days later this same essayist suggested that it "would be very impolite in Mr. Gerry to disappoint his patrons by any premature negotiation, which would prevent a *just, politic* and *necessary war*."[74]

While the opposition press made Pickering's life miserable with stories related to Gerry and the possibilities of peace, he was made more uneasy by some unfortunately timed British naval depredations. Here was another issue readymade for Republican manipulation. Jeffersonian newspapers gave splendid coverage to the activities of Richard Cambould, judge of the Vice-Admiralty Court on the island of Santo Domingo, who condemned ships and cargoes on the flimsiest pretexts. They further aroused their readers with reports of American ships seized by British cruisers. During June 1798, the British frigate *Thetis* alone took five vessels in just a few days while operating in American waters off Charleston.

These British depredations, especially the activities of the *Thetis,* which made headlines in the New York area, prompted Alexander Hamilton to intervene at the State Department. Aware of the negative impact that a soft attitude toward Britain would have upon public opinion, he advised Pickering to react firmly, even to the extent of sending warships to Charleston to defend American shipping.[75]

Hamilton deplored the actions of British courts and naval commanders who thus threatened the delicate political situation. "Cambauld at the Mole," he wrote, was "acting a part quite as bad as the directory and their instruments." Hamilton saw "a fatality in all this." Confident that the British government wanted to follow a conciliatory policy toward the United States, he could only hope that it would be able to bring its subordinates under control before too much damage had been done.[76]

Pickering was no less concerned about these problems than Hamilton. Indeed, he had lodged a strong protest with the Foreign Office over the activities of the admiralty court at Mole St. Nicholas long before Hamilton wrote.[77] But diplomacy takes time. Congress, therefore, debated the question of war or peace with France while Republican newspapers focused their attentions on some very real British depredations. The introduction of such an obvious ambiguity made it that much more difficult for Congress to take the last irreversible step.

British wrongdoing and opposition tactics notwithstanding, Secretary of State Pickering believed that with the negotiations in Paris now clearly at an end there was only one course left. In a letter to his son he explained, "The Rubicon is passed: War is inevitable."[78] But would Congress at long last proceed to a declaration of war? In faraway Boston another of Pickering's political intimates, Stephen Higginson, had his doubts. Enthusiastic at the militant tone and content of President Adams's addresses to the people, Higginson nevertheless warned Pickering on the dangers of congressional backsliding.[79] The merchant's fears were well founded, for although congressional Federalists could muster majorities to arm, increase the size of the army, lay new taxes, enact the Alien and Sedition Laws, and abrogate the treaties with France, they proved unable to put together even a simple majority for war, much less the decisive vote needed. In Dedham, Fisher Ames fretted. "Something energetic and decisive must be done soon," he wrote to Pickering. "Congress fiddles while our rome is burning."[80] The situation looked no better in Philadelphia, where the militant Congressman Theodore Sedgwick deplored the feebleness of those around him. It came as no surprise to him when Congress adjourned without voting for war.

Post-mortems on Congress's performance began even before the legislators had left the capital. Abigail Adams, perhaps reflecting the views of her husband, thought that on the whole it had been a productive Congress. She was particularly enthusiastic about the Sedition Law. What she thought "wanting," however, was "a declaration of war" which "ought undoubtedly to have been made." She blamed

Elbridge Gerry for this, believing that his decision to divide the peace commission had preserved hope for a settlement among some, making it that much more difficult to agree on war.[81] Pickering agreed but was not nearly so downcast as some other Federalists. He believed that Congress had not reacted properly to public opinion, "which is united behind the President." He predicted that in December, when Congress reconvened after having consulted its constituency, it would correct the oversight.[82] And to help Congress arrive at the proper conclusion, Pickering began the distribution of ten thousand copies of the second set of the envoys' dispatches along with related correspondence recently received from France.[83]

FOURTEEN

Schism

ALTHOUGH THERE HAD BEEN repeated disagreements between Pickering and the president during the first sixteen months of Adams's administration, until the summer of 1798 events had conspired to prevent their differences from becoming irreconcilable. Then, however, a clash over defense policy proved the first in a series of disputes upon which the relationship foundered. The original point at issue between Pickering and the president centered around proposals for enlarging the army. Adams was altogether opposed to a plan endorsed by Pickering for the creation of a large, well-trained provisional army.[1] Behind this difference of opinion lay a more significant disagreement over whether or not France posed a real military danger to the United States. Adams was skeptical about the Directory's ability to land and maintain a large force in North America while the Royal Navy dominated the Atlantic. Discounting the danger of a French invasion, the president naturally hoped to avoid a massive military build-up. He was keenly aware that the tax increases this would require would be especially unpopular if, as he suspected, no enemy appeared on American shores.[2]

The secretary of state, more overwrought than the president, gave greater credence to the French threat. When Congress emasculated the plan for a large provisional army, instead authorizing Adams to call up ten thousand men at such time as he judged a French invasion imminent, Pickering sent a highly emotional letter to Alexander Hamilton denouncing congressional shortsightedness. It was as though he could see the masts of a French invasion fleet already in Chesapeake Bay. And even if the assault did not come immediately, the danger was still very real. "The successful invasion of England ... would put us in jeopardy," he wrote. So too would a French descent upon Holland, for that would force the British to concentrate their fleet in the Channel, leaving the United States undefended.[3]

Pickering's fears extended well beyond thoughts of invasion, however. He was, for example, deeply troubled at the idea that the French Foreign Ministry might convince Spain to retrocede Louisiana, thus creating a base from which the Directory's agents might work their subversive schemes within the United States.[4] In fact, a favorite theme in Pickering's correspondence was that somehow French spies operating from Louisiana, or perhaps from Toussaint L'Ouverture's Santo Domingo, would arouse and organize the slaves of the South for a bloody revolution.[5] He suspected, too, that a connection existed between French operatives and western political dissidents. Pickering knew that two former French envoys, Genet and Adet, had been involved in western conspiracies and he suspected that the same was true of Joseph Letombe, the French consul general. Through James McHenry in the War Department he had access to information suggesting that a plot had been hatched between General James Wilkinson and the Spanish authorities at New Orleans aimed at separating Kentucky and Tennessee from the Union.[6] He also was monitoring the intelligence-gathering activities of General Victor Collot as well as two other French agents, one a mysterious General La Shaize, and another known only as Schweitzer.[7] There was of course no absolute proof of a connection between western separatists and the French, but a good deal of evidence pointed in that direction. Moreover, the secretary was aware that a similar scheme had been detected and thwarted by the British in Canada in 1797.[8] It was a simple extrapolation for Pickering, whose imagination thrived on suspicions of conspiracy, to conclude that like plottings were taking place in the American West.

By the summer of 1798 Pickering's hysteria had built to a furious crescendo, for he was convinced that the United States was confronted by a ruthless, diabolical enemy capable of using overt military force, espionage, and subversion in an ongoing attempt to overthrow the government and establish a revolutionary satellite. Given Pickering's frame of reference, congressional unwillingness to mobilize a large provisional force made it that much more important that the sixteen regiments of the regular army be well disciplined and ably commanded. He viewed it as certain that Adams would appoint the aged Washington as commander in chief of the "New Army" but recognized that whoever was appointed second to Washington would have effective control of the military. Anxious for the command to fall to an efficient officer, and fearful that Adams would appoint James Wilkinson, Henry Knox, or any one of a number of aging and incompetent revolutionary war generals, Pickering asked the president to appoint Alexander Hamilton Washington's second-in-command.[9] Adams's irate refusal should have put an end to the discussion, and it probably would have with any other man but the secretary of state. Gripped by an exaggerated fear of the French menace and persuaded that the president's personal hatred for Hamilton had blinded him to the national interest in a period of extreme danger, Pickering set out to force Adams to offer Hamilton the appointment.

There is little to be gained by recapitulating in detail the familiar story of how Pickering and James McHenry, with Washington's assistance, literally compelled the president to turn effective control of the army over to Alexander Hamilton.[10] Once Adams had agreed that Washington could select his own staff officers, it was no trouble at all for Pickering and the secretary of war to convince the aging and perhaps senile ex-president to place Hamilton's name first on his list of major generals, thus leaving Adams with no option save to appoint the New Yorker to a rank far higher than he would otherwise have been willing to contemplate.[11] Later, when Henry Knox, another of the designated major generals, claimed the right to outrank Hamilton and won Adams's support, Pickering again convinced Washington to intervene on the New Yorker's behalf this time charging that the president seemed about to renege on his earlier commitments.[12] Adams's contention that the power to appoint staff officers did not include the right to decide on the relative rank of the major generals had no influence on Washington. His threat to resign if Hamilton was not recognized as his second-in-command left the president no choice save surrender.[13]

In general, historians have assumed that Alexander Hamilton, who was skilled at behind-the-scenes manipulations, was responsible for this extraordinary conspiracy. There is strong reason to believe, however, that the central figure in the plot was Pickering. It was he who suggested Hamilton's name to Adams as second-in-command before the former treasury secretary knew anything about plans to officer the army. And, when Hamilton first wrote of the possibility of entering the army, he made no mention of a major general's commission, let alone the position just behind Washington. He explained in fact that he would be satisfied with an appointment as inspector general with a command in the line.[14] It was Pickering together with McHenry who convinced Washington to place Hamilton first on his list of proposed major generals. Moreover, when the dispute as to the relative rank of the major generals arose several weeks later, Hamilton expressed to Pickering his willingness to serve behind Knox or even third behind the other major general, Charles C. Pinckney, should that be necessary.[15] Pickering, however, adamant on the subject of Hamilton's claim to rank second only to Washington, withheld this letter from Adams.[16]

Nor can Pickering's extraordinary behavior be explained in terms of some sort of obsequious subordination to Hamilton's will. In fact, there is no reason to question the explanation he himself offered in a letter to the New Yorker. Writing at a moment when he believed that he might be dismissed by the irate Adams for his disloyalty, the secretary of state denied that friendship had anything to do with his efforts on Hamilton's behalf. Indeed, he maintained that he was not even Hamilton's friend, at least in "the proper strict sense of the word."[17] He had conspired against the president, he explained, because it was absolutely essential. Adams had allowed his hatred for Hamilton to cloud his perceptions. Pickering had then stepped in to set matters right: "I am not conscious that the risque [sic] of incurring the displeasure of any man ever deterred me from what I conceived to be my duty." He took up Hamilton's cause out of the conviction that the nation faced a serious danger to which the president was not attuned. Hamilton, he was certain, was the only man with the administrative skills and the capacity for leadership to prepare the army effectively for a threat that Pickering saw as imminent.[18]

Having won the major political victory, had Pickering been less the zealot, he would have allowed the president to have his way on lesser questions. But the secretary's opposition to the president on subjects relating to military appointments extended well beyond the question of Alexander Hamilton's rank. Thus, when Adams used his appointment power to nominate his son-in-law, Colonel William S. Smith, to a brigadier's rank, even though Smith's name did not appear on Washington's list of proposed general officers, Pickering again became the president's most vigorous opponent. Doubtful of Smith's political reliability as well as his personal character, the secretary of state lobbied so openly against the Smith nomination in the Senate that he expected the president to remove him from office for his trouble.[19] And well he might, for Adams was utterly humiliated when Smith's nomination was rejected. Although he was not at the time prepared to dismiss Pickering for his insubordination, neither was he ready to forget how and by whom he had twice been humbled.[20]

The incredible political risks that Pickering took on behalf of the army were of course predicated upon the existence of a serious French threat. Gripped by the emotionalism of the period and encouraged by the fact that discernible conspiracies against the Republic did indeed exist, Pickering magnified the dangers, overestimating the guile and resourcefulness of the potential foe. His misperceptions were extra-ordinary, his capacity for a realistic assessment of the military or diplomatic situation slight. Thus he became convinced that there could be no peace with revolutionary France, that she was averse to friendly relations with any nation she could not control.[21] This much given, it was a simple, even logical progression to the conclusion that full-scale war was not only inevitable but desirable.

Pickering had hoped that Congress would declare war before its adjournment in July. When the lawmakers balked, however, he thought that the disclosure of the XYZ affair might prompt the Directory to take the fateful step. Naturally, then, he was discomfited by the fact that during the summer and autumn of 1798 France made no move to widen the scope of the limited naval conflict then going on.

In the absence of a declared war, Pickering became increasingly sensitive to any indication that peace remained a possibility. In this connection he spent an anxious summer awaiting news of Elbridge Gerry, who was still in Paris. Originally, Pickering trusted that Gerry would not enter into negotiations without further instructions and counted on his letter of recall to bring the errant envoy home. But as the summer progressed and Gerry did not appear, the secretary came to fear that he might return from Europe bearing either a pledge that the Directory was ready to negotiate or, worse, a treaty.[22]

In late August Pickering was given a momentary lift by news of Gerry's belated departure from France, but the French foreign minister's swift publication of his correspondence with the American envoy put an end to that. In a careful review of the painful course of recent relations with the United States, Talleyrand emphasized his government's friendly inclinations. He expressed regret that Gerry would not remain to negotiate a treaty, but urged him to return to the United States with the message that France sought peace.[23] Talleyrand's letter, widely reprinted in the Republican press, seemed damaging enough to Pickering. But Gerry's published reply was far worse, for while he stoutly defended John Adams's foreign policy, he simultaneously expressed his own confidence in Talleyrand's sincerity. Peace through negotiations, he affirmed, was indeed within reach.[24]

The secretary of state was aghast. "You will have seen Mr. Gerry's correspondence with Talleyrand," he wrote to John Marshall. "This is the finishing stroke to his conduct in France by which he has dishonored & injured his country and sealed his own indelible disgrace."[25] Gerry's behavior, though he characterized it as "absurd and preposterous," nevertheless gave Pickering fits, for it was certain to have a profound effect on public opinion.[26] And so, without consulting President

Adams or waiting for explanations from Gerry, Pickering indulged his penchant for public controversy, this time publishing a scorching reproof in which he accused his one-time friend of having been duped by Talleyrand.[27]

One week after Pickering's diatribe appeared in the newspapers, Gerry arrived in the United States and set out immediately for Quincy and a conference with the president. Leaders in both parties waited anxiously to learn his views on the current status of Franco-American relations. John Marshall, for example, informed Pickering that the opposition in Virginia was ready "to receive him . . . or to drop him . . . as he may be French or American."[28] Marshall himself revealed more than a passing interest in what Gerry might say. Locked in a hotly contested congressional election campaign, his own future prospects were in some degree riding on Gerry's version of his Paris sojourn.[29]

Coffeehouses and other public gathering places in and around Boston buzzed with rumors of what Gerry had told the president and how the chief executive had responded. George Cabot was among those most avid in snatching up a rumor here and a reliable piece of information there. From these he was able to form a reasonably clear picture of what seemed to him an impending disaster. He informed the frustrated Pickering, who was powerless even to argue with the president as long as he remained away from the capital, that Gerry's position would be almost impossible to penetrate. The envoy, he reported, endorsed the vigorous foreign policy of 1798, urging continued national unity as well as strong measures of retaliation against French aggression. Simultaneously, however, he argued that the administration's display of strength had already accomplished its major purpose. Even though the publication of the XYZ dispatches had embarrassed his relations with Talleyrand, Gerry maintained that the French government had changed its position and was anxious to make peace.[30] Fisher Ames might wonder at some of Gerry's inconsistencies, but Cabot was despondent, for he realized that the envoy's views had a very wide appeal indeed. The president could feel gratified because his foreign policy had produced positive results without resort to all-out war, while the Republicans and the "half way men," as he called the moderate Federalists, would jump at a chance for peace. Such a coalition would be impossible to overcome.[31]

Depressed by Cabot's unconfirmed reports, Pickering soon received proof that much had gone awry in Braintree. Toward the end of October the president forwarded Gerry's long response to Pickering's published criticism. Adams asked the secretary of state to publish it, remarking, perhaps disingenuously, that it would satisfy Gerry and harm no one.[32] Pickering refused. He hadn't the least intention of publishing the vindication of someone he himself had publicly chastised. Moreover, he believed it would be a serious political error for the administration to in effect endorse Gerry's views by publishing his piece without comment. His emotions now fully aroused, Pickering began to improvise upon a theme he had only touched upon earlier in his published criticism of Gerry's behavior in Paris. He soon convinced himself that while in Paris Gerry had been more than Talleyrand's dupe, that he had knowingly collaborated with the French Foreign Ministry much to the disadvantage of Marshall and Pinckney. Pickering warned the president that if Gerry's remarks were published he was prepared to counterattack by pointing up not only the envoy's "pusillanimity, weakness, and meanness, . . . but his duplicity and treachery as well."[33]

Rather than provoke another cabinet crisis by insisting that Pickering publish Gerry's letter, the weary Adams let the matter drop. Simultaneously he asked Gerry not to publish the piece himself, for he wanted no newspaper controversies at that juncture.[34] It was fortunate for Pickering that Adams thus kept him from a public name-calling match with Gerry. The publication of the Talleyrand-Gerry correspondence and the spread of Gerry's view that peace was attainable were rapidly transforming the returned envoy into a figure of almost heroic stature. Had he run for the governship of Massachusetts in 1799, Adams's secretary, William S. Shaw, remarked, Gerry would in all likelihood have been elected by a very great majority.[35]

The effect of all this was almost more than Pickering could bear. Desperate, he sought the sympathetic ear of the British minister, Robert Liston, who duly reported these conversations to the Foreign Office. Recent events, Liston wrote, had created "a gloom over the minds of . . . members of the administration." Secretary of State Pickering sought war but France proved unobliging. She would neither attack the United States nor press for diplomatic advantage. Instead she returned Gerry with memorials which, Liston continued, "appear to demonstrate that the limits of French moderation have been farther stretched and that there is no meanness to which the Directory will not stoop when an important object is in contemplation."[36]

Pickering knew that of the three envoys originally sent to Paris only John Marshall had impressed President Adams with his performance. Having read and copied Marshall's journal of his stay in the French capital, he was also cognizant of the fact that the Virginia Federalist thought Gerry had been used by Foreign Minister Talleyrand. Aware that Marshall was the only man in the country with the stature to discredit Gerry, not only in the eyes of the president but possibly with the public as well, Pickering attempted to convince him to publish some "animadversions" that might bring Gerry's reliability into question.[37] As a candidate for Congress, however, Marshall had no intention of attacking Gerry, for though his ideas may have been incorrect, they were nevertheless enormously popular. Instead he attempted to put some distance between himself and the more militant Federalists, first by divorcing himself from the unpopular Alien and Sedition Laws and then by beginning to hedge on the peace issue.[38] Though insistent that when he left Paris there had been no possibility of a profitable negotiation, Marshall was willing to concede that the French might since have changed their attitude. Perhaps Gerry was not altogether wrong.[39] In keeping with his moderate approach, Marshall refused to allow Pickering to show President Adams those portions of his journal that were critical of Gerry's behavior in Paris.[40]

While the frustrated Pickering awaited further developments in Philadelphia, in faraway Braintree President Adams began to reconsider his foreign policy. The fact that Alexander Hamilton had effective control over the army gave the jittery president, who never discounted the possibility that the New Yorker might attempt a coup, good reason to seek a peaceful settlement with France and the swift demobilization of the army. A variety of political considerations pointed in the same direction. Aware of the disadvantages attendant upon maintaining a large and expensive army in the absence of an obvious military threat, Adams feared the rise of an "enthusiasm" against his administration if the tax burden were not lessened.[41] Nor was the political significance of Elbridge Gerry's sudden popularity lost upon him. Though Adams continued to distrust the French and does not appear to have been so credulous as was Gerry about the chances for peace, he could not afford to ignore his old friend.

The results of the congressional elections of 1798 offered further evidence of the political changes facing the administration. Though the Federalists won a twenty-vote majority in the House, the reliability of many newly elected southern Federalists was questionable. Moreover, in certain key states, including Pennsylvania, New Jersey, and Maryland, Federalism actually lost representation. Adams may well have seen this as an indication of growing public disenchantment with the costs of quasi war.[42] How else was one to evaluate the reelection of the militant Vermont Republican Congressman Matthew Lyon, or the election to the House of Dr. George Logan from Pennsylvania? When Logan had come to him after his notorious attempt at personal diplomacy in Paris, Adams had paid no attention to him at all. Evidently

Pennsylvania's voters took the self-appointed peacemaker more seriously.[43]

If political considerations encouraged Adams to think in terms of renewed talks, so too did foreign developments. There were, after all, positive signs that France might be reconsidering her earlier policy. Talleyrand's assurances to Gerry could not be completely ignored, especially since the Directory had given a substantive signal that it was interested in talks. Privateering had been sharply curtailed, and a long-established embargo on American shipping in French ports had been lifted.[44] Also, Adams received from William Vans Murray at the Hague a letter from Talleyrand to Louis Pichon, the French secretary of legation in Holland. This letter in some ways approximated the assurances he had insisted upon as a precondition to the renewal of negotiations. The cumulative effect of these considerations was not to convince the cautious Adams that he should suggest a reopening of talks. But with the opening of the December session of Congress just around the corner, it was enough to lead him to conclude that the door should be left open for French initiatives.[45]

If Adams's thinking strayed in the direction of peace, even Timothy Pickering was forced to conclude, albeit disconsolately, that there was no chance Congress would declare war that December. This is not to suggest, however, that he was willing to seek an accommodation with France. On the contrary, hoping that naval engagements and other incidents might yet produce full-scale war, he set himself the task of persuading the president that at the very least the undeclared naval war should be continued and every effort made to convince Congress to increase military spending. But when Adams finally arrived in Philadelphia, he showed little interest in serious discussions with his secretary of state. It was no wonder, for the president's opening address to Congress, in direct contradiction to Pickering's advice, was a clear signal to France that he was interested in reopening talks.[46]

The president's speech left Pickering confused and angered. Adams had made a terrible error, he complained. The crisis of 1798 had stimulated something akin to national unity, at least giving the administration a working majority in Congress. Now that advantage had been thrown away, and for nothing. Convinced that the French were insincere, Pickering believed that they wanted to reopen talks only in order to rekindle dissension within the United States. His fear of the Machiavellian qualities of French statecraft having long since led him to discount the utility of diplomacy, he continued to believe that no treaty could offer real security, since it would be violated when the Directory found the moment convenient. The only alternative to French domination, he thought, was "eternal animosity."[47]

What Pickering did not (and indeed could not) yet realize was that his serious difficulties with John Adams were just beginning. The president, having decided to pursue the possibility of further negotiations, knew that his cabinet would not approve. Rather than debate the issue pointlessly, he fixed on a policy of unilateral decision-making that left Pickering a mere observer, frustrated and unable to influence the course of events.

Shortly after his surprising December address to Congress, Adams took another step that revealed his determination to keep Pickering isolated and ineffective. The secretary of state was in possession of Elbridge Gerry's as yet unpublished correspondence with Talleyrand as well as a long memorandum that Gerry had written vindicating his behavior in Paris. Adams wanted these documents submitted to Congress and made public. But Pickering refused, fearing that in the wake of Adams's recent congressional address publication would strengthen the peace movement. During the following month he ignored three separate requests from the president to turn over the documents. Finally Adams did manage to extract them from the State Department, but only by sending his private secretary directly to Pickering with instructions not to take no for an answer.[48]

Pickering had not been altogether dilatory while resisting the president's requests for Gerry's papers. In fact he spent most of that month preparing a "report" designed to discredit Gerry. When the president forced him to relinquish the documents, Pickering asked Adams to include this statement as part of the package to be delivered to Congress. Adams wanted nothing to do with Pickering's report, informing him that neither he nor Congress needed the Talleyrand-Gerry correspondence explained to them. But Pickering persisted and Adams at last agreed, on the condition that he might read and abridge the statement before it was submitted.[49]

Adams was astonished at the nature and extent of Pickering's attack on Gerry. "I scarcely thought that prejudice and party rage could go so far," he later wrote.[50] Though the president lived up to his word, allowing publication of Pickering's report, he did act to undercut its effect. First, he submitted the Gerry-Talleyrand correspondence along with Gerry's carefully written vindication several days before Pickering's report, thus giving these documents a chance to have a public impact before the rebuttal appeared. In the interim he deleted whole sections that Pickering had written, in particular most of a long, slanderous attack on Gerry.[51] Before the report was sent to Congress,

Adams and Pickering had a bitter confrontation over the deletions. The secretary "reddened with rage or grief," Adams recalled, "as if he had been bereaved of a darling child." He even demeaned himself, begging the president to allow the unabridged report to go to Congress. Though the argument continued for half the night, Adams was adamant. The next morning Pickering was back again, demanding that the president restore the censored passages. But Adams was in no mood to compromise. The document seemed outrageous enough without the excised portions.[52]

Pickering vented his anger against the president in a spate of letters to Federalist friends. The deletions had made portions of his pamphlet seem disjointed, unconnected. But more important, in cutting out most of his references to Gerry, Pickering charged that Adams had struck at the heart of his work. Without those passages to guide them, he feared, many would "read and respect" Gerry's views.[53]

It is clear in retrospect that from the beginning of the December session of Congress, Adams, charting his own course, was unwilling to allow the secretary of state to play any significant role in policy formulation. If that was not obvious at first, it came crashing home to Pickering on February 18, 1799, when without any consultation the president nominated William Vans Murray to negotiate a settlement with France. Quickly Pickering sought to divest himself of any responsibility for what seemed to him another incredible blunder. Unwilling that anyone should think that he had endorsed this decision, he explained that prior to the nomination no one in the cabinet had the least notion of what the president intended.[54]

While Pickering fumed, a Senate committee, composed exclusively of staunch Federalists, undertook the delicate task of changing John Adams's mind. A conference was arranged at the president's house. At first the discussion was polite on both sides. But when Theodore Sedgwick momentarily lost his temper and suggested that Adams had been unduly influenced by Gerry, the president grew angry, refusing to withdraw the nomination. It was his duty as president, he exclaimed, "to defend against oligarchic influence." The full Senate, he insisted, would have to take action. Then, however, the reputedly headstrong Adams regained his composure and informed the committee that should Murray's nomination be rejected, he would appoint a negotiating commission. The commission members would remain in the United States until the Directory had given positive assurances as stipulated in his message of June 21, 1798, that they would be received and serious negotiations undertaken.[55]

The next evening Senate Federalists met in caucus at the home of

William Bingham. With Adams's offer of a compromise already before them, the senators agreed unanimously to vote against the Murray nomination. The next day, the committee drafted a report to the full Senate recommending rejection. Adams must have learned that the nomination was certain to be rejected, for at the last moment, even as a Senate clerk was making a final copy of the committee report, he withdrew Murray's name and nominated instead a negotiating commission to include Murray, Patrick Henry (who was later replaced by North Carolina's William R. Davie), and Chief Justice Oliver Ellsworth.[56] True to his word, Adams also stipulated that the two men selected to join Murray were not to sail until assurances had been obtained from France that they, like Murray, would be received in character and that purposeful negotiations would be undertaken. This, of course, meant that there would be a delay of several months as messages made their way back and forth across the Atlantic.[57]

At the State Department, Pickering was somewhat mollified by the fact that the president had been forced to compromise and that there would be a delay of some months before the envoys could sail for France. He even became momentarily optimistic when, after two months of unilateral decision-making, Adams again consulted his cabinet, this time inexplicably giving Pickering a free hand in drafting instructions for the envoys. To the secretary of state it seemed a heaven-sent opportunity to place peace out of reach by setting the price too high. And what a set of instructions they were! Even Oliver Ellsworth thought elements of them *"unusually* degrading" to France and warned Pickering that if the talks failed and the instructions were ever published, it would be nearly impossible to defend the administration against the charge that it had not sought an agreement in good faith.[58]

Elated for a time by the thought that the Directory would not accept the terms he had drawn up, Pickering soon reverted to a favorite theme. The Directory would undoubtedly agree to any conditions, even those he had drafted, if it suited their purposes. The problem was that France could not be trusted to live up to her agreements.[59] George Cabot was equally depressed. It made little difference, he thought, whether one or a trio of ambassadors was sent to Paris. The essential damage was done in either event, for Adams's decision led the nation to think in terms of negotiation rather than "resistance."[60] If it was any consolation to Pickering, he received like-minded messages from Federalists in all parts of the country. Washington disapproved of the decision to reopen the talks, as did Fisher Ames. "No one respects more sincerely the talents and virtues of our chief," Ames wrote, "But few know better than I do, the singularities that too frequently discredit his prudence." [61]

It would have been unlike Pickering finally to acquiesce in presidential decision-making without some further effort to undercut Adams. Thus, late in the spring of 1799 he and James McHenry, working together as they had during the struggle for control of the army, made a desperate and farfetched attempt to disrupt communications between the president and William Vans Murray, his only direct contact with Talleyrand. Hoping to prejudice Murray against the renewal of negotiations, Pickering regaled him with the general line then being taken by extreme Federalists. The nomination of a commission, he argued, had been a major blunder, for there could be no security in any treaty with France. "The Pentarchy of the Luxembourg must be overturned," he railed, "before any safe negotiation can take place with France." [62] Meanwhile McHenry, a personal friend of Murray's, tried to convince him to send no more information on French affairs directly to the president. The secretary of war told Murray that Pickering and "the old man" were very much at odds with "no love lost" either way. He further explained that Pickering knew of Murray's earlier correspondence with the president, but felt it would be "expedient" if in the future Murray addressed all "official business" to the State Department. The secretary of state was much distressed at Murray's earlier contacts with Louis Pichon, McHenry warned. He wanted no further contact with the Directory, at least for the immediate future. [63]

This outlandish attempt to undermine the negotiations at their source came to nothing. Near the end of July, Pickering received a dispatch from Murray enclosing a letter from Talleyrand that gave the precise assurances Adams had earlier required as a precondition to negotiations. [64] Given a different set of circumstances Pickering might have been tempted to suppress this letter. But having heard nothing from Murray about the plan to disrupt the Adams-Talleyrand connection, he had to assume that the president either already knew or would soon find out about the French foreign minister's recent concession. He had no choice but to forward the letter to the president. [65]

Adams responded promptly, instructing Pickering to proceed with the drafting of the envoys' instructions, which were to be sent to him at Braintree for his final approval. Though Pickering preferred that Adams return to the capital, the president, distracted by his wife's prolonged illness, saw no need to leave his home. The secretary could take care of any last-minute details. It was August 6, and Adams wanted the envoys on their way as quickly as possible. [66]

Aware of Adams's sense of urgency, Pickering nonetheless did not send a completed draft of the envoys' instructions to Braintree until the second week in September.[67] And though delay was in part the result of the government's flight from Philadelphia to Trenton to avoid an outbreak of yellow fever, the secretary of state was clearly seeking a way to forestall the sailing of the envoys. Although it seemed unlikely that Adams would listen, he nonetheless wrote to the president urging him to reconsider sending the commission.[68] Privately, the secretary of state admitted to Rufus King that he believed the time was long overdue for the United States to join England and her allies.[69] Cognizant of how such an argument would be received in Braintree, however, he confined himself to more cautious reasoning in his note to Adams. He pointed out that recent news from Europe indicated that the Directory had been overthrown, leaving France in a state of internal chaos. Meanwhile the Russians were driving into Italy and the English were planning an invasion of the Netherlands. The very least the administration should do, he argued, was to suspend the mission until the European situation was clarified.[70]

Pickering was not surprised when the president replied noncommittally.[71] On the contrary, he was utterly dumbfounded when, a few days later, Oliver Ellsworth informed him that Adams had decided to suspend the mission.[72] When he then learned that the president, who had earlier refused to come to the capital in spite of his urging, had suddenly changed his mind, he sensed something important in the wind. At a loss to understand Adams's sudden and unexpected departure from Braintree, the secretary of state assumed that European developments had convinced him to delay the mission indefinitely.[73]

Pickering, of course, had no way of knowing that Adams had decided to travel to Trenton because Secretary of the Navy Benjamin Stoddert had warned him that certain "artful and designing men" who were seeking to block his reelection were hatching a conspiracy against him there.[74] Nor did he catch the least glimmering of what was on Adams's mind during the six days between his arrival in the temporary capital and the cabinet meeting of October 16. Thus, four days after Adams's appearance in Trenton the secretary of state explained in a note to William Vans Murray that the news from Europe had been so disastrous as far as France was concerned that he fully expected the president would decide not to send the envoys.[75] Of course Pickering, who never mastered the art of fathoming Adams's real intentions, was again disappointed. On the sixteenth the president assembled his cabinet members, heard all their arguments in favor of further delay, and overruled them.

FIFTEEN

Humiliations

ON NOVEMBER 1, 1799, Oliver Ellsworth and William R. Davie sailed to join William Vans Murray in France. Their departure marked the end of any possibility for harmony between Pickering and Adams. In a flurry of letters to Federalist leaders, Pickering dissociated himself from the mission, urging that the president be dropped from the Federalist ticket in 1800. Only if Adams retired at the end of his term, Pickering wrote, would the party be able to reunite and perhaps yet "save the country from ruin."[1]

During the next half-year, relations between Adams and Pickering remained strained and excessively formal. There were, to be sure, infrequent moments during which the tension seemed to relax. Thus in March 1800, at a dinner given by Captain Stephen Decatur on board the new frigate *Philadelphia,* Connecticut's Roger Griswold noted with a mixture of pleasure and amazement that the "whole executive branch of the Government with the President at the head laughed until they wept."[2] But there were few such moments of camaraderie. By now Pickering had nothing but disdain for the president. And Adams, though he kept his own counsel, felt much the same about Pickering.

According to Abigail Adams, her husband was above harboring "the kind of resentments" that might have led another to dismiss such a disloyal subordinate. It seems more likely, however, that the president continued to tolerate Pickering because he hoped to avoid an open break with the extreme wing of his own party. From a purely political standpoint this was probably a mistake. Federalist unity was important, to be sure. But by the end of 1799 other considerations were more pressing. In the face of new taxes imposed to finance an augmented but unpopular army, the rigorous enforcement of the Sedition Law, the high interest rate paid on a large foreign loan, and the appearance on the streets of many cities of swaggering army officers, the electorate was losing patience with extremist policies. An early warning of what was to come was given in October 1799, when Thomas McKean, a former Federalist converted to Republicanism, won a landslide victory over the extreme Federalist James Ross in the race for the governorship of Pennsylvania. Another surprise was provided the following April when Elbridge Gerry, running against the popular Caleb Strong, almost won the governorship of Massachusetts.[3]

In spite of the growing popular disenchantment with radical measures, Adams made no move to separate himself from the extreme wing of his party until early in May 1800, after his reelection hopes were dealt a severe blow by a Republican victory in New York's legislative elections. Since in New York presidential electors were chosen by the legislature, Jefferson was assured of twelve votes that had gone to Adams four years earlier.[4] The president was desolated, while Abigail Adams gloomily predicted victory for Jefferson in November.

On May 3, news of the New York elections reached Philadelphia. Two days later the president allowed his temper to get the better of him, accusing Secretary of War James McHenry of being a tool of Hamilton, one of that small coterie of extremists who were the authors of his current political woes. The distracted McHenry, humiliated by this encounter, felt he had no choice but to resign.[5] Five days later Adams sent a curt note to the State Department requesting Pickering's resignation. On the morning of the twelfth, arrogant and self-righteous to the last, Pickering turned him down. Within an hour another note from Adams dismissing him was lying on the secretary's desk.[6]

Many Federalists agreed with Senator Benjamin Goodhue, who charged that Adams's decision to fire Pickering was an act of retaliation taken because he knew that he could not win the November election.[7] Adams may very well have acted in anger; indeed, he had a great deal to be angry about. Yet, whether or not he planned it that way, Pickering's dismissal did more than satisfy the president's emotional needs. Forcing McHenry, a total nonentity, out of the cabinet was not particularly significant in the broader political context. But dismissing Pickering, the enforcer of the Sedition Law and a symbolically important High Federalist, served as a formal declaration of Adams's break with the extreme wing of his party and was certain to strengthen his political appeal among moderates and Republicans during the remainder of the election campaign.[8]

Angry and embittered, Pickering immediately became an enthusiastic collaborator with Alexander Hamilton in the attempt to supplant Adams with Charles C. Pinckney.[9] Yet, although the two men agreed on the importance of dropping Adams, their approaches to this problem were wholly disparate. Hamilton sought an undifferentiated vote from New England's Federalist electors for both Adams and Pinckney, counting on South Carolina, which voted last, to drop a few Adams votes and give Pinckney the victory in the electoral count.[10] But that scheme was far too subtle for the angry Pickering, who sought personal vindication in a futile attempt to convince New England's Federalists to repudiate Adams entirely.[11]

As Pickering mobilized his emotions for the struggle against Adams, he magnified the president's past improprieties, distorting his purposes in grotesque ways until at last Adams became another of those diabolical enemies against whom he had battled throughout his lifetime. How easy it was for Pickering to convince himself of even the most outlandish perversions when he was aroused! And certainly never in his life had he been more bitter or felt greater humiliation than at that moment. Convinced that when the enemies of virtue were on the prowl they would seek to destroy him first, he soon came to believe that he had been the earliest victim of a massive political conspiracy.

After the New York elections, Pickering argued, the president realized that he could not win in November. But rather than leave office with dignity and give Pinckney the opportunity to succeed him and thus save Federalism and the country, he struck a bargain for the vice-presidency with Jefferson. Pickering claimed that his dismissal and the president's later decision to pardon Daniel Fries as well as other Northampton rebels constituted the price Adams had been required to pay for the vice-presidency.[12] "Mark my words," he wrote to his nephew, the Boston merchant Timothy Williams, "whatever interest Mr. Adams shall take in the choice of electors in Massachusetts, it will be to secure Mr. Jefferson's election & to exclude General Pinckney."[13] Through a process of repetition and elaboration Pickering moved beyond personal conviction to fixation. Federalists, he insisted, had no honorable choice left save to repudiate the president.

But New England's leaders were unwilling to follow where Pickering's frenzied imaginings led. Samuel Dexter, soon to accept an appointment as Adams's secretary of war, would have nothing whatever to do with the idea of abandoning the president. Such an attempt, he warned, would "crumble the Federal party to atoms."[14] From New Haven, Timothy Dwight alerted Pickering's friend Senator James Hillhouse to the importance of uniting behind Adams. "The old sore of the embassy is, or ought to be healed," he wrote. Otherwise Jefferson was certain to win in November.[15] Even George Cabot, who was bitterly disappointed by Adams's performance as president, saw no reasonable alternative but to support him.[16] On June 2, Senator Benjamin Goodhue, Pickering's emissary to the Federalist Party in Massachusetts, reported that it would be impossible to convince any of the state's electors to abandon Adams. "The attempt," he thought, "would throw the state into a convulsion."[17]

Pickering was utterly bewildered by his inability to persuade Federalist friends. Had the specter of Jefferson in the presidential mansion paralyzed their senses? He at any rate was convinced that even the Virginian was preferable to Adams, "whose self-sufficiency and capriciousness put everything at hazard."[18]

Pickering had only a short while to pursue his fanciful political schemes. Financial difficulties made it impossible for him to spend more than a few weeks in Philadelphia. What money he had been able to scrape together during his years in the capital had been sunk in worthless southern lands. Though he owned in excess of 120,000 acres in Pennsylvania, Kentucky, and North Carolina, he had nothing that could be converted into cash. Yet if Pickering was dismayed by this radical change in his circumstances, he gave no sign of it. Within a week after his dismissal, his future plans had matured. In company with his sons Henry and Timothy, he intended to develop his Pennsylvania holdings. Like some biblical patriarch he would clear a farm site, build a house, barn, sawmill, and gristmill, and begin life anew.[19]

But Pickering did not intend to remain isolated in the woods forever. Pennsylvania had at last enacted the Confirming Act that he had fought for thirteen years before. With the Wyoming dispute all but settled and the war in Europe over, he imagined a new wave of immigration would soon sweep into the back country. He would farm some of his lands, sell the rest at a great profit, and in the end probably return to Massachusetts a wealthy man.[20] It was the old vision revived, and despite strong opposition from family and friends he was determined once again to pursue it.[21]

Philadelphia had been the dream, and for years the family had lived it. They had not become rich, but neither were they poor. Moreover, Timothy and Rebecca Pickering had enjoyed something quite as important to them—cabinet status and social standing. Watching their household being dismantled, they must have felt as though life itself was being ripped and shredded. But the process was inexorable. Before the end of June all the necessary arrangements had been made. Furniture and other belongings that would not be needed or could not be fitted into the wagons hired to carry the family west were sold. There were a few farewells to old and dear friends, and then on June 28 the travelers were on their way.[22]

As the wagons rumbled through the streets of a city that had been home for so long, there was time for introspection, contemplation. How long ago was it that Pickering and his young wife had first ridden down from Salem to Philadelphia with baby John sleeping in the back of the wagon? Could he remember the songs they had sung along the way? Would there never come a time when he and Beckey would be able to forsake travel in wagons for the carriages that bore so many others? He ruminated over a wasted career and dwelt on his hatred for John Adams. Once out of the city the travelers became more cheerful. The countryside was beautiful in the early summer. It was easier to think about the future.

At Easton, Pickering left Beckey and his younger children with Samuel Sitgreaves, a Pennsylvania friend. Then, together with his son Henry and a few laborers, he began the assault upon the wilderness.[23] But four months of unremitting toil yielded little. Two small log houses, one for the laborers and the other for the family, were built from rough timber sawed on the site. Seven acres were cleared and planted and another twelve were cut over, the stumps prepared for burning during the coming spring. In all Pickering expected that even if he could keep two laborers working through the winter cutting trees he would still have no more than thirty acres ready for planting by the following year.[24]

Superficially at least the New Englander maintained his optimism. He wrote to his son John, then returning to the United States from London, that he was "not discouraged" by the slow start he had made. The family was in good health and neither he nor Rebecca had allowed themselves to "sink under misfortune."[25] But the fact was that by winter Pickering was already showing signs of discontent. Pioneering had been "more laborious, tedious, and expensive" than he had supposed. Moreover, he had expected a flood of German immigrants in western Pennsylvania and a consequent increase in land values. Their failure to appear heightened the gloom.[26]

In January Pickering set off for the East, stopping first in Philadelphia and then traveling on to New York, Boston, and finally Salem, where he received a warm welcome from family and friends. He had not returned home simply to renew old family ties, however. Desperate, he hoped to interest those closest to him in purchasing some of his Pennsylvania lands.[27]

In the past family members had always scoffed at Pickering's land speculations. This time, however, they seemed to recognize the psychological requirements of the situation. Nobody scoffed. Instead the family and Pickering became involved in a simple charade. Each side understood exactly what was at issue, but certain rites had first to be performed. Before Pickering could accept assistance it had to seem as though the people about to extricate him from his latest economic difficulties were really intent upon making a sound investment. They managed it very well, with first one and then another member of the family drawing Pickering out on the subject of his lands. Finally, when the appropriate psychological moment had been reached, Samuel Putnam proposed the organization of a subscription for the purchase of a large portion of Pickering's Pennsylvania holdings.[28] In no time at all thirty-four relatives and friends subscribed $25,000 for the purchase of 14,250 acres of largely worthless land. Part of the money was earmarked for the purchase of a farm for the Pickerings somewhere near Salem. The rest was to be managed by merchant friends. Pickering was to have no future opportunities for risky land-buying ventures.[29]

The list of subscribers who purchased lands from Pickering included some of the most prominent men in the state, among whom Stephen Higginson, George Cabot, John Lowell, Jr., and William Gray were only four. In effect, a significant element of the Massachusetts Federalist Party had banded together to bring Pickering back to his home state. Nor had they done this entirely out of charity. Among those who contributed to his return were many who viewed him as a distinct political asset. He was, in the first place, one among a declining number of active leaders of the revolutionary generation with a tie to the immortal Washington as well as a national political reputation. His significance extended beyond this, however, for to an older generation of Massachusetts Federalists, men whose eighteenth-century values were rapidly becoming anachronistic as a result of social and political change, he was the incarnation of an elitist past—their link with tradition. A "gentleman of the old school," he was resuscitated politically by men of similar convictions, who believed that even in an increasingly democratic age Massachusetts society was still sufficiently deferential to ensure that a man of Pickering's stature could win elections.[30]

Specifically, these old-line Federalists hoped that Pickering would be able to win the congressional seat from the Essex South district in the elections to come in 1802. But success was no foregone conclusion. During the preceding two years Republicanism had made enormous gains in Massachusetts. Even normally Federalist Essex County was showing signs of disaffection. There, led by the powerful Crowninshield family of Salem, the Jeffersonians had stolen a march on the old oligarchy, organizing themselves for a serious challenge to the established order. With a newspaper of their own, the *Salem Impartial Register,* and a vigorous congressional candidate, Captain Jacob Crowninshield, the Republicans had come within a few votes of winning the formerly safe Essex South district in the preceding congressional election.[31] Crowninshield was certain to run again in 1802. But would the Federalists be able to win this time? Obviously some thought Pickering was the key.

To all intents and purposes Timothy Pickering had been bought and paid for. Any doubts he himself may have harbored on this account were resolved early in 1802 as he searched for a suitable farm in the vicinity of Salem. At that time Theodore Lyman, his nephew and one of the subscribers, told him that he need not be too seriously concerned about the size of the farm or the quality of its land. He would be in Congress much of the time in any event and unable to manage a large place. Sometime later Pickering explained to Beckey that his friends, "whose liberal conduct enabled me to pay my debts and remove to Massachusetts," seemed "to have had in view my engaging in public affairs."[32]

Toward the end of 1801 the Pickering family moved once more, this time to Danvers, a few miles from Salem, where they rented a small farm. A kinder fate would have left Pickering to live out the remainder of his days pouring over his papers, planning his various vindications, nursing his hates, and pontificating on the evils of Jeffersonian America. Instead, however, he was soon back in political harness as the Federalist candidate for Congress from the Essex South district. As expected, the Republican nominee was again Jacob Crowninshield. The *Salem Gazette*, which endorsed Pickering, predicted an extremely close race. Every Federalist, the *Gazette* intoned, would have to do his duty.[33]

The election was hotly contested, with the Jeffersonians showing far more in the way of party organization than the Federalists.[34] While Crowninshield and his friends campaigned through the district, William Coleman's newspaper, the *Register*, attacked Pickering mercilessly. His indecisiveness at the Battle of Lexington was used against him. He was pilloried for his support of the Alien and Sedition Laws, for his failure to defend American seamen impressed into the Royal Navy, and for his endorsement of large-scale military spending as well as tax increases during the Adams administration. He had quarreled with Washington and he had quarreled with Adams, who "dismissed him," one author wrote. And now "the Tories want to send him to quarrel with Mr. Jefferson."[35]

While the Republicans fought a vigorous, rough-and-tumble campaign, Pickering played the role assigned to old-style eighteenth-century elitists who believed that candidates stood but did not run for office. He remained rooted to his little farm like Cincinnatus awaiting the call of his people.[36] Thomas Cushing's *Salem Gazette* tried to fight back against the *Register's* raucous attacks but was largely ineffective because Cushing too sought to project a genteel image. On October 1 the *Gazette* published a list of candidates. Pickering's name, along with others described by the *Gazette* as "friends of the system of Government represented by Washington and Adams"—an irony that was not lost on the opposition—was capitalized. Voters were urged to support them.[37] In subsequent issues, in a column carefully labeled *"Electioneering,"* polite letters either endorsing or defending Pickering regularly appeared.[38]

Election day 1802 was a sad one for Federalism in Massachusetts. Pickering lost the Essex South district by 107 votes. In Suffolk County, John Quincy Adams, also standing for Congress, went down to defeat, as did Federalist candidates in two other districts. For the first time in history the Massachusetts congressional delegation was divided evenly between Federalists and Republicans. The *Salem Gazette,* surveying the postelection ruins, lamented that "the cause of federalism is lost in this state. . . . The devil is in Massachusetts!"[39]

Satan had not yet managed, however, to overwhelm the state legislature, where the Federalists still clung to a majority. Early in 1803 they had the opportunity to strengthen the party's national representation by appointing two United States senators, one to a full six-year term and a second to the unexpired term of the retiring Dwight Foster. In the state house of representatives, where nominations were decided, rival factions within the Federalist Party, one supporting Pickering and the other predisposed to John Quincy Adams, immediately began to war with each other over which candidate was to have the full term. Disputes between Pickering and the Adams family always had a tendency to get out of hand, and this was no exception. On February 2, the Federalist caucus met to work out a compromise. It was agreed that Federalists in the House would unite behind Pickering for the first two ballots but that if he had not won the nomination by that time, they would shift their support to Adams.[40] During the first two trials, Pickering proved unable to defeat his Republican opponent. On the third ballot many Federalists, though not all, deserted Pickering. On the fourth test Adams won nomination for the full six-year Senate term by just one vote.[41] A humiliated Pickering was subsequently chosen to fill out Dwight Foster's unexpired Senate term.

SIXTEEN

Hysteria, the First Secessionist Conspiracy

THE JUNIOR SENATOR from Massachusetts arrived in Washington in October 1803. Though chagrined by his recent humiliation at the hands of the younger Adams, he was nevertheless delighted to be back at the focus of national affairs. The return from exile was a kind of personal vindication that left him, at least momentarily, in high spirits. Even his first view of the new capital did not dampen that enthusiasm. Most observers were appalled on catching their earliest glimpse of Washington, for the town, situated on a virtual swamp, was at best uninviting. But Pickering thought it a "delightful site for a large city."[1] He moved in at Coyle's, a boarding house on Capitol Hill that catered exclusively to Federalists, quickly renewed some old acquaintanceships, and soon felt quite at home.[2]

The Federalist Party in Congress was badly in need of regeneration. During the preceding two years Federalists had shown no understanding of the role of the minority in a two-party system. They acted as individuals bound together by a loosely defined set of principles, rather than as a cohesive political coalition. Worse, they seemed unconcerned with the development of alternatives to Jeffersonian policies, confining themselves instead to a pointless obstructionism that only damaged their reputation with the electorate.[3]

Pickering, a nationally known political figure, was in a unique position to offer the leadership congressional Federalists lacked. Yet, although he seems to have expected to lead, he was utterly unsuited to the task. Some younger congressional Federalists—John Quincy Adams and New Hampshire's William Plumer, to name two—realized that the art of politics in the republic was changing, and that if Federalism was to survive it would have to change, too. But Pickering was of an older generation. No more penetrating than most of the antique gentlemen he had come to join, he committed himself to a generally ill-considered and futile opposition to all measures of Republican origin. Nor would he be bound by that fundamental principle of modern politics, party unity. On the contrary, where harmony was essential he allowed his personal hatred for John Quincy Adams to intrude, further weakening the Federalist coalition in the Senate.[4]

The great majority of Pickering's senatorial colleagues wanted little to do with him, consigning him to that backwater of bitterness he and a few other Federalist extremists had marked out for themselves. He was never placed on committees of any importance; in fact, he was seldom chosen to serve on committees at all. Moreover, though he often played an active part in the debates, his speeches, bitter and vituperative, frequently did the Federalists more harm than good. Pickering, William Plumer noted, was honest enough, but "passionate and imprudent." His "manners and habits" were "too abrupt," even to the point of "disgusting" many in the Senate. As a result, when he spoke the effect was usually to turn at least "some of the Senate against him." Plumer was nonplused: "I really wish he had more prudence & would content himself with voting only."[5]

Pickering found it frustrating to be part of a tiny and largely inconsequential minority. To a degree this was the normal reaction one might expect from a senator who found himself politically impotent. But his agonies ran deeper, for he sensed that a revolution had taken place in 1800, that he had become part of a dwindling collection of displaced and repudiated leaders. It seemed to him the ultimate tragedy that in the end the Revolution should have come to nothing, that "the real patriots of '76" should have been "overwhelmed by the modern pretenders to that character."[6]

Strangely, however, Pickering was unwilling to take any action to reverse this. Some other Federalists (Alexander Hamilton and Fisher Ames were the most prominent) urged the creation of a national political organization as the only feasible solution to their difficulties. In Massachusetts a group of younger Federalists aided by Ames, George Cabot, and some others of Pickering's generation went further, actually organizing a modern political party that functioned efficiently at the state level. But the incurably individualistic Pickering played no part in these efforts, preferring instead to remain a political anachronism. He would not support efforts to create a national Federalist Party. Nor (save for a brief period in 1808) did he play any influential role in Massachusetts party councils where more practical men ruled.

Of course, the frustrations created by membership in a permanent and increasingly irrelevant minority required some form of adaptation.

And so in a move which, if it did not accomplish anything of a practical nature nevertheless fulfilled certain pressing psychological needs, Pickering made the quantum jump into political fantasy. Typically, his was a world of distorted images where evil was arrayed against good and there was no room for compromise.

One of Pickering's most tortured misperceptions was an elaborate conspiracy theory that he developed to explain the changes that had occurred in American political life since 1800. Incapable of viewing Republicanism as a legitimate political alternative to Federalism, he argued instead that Jefferson headed a diabolical plot designed to overthrow the virtuous political order established during the Federalist era.[7] The sole aim of the Jeffersonian leadership, Pickering insisted, was to perpetuate itself in power. To accomplish this, "our masters" (he was fond of the obvious double entendre) would always curry favor with the ignorant public, even at the expense of the national interest. This was especially true of Jefferson, who he believed was bent upon making himself "President for life." Nor was the Constitution any defense against the Republican assault; it had become nothing more than "clay in the hands of the potter." When it was not convenient to violate it, as Jefferson and his followers had done in the case of the Louisiana Purchase, they had the votes to alter it to meet their needs, as they had done in passing the Twelfth Amendment.[8]

Obviously Pickering's fantasies reflected his deeply rooted moral self-image. But they served one other important psychological function, too. As a representative of truth and virtue in a corrupt society, he was given the opportunity for martyrdom. "Virtue in the country has been lost," Pickering declared. His only consolation came from being associated with those few who had not yet "bowed" before "Baal" and who still held "fast their integrity."[9] Federalism, he thought, would probably be overwhelmed by the Jeffersonian leviathan. Nevertheless, it was better to end virtuously than to surrender to corruption and survive. If Pickering's imagery was magnificently heroic, his prediction was for ultimate defeat. Yet his clear intention was to make no compromise where principle was involved. More practical minds would not understand, but Pickering found something very fulfilling in this.

The New Englander was able to sustain and nurture his distorted perceptions with regard to both Jeffersonian purposes and his own role in national affairs because he lacked the capacity for empathy. He was incapable of sharing, even vicariously, perceptions held by members of the opposition. Moreover, he proved a past master at what psychologists sometimes refer to as "selective inattention."[10] Quick to focus on those aspects of Republican public policy that supported his already established and flourishing fantasies, he was equally innovative at twisting the meaning of events to meet psychological needs, while ignoring developments that challenged rooted notions.

Consider, for example, Pickering's reaction to Jefferson's policy regarding the removal of Federalist office holders. It is generally conceded that the president acted with a degree of restraint, even to the point of angering many of his more ardent supporters.[11] Pickering, however, viewed the president's moderate policy as brilliantly Machiavellian. Had he proceeded at once to act against the entire Federalist bureaucracy, replacing its members with such "creatures" as he chose, Pickering wrote, "even his followers . . . would have been shocked." By proceeding slowly, he avoided rebellion in the ranks. Moreover, by making it clear that public office would go only to those who collaborated with him, Jefferson corrupted good men who became apostates not only to Federalism but "to virtue, . . . religion, . . . and to good government" as well. In this way "Mr. Jefferson's plan of corruption" moved toward its real end, "the subversion of the Constitution, and the prostration of every barrier erected by it for the protection of the best . . . part of the community."[12]

Pickering structured his life in Washington as though determined to diminish the possibility that any of his misperceptions might be challenged. He seldom attended social gatherings where Jeffersonians might be present and exchanged views with members of the opposition only on the floor of the Senate. Living at Coyle's was in itself a defense against foreign ideas. There, the little group of embattled Federalists spent evenings by the hearthside reinforcing one another's prejudices. Uriah Tracy, the senator from Connecticut, could ramble by the hour, entertaining his fellow lodgers with that humorous banter for which he was justly famous. But it was a cynical patter, gallows humor.[13]

Like the besieged defenders of a castle nearly in ruins, Pickering, Tracy, James Hillhouse, and most of the others living at Coyle's fought to keep aliens and their ideas out. Senator William Plumer, more open-minded than the rest, found the situation increasingly difficult. He welcomed exchanges with Jeffersonian congressmen but found his opportunities limited because he could not invite members of the opposition to visit him at his lodgings. "I dare not invite a gentleman to call upon me whose politics are different," he wrote, "lest those violent inmates should treat him with rudeness and insults." Pickering was among the worst in this regard. His "prejudices," Plumer wrote, were "oftimes too strong for his reason." As Plumer drifted away from the Federalists, he at last concluded that this was more than a simple matter of imprudence. Pickering, Tracy, and the rest were, in fact, political bigots who had lost all perspective.[14]

Satisfied that the Jeffersonian conspiracy was aimed not only at permanent hegemony but also at "the destruction of every influential Federalist, and of every man of considerable property who was not of the reigning sect," Pickering grew hysterical.[15] Within three months of coming to Congress, he had seen enough to convince him that only by seceding from the Union could the northern states escape the clutches of this villainous force.

Three issues—the acquisition of Louisiana, the enactment of the Twelfth Amendment to the Constitution, and the Jeffersonian attack upon the judiciary—outlined for Pickering the parameters of the Jeffersonian conspiracy. The obvious economic and diplomatic advantages that accrued to the United States on acquiring Louisiana are too well understood to deserve mention here. It is important to note, however, that on more than a few occasions during his tenure in the State Department Pickering himself had had cause to wish that this strategically important region were securely in American hands. Yet in 1803, as he speculated on the reasons behind Jefferson's decision to purchase the area, the former secretary of state ignored all such considerations. His analysis of the president's purposes was cast narrowly within the context of his fears of conspiracy. This frame of reference left room for only one explanation of the purchase: it was designed to lay the basis for a permanent southern majority in Congress. The new states to be carved from this huge tract would, Pickering predicted, be developed as slave states. Thus, even if at some time in the future states such as New York and Pennsylvania returned to the Federalist fold, the South would still be able to dominate the nation politically.

Pickering exhibited a similar narrowness in evaluating the Twelfth Amendment to the Constitution, which altered the method of selecting the president and vice-president. The basic motive of those who supported the amendment was to avoid another crisis similar to the one that shook the body politic in 1800, when the presidential election was thrown into the House of Representatives. But Pickering, again influenced by his conspiratorial vision, ignored that very important issue. He was certain, in fact, that the real, though unstated, purpose of the amendment was to exclude the Federalists from winning even the vice-presidency in 1804.[16]

The Jeffersonian attack on the judiciary was the final element in what Pickering conceived to be a many-faceted assault on constitutionalism and virtue in America. The impeachment of the demented Judge John Pickering of New Hampshire (no relation), and rumors to the effect that Justice Samuel Chase of the Supreme Court would be next, convinced the frightened New Englander that the courts were destined to be undermined, too. Soon all the branches of government would be under the control of the atheist Thomas Jefferson. How long would it be before he declared himself "President for life?"[17]

Throughout his long and very active political life, Timothy Pickering had habitually elevated those he opposed to the status of diabolical enemies involved in deeply laid, nefarious conspiracies. His analysis of Jeffersonian purposes is, then, not surprising. It is important to note, however, that he was by no means singular. Rather, he stood as one of the more passionate exponents of a pattern of thinking widely shared in Federalist circles. Shorn of their power at the national level, threatened by the rise of Republicanism in their home states, and with their elitist views becoming increasingly irrelevant in Jeffersonian America, a great many Federalists found psychological refuge in characterizing themselves and their values as the victims of a conspiracy. Thus both George Cabot and Stephen Higginson explained the Louisiana Purchase as part of a "deliberate plan" to diminish New England's influence in an expanded union of states.[18] An equally hysterical Andrew Ellicott denounced the Twelfth Amendment because he was certain that it would "first lead to a consolidation, and then by quick strides to either a consular government, or monarchy." The "torrent of innovation which is now let loose," Ellicott warned, "will overwhelm, and break down every barrier of liberty, open a passage for despotism, and destroy the last and best hope of freedom in the world."[19] Nor were southern Federalists immune from such fears. Henry Laussure, a South Carolinian, viewed the repeal of the Judiciary Law of 1801, the Chase impeachment, and a variety of similar developments at the state level as clear proof "that no paper sanctions" would be sufficient to "guard . . . that feeble branch of government." The Jeffersonians, he was certain, were aiming at "the complete overthrow of the . . . independency of the judiciary."[20]

It is by no means surprising, then, that Pickering's hysteria spread like a contagion through the closed environment of Coyle's. Soon Roger Griswold, William Plumer, Uriah Tracy, James Hillhouse, and most of the others living there as well came to share his fears. These men formed the nucleus of an embryonic secessionist movement, each contacting friends in his home state, attempting to sound the alarm. Interestingly enough, Plumer, who within two years would join the Jeffersonians, was among the most frantic and despairing. Affairs had reached an "important crisis," he explained in a letter to his New

Hampshire friend Jeremiah Mason. The time for action was at hand.[21]

In spite of his frenzy, or perhaps because of it, Pickering gave little thought to the many obstacles that would have to be overcome before his envisioned northern confederacy could become a reality. Thus he simply assumed that once Massachusetts had led the way the other New England states, as well as New Jersey, would quickly follow.[22] As for New York, a state he considered critical to the scheme, the best he could do was to develop a farfetched plan wherein New York's Federalists were to throw their support to Aaron Burr in his coming bid for the governorship there. The quid pro quo was to be Burr's postelection collaboration in the secessionist movement. Nor had Pickering considered methods of responding to military intervention by the national government if the plan were actually attempted. Finally, and perhaps most unrealistically of all, he was thinking of leading Massachusetts out of the Union during a period of economic prosperity and at a time when the Jeffersonians seemed on the verge of becoming the majority party in that state.

The aura of unreality that still hangs over Pickering's disruptive plans notwithstanding, he was in deadly earnest. In fact, his emotions were so completely involved that when confronted by a serious personal crisis that threatened to interfere with his designs he could not bring himself to respond appropriately. The senator's seventeen-year-old son William had always been the slowest, least adept of the children; perhaps he was even mentally retarded. And Pickering, who had long been aware of his son's problems, had been understanding and quite protective of him.[23] Nevertheless, when in 1803 William began to show signs of emotional instability as well, Pickering became obsessed by the belief that somehow his ambition for his children, especially the emphasis he placed upon the importance of education, was a critical factor in the boy's evident emotional difficulties. He tried to talk with William about what was troubling him. He "had got no learning," was the boy's only explanation. Pickering tried to encourage him. There was still the opportunity to go back to school. But William answered sadly, "Tis too late."[24]

The boy's depression grew, becoming increasingly pronounced until at last Pickering sent him to live for a time with his brother, Timothy Jr., who owned a farm at Starucca in western Pennsylvania. Perhaps a change of scene and the beauties of an uncorrupted forestland would relieve some of his son's emotional burden. Unhappily, this proved to be a mistake for, having been sent away from home, William felt only rejection. In December 1803, he ran away from his brother's farm intending to walk back to Massachusetts. He became lost, however, and now, completely distracted, wandered aimlessly in the wilderness for some time before coming upon the home of Dr. Joseph White, an Irish immigrant who lived in Cherry Valley in western New York.

On December 22, 1803, Pickering received a letter from White, informing him of what had befallen his son. The boy, he reported, would say little save to repeat again and again that his father would never forgive him for what he had done. White thought it imperative that he come at once in order to relieve William's awful anxieties.[25] Pickering had been dressing for a dinner to be held later that evening at Secretary Madison's home when White's letter arrived. But he gave up any thought of dining out that night and sat down instead at his writing desk. "Merciful God! Interpose for the relief of our dear son!"[26] The words, part of a letter written to Beckey, spilled across the paper, testimony to his grief.

It was winter and Dr. White's home was nearly five hundred miles from Washington. Nevertheless, Pickering's first instinct was to go at once. James Hillhouse, who shared a room with him at Coyle's, was deeply impressed. "With him the difficulties that attend a journey of four hundred and fifty miles at this inclement season vanish when he hears the voice of his child in distress."[27] Yet despite William's need and his own feelings of guilt, Pickering did not make the trip. There were, to be sure, some predictable rationalizations. But certainly Pickering realized that William was calling for him, that only he might assuage the afflicted boy's overwhelming sense of guilt. His letters, literally imploring Beckey to set William's mind at rest by assuring him that there was nothing to forgive, that his father loved him, testify to this.[28] When he decided against leaving Washington it was not because it made sense to await further news from home, or even because it was winter and travel would be difficult. He stayed because his secessionist plottings had become an overwhelming obsession.

His own extraordinary emotional commitment to secession notwithstanding, Pickering received no encouragement from other frequently like-minded men. His friend Richard Peters remarked on the futility of Federalists attempting any form of political opposition, let let alone leading a secessionist movement. Federalism, he thought, was dead and could never be revived. "The mass of mankind are governed by names, not things," he wrote. "The million have been taught that everything vituperative is meant by federal and Federalist. They will not be saved that way." Unlike Pickering, Peters was not, however, completely despairing. The nation was enjoying "a tide of general prosperity" which, he thought, would "carry the ship on her voyage." He urged

Pickering to "philosophize." Regardless of who was at the helm, things would probably work out reasonably well for the country.[29]

Pickering's closest contacts in New England, though they did not share Peters's optimistic outlook, nevertheless argued that any attempt at secession would be futile. Stephen Higginson warned that not even a majority of Federalists in Massachusetts could be convinced to go along. "Many men of our own party have much . . . of the Democratic taint about them," he wrote. With the Adams family to lead the moderates and thus "keep up a division in the Federal Party here," he predicted, those who advocated secession would lose their influence as soon as they broached the idea.[30]

George Cabot, undoubtedly the most acute observer among Pickering's correspondents, added significantly to Higginson's analysis. There was a flaw in Pickering's understanding of the political situation, which he defined as a sectional conflict between the northeastern and the southern and western states. Cabot noted that the problem crossed regional lines. The critical issue was democracy, which Cabot defined as *"Government of the worst"* and which had firm roots in New England. Under current circumstances, he continued, secession offered no solution at all.[31]

If those in New England who were friendly to Pickering tried gently to persuade him that secession was impossible, Harrison Gray Otis, Josiah Quincy, and other younger Federalist Party leaders in Massachusetts simply ignored him. As one historian has noted, they "went their own way, with the party behind them."[32] But they must have wondered, too, what good it was to have a senator in Washington who was so out of touch with the realities of the political situation in his home state.

In spite of almost universal opposition, Pickering refused to give up his plot. In March he began the serious cultivation of Aaron Burr, whom he had come to view as the crucial figure in his projected new confederacy. Meanwhile he urged Rufus King to support Burr's gubernatorial ambitions and to convince other New York Federalists to do the same.[33] This—as Roger Griswold, a confidant of Pickering's, explained—was a last desperate attempt to accomplish something before democracy overcame them all.[34] It was not only desperate, it was admittedly self-defeating. In throwing their support to Burr, Pickering and other extremists granted him a legitimate claim to become the dominant political figure in the projected northern confederacy. As even Griswold noted, this in itself would probably be enough to discourage many otherwise sympathetic Federalists from supporting the plot.[35]

Pickering found it impossible to convince New York's leading Federalists either to endorse secession or to give Burr their support. Alexander Hamilton especially wanted no part in a plan that projected not only the destruction of the federal union but the political advancement of his archenemy Burr. Aware of Hamilton's unfulfilled military ambitions, Pickering attempted to entice him into cooperation by offering him the command of the army of his phantom confederacy. But Hamilton refused to take the bait.[36] When it was proposed that a meeting of a select group of Federalists be held in Boston in the autumn of 1804 to discuss the possibility of secession, Hamilton did agree to attend. In all likelihood, however, had he lived into the autumn he would only have attempted to discourage the extremists.[37]

There was no conspiratorial meeting in Boston that autumn, but the nation did hold a presidential election that demonstrated just how wrapped in fantasy Timothy Pickering's plans for disunion actually were. Jefferson buried Charles C. Pinckney under a popular landslide. Even Massachusetts gave the Virginian all nineteen of its electoral votes. Stunned, Pickering was forced to acquiesce in the judgment of those who believed that the moment for secession had not yet arrived.

It has often been alleged that Timothy Pickering was a political and ideological leader among New England Federalists.[38] But if the secessionist conspiracy of 1804 demonstrates anything, it proves that even in New England he was no more than one among equals. When his emotions got the better of him, other more practical men of his own generation tried to bring him back to reality, while the younger leaders of the Federalist Party in his home state simply ignored him. As a United States senator, one of the few members of the revolutionary generation who remained active in national politics, Pickering sometimes proved to be a useful political symbol. But he was not an important leader.

SEVENTEEN

Battling the Embargo

IN THE SPRING OF 1805, as Pickering's abbreviated term in the Senate neared its expiration, he toyed with the idea of retirement. At sixty he was weary and depressed. Everywhere, even in Massachusetts, Federalism was in retreat before a rising Republican tide. At home in New England there would be more time for his family; he would be able to take up farming seriously and enjoy the grandchildren that were certain to come along now that both John and Tim Jr. had decided to marry. Such thoughts spun through his brain as he considered the alternative, another six years in Jefferson's capital. Yet they proved in the end no more than the idle speculations of a habitual politician.

After his reelection to the Senate, rationalizations came easily. But they were beside the point, for Pickering thrived on the prestige of being one of a diminishing number of first-generation revolutionaries who remained politically active. In a curious way, too, he was reliving the pattern of his father's life. He persisted in his struggle against the Jeffersonians just as the deacon had pursued a forty-year campaign to reform Salem's First Church. Personal fulfillment in each generation, it seemed, required the continued presence of a diabolical enemy.

In November 1805, Pickering again journeyed to Washington. As before, he and James Hillhouse shared a room at Coyle's, where more than a dozen other Federalists also lived.[1] But the capital was a changed place. Foreign policy problems obscured the domestic issues that had been the focus of political life during Jefferson's first administration. British seizures of American merchant vessels escalated sharply after the famous *Essex* decision, and talk of armed retaliation was heard even among the Federalist merchants of Boston, Salem, and Philadelphia.[2] Theodore Lyman, for example, predicted "hostile proceedings" if England persisted, while denouncing the administration for its failure to arm.[3] Benjamin Goodhue was even more strident. "Rather than have our national rights trampled upon," he stormed, "recourse should be had to arms."[4]

Pickering sympathized with his merchant friends for, like many others, he believed that British policy was not altogether the result of military necessity. It seemed also to be aimed at recapturing a part of world trade once dominated by British interests but lost to the United States as a result of the war.[5] He therefore submitted a memorial to the Senate from Boston's mercantile community attacking the "new constructions of International law" currently "emanating from British courts of admiralty."[6] He also endorsed a resolution sharply critical of Britain's "unprovoked aggression" and helped defeat a move to soften the language of a second resolution instructing the president to "demand and insist upon" reparations as well as "indemnifications" for losses sustained by Americans at the hands of the Royal Navy.[7]

Protest was one thing, but when Republicans in Congress responded to the British challenge with a spate of resolutions aimed at economic retaliation, Pickering decided things had gone too far.[8] Taking his cue from Fisher Ames, George Cabot, and the many merchants who now paused to reconsider their earlier rhetoric, he suddenly shifted his line of reasoning entirely in an effort to check Republican emotionalism before events got out of hand. Had the European conflict been simply another "ordinary" war, he now wrote, resistance would be justified. But this war was no mere dynastic squabble. England was in a struggle for her very existence against an enemy whose ultimate ambition was "to rule the world." She was in fact "fighting our battles with her own blood and treasure." Americans ought, therefore, to be satisfied with that portion of world trade left to them by Great Britain.[9] It might not be an ideal situation, but Pickering had concluded that living within the constraints established by British blockade practices was a more attractive option than war and the total destruction of America's foreign trade.

Timothy Pickering believed that he understood where the genuine national interests of the United States lay. He was equally confident that his perceptions were shared by Jeffersonian leaders. Yet, despite the fact that acquiescence in British depredations seemed the wise course, the administration appeared intent upon defending America's neutral rights. Surely Jefferson was not acting from old sympathies for the French Revolution. Nor did it occur to Pickering to credit the government's avowed concern over impressment and British trade restrictions. Instead, in an analysis that revealed the depth of his contempt for America's new "rulers," he argued that in order to gain power the

Republicans had originally endorsed an Anglophobic foreign policy which, if it satisfied an emotional public, nevertheless ran directly contrary to the national interest. Now they were committed to that policy. Thus, even though administration leaders understood just as clearly as did he that America's "only defense against France" was "Great Britain and that without Britain we would quickly fall subject to Napoleon," they were unwilling to adapt their foreign policy to this reality. To do so would be to admit that the Federalists had been correct all along. Rather than "hazard their popularity" and the political offices that went along with it, Pickering contended, Jefferson and Madison remained locked into a policy they themselves realized could lead to catastrophe.[10]

The members of a dispossessed ruling group are likely to despise their successors even to the point of irrationality. This was undoubtedly true in Pickering's case. Moreover, he did not occupy these darker intellectual regions in complete isolation. Nevertheless, even within the context of early nineteenth-century Federalism, Pickering qualified as an extremist. Nothing reveals this more clearly than his reaction to *H.M.S. Leopard*'s unprovoked attack on the American frigate *Chesapeake* in June 1807. Not only Jeffersonians but a great many staunch Federalists became aroused on learning of the incident.[11] Pickering, however, set himself the formidable task of justifying England's use of force to impress the alleged deserters serving on board the *Chesapeake*.[12] And he did this at considerable personal cost, for during the entire period of his service in the State Department, he had vehemently protested acts of impressment.[13] Indeed, on one occasion when seamen were impressed from an American national vessel, he had even threatened the Foreign Office with retaliation.[14] But by 1807 all of that was an age ago. Pickering's fears of a war with England and his antipathy to the Jeffersonians had long since robbed him of whatever ability he once had to judge the diplomatic situation impartially. The defense of neither neutral rights nor American nationality on the high seas seemed any longer in the national interest. The "many" who "call for free trade and sailors' rights," he wrote, "don't know what are meant by these ideas."[15] Aware of his own inconsistencies, Pickering ransacked his personal papers in an unsuccessful search for proof that he had not changed his position on impressment. Finding no support in the documents, however, he was reduced to the pathetic contention that there was nothing to be gained by "consistency" if it was "in error."[16]

In October 1807, with the threat of war very much in the air and Congress preparing to convene two months ahead of schedule, Pickering's heart was filled with gloom and foreboding. The president's opening message to Congress should have boosted his spirits, for as the militant John Quincy Adams unhappily noted, it called for "caution" not "ardour."[17] But Pickering's overweening fear of the Machiavellian quality of Jeffersonian statecraft allowed him no room for relaxation. The government's insistence that a settlement to the *Chesapeake* affair be linked to an agreement on impressment and the news which arrived in mid-November that talks between Foreign Secretary Canning and James Monroe were deadlocked reinforced his view that ultimately the administration intended war.[18]

To counteract this, Pickering became a leading participant in a propaganda campaign designed to lay responsibility for the *Chesapeake* affair at Jefferson's feet. In his search for collaborators he contacted Captain Thomas Truxton, one-time commodore of the American Mediterranean Squadron and a naval hero during the quasi war. Pickering hoped that the prestigious Truxton would support the view that Commodore James Barron, the commander of the *Chesapeake,* should have returned the deserters claimed by the captain of the *Leopard* and that his refusal to do so justified the attack that followed. Unhappily, Truxton was of little use on that score.[19] He did, however, offer the allegation that the Jefferson administration was applying a double standard with regard to the return of deserters to the belligerents. Relying heavily on unsubstantiated newspaper reports, Truxton insisted that the administration always cooperated with the French but seldom with the English.[20]

Pickering rushed these charges into print and forwarded Truxton's letter to John Lowell, the foremost Federalist pamphleteer in New England, who used the commodore's views in several of his own writings.[21] But whatever hopes the Massachusetts senator had for these propaganda efforts were dashed by a humiliation that might have left a more sensitive politician thinking seriously of retirement. Having first been grotesquely inconsistent in defending the British "right" to impress seamen from American war vessels, he suddenly had the ground cut out from under him by, of all people, George Canning. Not only did Britain's foreign secretary renounce the view that England had a right to search foreign national ships or impress their seamen, he sent a special envoy, George Rose, to the United States to negotiate a settlement.

Astonishingly this embarrassment hardly fazed Pickering, who seems not to have noticed just how foolish Canning's announcement made him appear. What he did perceive was that the British initiative had given many in Congress cause to step back from the precipice.[22] Jefferson might still want war, but Pickering felt sure that he could no longer command the necessary congressional majorities. His confidence growing almost moment by moment, the New Englander soon convinced himself that Jefferson had never intended to fight. Though at best indecorous in one who in October had been a Cassandra issuing dire warnings of a destructive conflict, he now arrogantly maintained that the cowards who headed the American government had no stomach for a contest with Britain. All of the bustle and warlike rhetoric of the summer and fall had been nothing more than an elaborate but mercifully ineffective "finesse" designed to maneuver the English into undesirable concessions.[23]

Pickering's confidence in Jeffersonian pusillanimity lasted only until mid-December when, with lightninglike efficiency, administration supporters in Congress enacted the Embargo. Refusing once again to credit the reasons given by the president for this extraordinary measure, the senator from Massachusetts dismissed King George III's recent royal proclamation reaffirming and expanding British claims to the right of impressment as of no consequence.[24] Nor would he accept the administration's contention that the Embargo was partially designed as retaliation for Napoleon's recent decision to apply the Berlin Decree to ships flying the American flag. In fact, he maintained that the reverse was actually the case. News that Napoleon intended to implement his decree against the United States arrived in Washington on December 16. Pickering suspected that, because he was taking orders from the French emperor, Jefferson responded two days later with the call for an embargo.[25] The law should have been named, he thought, "An act to render complete the Continental System of his imperial & royal majesty the emperor of the French, King of Italy &c. in order to destroy the commerce of G. Britain, & thereby facilitate her subjugation to his said imperial & royal majesty."[26]

The destructive implications of Jefferson's Embargo, with regard to both the national economy in general and New England's interests in particular, were immediately apparent to Pickering. But he was more intrigued by the political possibilities it presented. Four years before, a whole spectrum of Federalist leaders had warned that the time was not right to take the political initiative because the Jeffersonians had not yet made any serious mistakes. Pickering seized upon the Embargo as the blunder that he and others had been waiting for. Not only merchants, but planters and farmers who produced for the national and world markets were bound to be hurt. Enormous surpluses would soon create a glut, driving domestic prices down. One result of such artificially induced economic hard times that Pickering foresaw was a growing popular disenchantment with the Republicans.[27]

But this was not to be 1804 all over again. This time there would be no thoughtless demand for New England's secession. The public's reaction to the Embargo suggested the possibility of overthrowing the Virginia dynasty at the polls. Pickering therefore opted to seek change within the established political system. He would not, it is true, support a scheme hatched by Federalist Party leaders in Massachusetts that was designed to unite dissident northern Republicans and Federalists in support of the presidential candidacy of the apostate Republican governor of New York, George Clinton.[28] But unlike Theodore Sedgwick and a number of other "gentlemen of the old school," he was not opposed to the idea on ethical grounds. It was simply that Clinton was unacceptable to him. Down to the eve of the presidential election he was prepared to support a "moderate northern democrat" of "sound disposition," provided one could be found.[29]

Though Pickering spoke frequently and at length regarding presidential politics during 1808, he had little to do with that year's national election campaign. In Massachusetts, however, he played a very active role in working to dislodge the Republicans who at that time controlled both the state legislature and the governorship. On February 16, Pickering addressed an inflammatory letter to the Massachusetts legislature. Charging that the administration meant to provoke a needless war with England, he maintained that the ostensible reasons for the Embargo—impressment, the *Chesapeake* affair, and the British Orders in Council issued in November 1807—were not genuine. Instead, he asserted, French influence was behind it. "Has the French Emperor declared that he will have no neutrals? Has he required that *our* ports, like those of his vassal states in Europe, *be shut* against British commerce? Is the Embargo a *substitute, a milder form* of compliance with that harsh demand?" Exhorting Massachusetts lawmakers to lead northern state legislatures in taking united action against the Embargo, he concluded with the demand that Jefferson make public recent dispatches from John Armstrong, the American minister in Paris, confident that they would reveal once and for all that Napoleon was actually in control of the administration's foreign policy.[30]

Nearly a century and three-quarters after the fact, these charges seem insane. But at the time it was accepted doctrine among committed Federalists that a "French influence" governed in Washington.[31] With their ships rotting at wharfside and their entire economy in disarray, there was ample reason to believe that a substantial majority of the voters of Massachusetts might come to agree.

Instead of forwarding his letter directly to the legislature, Pickering sent it to James Sullivan, the popular Republican governor of Massachusetts. Claiming that the governor was the only channel through which he as a senator might *legitimately* address the lawmakers, Pickering asked Sullivan to forward it. When, as Pickering and other Federalist strategists supposed he would, the governor refused, George Cabot published the letter in the newspapers. Massachusetts Federalists then charged that Sullivan had attempted to suppress it. This strategy was intended not only to strengthen the effect of Pickering's arguments on the public, but also to damage Sullivan's chances in the coming election.[32]

The Federalist Party organization in Massachusetts distributed Pickering's letter with great speed, first throughout New England and then nationally. On March 25, not two weeks after publication, the *Salem Gazette* estimated that seventy thousand copies had appeared in the Northeast alone.[33] Packets of the letter were sent to trustworthy Federalists in every state in the Union with instructions for distribution. Jacob Wagner, editor of the *Baltimore Federal Republican*, Pickering's Maryland mouthpiece, published the letter in a regular issue of his paper and printed an extra thousand copies for circulation throughout the state. The Pickering letter even crossed the Atlantic, going through several editions in England.[34]

For the life of him, young Thomas Boylston Adams could make neither head nor tail of the "great *rumpuss* and fuss" some Massachusetts Federalists were making over Pickering's letter. He rather liked the *Boston Independent Chronicle*'s pithy comment that "Timothy" was "at his old tricks again."[35] If Adams passed the Pickering letter off lightly, however, the Jeffersonian Republicans in Massachusetts, distressed by the audience it was attracting, took it more seriously. "So copious and overwhelming was its issue," Levi Lincoln later remarked, "so extensive, sudden and rapid its spread that there was scarcely time or the means of a general counteraction."[36]

The Republican press nevertheless did its best. Although Pickering had carefully avoided all mention of secession in his letter, most alleged that it was the opening gambit in a new conspiracy.[37] One writer in the *Essex Register* termed the letter "Incendiary" and "dictated by the malignity of a factious spirit and the spleen of disappointed ambition."[38] Another charged that "Timothy's letter" had been designed "to touch the train which had been secretly laid to blow up our Republic."[39] It was, in the words of still a third pseudonymous author, "a scandalous and disorganizing libel on the government of the United States." It degraded "the character of a Senator," this same writer continued, "to that of a scavenger of Party violence."[40] Governor Sullivan himself denounced Pickering's letter as an open invitation to sedition and rebellion. For what other purpose, the embattled Sullivan queried, had Pickering appealed "from the sovereign power of the nation to the authority of one of the states?" There could be only one reason, he maintained, "to disunite, divide, and dissolve the nation."[41]

It is by no means simple to assess the political effect of a single initiative such as Pickering's letter on the outcome of a major political campaign. Most Federalists, however, believed that the letter had a considerable effect, for even though Christopher Gore lost to Sullivan in a close race, their party made substantial gains in the legislature. Caleb Strong, writing from Northampton in the western part of the state, credited the Embargo and Pickering's letter for the Federalists' impressive showing.[42] James Hillhouse, watching the Massachusetts situation from nearby New Haven, was actually jubilant. Soon, he predicted, "we may place our country in a better situation and our government in better hands."[43]

While there can be no doubt that Pickering intended his letter to have its primary effect in Massachusetts, it is nevertheless clear that he also intended it to serve certain other purposes beyond the borders of his native state. The national distribution it received and its appearance at the precise moment that a resolution was introduced in the House of Representatives calling for the repeal of the Embargo demonstrate beyond question that it was one element in an overall Federalist attack on the law. It is reasonable to assume too that a substantial portion of the letter's content, as well as the timing of its appearance, was intended to serve certain British purposes in the United States. At the very moment that Pickering's letter appeared in print, George Rose, the British envoy, announced that his negotiations with Secretary of State Madison relative to the *Chesapeake* affair had broken down. It strains credulity to believe that it was mere happenstance that in his letter Pickering was at pains to blame the State Department for the failure of these talks. The timing was too perfect. Moreover, it is beyond question that prior to the appearance of the letter Pickering and Rose, who got on well together, spent an inordinate amount of time in each other's company.[44]

Many in Washington believed that consultations between Rose and Pickering regarding the contents of the letter and the timing of its appearance had taken place in advance of its publication. A rumor circulating widely in the capital had it that prior to writing his letter Pickering spent an entire evening with Rose in secret conversations, and that they met again just before Rose announced the failure of his mission. Republicans, at least, had no difficulty believing these charges. Benjamin Crowninshield thought Pickering "would sell his country" to the English "for fewer pieces of silver than Judas did his Master."[45]

And Massachusetts' Henry Dearborn, in language less colorful, explained that there was "reason for suspecting that Pickering's letter, a motion in Congress by Mr. Livermore to take off the Embargo, combined with the final answer of Mr. Rose, were intended to operate in concert."[46]

Whether or not Rose collaborated with Pickering in drafting and timing the release of the letter, he certainly put it to good use, carrying a copy with him to England where it was published and widely disseminated. It served the embattled Perceval government well at a moment when English Whigs, including the influential Lord Erskine and the Baring brothers, were seeking the repeal of the Orders in Council.[47] Rose congratulated Pickering on the "sensation" his letter had caused.[48] The *Washington Monitor,* meanwhile, reported that Pickering was "all the rage in the ministerial prints" in England. And the American envoy in London, William Pinkney, enquired wryly of Secretary Madison whether there was some sort of ban on the exportation of writings favorable to administration policy.[49]

Though Pickering was cautioned by one Federalist observer in London that his letter had done more harm than good there, he paid no attention.[50] He was too emotionally caught up in the battle against the Jeffersonians, and in any event his vanity would not allow it. All his life he had sought notoriety, publishing his views on an astonishing variety of issues great and small. At last his letter to the Massachusetts legislature had attracted the sort of national and international audience that he had always hungered for. He would not willingly surrender what he had so long sought.[51] Thus, instead of laying down his pen, he published several more letters before George Cabot and other Massachusetts Federalists, who realized that overexposure was undermining his effectiveness, managed to rein him in.

On March 22, 1808, only a week after the publication of Pickering's letter, President Jefferson submitted a massive collection of foreign policy documents to Congress. Included were the Rose-Madison letters as well as recent Franco-American diplomatic correspondence that Pickering had maintained would prove the effect of French influence on American policy makers.[52] For six days congressional clerks read the documents aloud before the Senate. When they had finished Pickering was left in a state of total dismay. He had been certain that the French were responsible for the Embargo—so certain, in fact, that he had made the allegation in print. Yet nothing in the mass of documents in any way substantiated that charge. Pickering was even more taken aback by the correspondence between George Rose and James Madison, for he had publicly insisted that the secretary of state was responsible for the failure of the talks. Unhappily, even confirmed Federalists were forced to admit that the documents corroborated the government's claim that the British were responsible for the collapse of the negotiations.[53]

Though discouraged, Pickering remained intent on proving that the Embargo had been the result of French influence operating upon the administration. Naturally, then, he was very much interested in a letter he received from William Cooke, a retired Baltimore attorney and the president of a Maryland bank, claiming that Jefferson was holding back information that would prove Napoleon had masterminded the Embargo. Cooke's son, a merchant at Leghorn, had seen and extracted parts of a letter from France's foreign minister, Champagny, to John Armstrong. According to Cooke, Champagny expressed the emperor's regret at the recent seizure of numbers of American ships but indicated that redress would be forthcoming only if the United States took steps to defend its neutral rights against the English.[54] After checking on the reliability of his informant, Pickering began circulating the story. Soon the rumor was abroad that the administration was withholding information that would prove the Embargo was the result of French pressure.

The State Department archives contain no such letter as the one described by Cooke. However, late in March 1808, the administration did receive a letter from Champagny to Armstrong dated January 15, 1808, which closely approximated the one that Cooke charged was being withheld. Jefferson would no doubt have preferred to keep this letter out of the newspapers, not only for political reasons, but also because its publication was bound to damage future relations with France. But with the capital already buzzing he could not risk having the letter leak. Instead, he forwarded the Champagny letter to Congress where, after a short and bitter debate, it was published.[55]

Pickering derived enormous personal satisfaction from the publication of the Champagny letter, for he interpreted it as proof of his long-standing contention that the French were exerting enormous pressure upon the administration. Few others viewed it in this light, however. In fact, in the broader political context, this letter was of little consequence. Of far greater importance was the internal economic effect of the Embargo, which seriously weakened the Republican majority and made possible the Federalist revival that began in 1808. Before the end of the year some sensed an incipient rebellion forming in New England, where "extremists" advocated secession while "moderates" thought in terms of some sort of sectional convention to discuss methods of opposing the Embargo. Perhaps even more significant, areas outside New England were joining in the protest. Samuel Smith's

Baltimore was no longer securely in the Republican fold, while in New York the powerful Clinton faction was in open rebellion against the Republican Party's southern leadership.

It seemed clear to a great many whose political views were far different from Pickering's that the Embargo would have to be repealed. John Quincy Adams, driven from the Senate by the Massachusetts legislature because he had voted for the Embargo, warned friends in Congress that the law could not "possibly be continued much longer without meeting direct & forcible resistance" in New England.[56] Old John Adams, too, thought the situation nearly out of hand. Although he did not believe it would be a simple matter to stimulate a rebellion in Massachusetts, "to carry such laws into effect against the universal bent of a whole people would require armies and navies sufficient to carry on a foreign war."[57] And Albert Gallatin, watching over the tense situation from the vantage point of the Treasury Department, was equally concerned. The majority of the people would "not adhere to the embargo much longer," he explained to his friend Joseph Nicholson. War or "submission" to the belligerents seemed to him the only two possibilities for the future.[58]

In November 1808, following Madison's victory in the presidential election, Timothy Pickering returned to Washington for what he confidently expected would be the last act in the struggle against the Embargo. Four days after Congress convened, his friend James Hillhouse introduced a resolution calling for repeal, and the battle was joined.

Pickering's speech in support of the Hillhouse resolution, done up in pamphlet form and even translated into German for "electioneering work," won enthusiastic applause from a number of Federalists.[59] None other than John Marshall lent at least a private endorsement to his argument that the Rule of 1756, upon which the British based their claim to interfere with America's trade in reexports, was a legitimate reading of international law. He thought too that Pickering was correct when he alleged that French influence was responsible for Jefferson's decision to enact the Embargo in the first place.[60] Bushrod Washington was so captivated by Pickering's speech that he had copies circulated throughout Virginia.[61] From Blandensburg in Maryland, former Secretary of the Navy Benjamin Stoddert rhapsodized over the speech, while George Cabot and John Lowell sent gushing letters of support from Boston.[62] Even Richard Peters, who had earlier endorsed the Embargo, joined in the chorus. "I really sympathize with you & those whose political opinions I respect," he wrote. But though he believed his friend deserved "success," Peters was pessimistic about the prospects for winning a political victory.[63]

Pickering's speech won the wholehearted support of a number of Federalists, but it had no effect on Congress. On December 2 the Hillhouse resolution was smothered by a vote of 25 to 7.[64] A few days later, adding insult to injury, Senator William Branch Giles submitted a new proposal for a more stringent enforcement of the Embargo.[65] The enforcement bill, with its "sweeping grant of arbitrary power" to the national government, provoked an anguished cry from Federalists in the Senate who found themselves in the enviable political position of defending basic civil liberties against an overweening central authority. Chauncey Goodrich, senator from Connecticut, attacked the bill as a blow to "the vital principles of our republican system."[66] James Lloyd found the proposal more closely akin "to the bowstring discipline of a Turkish despotism, than to the pure and wholesome laws of a free and elective Republic."[67] And Timothy Pickering, who ten years before had been energetically enforcing the Sedition Law while urging a general crackdown against dangerous aliens, now warned that "despotism," which seemed to be "advancing with rapid strides," would gain a great new victory with the passage of the bill.[68]

Pickering's speech in opposition to Giles's bill was a wild and intemperate performance filled with slanderous reproaches hurled not only against the president and the secretary of state but even against his old political enemy, John Quincy Adams.[69] Congressional Republicans were outraged. Senator Giles was the first to respond, taking it upon himself to reply for Adams who, having been replaced by the Massachusetts legislature, was of course not present to defend himself. But sparks really flew in the House of Representatives, where first John G. Jackson, Madison's brother-in-law, and then John W. Eppes, the president's son-in-law, delivered slashing retorts. Eppes in particular held nothing back. That the man who in 1798 had conspired to involve the nation in a war with France should, ten years later, accuse the Jefferson administration of attempting to provoke a war with Britain was beyond enduring, Eppes stormed. Then, resorting to the sort of trashy accusation that he believed Pickering would best understand, he revived the old allegation that during the quasi war Pickering had withheld crucial diplomatic correspondence from President Adams because it would have alleviated tensions with France when he wanted war.[70]

In exchanging slander for slander Eppes struck with devastating accuracy, for although Pickering was among the most combative politicians of his generation, he had never been able to withstand the slightest criticism. Accusations such as Eppes's sent him into fits of despair. His ego a ruin, he searched for the diabolical purpose behind the Virginian's speech. For psychological reasons Pickering found it impossible to believe that Eppes, a man of no great consequence in his eyes, could have been acting on his own. He quickly surmised, therefore, that his own remarks had stung Jefferson, "the Devil always behind the scenes." It must have been "the old hypocrite" himself who had ordered retaliation.[71] Obviously, Pickering had played Don Quixote to the Jeffersonian windmill for too long. Nevertheless, he did not intend to remain silent. Buoyed by the thought that he had actually offended the president, he steadied himself for another round. With his "next thrust," he predicted, in a particularly apt metaphor, the "javelin will reach his heart."[72]

Before Pickering had a chance to react to Eppes's speech, however, the Force Act became law. Though that development should have triggered another outburst, it didn't. Perhaps the aging zealot had become chary after his painful encounter with Eppes, Jackson, Giles, and others. Or it may have been that some of his Federalist colleagues cautioned him against perpetuating the contest. Whatever the cause, Pickering remained silent while anticipating the popular reaction to the Force Act. He thought this latest attempt to strengthen the Embargo could only increase the gap between the government and the people, who "suffer and will no longer submit to be dragged along the road to ruin."

Though often in the past Pickering had misjudged what the people would or would not stand for, he was correct about the Force Act. Early in February 1809, while he watched from the sidelines, Jeffersonian ranks in Congress crumbled. Congressional Republicans had "become too restive to be controlled any longer," Pickering reported to Tim Williams. Though the president was doing everything in his power to defend the Embargo, his supporters simply wouldn't "follow any more." They realized that it would mean the end of their party if they didn't change the law.[73]

Pickering expected a clean victory: the repeal of the Embargo. When he first heard total nonintercourse with the belligerents proposed as a substitute measure by Senator Giles, he scoffed. "The administration dies hard," he wrote, "but die it must." Public opinion would "assuredly defeat the project."[74] After passage of the Nonintercourse Act, however, Pickering wondered what sort of victory, if any, had been won. The new law might prove more aggravating to England than the Embargo. If properly enforced, nonintercourse would deny her not only American exports but the valuable American market as well. The loss of both could be such a blow to the British economy as to prompt the

Perceval government to take retaliatory action. If that was decided upon there would be the American merchant fleet, nearly a million tons in all, ripe for the picking.

He was distressed, too, at the loss of a valuable political advantage. The Embargo had been an essential ingredient in Federalism's modest revival and had simultaneously helped disrupt the ranks of the opposition. Without it, who could tell what the future might bring. Many others were equally upset. Tim Williams, for example, who like Pickering had long inveighed against the injustices of the Embargo, paused now to mourn its passing. It had been such a useful political tool. Had it remained in effect a bit longer, he remarked, it would surely have produced a complete political "regeneration" not only in New England but in New York as well. He, too, wondered whether the change was for the better: "G. Britain says the Embargo is no cause of war with her. A substitute for it might be."[75] Even John Quincy Adams, who had long urged his congressional friends to replace the Embargo with nonintercourse, admitted that if it were maintained for any great length of time it might provoke England into a declaration of war. That, however, was a risk he thought worth taking in order to relieve some of the pressure at home and forestall the civil war he believed was brewing.[76]

Such misgivings notwithstanding, Federalists in all parts of the United States celebrated the Embargo's repeal at dinners and public gatherings. In Philadelphia Thomas Fitzsimmons and Thomas Truxton headed a list of prominent leaders who hosted a gala political dinner in honor of the event. A distinguished guest returning from Washington to his new home in Wenham was Timothy Pickering. In his honor the group sang a new lyric, "The Pilots whom Washington plac'd at the Helm," written especially for the occasion. But even as he raised his glass Pickering wondered whether he should be celebrating.

EIGHTEEN

The Crucible of War

AFTER THE ENACTMENT of the Nonintercourse Law, Pickering assumed that relations between the United States and Britain would deteriorate still further. Naturally, then, he was utterly confounded when the new president, James Madison, announced in his premier message to Congress that he and the British minister, David Erskine, had arranged an accommodation between their two countries.[1] A president he despised and an envoy for whom he had not a shred of respect had somehow managed to achieve the unattainable. It was all very perplexing.

Amazement, however, soon gave way to euphoria, as Pickering's entire attitude toward the new administration underwent a radical change. He now dined willingly at the presidential mansion, noting in a self-satisfied manner that the Federalists seemed more friendly to the president than many in his own party.[2] And when Dolley Madison revived the old custom of holding a weekly drawing room, he attended "to do honor to former times," he explained to Beckey.[3] His conciliatory attitude even came to embrace John Quincy Adams, chosen by Madison for the ministry at St. Petersburg. Normally Pickering would have opposed this nomination. Under the circumstances, however, he made no objection, though he was heard to grumble that "upon the whole the best thing that could be done" with Adams was to send him "out of the country."[4]

Pickering was at home in Wenham when this honeymoon period at last came to an end. In mid-July 1809, the newspapers announced that Foreign Secretary Canning had repudiated the Erskine Agreement, claiming that in signing the compact his young envoy had exceeded his instructions. Less than three weeks later the president revived nonintercourse against England. Though furious with Erskine, Pickering laid primary responsibility for this diplomatic debacle upon the president. The British envoy, "a weak young man," had no doubt been "the dupe of the cunning and deceit of an administration" intent upon "pursuing the mischievous system of Jefferson," he wrote.[5]

Pickering's chagrin over the abortive agreement with Great Britain was only the latest in a long series of frustrations that he had experienced as a member of the Federalist minority. Everything considered, it is remarkable that he remained politically active. Many other prominent Federalists had long since stacked their lances and retired to private life. But that was not the way Pickering functioned. Being one of a diminishing number of active Federalists reinforced his martyr's self-image while new disappointments only strengthened his will to persist in the struggle against the Jeffersonians.

And so Pickering continued to preach and publish the gospel of extreme Federalism. The Republicans, who had already made him the most reviled politician of his generation, responded mercilessly, not only because they detested him, but because they had learned that it was politically advantageous to provoke him. Pickering's views were so extreme, his allegations so unbelievable, that he became in effect the perfect political opponent. A leading student of Federalist Party organization has written that "a single 'outrageous pamphlet' by Pickering could be more influential in its operation upon the public mind than a dozen carefully contrived young Federalist efforts to establish a popular base" for their party.[6]

And it was true. Republicans much preferred to run their campaigns against Pickering rather than against their real but less vulnerable opponents. Thus, in 1809 Pennsylvania Republicans hanged and burned him in effigy as part of their campaign during that year's state elections.[7] In New York the opposition sought to offset an efficient Federalist political organization by employing similar tactics in the elections of 1810. A handbill was circulated implying that New York's Federalists were being financed by Pickering. It was claimed that he had embezzled seventy-five thousand dollars while in the State Department and was using the money to support Federalist political campaigns.[8]

Pickering was helpless in the face of such tactics. He instituted libel suits to vindicate his good name and solicited statements from the Treasury Department certifying that his accounts were in order.[9] Inevitably, too, just as Republican strategists hoped, he was very active in defending his treasured integrity. It was all quite pathetic, for he hadn't the vaguest idea of how he was being manipulated. Thus, after his "burning" in Philadelphia, he wrote to his friend Richard Peters proclaiming his "innocence" of all malfeasance. Self-righteous as ever, he begged Peters to find the man responsible for the recent demonstration against him. He wanted this person to know that it was not the first time that he had "opposed tyrannical acts." Nor would it be the last. No "burning in effigy or threat of real burning," he wrote, "will stop my mouth or make me crop my pen."[10]

On no occasion did Pickering play more completely into Republican hands than when he linked his reputation and that of a substantial element of the Federalist Party to Francis James Jackson, the British minister sent to replace David Erskine. Pickering's enthusiasm for the haughty Jackson was the result of a rather extraordinary turn of mind. The American people, he maintained, had been unable to penetrate the hypocrisy of those they had raised to power in 1800. Federalism had failed to awaken the people and seemed itself incapable of a return to power. But the English remained strong. By backing the Republicans to the wall they might yet reveal the hollowness of Jeffersonian leadership. The British Foreign Office and Jackson had in effect become Pickering's last resources in the internal political contest with the Republicans.

Not surprisingly, relations between Jackson and the Madison administration broke down in short order. From the very outset the British envoy was arrogant and unfriendly. More to the point, in letters to Secretary of State Robert Smith he repeatedly insinuated that during their negotiations the president had knowingly encouraged David Erskine to violate his instructions. When it became clear that Jackson was not prepared to renounce this charge, the president dismissed him and published his correspondence with the State Department.[11]

The public's reaction to the Jackson-Smith letters should have convinced Pickering to break with the British minister for, as he himself unhappily remarked, a great majority of Republicans and Federalists alike supported the administration's position.[12] Insensitive to the political impact of Jackson's gratuitously insulting behavior, however, Pickering rushed to the Englishman's defense. Jackson, he maintained, had been no more than accurate when he charged that Madison had tricked Erskine into violating his instructions. Incredibly, he found the recently published documents so persuasive on this point that he actually urged their wider distribution.[13]

Not content to let matters rest there, Pickering also helped initiate a campaign to turn Jackson's dismissal into a political *cause célèbre,* the central issue in that year's New England state elections. From his Senate seat he provided inspiration for Federalist writers then defending Jackson in the regional press. The "discerning reader," he remarked to one Boston correspondent, would look between the lines of the secretary of state's letters to Jackson. They were, he claimed, "supercilious," written in a "petulant style as if designed to irritate" Jackson "into some indiscretion which might furnish a pretense for putting an end" to talks.[14] He even helped arrange a tour of the Northeast for Jackson, envisioning it as a sort of triumphant finale to the year's political campaigning.[15]

On the eve of the voting in Massachusetts, despite the recent Republican upset victory in nearby New Hamsphire, the Boston Insurance Company was giving odds of 3 to 1 that Christopher Gore would defeat the Republican Elbridge Gerry for the governorship.[16] But when the last ballot had been counted, the Republicans had elected not only a governor but a lieutenant governor as well. Later they also won control of the lower house of the state legislature. The Federalists, meanwhile, clung to a precarious one-vote majority in the state senate. Even this was not the worst of it. After the spring elections elsewhere, the entire Northeast save Connecticut was in Republican hands.[17]

Pickering, who remained blind to his own failings, blamed the debacle upon the skillful political legerdemain of the opposition.[18] Nor would he dissociate himself from that millstone round his neck, Francis James Jackson. Instead, when the former envoy reached Boston on what turned out to be something less than a triumphal tour of the northern United States, Pickering was there to greet him. In fact it was in Boston, at a dinner given in Jackson's honor and attended by some three hundred faithful Federalists, that he gave his famous toast: "The World's last hope—Britain's Fast-anchored Isle."[19] But the Massachusetts senator's flamboyant remark, a gauntlet hurled in the face of his enemies, was mere bravado. Inwardly he was depressed.[20]

Pickering stumbled from one defeat to another, never questioning his anachronistic political ways, never learning any of the lessons of partisan politics. Thus he returned to Washington in December 1810, battered but still searching for a method of proving to the electorate that their leaders were charlatans. He had only just arrived in the capital when opportunity seemed to beckon. Six weeks earlier a group of American settlers living near Baton Rouge had declared West Florida independent of Spain and requested annexation by the United States. The president immediately took possession of the region, claiming it as part of the Louisiana Purchase.[21] Pickering, who thought the seizure an unconstitutional act of aggression against a friendly power, sensed an opportunity to embarrass the government.

Administration supporters in the Senate wanted no part of a long, potentially embarrassing public debate over the seizure of West Florida.

But they did want action to legitimize it and therefore sought to rush a resolution endorsing the president's action through Congress. During the debate, Pickering took the floor of the Senate intent upon highlighting the questionable aspects of the administration's Florida policy. His strongest card was a letter written by former French Foreign Minister Talleyrand that had been submitted to the Senate by President Jefferson five years before. The United States, Talleyrand wrote, had no legitimate claim to the Floridas stemming from the Louisiana Purchase.

Though he had prepared a long speech, Pickering got no further than the reading of Talleyrand's letter. Maryland's Samuel Smith interrupted to inquire whether the letter had ever been transmitted publicly to the Senate. Suddenly, and much to his horror, Pickering realized that he had violated a Senate rule by revealing a document that still bore the seal of confidentiality. Senate Republicans, delighted by the same discovery, and aware that they had caught Pickering in a punishable indiscretion, voted immediately to clear the galleries. The debate then continued for an hour behind closed doors. When the public was readmitted to the Senate chamber, the young Republican senator from Kentucky, Henry Clay, introduced a resolution of censure against Pickering that passed, after much partisan wrangling, by a vote of 20 to 7.[22]

There is a certain irony in the fact that when the obstreperous Pickering was finally censured by his Senate colleagues, it came not as a result of his frequently outrageous misrepresentations of administration policy but because he was striking too near the truth. The vote of censure, as Pickering himself remarked, was a "put up affair" and was perhaps designed to distract the public's attention from the more important yet embarrassing Florida question. Pickering had violated Senate rules, to be sure. But he had certainly not infringed on their true spirit, since the original reason for insisting upon the confidentiality of the Talleyrand letter—the fear that its revelation might jeopardize negotiations taking place in 1805 between France and the United States over Florida—had long ago ceased to pertain.[23] But in 1810 Senate Republicans were not only anxious to avoid drawing public attention to the French diplomat's letter, they were even more touchy about the constitutional issues raised by Madison's decision to seize West Florida without first requesting congressional authorization. Indeed, they were so sensitive on these points that after Pickering's censure, rather than renew the debate on the resolution and thus risk further public discussion, they let the entire matter drop.

Although Pickering gave no outward sign of losing his composure, privately he seethed with fury at those "slanderers" who were constantly attempting to destroy his reputation. Continued references in the press to his questionable role during the Battle of Lexington, the oft-repeated charge that John Adams had dismissed him because he had withheld important diplomatic correspondence, and now the censure were all, he was certain, parts of an ongoing conspiracy. He had been singled out for punishment, he maintained, because he alone had penetrated Republican hypocrisy and had worked to expose it to the people.[24]

The moment was opportune for the sixty-six-year-old Pickering to preserve some shred of his dignity by announcing his retirement. His term in the Senate was soon to expire. Nor did it appear that he would be reelected, for as the 1811 elections in Massachusetts approached, indications were that the Republicans would not only maintain their control over the governor's office and the lower house, but would win the state senate as well. Nevertheless, though humiliated and facing defeat, Pickering could not bring himself to drift quietly out of political life. He encouraged friends in the state senate, where the Federalists clung tenuously to a slender one-vote majority, to help his reelection efforts by holding the Senate election early. The attempt failed, however, when the upper chamber, dividing its votes equally, was unable to choose between Pickering and the Republican candidate Joseph Varnum.[25] Benjamin Waterhouse, the lone Jeffersonian on the Harvard faculty, rejoiced to his former colleague John Quincy Adams that the plot had been foiled. The legislature would make no decision until the next session, when he felt confident the Republicans would be in control. Meanwhile, he laughed, Pickering, "like spoilt wine, grows every day more sour, & is in a fair way to becoming first rate vinegar."[26]

Long before the legislative elections of 1811 had been held, Pickering realized that there was no hope of his reelection. He turned bitterly to other pursuits. For some time he had toyed with the idea of writing a history of the United States. It would be the perfect format for one last attack upon a vast collection of enemies including Washington, Adams, Jefferson, Madison, Gerry, and others with whom he had quarreled over a long lifetime. Though his manuscripts are filled with notes and thoughts pertaining to the project, Pickering never wrote that history. In the spring of 1811, however, he did publish an extensive series entitled *Letters to the People of the United States*. Originally conceived as a final valedictory, these letters, which were printed in the *Boston Columbian Centinel,* quickly deteriorated into the hysterical ravings of a man who sensed, prematurely as things turned out, that the last battle had been fought, that there was nothing left to lose.[27]

Many of those victimized by Pickering's slanderous accusations were thoroughly outraged. Abigail Adams, for example, was furious with Benjamin Russell for having agreed to publish his vituperations. "He throws about arrows, fire brands, and darts with the venom of a serpent, and dips his pen in the gall of the asp," she wrote.[28] Her husband, one of Pickering's many targets, was at first tempted to reply.[29] He finally rejected the idea, however, as beneath his dignity and warned the irritated Benjamin Waterhouse against making any sort of public response in his defense. "When a man who has been thought honest, tho' passionate & fiery, begins to be crazy," the ex-president explained, "I have often observed that one of the first decisive symptoms of insanity is knavery." Waterhouse responded that if not he then John Quincy ought to reply to Pickering's slanders. But Adams wrote, *"I hope he would not foul his fingers in such dirt."* [30]

The aging ex-president may have sensed that there was no need to reply. Pickering's charges were so extreme, his writing so passionate, that even his supporters winced on reading these letters. Virginia's Henry Lee actually took the unusual liberty of warning the ex-senator that his "Achillean ire" was undermining his effectiveness.[31] Abigail Adams probably did not miss the mark by much when she noted that "sober federalists" condemned Pickering for his excesses while the Republicans were actually "gratified that he had shown his teeth." As usual he was doing them "a world of good." [32]

Although Pickering's senatorial career came to an abrupt conclusion in 1811, foreign policy remained his obsession. From his enforced retirement in Wenham he kept in contact with former British envoys Jackson and Rose, read the newspapers avidly, and carried on a regular correspondence with acquaintances in Congress. Pickering exhorted his Washington contacts to unite in opposition to defense appropriations as well as other measures that might move the nation closer to war. But he soon learned of sharp divisions within the Federalist Party that made unity impossible. Some, overwhelmed by apathy, were unprepared to take any action. Others, however, led by Josiah Quincy, one of the more venturesome Federalists in the House, decided to endorse all military appropriations sought by the administration. Though they would not support an actual declaration, Quincy and his followers were determined to collaborate with congressional war hawks even to the verge of war if necessary. This time there were to be no convenient Federalist whipping boys about when the administration sought to lay responsibility elsewhere for the bankruptcy of its foreign policy.[33]

Pickering was disheartened that at this critical time congressional

Federalists should be so ineffectively led. Federalists who chose the course of unprotesting acquiesence were abdicating their responsibilities. But he reserved his strongest criticisms for Quincy and his followers. What sense did it make to support defense appropriations and then vote against a declaration of war? Aware that the Adams administration had foundered at least in part because it had increased taxes to support the military, he now saw Quincy and his supporters throwing away a golden opportunity. If they joined the Republicans in supporting larger defense budgets, certainly they would have to support the new taxes that would be required to finance them. Were the Federalists in Congress such fools that they were willing to "bear the odium . . . of the majority in imposing the unpopular taxes" needed to increase the size of the army and then vote against using it? A dignified opposition to all war measures was, Pickering thought, the best strategy.[34]

Federalists may have been divided over tactics, but from Pickering to Quincy they agreed on one essential point: in all likelihood Madison was not prepared to fight. Even the report recommending war that was submitted for the House Committee on Foreign Affairs by Peter B. Porter of New York did not convince them that the threat was serious. William Reed, one of Quincy's disciples in the House, actually predicted that the committee's report would be for war but thought this simply another device designed to frighten the Federalists and the people at large into accepting further trade restrictions.[35] Pickering was no more impressed. "Porter & his whole gang of bullying warriors," he wrote, had "no intention" of going "to war with G. Britain."[36]

When at last it became apparent that the administration actually meant to fight, Pickering did not despair. On the contrary, he sought to take political advantage of the situation. At last, he gloated, the Republican Party had overreached itself. He hurried his son Henry off on a private errand to London, carrying letters for both George Rose and Francis James Jackson. Pickering informed his British friends that the threat of war was contributing to a Federalist revival in the United States. If England would but remain on the defensive militarily, at least for the time being, he predicted that there might soon be a change of government in Washington.[37]

Next, Pickering plunged back into state politics. His *Letters to the People of Massachusetts,* published in April 1811, prompted the *Salem Register* to hoot mockingly that the "lie-on of Federalism" had again "entered into the political world seeking whom he may devour."[38] But Pickering had the last laugh, for the Federalists registered impressive victories at the polls. Only the state senate remained in Republican hands, and only because of the gerrymander. Furious that this clever act of redistricting should have thwarted a potential political sweep, Pickering raged that the "senatorial usurpers would be thrown out of office next year if not peacefully, then by more violent means."[39]

Not surprisingly Pickering became very much a part of the hysterical opposition that swept New England following the June 18 declaration of war. He chaired an Essex County convention in Ipswich and drafted the militant antiwar resolutions adopted there.[40] He also exhorted his Massachusetts friends to call a state convention as a preliminary step to the convocation of all the northeastern states. For a decade Pickering had clung tenaciously to the view that differences between Federalists and Republicans were fundamentally sectional and that a return to political orthodoxy depended upon driving the southern leadership from power. Now if ever, he thought, the time had come to act. The threat of secession, he maintained, was essential to the reformation of the government. Once "the *idea*" was clearly presented to the South that the northern states actually meant to separate, he argued, reconciliation on northern terms might easily be achieved and the war brought to a swift conclusion.[41]

Pickering's goal of a state convention took a major step toward fruition when Boston's town meeting elected delegates. The idea was subsequently dropped, however, when Harrison Gray Otis and several of Boston's less extreme Federalist leaders intervened to block it.[42] Pickering, who never had much use for Otis and the "timid" Boston leadership, was completely out of sympathy with their strategy.[43] Still, he was not altogether displeased with political developments in 1812. To be sure, DeWitt Clinton, the dissident Republican, lost the presidency to Madison, but by a mere nineteen electoral votes. The Federalists meanwhile made substantial gains in New Jersey, Massachusetts, New Hampshire, and New York. The revival of Federalism even carried Pickering back to political prominence. In November he ran unopposed for Congress from the Essex North district and won a strong vote of confidence from the voters.

Pickering spent the six months following his election at home in Wenham awaiting the opening of the next session of Congress. Much of his time was taken up working on the land and preparing for the marriage of Mary, one of his twin daughters, to a young Salem attorney, Benjamin Ropes Nichols. But the aging revolutionary, now a sixty-seven-year-old freshman congressman, kept politically active, too, indulging his penchant for newspaper controversy with still another series of public letters. These were intended to persuade New England's investing public not to contribute to the war loans so desperately needed by the national government.[44] The old man had a particular loathing for Federalists who took advantage of the high interest rates being offered by the Treasury Department. "I know not any punishment they do not deserve," he wrote. At the very least they should be publicly exposed in order to "discourage and prevent" others from participating in future loans.[45]

In May 1813, just after his daughter's wedding, Pickering caught the stage wagon that would carry him on the first leg of his journey to Washington. He was in high spirits—so exuberant, in fact, that when vice-president-elect Elbridge Gerry caught the same stage just a few miles beyond Boston, it hardly fazed him. Enemies for so long, Gerry and Pickering were forced to endure each other at close quarters all the way to Philadelphia. Though each hated the other, they nevertheless got on well, largely because they were wise enough not to discuss politics.[46] Pickering, who sensed the humor of the situation more clearly than did Gerry, was on his best behavior. The vice-president was "remarkably civil," he reported in a letter to his son Henry. "I could not be a churl."[47]

The comedy became even broader around midnight on the first day of their journey, when the stage reached Hartford. The Connecticut general elections had just been held, and inns and boarding houses were filled almost to capacity. Between them the vice-president of the United States and a distinguished member of the House of Representatives could command but a single bed. After each had offered to surrender the prized resting place to the other, it was agreed that they would share it. And so they did. "[We] slept from one to four without touching each other," an embarrassed Elbridge Gerry later informed his wife.[48] Pickering, amused by the whole experience, told and retold the story, chortling when one of his Connecticut friends remarked that "the millennium must be near at hand" for Gerry and Pickering "had lain down together."[49]

In Philadelphia the two discomfited traveling companions at last separated, Pickering going by land to New York where he took the steamboat to Brunswick. It was his first venture on board a steam-driven vessel and he was impressed. Once ashore, however, he plunged back into the eighteenth century, traveling by stage over rain-soaked roads worse than any he had ever seen. Between Brunswick and Princeton they were so bad that the horses could not pull the loaded stage. Pickering and his traveling companions were forced to walk several miles through thick "miry clay." It was difficult going for a man of his years. But Pickering, always proud of his stamina, walked the painful miles without complaint.[50]

The discomforts of travel notwithstanding, it was deeply satisfying to be back in Washington. Most of Pickering's old congressional friends were gone, to be sure, but the veteran legislator soon found accommodations with a group of younger Federalists at Mrs. Wadsworth's rooming house, hardly a stone's throw from the capitol building. And of course there were old friends living in nearby Georgetown, Alexandria, and Maryland to welcome him back. It was especially pleasing to be in Washington at this time because news of important Russian victories against the French had just arrived. Three hundred exuberant Federalists held a public dinner in Georgetown to mark the event and also to welcome Pickering. The old man was genuinely touched by the "cordial greeting" he received. It was especially pleasing, he admitted in a note to Beckey, "to witness such proofs of esteem, affection, and respect" coming even "from strangers."[51]

Though he thoroughly enjoyed his triumphal return, there was little for Pickering to do in Washington. He observed the factional infighting among Republicans and voted consistently as part of a futile opposition. But only once did he participate in any significant way in House debates, endorsing a war protest sent by the Massachusetts legislature. The Massachusetts Remonstrance, with its vague, partially formed threat of secession, was an embarrassment to Pickering. He craved action, not more words, and thought it hopeless to expect such an obviously empty gesture as the Remonstrance to be taken seriously. Nor was he surprised when the House majority ignored it.[52]

At home in Wenham between congressional sessions, Pickering was far more active in seeking to exacerbate popular discontent. Months before, the *Baltimore Federal Republican* had charged that the Russian czar's 1813 offer to mediate a peace settlement between Britain and America had been an administration hoax. Pickering had received similar information from Richard Söderström, the Swedish consul, whom he had known since his days in the State Department.[53] Without bothering to test the reliability of his source, and in spite of warnings from both Tim Williams and George Cabot, Pickering now revived the charge in yet another wearisome series of letters to the public. This, Pickering's latest bit of political ineptitude, came to a swift and embarrassing conclusion when the Madison administration produced documents proving that the offer of mediation had come directly from the Russian court.

If Massachusetts' Federalists were chagrined at Pickering's gaffe, the opposition was of course delighted. Thomas Boylston Adams, amused at this most recent bit of "political eccentricity" on the part of the "old Epistolary of Essex," wondered how the Federalists would extricate him from his latest predicament.[54] And P. P. F. Degrand, a Boston Republican, maintained that the recent publication of documents by the administration would prove to a great many not only the "daring imprudence of Timo. Pickering" but "the integrity and fairness of the Govt. of the U.S." as well.[55] Degrand in fact predicted that repercussions from Pickering's faux pas would be felt in the upcoming state gubernatorial election. But not even Pickering's political ineptitude could overcome popular antagonism to the war in Massachusetts, especially after the enactment in December 1813 of a new trade embargo.[56]

His own discomfiture notwithstanding, the year 1814 opened on a most optimistic note for Pickering. The president announced that the British had offered and he had accepted an invitation to hold direct peace talks. For once the Massachusetts congressman believed the administration to be in earnest. A British dispatch vessel had just brought news of Napoleon's defeats in Germany and his hasty withdrawal from Leipzig. With the tyrant about to fall, Pickering was certain the administration would act to end the fighting before England was able to concentrate all of her vast power against the United States. The New Englander delighted in a vision of the Jeffersonians humbling themselves before the English. Then, he exulted, they would have "abundant cause to mourn in sack cloth and ashes."[57] Nor did he show any concern for the impending humiliation of the United States, viewing it as a vindication both of himself and of Federalism. He had for some time believed that it would take a traumatic experience to awaken the people to their past errors. He now expected that out of defeat and national degradation would come a return to political orthodoxy that would restore Federalism to power.[58]

Political developments later in January quickly disabused Pickering of these self-indulgent fantasies but simultaneously sent him reeling off in an equally unrealistic direction. When Madison first announced talks with Britain, he cautioned Congress that it would nonetheless be essential to make "vigorous preparations for carrying on the war."[59] Pickering had taken Madison's warning to be nothing more than window dressing designed to disguise the impending collapse. But when the president announced that two war hawks, Henry Clay and Jonathan Russell, had been added to the negotiating commission, he began to suspect that they had been included to hamstring the peace commission.[60]

Pickering's fear that the talks would fail grew stronger as the Republican majority in Congress passed a variety of laws strengthening the armed forces. Then came the defeat of a Federalist-sponsored resolution stipulating that it would be "inexpedient" to attempt an invasion of

Canada pending the outcome of negotiations. That was enough for Pickering, who concluded that Madison planned to continue the war.[61] Only a combination of "wickedness and stupidity," he wrote, could account for this.[62]

Two years before, Pickering had advocated the threat of secession as a method of forcing political change in the United States. Now, faced with the prospect of a continuation of the war, he began his last and most serious attempt to encourage the actual creation of a northern confederacy. In a confidential letter circulated among Federalist leaders in Massachusetts, he warned that further protests would produce only "abuse" in Washington. The people of New England would have to act if they expected redress. Massachusetts, he wrote, ought to make one last formal protest against continuing the war. Simultaneously, he urged that the legislature address the people, assuring them that the state's leaders had every intention of preserving the Union if the national government responded positively, but preparing them for secession if it did not. He realized, of course, that the Bay State could not secede unilaterally. The attempt would surely be crushed, and the example would convince like-minded states not to follow in her footsteps. But he thought there was a good chance for success if Massachusetts took the lead in calling for an interstate convention to include New York and all of New England.[63]

Though Pickering was encouraged by the fact that there was strong sentiment for secession in Massachusetts, the divided reaction of the people there to British military activity during the summer of 1814 made it apparent that the road to disunion would be difficult. The Royal Navy, striking at will along an undefended coast, raided Connecticut and Massachusetts, and then landed troops in the District of Maine.[64] Until then the state's Board of Seacoast Commissioners, controlled by Pickering and four other like-minded Federalists, had successfully thwarted every attempt at military preparedness.[65] Now, however, moderate Federalists joined with Republicans in demanding that something be done. The continued obstructionism of Pickering's Seacoast Commission provoked a political battle in Boston, where advocates of preparedness won a court order requiring the unwilling selectmen to hold a town meeting. At this meeting, however, those who urged defensive measures were overruled by the well-organized opposition. Not even the news that the British had taken Washington, burning all of the public buildings there, had any effect on the voting. "Such is the baneful influence of the British partizans," wrote one downcast Republican.[66]

However, on the day following the town meeting, Pickering and other opponents of preparedness suffered a serious reversal when Boston learned of the capture of Alexandria, Virginia, by the British. The city fathers of this staunchly Federalist stronghold had offered no opposition, even ransoming the town. Nevertheless, Admiral Sir George Cockburn made off with the merchant ships at anchor there together with their cargoes. This news led to a spontaneous demand in Boston that something be done to defend Massachusetts.[67] Suddenly, one delighted Republican noted, Pickering and others who opposed defending the state against a British attack "were left in the background." Even Governor Strong reversed himself. With the state in a panic, fifteen thousand militiamen were mobilized and frantic efforts were made to strengthen the forts defending the sea approaches to Boston. For one brief moment Massachusetts knew a unity that it had not enjoyed for more than a decade. "However we may squabble about the loaves and fishes," Benjamin Waterhouse rejoiced, "we all agree to fight the common enemy the English." Old John Adams, too, sensed the changed atmosphere. There were, after all, "symptoms that the germ of virtue is not destroyed," he wrote.[68]

To be sure, this new consensus lasted only a short while. Before long the fear of a British attack dwindled and old patterns reappeared. Governor Strong demobilized the militia and the legislature turned its attentions to the forthcoming convention at Hartford. Nevertheless, in that moment a sense of nationalism was revealed that Pickering and other disunionists would be hard-pressed to contend with.

By the middle of October Pickering's secessionist hopes were being buffeted from a number of directions. At sea, two American warships, the *Wasp* and the *Peacock*, won victories over British vessels in heroic single-ship actions. More significant, the British were humiliated before Baltimore; General Sir George Prevost was forced to retreat from Plattsburg, New York, back into Canada; and America's Captain Thomas MacDonough won naval control of the Great Lakes. As one shrewd Republican observer noted, much had happened "to elevate the national character and the national government" in the eyes of all the people, North and South.[69]

Of course, none of these developments influenced Pickering. Not even the sight of the capital in ruins shook his willingness to overlook British outrages. England, he insisted, was merely demonstrating the futility of continuing the war before making peace.[70] But a growing number of Federalists were wondering how much of a lesson the English intended to inflict. Even Rebecca Pickering grew terrified. Perhaps Admiral Alexander Cochrane really intended to carry out the threat he had reportedly made to burn and pillage the entire coastline.

Even as Pickering attempted to soothe the jangled nerves of his wife and other Federalists, more disconcerting news arrived. Dispatches from the envoys at Ghent detailing British peace terms made it evident that they sought nothing short of national humiliation for the United States.[71] Aware that the British demands were of considerable domestic political importance, Madison quickly published them along with the American negotiator's instructions. Together they made it clear that while England seemed intent upon a victor's peace, the United States sought nothing at Ghent but a settlement based on the principle of the *status quo ante bellum.*

On October 10, Pickering was in his seat in the House chamber when the clerk read Madison's message submitting the dispatches from the envoys as well as their instructions. John Forsyth, a Georgia Republican, moved to print five thousand copies of the dispatches. Alexander Conte Hanson then took the floor. This Maryland Federalist was perhaps closer politically to Pickering than anyone else in either house. His newspaper, the *Baltimore Federal Republican,* had for years been Pickering's mouthpiece in the South. Yet Hanson now urged the House to double the number of copies of the dispatches to be printed. In the past, he said, he had opposed the war, supposing that the administration had not honestly sought peace. But now there was no room for doubt. The United States had made a fair bid for a settlement and had been rebuffed because the English insisted upon "degrading and humiliating conditions." From "that moment," Hanson continued, the conflict ceased to be "a party war" and became "national." [72]

Unlike Hanson, Pickering was neither surprised nor irritated by the British demands. In fact, he defended them as completely reasonable.[73] He found few others, however, who agreed with him. He contacted John Jay, hoping for an endorsement of Britain's terms from that prestigious quarter. But the aging statesman thought the proposals so extreme that he refused to take them seriously. Since for some arcane reason England seemed determined to continue the war, Jay hoped the people would unite in the nation's defense.[74] Even Gouverneur Morris, as much a political extremist as Pickering, was appalled at the British proposals, believing that to submit to them would be a national disgrace.[75] Most congressional Federalists agreed with Jay and Morris. At a caucus held after publication of the dispatches, an overwhelming majority insisted that, the war having changed in nature, they could no longer oppose the loans or tax increases needed to finance it.[76]

Changed political circumstances, and the realization that most Federalists had a stronger sense of national loyalty than he had imagined, led Pickering to modify his attitudes. Neither in his personal correspondence nor in public did he chastise Hanson or those who rushed to the colors after publication of the British terms. At the Federalist congressional caucus, though a dissenter, he did not categorically oppose support for new taxes or war loans.[77] Moreover, claiming to have been misunderstood, he reverted once again to the argument that secession should be employed only as a tactic, a temporary expedient designed to preserve "the just rights of the North" within the Union.[78]

Pickering remained convinced, however, that the South and the West dominated national political and economic affairs to the detriment of the Northeast. Confident that the South would quickly be reduced to the status of a minority section if shorn of its connection with the West, he exhorted the delegates about to assemble at the Hartford Convention to endorse a division of the nation into separate confederacies divided by the mountains. In order to accomplish this as well as the enactment of a series of radical constitutional changes that he believed were also necessary, Pickering argued that the delegates would have to vote to secede.[79]

But Pickering had no confidence in the willingness of the majority at Hartford to support such action. Even the Massachusetts contingent seemed weak and unreliable. He despised Harrison Gray Otis.[80] Nor had he much faith in George Cabot, the head of the delegation. His old friend had a fine mind, perhaps the best in all of New England; but he was tired and a cynic. He thought democracy too far advanced for the society to be saved. "Why can't you and I let the world ruin itself in its own way?" Cabot had once inquired of Pickering. The words "sunk deep in my mind," the Massachusetts congressman later recalled. "In this wicked world it is the duty of every good man, tho' he cannot restore it to *innocence,* to strive to prevent its growing worse."[81] And so, with little enthusiasm, Pickering awaited the results of the Hartford Convention.

On the very day that the delegates were scheduled to begin their deliberations in far-off Connecticut, Pickering learned of military developments that gave him some hope. A large British expeditionary force was reported to be descending upon New Orleans. Pickering viewed both the English invasion and the Hartford Convention as driving at the same point, the restructuring of the Union. His fertile imagination quickly fashioned an exciting new scenario. Britain would take the state of Louisiana and West Florida as colonies. But her command of the Mississippi and the Gulf would lead to the creation of a new satellite republic in the West. With Kentucky, Tennessee, and the rest of the transmontane region gone, the South would at last be forced to come to terms with the northern states, assuming a subordinate position in the old Union.[82]

Pickering also sensed that news of the impending British attack upon Louisiana might strengthen the hand of those at Hartford ready to take decisive action. He urged his friend James Hillhouse, a leader among the more extreme delegates, to be bold. The time was right to strike, he wrote. Only the "mystical word union" had prevented New England from seizing the initiative earlier. Now, Pickering insisted, the magic of the word had largely worn away. The northern states must demand concessions and, if necessary, secede to win their point. Nor need they fear retaliation from the national government, weakened as it had been by the war.[83]

Pickering's extraordinary burst of enthusiasm was clearly not shared by the majority of the delegates at Hartford. The efforts of Hillhouse and other extremists notwithstanding, nothing substantive was accomplished during the convention. Pickering, however, refused to become discouraged, for the overall antiwestern and antiexpansionist flavor of the convention report pleased him, as did the inclusion of a series of proposed radical constitutional amendments similar to those he had recommended earlier to Hillhouse. The fact that the delegates endorsed the idea of a second meeting, this time to be held at Boston, also encouraged him, for it suggested a willingness to take action in the near future if proper redress were not forthcoming from the national government.[84] Finally, and perhaps most important, Pickering was counting on a British triumph at New Orleans. If the delegates at Hartford hadn't yet taken steps to confront the federal government, he was confident that those attending the projected Boston meeting would do so after the British had won their inevitable victory in the West.

During December and January, as he awaited news of the expected blow against New Orleans, Pickering's emotionalism built in a furious crescendo. He fought wildly against a Republican-sponsored measure to strengthen the armed forces by conscripting militia. And when it seemed that the national government might attempt to bring elements of the Massachusetts militia into national service, he advised Governor Strong to resist, forcefully if necessary.[85] But perhaps nothing more clearly demonstrates the extent of his passion and, not incidentally, the degree to which he had lost sight of human values, than his reaction to the sudden death of Elbridge Gerry. Pickering, who had known Gerry longer than anyone else in Congress, was asked to introduce a resolution expressing the House of Representatives' sorrow at the death of the vice-president. Although it is not uncommon for even the most bitter enmities to be dissipated by death, Pickering was not so forgiving.

Gerry had transgressed during the quasi war and later when he became a leader among Massachusetts Republicans. Now he was dead and Pickering wasn't sorry. He absolutely refused to engage in what he described as hypocrisy, and would have nothing whatever to do with the House of Representatives' resolution.[86]

When the long-awaited news from New Orleans at last filtered through to Washington, it was of course not at all what Pickering had expected. The first indication that things had gone awry for General Packenham and the British expeditionary force came late in January, when the *National Intelligencer* carried early reports that New Orleans had been saved.[87] A week later more authoritative accounts of the victory arrived.[88] This should have been the final disappointment for Pickering, the crushing blow from which there could be no recovery. Incredibly, however, he was literally transformed by the news of Andrew Jackson's miraculous victory. The virtual annihilation of Packenham's army touched Pickering's sense of national pride, which until then had been hardly noticeable. He culled the newspapers for every scrap of information relating to events at New Orleans. And in a long letter to Beckey in which he described the battle in great detail, he exulted at how the "Americans mowed" the British "down."[89] The victory at New Orleans affected Pickering's attitude toward a number of related issues as well. Where only a short while before he had rebuked Massachusetts Senator James Lloyd for even suggesting that the United States seek a settlement based on the prewar status quo, he now explained excitedly to Beckey that the victory would surely force the Foreign Office to reconsider its earlier demands.[90] Nor did he ever again mention Hartford or the idea of a New England confederacy.

This extraordinary turnabout begs for and simultaneously defies explanation. It is of course possible to contend that Pickering, who saw the handwriting on the wall, changed his opinions to reflect new political realities. Yet he so frequently ignored political considerations that this cannot be a totally convincing argument. Moreover, such a view must of necessity discount the honest enthusiasm of his letter to his wife. Perhaps the best that can be done is to suggest that at certain critical moments Pickering did have conversion experiences that incidentally served to protect him politically. In this regard it should be noted that such radical shifts were characteristic of Pickering's long political career. Thus, forty-five years before, he had moved swiftly out of the Tory faction to become an outspoken Whig. And during the 1790s, under the pressure of a virulent Republican attack, he repudiated his earlier opinion of the French Revolution and became an extreme Federalist. Certainly Jackson's victory could have induced a similar change. In any event, the significant fact is that after New Orleans, Pickering was a much different man. Contemporaries then and historians since have commented upon the power of the nationalist outburst that came on the heels of Jackson's triumph. Surely there is no stronger evidence for this than the remarkable transformation of Timothy Pickering.

NINETEEN

Epilogue

FOR MORE THAN A DECADE prior to 1815 Pickering had lived with great tension, much of it self-induced, the product of a rich political fantasy life. Now, with the coming of peace, he relaxed into an amiable social existence spent in the company of well-to-do Federalists in Georgetown and nearby Maryland.[1] He came to view the political opposition in a new and more tolerant light as well, explaining to Beckey that the democrats seemed "more cordial" than before, when in truth he too had changed. Not only was there less to quarrel about, but he was less quarrelsome.[2]

Though in some ways he was a different person, Pickering's economic frame of reference remained very much the same. Despite the fact that cotton manufacturing had taken root in his native soil and there was a new sugar refinery in Salem, one of six that had recently grown up in New England, he remained the representative of Massachusetts' merchant community. Predictably, then, he opposed the Tariff of 1816 because the protection it offered New England's textile manufacturers threatened the merchants' lucrative trade in East Indian fabrics.[3] Nor was he sympathetic to President Madison's scheme to force the English to open the West Indies to American trade through a program of discrimination against British ships and goods.[4]

Pickering's failure to adapt to the economic changes taking place in his congressional district undoubtedly contributed to his final undoing. However, the specific issue that at last finished him politically was his uncompromising support for a congressional salary increase that proved to be extremely unpopular with the voters.[5] Other congressmen, surprised by the outraged public reaction to the enactment of the new salary law, moved quickly to mend fences, and repeal of the act soon became a certainty. Yet, characteristically, Pickering refused to adjust to the current of opinion, even though he realized that it ran more strongly in Massachusetts than in many other states. He was appalled that legislators in his home state should have made so much of this "piddling" affair. Nor would he act on direct instructions from the state legislature to vote for repeal of the new statute. Instructions to a representative, he insisted, were not only "improper and impertinent," they were "repugnant to the great principle of representation in a free government."[6]

This reaction was typical of an older generation of Federalists who prided themselves on being independent of the whims and fancies of public opinion.[7] It was also, one senses, the response of a man who craved the extra money. But above all it was fatally anachronistic, for politics had changed fundamentally since the Federalist era, and congressmen who refused to respond appropriately to constituent demands courted disaster.[8] Pickering's uncompromising refusal to respond to either public pressure or legislative instructions was too much for his constituents. In the autumn of 1816 they made it apparent that he would not be nominated for a third congressional term.[9] Only then did Pickering attempt to save some shreds of his dignity by announcing his retirement. And so, fittingly, he left national politics, toppled like some great oak in a democratic storm, his career finally ended over an issue that even he admitted was of no real consequence.

Pickering lost none of his fiery enthusiasm in retirement. To be sure, the long fringe of hair around his bald head had grown white. But the fire in his eye that Gilbert Stuart had seen and captured in his 1808 portrait remained unchanged, and his physical vigor was undiminished. He ate sparingly, walked long distances easily, and continued to do most of the hard labor on his farm even when past the age of eighty. Quite literally, Pickering sought to deny physical or mental decline, to exercise power over death. It was his last great struggle.[10]

Although the old man was treated with some deference by the majority of those who lived along Massachusetts' North Shore, he had finally lost his political influence, his significance having become largely symbolic. No one, after all, was better suited to deliver the July 4 address in Salem during the Jubilee Year than this aging relic of the revolutionary generation.[11] And when a committee was organized to collect food, clothing, and other essentials for the Greeks suffering under Turkish oppression, it seemed altogether fitting that Pickering should be at its head.[12] But when friends attempted to send him back to the House of Representatives in 1818 the movement attracted no support, for he was an anachronism whose views on politics, commerce, and manufacturing appealed only to a diminishing number of unreconstructed Federalists.[13]

Pickering, who appears not to have noticed that he had become little more than a curiosity, continued to play the role of the restless activist. He read the *National Intelligencer* avidly and corresponded with congressional contacts, in this way maintaining a sort of quasi connection with a political life that he could no longer enjoy firsthand. An early convert to William Ellery Channing's brand of rational Christianity, he was soon in the thick of the Unitarian controversy as well.[14]

The moral and political issue that most interested Pickering during his long years in retirement, however, was slavery. Because he viewed black emigration as a potential solution to the dilemma posed by the race question, he at first became an enthusiastic spokesman for the recently organized American Colonization Society.[15] Unlike those others who clung to colonization long after it had become irrelevant, however, Pickering lost his enthusiasm for the idea after the enactment of the Missouri Compromise. What sense did it make to promote colonization, he wondered, while simultaneously opening millions of square miles to slavery? For every black who emigrated, "the profit hungry slave breeders" of the upper South would raise up a thousand to fill these empty lands.[16] Assuming the rapid growth of the black population, Pickering concluded that since slavery would have to be abolished sooner or later, the only option left for Americans was to face up to the prospect that ultimately Negroes and whites would have to live together in a free society. He therefore turned away from colonization, advocating instead a system of gradual emancipation with slave owners bearing the responsibility of preparing blacks for freedom.[17]

During the 1820s, as America's slave population multiplied, Pickering became increasingly skeptical about the possibility of heading off some sort of great social catastrophe. "I can think of no cause of gloomy foreboding so dreadful as the extensive and rapidly increasing population of" blacks kept in "a state of slavery," he explained to John Marshall.[18] The South's "peculiar institution," he thought, was a "portentous evil, swelling to a magnitude appalling to contemplate and surpassing any other that can be conceived."[19]

Although Pickering's abolitionism was genuine enough, he did not approach the problem with the zeal that he usually reserved for truly compelling issues. The point, one supposes, is that as he grew older his life narrowed and he found it difficult to become aroused by questions that were not of immediate personal importance. Thus, of far greater moment to Pickering than Unitarianism, slavery—or any other moral, religious, or political issue, for that matter—was the gnawing concern he felt about his place in history. It is difficult to judge what bothered him more, the fact that he was not included among the exalted few destined to be remembered as the giants of his era, or the fact that others whom he had despised were. The effect was the same in either event. As Americans went about the business of fabricating the myths that were to transform the leaders of the revolutionary generation into a republican pantheon, he grew bitter and, characteristically, resolved to expose to the harsh glare of "truth" the fallacies perpetrated by such popular authors as Mason Weems and William Wirt.

Perhaps inevitably, Pickering reacted most violently to George Washington's growing historical reputation. He insisted that the Virginian had been badly educated, that he was at best intellectually mediocre, that he had been inept as a general and undistinguished as the nation's chief executive officer.[20] The men around Washington, Pickering contended, had time and again saved him from terrible mistakes. During the Revolution, Nathanael Greene, Alexander Hamilton, Robert Harrison, and a few other aides had made many of the most critical decisions, while simultaneously carrying on almost all of Washington's very extensive correspondence for him. And Hamilton, not Washington, had been the author of the important policies of the precedent-setting first administration. Washington had not even written his own immortal Farewell Address. That too, Pickering insisted, had been the exclusive product of Hamilton's genius.[21]

For years Pickering fumed over Washington's unjustified reputation, while carrying on a spirited private correspondence with Richard Peters and a few other close friends who were willing to debate the issue with him.[22] During that same period Washington's myth grew until at last he had been elevated to the status of a demigod, truly the father of his country. Virtually beside himself, Pickering began to speak openly of his contempt for the dead leader.[23] Friends warned him that in attacking the mythologized hero, he was doing his country no favor, and was in any event doing more harm to himself than to the memory of the departed president.[24] But Pickering persevered, proclaiming his intent to publish the truth, not only about Washington, but also about the "supreme hypocrite" Thomas Jefferson, as well as Samuel Adams, John Adams, and other overrated leaders of the revolutionary era.[25]

All of his threats notwithstanding, Pickering would probably have been content to compose angry letters and scribble diatribes in his political notebooks to the end of his days had not a particularly annoying pamphlet appeared in October 1823. It was a compendium of more than sixty letters exchanged between John Adams and his cousin William Cunningham from 1803 to 1812.[26] The elder Adams had not intended that these letters should be made public. On the contrary, he had specifically prohibited their publication, at least until after his death.[27] Adams had good reason, for he had written with great asperity not only about Jefferson and Madison, but also about numbers of Federalists with whom he had worked during his long career, among them Fisher Ames, George Cabot, and Alexander Hamilton. No one came in for more abuse than Pickering, who was characterized by Adams as having been the principal conspirator against peace with France during his administration. Adding insult to injury, Adams further suggested that one very good reason for removing Pickering in 1800 had been that he was intellectually deficient—that is, without sufficient background or learning to carry out the responsibilities of his office. Though Pickering had "a strong desire for celebrity," Adams acridly remarked, he had only "feeble means of obtaining it."[28]

Not surprisingly, Pickering was infuriated on reading the Adams-Cunningham correspondence. "In all of my life I have never met with such a mass of calumny," he raged. "The whole noble family of Adams will regret this act of the ex-president, alike imprudent and malevolent."[29] Encouraged by a number of friends, Pickering was soon at work on a pamphlet designed to serve at once as a rebuttal to Adams, a corrective to the myths growing up around Washington and Jefferson, and an attack upon the presidential aspirations of John Quincy Adams. The seemingly indefatigable old man was back in politics again.[30]

When finally Pickering's review of the Adams-Cunningham correspondence appeared in May 1824, the Salem Gazette congratulated the aging zealot for having "defended himself, fully and completely, from the virulent reproaches of Mr. A."[31] But unrestrained enthusiasm for Pickering's pamphlet was confined to a very few. A more characteristic response was that of the Baltimore Patriot, whose editor deplored the fact that in their dotage Pickering and Adams should be at it again and advised his readers to pay no attention. The pity was, the editor continued, "that there were Iagoes enough in our country to excite such a controversy between too such hoary heads."[32]

Some of John Quincy Adams's supporters in Massachusetts advised him to respond to the charges leveled against him by the querulous old man. But Adams, who believed Federalism dead and Pickering's malicious attack politically irrelevant, refused to take the situation seriously, passing the pamphlet off as an example of Pickering's personal animus against his father. Though the younger Adams would not be enticed into a public name-calling match, pro-Adams newspapers were not always so sensible. Charles King's New York Journal and Robert Walsh's National Gazette were swift to counterattack, the Gazette charging that Pickering seemed willing to accept yet another president handpicked by the Virginia aristocracy simply to satisfy his desire for revenge "against the father of the eastern candidate."[33]

Pickering reacted characteristically to the *National Gazette*'s accusations. Editor Walsh, he maintained, had been corrupted. Adams had undoubtedly promised him the State Department job in return for his aid. Of course the old man would not be silenced. "With *truth* for my shield and spear I fear none of them," he exclaimed to Ebenezer Bowman.[34] Soon, though none of the contending factions was anxious to claim him, Pickering became involved in the presidential campaign, publishing pseudonymously in an Essex County newspaper in support of William H. Crawford, the regular Republican Party candidate. Later, when the election was thrown into the House of Representatives, Andrew Jackson became Pickering's last hope against Adams.

During the 1820s a number of old Federalists turned up in Jacksonian ranks. Surely, however, the new Democratic Party had no stranger recruit than Timothy Pickering, whose conversion was the result of a single passion, his hatred for the Adams family.[35] Thus, this old man, who had begun his political life sixty-five years before as one of Salem's more promising young Loyalists, and who spent his mature political years struggling against the egalitarian tendencies of Jeffersonian democracy, made his last political act a commitment to Andrew Jackson in the presidential election of 1828.

Pickering's conversion to Jacksonianism required some major intellectual as well as emotional adaptations, for as an extreme Federalist he had long held to elitist political views. He proved sufficiently flexible, however. Thus, when Adams's supporters charged that Jackson was not learned enough to be president, Pickering retorted in a way that can only be described as typically Jacksonian. Learning, he maintained, was not essential in a president. Washington and Monroe had both proven that. Moreover, Jackson had qualities of leadership that were of far greater importance than any intellectual attainments. His generalship at New Orleans, Pickering contended, proved beyond question that he possessed "a capacity for any . . . office . . . requiring only good sense, a sound judgment and a firmness of purpose in the execution."[36]

During the heated campaign of 1828, Pickering, aged eighty-two, even participated in the seamier side of democratic politics. He set friends in Boston to work searching the records of all the Masonic lodges in the area in hopes of proving that John Quincy Adams had lied in declaring that he had never been a Mason. It was, Pickering admitted, "disgraceful to resort to such pitiful means" in the struggle against the president. But it was nonetheless necessary, for Jackson, who made no secret of his Masonic affiliation, was being hurt politically in several counties of western New York where anti-Masonry was a powerful force.[37] When Pickering's diligent search for proof of the president's connection with the Masons failed to produce anything incriminating, he tried to turn the tables by using anti-Masonry against Adams. It was an outrage, Pickering railed, that the president and his supporters should attempt to turn Jackson's Masonic connection to political advantage. He was certain, however, that "given time to reflect," the people in western New York "would repel with disdain the imposition which has been practiced on them."[38]

Jacksonian leaders seem to have been of two minds about accepting Pickering's help during the campaign. They actually solicited his aid in ascertaining the facts surrounding Adams's alleged Masonic affiliation. Nor were they reluctant to publish one of his pseudonymous essays lauding the general's leadership at New Orleans.[39] However, they seem to have been anxious to keep the public ignorant of Pickering's connection with the Democratic Party. Thus the editor of Boston's *Jackson Republican* refused to publish one of Pickering's essays simply because he had signed it. Boston's Democrats feared a popular backlash if it became too widely known that he was in their camp.[40]

On August 14, 1828, while the campaign was in full swing, Rebecca, Pickering's wife of fifty-two years, died. During that same week in distant Philadelphia, Richard Peters too passed away, and for just a moment the old man felt very much alone. But he refused to bend or stumble, even under the weight of such sorrows. On the contrary, he took sustenance from his small role in the election campaign and was of course enormously pleased when Jackson won. Nor did other aspects of his life change significantly after his wife's death. He continued as an active member of the Essex Agricultural Society and was to be seen regularly striding easily along the Salem-Wenham Road on his way to or from his farm.

By the same token he remained intent on revealing the "truth" about the revolutionary generation. His review of the Adams-Cunningham correspondence had been a beginning, nothing more. When not preoccupied with his agricultural pursuits, he spent long hours at his desk writing political essays in his notebooks. His most important historical project, however, was a biography of Alexander Hamilton that he began planning in 1827.[41] The Hamilton biography, which he never wrote, was to be the vehicle for redressing the historical balance. It was a fixation he would carry with him to the grave that somehow the growing myth of the Founders would have to be punctured, that

Washington's mediocrity, Adams's vanity, and Jefferson's hypocrisy would have to be brought home to the people.[42]

It may seem amazing that at eighty-two Pickering should have undertaken to write a major work of biography. But his instinct for survival, his continued vigor and good health, and the fact that many of his siblings had arrived at extreme old age, encouraged him to think in terms of living for many more years.[43] He was not, however, to survive as long as he hoped. His magnificent physical constitution would fail before he could complete his attack on the myths that had grown up around the heroes of the revolutionary generation.

Sunday, January 4, 1829, was one of those bright, deceptively clear wintry days that makes one think longingly of spring. As was his habit, Pickering rose early, dressed, and walked to church. But the cold air of the morning, more penetrating than he had imagined, left him with a chill. He returned home unwell and went to bed. Confident that, as in the past, by resting and eating sparingly he could overcome whatever was troubling him, the old man refused all medical help for almost three weeks. But a pain developed in his left side; he grew feverish and found it increasingly difficult to breathe. At last he gave in to his family's importunings and summoned a doctor, and then another, and another. He was bled, and mustard plasters as well as leeches were applied to his side, but without any positive result. Timothy Pickering was in fact dying, slowly and painfully.[44]

Tenacious to the last, he summoned all of his remaining strength and actually rose from his deathbed to spend two final days sitting up with his family. It was as though through an act of sheer will he could bring himself back to good health. But on January 27, his last reserves having been expended, he retreated to his bed and asked to see a minister. When Charles Upham arrived at Pickering's bedside, he could see that the old man's time on earth was short. With his breath now coming in short gasps, Pickering explained to Upham that he had hoped to live at least a few more years. There were some "truths, important in an historical point of view," that he wanted to make known to the people. Then he added sadly, "perhaps it is of no matter." Recalling two lines from his still unclouded memory, he concluded: "Truths would you teach, or save a sinking land, / All fear, none aid you, and few understand."[45] Two days later Timothy Pickering was dead.

NOTES

A NOTE ON THE SOURCES

INDEX

Abbreviations in the Notes

AC	*Debates and Proceedings in the Congress of the United States (Annals of Congress)* (Washington, 1834–1856).
AP	The Adams Family Papers, Massachusetts Historical Society (microfilm).
APS	American Philosophical Society Library.
ASPFA, ASPIA	*American State Papers* . . . Foreign Affairs and Indian Affairs series (Washington, 1832–1861).
CL	Clements Library, University of Michigan.
DIDSNA	Diplomatic Instructions, Department of State, R.G. 59, National Archives (microfilm).
DLDSNA	Domestic Letters, Department of State, R.G. 59, National Archives (microfilm).
EI	James Duncan Phillips Library, Essex Institute.
GWPLC	Papers of George Washington, Presidential Microfilm Collection, Library of Congress.
LC	Library of Congress.
MHS	Massachusetts Historical Society.
PCCNA	Papers of the Continental Congress, National Archives (microfilm).
PP	Papers of Timothy Pickering, Massachusetts Historical Society (microfilm).
RWRNA	War Records Collection of Revolutionary War Records, Miscellaneous Numbered Records (the manuscript files), National Archives (microfilm).
SP	*The Susquehannah Company Papers,* ed. Robert J. Taylor (Ithaca, 1969–1971), vols. 8–10.

Notes

Chapter 1. From Loyalist to Whig

1. George D. Phillips, *Salem in the Eighteenth Century* (Boston: Houghton Mifflin 1937), pp. 166–88; G. L. Streeter, "Salem Before the Revolution," *Essex Institute Historical Collections,* XXXII (1896): 47–48.

2. Octavius Pickering and Charles W. Upham, *The Life of Timothy Pickering* (Boston: Little Brown, 1867), I 3–5.

3. Ibid.

4. Ibid., p. 5*n;* Phillips, *Salem,* p. 262.

5. Clifford K. Shipton, *Sibley's Harvard Graduates* (Boston: Massachusetts Historical Society, 1873–), VI, 331–35.

6. Pickering and Upham, *Pickering,* IV, 393–94.

7. Pickering to Williams, Nov. 1789, *PP,* reel 6.

8. John Adams, *The Diary and Autobiography of John Adams,* ed. Lyman Butterfield (Cambridge, Mass.: Belknap Press, 1961), III, 320–21.

9. Phillips, *Salem,* p. 267.

10. Joseph B. Felt, *The Annals of Salem* (Salem: W. & S. B. Ives, 1827); II, 416; Pickering and Upham, *Pickering,* I, 6*n; Essex Gazette,* Nov. 1–8, 1768; March 14–21, 1769, microcard, University of Missouri Library.

11. Felt, *Annals,* II, 453–54.

12. Phillips, *Salem,* pp. 102–12; Whitaker to Pickering, Apr. 17, Dec. 2, 1771, *PP,* reel 39; Timothy Pickering, "Letters to Congregational Churches," *Essex Institute Historical Collections,* XLIX (1913): 85–90.

13. Pickering to R. Pickering, Sept. 11, 1778, *PP,* reel 1; Pickering and Upham, *Pickering,* I, 5–6.

14. Pickering's memo on Harvard, Oct. 1828; T. Pickering, Sr., to T. Pickering, Jr., March 12, Dec. 8, 1762, *PP,* reel 53.

15. Ibid; Josiah Quincy, *The History of Harvard University* (Cambridge, Mass.: J. Owen, 1840), II, 98–99.

16. Samuel Eliot Morison, *Three Centuries of Harvard* (Cambridge: Harvard University Press, 1936), pp. 83–84.

17. Ibid., p. 92.

18. Ibid., p. 90.

19. Harvard Faculty Records (Harvard University Archives), May 1, 1760, Dec. 12, 1762, II, 113, 182.

20. Ibid.

21. Pickering's memo on Harvard, Oct. 1828, *PP,* reel 53.

22. Ibid; Shipton, *Sibley's Harvard Graduates,* XIII, 97–100.

23. Pickering's memo on Harvard, Oct. 1828, *PP,* reel 53.

24. Ibid.

25. Page Smith, *John Adams* (Garden City, N.Y.: Doubleday, 1962), I, 15–16.

26. Pickering was admitted to the Massachusetts Bar in 1768; memo, Dec. 31, 1768; *PP,* reel 33; Pickering and Upham, *Pickering,* I, 31.

27. Pickering's journal, April 9, 1768, *PP,* reel 53.

28. Salem Social Library Record Book (Essex Institute), May 27, 1765; receipt dated May 27, 1765, Pickering Papers, *EI.*

29. *Essex Gazette,* Oct. 23–30, 1770.

30. Pickering and Upham, *Pickering,* I, 16.

31. Merrill Jensen, *The Founding of a Nation* (New York: Oxford University Press, 1968), pp. 256–57; Bernard to Lord Barrington, June 29, 1768, *Barrington-Bernard Correspondence,* ed. Edward Channing and Archibald G. Collidge (Cambridge: Harvard University Press, 1912), p. 161.

32. *Essex Gazette,* Aug. 2, 1768; Phillips, *Salem,* p. 294.

33. Pickering and Upham, *Pickering,* I, 16.

34. *Essex Gazette,* Aug. 28–Sept. 4, Sept. 18–25, 1770; Pickering and Upham, *Pickering,* I, 506.

35. *Essex Gazette,* Oct. 23–30, 1770.

36. Ibid.

37. Salem Town Records (transcripts in *EI*), March 9, 1772.

38. Richard D. Brown, *Revolutionary Politics in Massachusetts* (Cambridge: Harvard University Press, 1970), pp. 79–80.

39. Adams to Gerry, Nov. 14, 1772, cited in James T. Austin, *The Life of Elbridge Gerry* (Boston: Wells & Lilly, 1828–29), I, 21.

40. Salem Town Records, June 7, 1773.

41. Ibid.

Chapter 2. The Revolution Closes In

1. *Essex Gazette,* May 10–17, 1774.

2. Pickering to Clarke, June 15, 1774, *PP,* reel 33.

3. *Essex Gazette,* May 10–17, 1774; Merrill Jensen, *The Founding of a Nation* (New York: Oxford University Press, 1968), pp. 464–66.

4. Salem Town Records (transcripts in *EI*), May 16, 1774; *Essex Gazette,* May 10–17, 1774.

5. *Essex Gazette,* May 10–17, 1774.

6. Salem Town Records, May 17, 1774; *Essex Gazette,* May 17–24, 1774.

7. *Essex Gazette,* May 31–June 7, 1774; George D. Phillips, *Salem in the Eighteenth Century* (Boston: Houghton Mifflin, 1937), p. 323.

8. Gage to Johnson, June 26, 1774, Thomas Gage Papers, *CL.*

9. John Adams to Abigail Adams, July 2, 1774, *Adams Family Correspondence,* ed. Lyman Butterfield (Cambridge, Mass.: Belknap Press, 1963), I, 120.

10. *Essex Gazette,* June 7–14, 1774.

11. Gage to the Merchants and other inhabitants of Salem, June 11, 1774; address to

Gage from the wardens and Vestry of St. Peters Church; Salem, June 3, 1774, Thomas Gage Papers, *CL*.

12. *Essex Gazette,* June 14–21, 1774; Octavius Pickering and Charles W. Upham, *The Life of Timothy Pickering* (Boston: Little Brown, 1867), I, 49–52.

13. Phillips, *Salem,* pp. 327–28; John C. Miller, *Sam Adams: Pioneer in Propaganda* (Boston: Little Brown, 1936), p. 308.

14. John R. Alden, *General Gage in America* (Baton Rouge: Louisiana State University Press, 1948), p. 209.

15. *Essex Gazette,* July 12–19, 1774.

16. Ibid., Aug. 9–16, 1774.

17. Ibid., Aug. 16–23, 1774.

18. Flucker to Pickering, Aug. 24, 1774, *PP,* reel 17.

19. Pickering to Wingate, Aug. 25, 1774, *PP,* reel 33.

20. Ibid.

21. Ibid.

22. Pickering's recognizance, Aug. 25, 1774, *PP,* reel 53.

23. Pickering to Wingate, Aug. 25, 1774, *PP,* reel 33.

24. Andrews to Barrell, Aug. 26, 1774, "Letters of John Andrews Esq. of Boston," ed. Winthrop Sargeant, *Massachusetts Historical Society Proceedings,* VIII (1864, 1865): 347.

25. Ibid.

26. Pickering to Wingate, Aug. 25, 1774, *PP,* reel 33.

27. Andrews to Barrell, Aug. 26, 1774, "Letters of Andrews," p. 347.

28. "The Montresor Journals," *Collections of the New York Historical Society,* 1889, p. 123.

29. Gage to Frye, Aug. 27, 1774, Thomas Gage Papers, *CL.*

30. *Boston Evening Post,* Aug. 29, 1774.

31. Andrews to Barrell, Aug. 25, 1774, "Letters of Andrews," p. 347.

32. "A Freeholder," Aug. 1774, *PP,* reel 33.

33. Ibid.

34. *Essex Gazette,* Sept. 6–13, 1774.

35. Ibid.

36. Ibid.

37. Marblehead Committee of Correspondence to Salem Committee of Correspondence, Sept. 6, 1774, *PP,* reel 39.

38. Boston Committee of Correspondence to Salem Committee of Correspondence, Sept. 6, 1774, ibid.

39. Ibid.; Richard D. Brown, *Revolutionary Politics in Massachusetts* (Cambridge: Harvard University Press, 1970), pp. 122–23.

40. *Essex Gazette,* Sept. 6–13, 1774.

41. Ibid., Sept. 28–Oct. 4, 1774.

42. Ibid., Oct. 4–11, 1774.

43. Ibid.

44. Ibid., Sept. 6–13, 1774.

45. Ibid., Oct. 4–11, 1774.

46. Pyncheon to Browne, 1775, cited in Pickman, *The Diary and Letters of Benjamin Pickman* (Newport, 1928), p. 56.

47. Higginson to Pickering, April 1775, *PP,* reel 5.

48. A draft of the retraction as it appeared in the *Gazette* may be found in Pickering's hand in *PP,* reel 33.

49. *Essex Gazette,* Oct. 4–11, 1774.
50. Ibid.; Phillips, *Salem,* pp. 340–42; Salem Town Records, Oct. 6, 1774.
51. Ibid.
52. Jensen, *Founding of a Nation,* p. 536.
53. *Essex Gazette,* Sept. 28–Oct. 10, 1774.
54. Ibid., Nov. 8–15, 1774.
55. *Essex Gazette,* Oct. 25–Nov. 1, 1774.
56. Higginson to Pickering, Apr. 1775, *PP,* reel 5; Pickering to Higginson, May 2, 1775; Higginson to Pickering, May 3, 1775, *PP,* reel 39; Wingate to Pickering, Mar. 1, 1775, *PP,* reel 17.
57. Ibid.
58. Timothy Pickering, "An Easy Plan of Discipline for a Militia," *Early American Imprints,* microcard, University of Missouri Library, pp. 10–11; Don Higginbotham, *The War of American Independence* (New York: Macmillan, 1971), pp. 4, 12–13, 47–48.
59. Ibid. ˙
60. *Essex Gazette,* Feb. 14–21, 1775; Pickering to the Officers of the Essex Militia, Dec. 26, 1774, *PP,* reel 5.
61. Phillips, *Salem,* pp. 354–55; George A. Billias, *General John Glover* (New York: Holt & Co., 1960), p. 64.
62. Phillips, *Salem,* pp. 358–60; *Essex Gazette,* Feb. 28–March 7, 1775.
63. Ibid.
64. Pickering's recollections of Apr. 19, 1775, dated 1807, *PP,* reel 53.
65. Christopher Ward, *The War of the Revolution* (New York: Macmillan, 1952), I, 49.
66. Pickering's recollection of Lexington, 1807, *PP,* reel 53.
67. Ibid.
68. Ibid.; Richard McKee, "Elias Hasket Derby, Merchant of Salem, Massachusetts, 1733–1799" (Ph.D. dissertation, Clark University, 1961), pp. 97–98.
69. William Heath, *Memoirs of Major General William Heath,* (New York: A. Wessels Co., 1904), p. 9.
70. Pickering's recollections of Lexington, 1807, *PP,* reel 53.
71. Pickering to Wingate, Apr. 23, 26, 1775, *PP,* reel 33.
72. John Cary, *Joseph Warren, Physician, Politician, Patriot* (Urbana: University of Illinois Press, 1961), p. 187.
73. Ibid.; Pickering's recollections of Lexington, 1807, *PP,* reel 53.
74. Cary, *Warren,* p. 187.

Chapter 3. A Taste of Battle

1. Higginson to Pickering, May 3, 6, 1775, *PP,* reel 39; Pickering to Higginson, May 2, 1775, *PP,* reel 5.
2. Pickering to Higginson, May 2, 1775, ibid.
3. Pickering to Holton, Oct. 16, 1775, ibid.
4. Ibid.
5. Holton to Pickering, Nov. 3, 1775, ibid.
6. Pickering to White, Nov. 2, 14, 1775, *PP,* reel 1.
7. Pickering to White, Nov. 29, Dec. 27, 1775, ibid.
8. Douglas S. Freeman, *George Washington* (New York: Scribner's, 1948–57), IV, 299–300.
9. Octavius Pickering and Charles W. Upham, *The Life of Timothy Pickering* (Boston: Little Brown, 1867), II, 21–22.

10. Pickering to R. Pickering, Jan. 30, 1777, *PP*, reel 1.

11. Washington to Heath, Dec. 18, 1776, *The Writings of George Washington*, ed. John C. Fitzpatrick (Washington, D.C.: U.S. Government Printing Office, 1939), VI, 392–94.

12. Washington to Heath, Dec. 28, 1776, ibid., pp. 449–50.

13. Pickering to R. Pickering, Jan. 14, 1777, *PP*, reel 1; Pickering and Upham, *Pickering*, I, 96–107.

14. Pickering and Upham, *Pickering*, I, 103; Pickering to J. Pickering, Jan. 31, 1777, *PP*, reel 5.

15. "The Journal of Lt. Colonel Stephen Kemble," *New York Historical Society Collections*, 1883, pp. 108–09; Ambrose Serle, *The American Journal of Ambrose Serle*, ed. Edward Tatum (San Marino, Calif.: Huntington Library, 1940), p. 181.

16. Pickering and Upham, *Pickering*, I, 103; Pickering to J. Pickering, Jan. 31, 1777, *PP*, reel 5; Parsons to Washington, Feb. 3, 1777, *GWPLC*, reel 39; Washington to Heath, Feb. 4, 1777, *Writings of Washington*, VII, 99–100; Graham Dolan, "Major General William Heath" (Ph.D. dissertation, Boston University, 1966), pp. 275–80; William Heath, *Memoirs of Major General William Heath* (New York: A. Wessels Co., 1904), pp. 97–106.

17. Pickering and Upham, *Pickering*, I, 115–18.

18. Pickering to Washington, Apr. 9, 1777, *PP*, reel 33.

19. Pickering to Washington, Apr. 14, 1777, ibid.

20. Pickering to R. Pickering, June 23, 1777, *PP*, reel 1; Pickering to J. Pickering, June 23, 1777, *PP*, reel 5.

21. After Orders by Timothy Pickering, June 28, 1777, Benjamin Lincoln Papers, *MHS*, reel 2; Freeman, *Washington*, IV, 426–27.

22. J. Adams to A. Adams, Aug. 13, 1777, *Adams Family Correspondence*, ed. Lyman Butterfield (Cambridge, Mass.: Belknap Press, 1963), II, 310.

23. Pickering to R. Pickering, Aug. 10, 1777, *PP*, reel 1.

24. Pickering to J. Pickering, Sept. 25, 1777, *PP*, reel 5.

25. Pickering to R. Pickering, Aug. 29, 1777, *PP*, reel 1.

26. Adams to A. Adams, June 2, 1777, *Adams Family Correspondence*, II, 253–54; Rush to J. Adams, Aug. 8, 1777, *Letters of Benjamin Rush*, ed. Lyman Butterfield (Princeton: Princeton University Press, 1951), I, 152–53.

27. Pickering and Upham, *Pickering*, I, 152–53.

28. Ibid., pp. 158–61; Freeman, *Washington*, IV, 490–94; Pickering to Peters, Jan. 17, 1811, *PP*, reel 14.

29. Freeman, *Washington*, IV, 484; Pickering to J. Pickering, Sept. 25, 1777, *PP*, reel 5.

30. Pickering to R. Pickering, Sept, 30, 1777, *PP*, reel 1.

31. Pickering to Peters, Jan. 17, 1811, *PP*, reel 14.

32. Ibid.

33. Pickering and Upham, *Pickering*, I, 168; Christopher Ward, *The War of the Revolution* (New York: Macmillan, 1952), I, 366; North Callahan, *Henry Knox: General Washington's General* (New York: Rinehart, 1958), pp. 119–24.

34. Ward, *War of the Revolution*, I, 368–69; Callahan, *Knox*, p. 122; Freeman, *Washington*, IV, 510–12; Pickering and Upham, *Pickering*, I, 169.

35. Pickering to R. Pickering, Oct. 13, 1777, *PP*, reel 1; Theodore Thayer, *Nathanael Greene: Strategist of the American Revolution* (New York: Twayne, 1960), p. 204.

36. Pickering to Pickman, Mar. 24, 1778, *PP*, reel 5.

37. Pickering to J. Pickering, Sept. 25, 1777, ibid.

Chapter 4. The Board of War

1. A copy of the returns for the army for Dec. 2, 1777, may be found in *PP*, reel 56.

2. Thaxter to Adams, Jan. 28, 1778, *Adams Family Correspondence*, ed. Lyman Butterfield (Cambridge, Mass.: Belknap Press, 1963), II, 387–88.

3. Craik to Pickering, Oct. 13, 1777, *PP*, reel 17; David F. Hawke, *Benjamin Rush: Revolutionary Gradfly* (Indianapolis: Bobbs Merrill, 1971), pp. 210–23, 237–38, 245–52.

4. J. Pickering to Pickering, Nov. 11, 21, 1777; Williams to Pickering, Nov. 13, 26, 1777; Goodhue to Pickering, Dec. 15, 1777, *PP*, reel 17.

5. Pickman to Pickering, Jan. 17, 1778, ibid.

6. Pickering to R. Pickering, Jan. 18, 1778, *PP*, reel 1.

7. Pickering to R. Pickering, Feb. 14, 1778; ibid.

8. Lovell to Trumbull, Jan. 27, 1778, *Letters of Members of the Continental Congress*, ed. E. C. Burnett (Washington, D.C.: Carnegie Institution, 1921–36), III, 54; Douglas S. Freeman, *George Washington* (New York: Scribner's, 1948–57), IV, 559, 573, 585.

9. Some useful studies on the Conway cabal include Don Higginbotham, *The War of American Independence* (New York: Macmillan, 1971), pp. 216–22; Freeman, *Washington*, IV, 586–612; Edmund Burnett, *The Continental Congress* (New York: Macmillan, 1941), pp. 279–97; Kenneth Rossman, *Thomas Mifflin and the Politics of the American Revolution* (Chapel Hill: University of North Carolina Press, 1952), pp. 116–39; and Paul Nelson, *General Horatio Gates: A Biography* (Baton Rouge: Louisiana State University Press, 1976), pp. 157–85.

10. Scammell to Pickering, Apr. 21, 1778; Carlton to Pickering, Apr. 22, 1778, *PP*, reel 17.

11. Pickering to J. Pickering, Apr. 26, 1778, *PP*, reel 5.

12. Ibid.

13. Pickering to R. Pickering, June 6, 12, 1778, *PP*, reel 1.

14. Pickering to R. Pickering, Apr. 18, 1778, ibid.

15. Gates to the President of Congress, Feb. 10, 1778, *PCCNA*, R.G. 360, reel 157; Pickering to Congress, Feb. 10, 1778, *PP*, reel 33.

16. Scammell to Pickering, Apr. 21, 1778, *PP*, reel 17.

17. Pickering to Washington, Jan. 9, 1779, *PP*, reel 33; Freeman, *Washington*, IV, 452–54; Burnett, *Continental Congress*, pp. 276–78.

18. Greene to Marchant, Oct. 15, 1778, in George W. Greene, *The Life of Nathanael Greene* (Boston: Little Brown, 1846), II, 156; Theodore Thayer, *Nathanael Greene: Strategist of the American Revolution* (New York: Twayne, 1960), p. 271.

19. Ibid.; E. James Ferguson, *The Power of the Purse* (Chapel Hill: University of North Carolina Press, 1961), pp. 95–97. See also "A Report by a Congressional committee on the conduct of the Quartermaster Respecting the Transportation of Provisions and Stores from Philadelphia to Trenton," June 16, 1780, *PCCNA*, R.G. 360, reel 30.

20. Pickering to Orne, Apr. 29, 1778, *PP*, reel 5.

21. Peters to Greene, Oct. 21, 1779, Greene Papers, II, *APS*.

22. Pickering to the President of Congress, Oct. 12, 1778, Mar. 9, 1779, June 1, 1779, *PCCNA*, R.G. 360, reels 157, 158; Pickering to the President of the Council of Massachusetts Bay, June 23, 1778; Pickering to Washington, Apr. 9, 1779, *PP*, reel 33.

23. Pickering to the President of Congress, Mar. 30, 1779; Board of War to President of Congress, July 22, 1780, *PCCNA*, R.G. 360, reel 158.

24. Gates to the President of Congress, Feb. 26, 1778, *PCCNA*, R.G. 360, reel 157; Pickering to Scammell, Feb. 11, 1778, *PP*, reel 33.

25. Pickering to R. Pickering, Jan. 18, 1778, *PP*, reel 1; Pickering to Scammell, Feb. 11, 1778, *PP*, reel 33.

26. Board of War to President of Congress, Oct. 5, 1778, *PP*, reel 33.

27. Greene to Board of War, June 30, 1779, Greene Papers, IV, *APS*.

28. Greene to Pettit, June 30, 1779, ibid.

29. Pickering to J. Pickering, Sept. 6, 1779; Pickering to Derby, Feb. 21, 1779; Pickering to Dodge, Dec. 11, 1779; Pickering to Williams, March 1, 1780, *PP*, reel 5; Pickering to J. Pickering, Sept. 6, 1779, Pickering Papers, Houghton Library.

30. Pickering to R. Pickering, July 5, 8, 1778, *PP*, reel 1.

31. Ibid.

32. Board of War to President of Congress, Aug. 14, 1778, *PCCNA*, R.G. 360, reel 157.

33. Pickering to R. Pickering, May 19, June 6, 12, 1778, *PP*, reel 1.

34. Pickman to Pickering, Jan. 22, 1778; Sargeant to Pickering, May 28, 1778, *PP*, reel 17.

35. Pickering to T. Pickering, Sr., Feb. 23, 1778, *PP*, reel 5.

36. J. Pickering to Pickering, July 4, 1778, *PP*, reel 17.

37. Pickering to R. Pickering, Sept. 11, 1778, *PP*, reel 17.

38. Ibid.

39. Pickering to J. Pickering, Jan 1, 1779, *PP*, reel 5.

40. Pickering to President of Congress, Oct. 8, 1778, *PP*, reel 5; Pickering to R. Pickering, Oct. 12, 1778, *PP*, reel 1.

41. Ferguson, *Power of the Purse*, p. 32.

42. Pickering to Committee of Congress on Salary, Nov. 22, 1779; Pickering to J. Pickering, Dec. 13, 1779, *PP*, reel 5.

43. Board of War Report to Congress, March 1779, *PCCNA*, R. G. 360, reel 158.

44. Ibid.

45. Board of War to President of Congress, Mar. 23, 1779, ibid.

46. Ibid.; Clarence L. Ver Steeg, *Robert Morris, Revolutionary Financier* (Philadelphia: University of Pennsylvania Press, 1954), pp. 10–11, 22–27.

47. Board of War to President of Congress, Sept. 8, 1779, *PCCNA*, R.G. 360, reel 157.

48. Ibid.; Ferguson, *Power of the Purse*, pp. 46–56; Higginbotham, *War of American Independence*, pp. 194–96.

49. Christopher Ward, *The War of the Revolution* (New York: Macmillan, 1952), II, 695–703; Piers MacKesy, *The War for America* (Cambridge: Harvard University Press, 1964), pp. 340–41.

50. Pettit to Greene, Oct. 15, 1779, Greene Papers, III, *APS*.

51. Pickering to President of Board of War, Dec. 7, 1779, *PCCNA*, R.G. 360, reel 157.

52. Pettit to President of Board of War, Apr. 24, 1780, ibid., reel 159.

53. Pickering to J. Pickering, June 13, 14, 1780, *PP*, reel 5; Ward, *War of the Revolution*, II, 703; MacKesy, *War for America*, pp. 340–41; John Cavanagh, "The Military Career of Major General Benjamin Lincoln" (Ph.D. dissertation, Duke University, 1969), pp. 177–202.

54. Board of War to President of Congress, Mar. 23, 29, 1780, *PCCNA*, R.G. 360, reel 159; Elias Boudinot to Pickering, Jan. 6, 1780, *PP*, reel 18.

55. Board of War to President of Congress, Mar. 23, 1780, *PCCNA*, R.G. 360, reel 159.

Chapter 5. Quartermaster General

1. Clarence L. Ver Steeg, *Robert Morris, Revolutionary Financier* (Philadelphia: University of Pennsylvania Press, 1954), pp. 45–47; E. James Ferguson, *The Power of the Purse* (Chapel Hill: University of North Carolina Press, 1961), pp. 51–52.

2. Pettit to Greene, Jan. 26, 1780, Greene Papers, II, *APS.*

3. Greene to Marchant, Oct. 15, 1778, in George W. Greene, *The Life of Nathanael Greene* (Boston: Little Brown, 1846), II, 156; Douglas S. Freeman, *George Washington* (New York: Scribner's, 1948–57), V, 152.

4. The Pickering-Mifflin Plan, Mar. 27, 1780, *PCCNA,* R.G. 360, reel 22.

5. Ibid.; Pettit to Greene, July 23, 1780, Greene Papers, *CL.*

6. Ibid.; Greene to Washington, Mar. 28, 1780, in Greene, *Life of Greene,* II, 275–76.

7. Ibid.

8. Washington to President of Congress, Mar. 26, 1780; Washington to Greene, Mar. 26, 1780, *The Writings of George Washington,* ed. John C. Fitzpatrick (Washington, D.C.: U.S. Government Printing Office, 1939), XVIII, 151, 152–53.

9. Greene to Greene, Sept. 3, 1780, Greene Papers, *CL.*

10. Congressional Resolution of Apr. 14, 1780, *PCCNA,* R.G. 360, reel 42.

11. Laurens to Lee, Aug. 1, 1780; Schuyler, Matthews, and Peabody to President of Congress, July 27, 1780, in *Letters of Members of the Continental Congress,* ed. E. C. Burnett (Washington, D.C.: Carnegie Institution, 1921–36), V, 306, 297; Edmund Burnett, *The Continental Congress* (New York: Macmillan, 1941), pp. 461–64; Theodore Thayer, *Nathanael Greene: Strategist of the American Revolution* (New York: Twayne, 1960), pp. 276–77.

12. Pickering to Sherman, Aug. 6, 1780, *PP,* reel 5; Pickering to President of Congress, Aug. 7, 1780, *PP,* reel 33; Pickering to J. Pickering, Aug. 29, 1780, Pickering Papers, *EI.*

13. Flower to Pickering, Aug. 20, 1780, *PP,* reel 18.

14. Cox to Greene, Aug. 7, 1780, Greene Papers, *CL.*

15. Peabody to Greene, Sept. 8, 1780, ibid.

16. Claiborne to Greene, Oct. 16, 1780, ibid.

17. Pickering to J. Pickering, Sept. 3, 1780, *PP,* reel 5.

18. Pettit to Greene, July 23, 28, Aug. 1, 1780, Greene Papers, *CL*; Washington, to Pickering, Sept. 15, 1780, *PP,* reel 39; Freeman, Washington, V, 185. For some of the many reprimands Washington issued for absenteeism see Washington to Pickering, Sept. 6, 8, 1781; May 15, Dec. 24, 1782; Feb. 8, Mar. 10, 1783, *GWPLC,* reels 21, 83, 90; Washington to Lincoln, May 15, 1782, ibid., reel 85.

19. See, for example, Nielson to Pickering, Oct. 6, Nov. 1, 1780, *RWRNA,* M. 859, reel 66.

20. Pickering to Pettit, Dec. 1, 1780, *PP,* reel 33.

21. Pickering to Hubbard, Jan. 13, 1781, ibid.

22. Neilson to Pickering, Oct. 1, 1780; Hay to Pickering, Nov. 12, 1780; Hatch to Pickering, Nov. 16, 1780, *RWRNA,* M. 859, reel 80.

23. Pickering to Huntington, Sept. 29, 1780, *PCCNA,* R.G. 360, reel 199.

24. Fooks to Pickering, Nov. 21, 1780, *PP,* reel 39; *Journals of Congress,* Nov. 15, 1780, XVIII, 1055–56.

25. Pickering to President of Congress, Oct. 30, 1780, *PCCNA,* R.G. 360, reel 199.

26. Knox to Knox, Dec. 2, 1780, Knox Papers, reel 5, *MHS.*

27. Heath to Washington, Dec. 9, 1780, Papers of General William Heath, *Massachusetts Historical Society Collections,* ser. 7, vol. 5 (1905): 139–41.

28. Heath to Washington, Dec. 18, 28, 1780, ibid., pp. 144, 146.

29. Washington to Pickering, Jan. 21, 1781, *PP,* reel 39.

30. Pickering to Washington, Dec. 29, 1780, *GWPLC,* reel 73.

31. Pickering to Washington, Apr. 25, May 9, 1781, *PP,* reel 33.

32. Washington to Pickering, Apr. 11, 1781, *PP,* reel 39.

33. Washington to Pickering, Apr. 12, 1781, ibid.

34. Pickering to Humphreys, Apr. 13, 1781, *PP,* reel 33.
35. Pickering to Washington, Jan. 22, 1781, ibid.
36. Pickering to Hughes, Apr. 17, 1781, *PCCNA,* R.G. 360, reel 100.
37. Pickering to President of Congress, Apr. 21, 1781, ibid.
38. Washington to Pickering, Apr. 25, 1781, *PP,* reel 39.
39. Humphreys to Pickering, Apr. 24, 1781, ibid.
40. Pickering to Heath, May 11, 1781, Heath Papers, pp. 193–95.
41. Washington to Pickering, Apr. 25, May 4, 1781, *PP,* reel 39.
42. Pickering to Washington, Apr. 25, 1781, *PP,* reel 33.
43. Washington to Pickering, Apr. 25, 1781, *PP,* reel 39.
44. Washington to Pickering, Apr. 28, 1781, ibid.
45. Washington to Pickering, May 6, 1781, ibid.
46. Ver Steeg, *Robert Morris,* pp. 72–73; Ferguson, *Power of the Purse,* pp. 132–33.

Chapter 6. Peace and Disillusion

1. Pickering to J. Pickering, Feb. 7, 1783, *PP,* reel 34; Pickering to Williams, Feb. 17, 1783, *PP,* reel 5.
2. Ibid.
3. Pickering to R. Pickering, *PP,* Feb. 19, 1782, reel 4: I; Pickering to J. Pickering, Mar. 20, 1782, *PP,* reel 5.
4. Pickering to J. Pickering, Sept. 22, 1782, *PP,* reel 34; E. James Ferguson, *The Power of the Purse* (Chapel Hill: University of North Carolina Press, 1961), p. 115; Edmund Burnett, *The Continental Congress* (New York: Macmillan, 1941), pp. 391–93.
5. Washington to Lincoln, May 15, 1782, *GWPLC,* reel 85; Pickering to J. Pickering, Aug. 6, 1782; Pickering to Washington, Aug. 6, 1782, *PP,* reel 34.
6. Washington to Lincoln, May 15, 1782, *GWPLC,* reel 85.
7. Pickering to J. Pickering, Sept. 22, 1782, *PP,* reel 34.
8. A copy of a series of congressional resolutions dated April 22, 1782, and relevant to the question of the reorganization of the Quartermaster General's Department may be found in *PP,* reel 5; Pickering to Congressional Committee on the Reorganization of the Quartermaster General's Department, Apr. 20, 29, 1782, ibid.; Pickering to Hodgdon, Oct. 24, 1782, *PP,* reel 34.
9. Pickering to Hodgdon, Oct. 24, 1782, ibid.
10. Ibid.
11. *Journals of Congress,* Oct. 23, 1782, XXIII, 682–86; Jan. 13, Mar. 7, 1783, XXIV, 44–45, 176–77.
12. Pickering to R. Pickering, Jan. 18, 1783, *PP,* reel 1; Pickering to Washington, *PP,* reel 34; Benson to Pickering, Jan. 8, 1783, *GWPLC,* reel 89.
13. Pickering to R. Pickering, Jan. 19, 1783, *PP,* reel 1; Pickering to Hodgdon, Jan. 20, 1783; Pickering to J. Pickering, Feb. 7, 1783, *PP,* reel 34.
14. Douglas S. Freeman, *George Washington* (New York: Scribner's, 1948–57), V, 430–47; Paul Nelson, *General Horatio Gates: A Biography* (Baton Rouge: Louisiana State University Press, 1976), pp. 266–97; Don Higginbotham, *The War of American Independence* (New York: Macmillan, 1971), pp. 398–412; Richard H. Kohn, *Eagle and Sword: The Federalists and the Creation of the Military Establishment in America* (New York: Free Press, 1975), pp. 17–39.
15. Nelson, *Gates,* pp. 266–97; Kohn, *Eagle and Sword,* pp. 28–34.
16. Pickering to Hodgdon, Mar. 16, 1783, *PP,* reel 34.
17. Ibid.; Washington to the officers of the army, Mar. 15, 1783, *The Writings of*

George Washington, ed. John C. Fitzpatrick (Washington, D.C.: U.S. Government Printing Office, 1939), XXVI, 222–27.

18. Ibid; Pickering to R. Pickering, Mar. 16, 1783; *PP,* reel 1.

19. Ibid.

20. Ibid.

21. Ibid. Later Pickering wrote that he alone among the officers had spoken out against the fifth resolution. But in this letter to Hodgdon he states categorically that he realized at the time opposition would be futile and so remained silent. For more on Pickering's thoughts see Pickering to R. Pickering, Mar. 20, 1783, *PP,* reel 1.

22. Knox to Lincoln, Mar. 16, 1783, Knox Papers, reel 12, *MHS.*

23. Lincoln to Knox, Mar. 22, 1783, Lincoln Papers, reel 6, *MHA.*

24. Ibid.

25. Ibid.

26. Gates to Pickering, May 19, 1783, *PP,* reel 18. The scholars who have most recently evaluated Gates's role at Newburgh disagree sharply. See Paul Nelson and Richard Kohn, "Horatio Gates at Newburgh," *William and Mary Quarterly,* ser. 3, XXIX (January 1972): 143–58.

27. Pickering to R. Pickering, Mar. 16, 1783, *PP,* reel 1.

28. Freeman, *Washington,* V, 440.

29. Burnett, *Continental Congress,* p. 573.

30. Ibid.

31. Merrill Jensen, *The New Nation* (New York: Knopf, 1950), 81; Freeman, *Washington,* V, 441–42.

32. Pickering to Hodgdon, June 3, 7, 1783, *PP,* reel 34.

33. Pickering to J. Pickering, June 18, 1783, ibid.

34. Pickering to Hodgdon, June 12, 1783, ibid.

35. Miller, *Triumph of Freedom* (Boston: Little Brown, 1948), p. 677.

35. John C. Miller, *Triumph of Freedom* (Boston: Little Brown, 1948), p. 677.

36. Pickering to Hodgdon, Nov. 5, 1783, *PP,* reel 34.

37. Ibid. Octavius Pickering and Charles W. Upham, *The Life of Timothy Pickering* (Boston: Little Brown, 1867), I, 488–91.

38. Pickering and Upham, *Pickering,* I, 488–89.

39. Ibid., p. 490.

40. Ibid., pp. 490–91.

Chapter 7. The Allure of Western Lands

1. Curtis Nettles, *The Emergence of a National Economy* (New York: Holt, Rinehart and Winston, 1962), p. 61.

2. Ibid.; Gerry to Hodgdon, July 14, 1784, *RWRNA,* M. 859, reel 104.

3. Nettles, *Emergence of a National Economy,* p. 61; Merrill Jensen, *The New Nation* (New York: Knopf, 1950), pp. 185–93; Robert A. East, *Business Enterprise in the American Revolutionary Era* (New York: Columbia University Press, 1938); Jacob Cooke, *Tench Coxe and the Early Republic* (Chapel Hill: University of North Carolina Press, 1978), pp. 62–82.

4. Pickering to Mifflin, Mar. 5, 1784; Pickering to Holton, Dec. 7, 1784, *PP,* reel 5; Pickering to Hodgdon, Dec. 6, 1784, *RERNA,* M. 859, reel 108.

5. Pickering to Hodgdon, Dec. 25, 1783, *PP,* reel 34; Pickering to Hamilton, Mar. 25, 1825, Pickering Papers, Houghton Library; Norman B. Wilkinson, "Land Policy and Speculation in Pennsylvania, 1779–1800" (Ph.D. dissertation, University of Pennsylvanias 1958); Aaron Sakolski, *The Great American Land Bubble* (New York: Harper and Bros., 1932), pp. 31–36.

6. Pickering on land purchases, 1784–85, July 15, 16, 1822, *PP,* reel 65.

7. Pickering to Hamilton, Mar. 25, 1825, Pickering Papers, Houghton Library; Cooke, *Coxe,* p. 81.

8. Wilkinson, "Land Policy," pp. 46–49.

9. Gerry to Pickering and Hodgdon, Apr. 24, 1785, *RWRNA,* M. 859, reel 108.

10. Ibid.; Gerry to Hodgdon, July 5, 1784, ibid.

11. Pickering to Hodgdon, Apr. 13, 17, 1785; Pickering to J. Pickering, June 11, 1785, *PP,* reel 34; Wilkinson, "Land Policy," p. 39.

12. Potter to Pickering, July 20, 1789, Potter Papers, Draper Collection, State Historical Society of Wisconsin (microfilm).

13. Orne to Pickering, Oct. 16, 1784; Sargeant to Pickering, May 10, 1785, *PP,* reel 18; Pickering to Williams, Jan. 26, 1786, *PP,* reel 35.

14. Pickering to Gerry, Feb. 20, 1784; Pickering to Mifflin, Mar. 5, 1784, *PP,* reel 5; Gerry to Pickering, Feb. 26, 1784, *PP,* reel 18.

15. Gerry to Pickering, Feb. 26, 1784, *PP,* reel 18.

16. Pickering to Gates, Mar. 31, 1785, Pickering Papers, New York Public Library.

17. Holton to Pickering, Dec. 4, 1784, *PP,* reel 18.

18. Holton to Pickering, Dec. 14, 1784.; Pickering to Holton, Dec. 7, 1784, Jan. 26, 1785, *PP,* reel 5; Hodgdon to Pickering, Apr. 13, 1785, *PP,* reel 40.

19. Pickering to Gates, Mar. 31, 1785, Pickering Papers, New York Public Library; Robert Ernst, *Rufus King: American Federalist* (Chapel Hill: University of North Carolina Press, 1968), p. 49.

20. Hodgdon to Pickering, May 22, 27, 1785, *PP,* reel 40: King to Pickering, May 30, 1785, *PP,* reel 18; Pickering to Mifflin, Mar. 5, 1784, *PP,* reel 5.

21. Hodgdon to Pickering, Aug. 6, 1785; Gerry to Hodgdon, Sept. 2, 1785, *PP,* reel 40.

22. Pickering's journal of his trip into the Pennsylvania wilderness, Aug.–Sept. 1786, *PP,* reel 57.

23. Ibid.

24. Under its sea-to-sea charter of 1622, Connecticut laid claim to the northern portion of Pennsylvania between the 41st and 42nd degrees north latitude, about 40 percent of the total territory of the colony. In 1753 a group of Connecticut farmers and land speculators organized the Susquehannah Land Company and in the year following purchased the preemption rights to more than five million acres of this land from several sachems of the Six Nations. In 1755 Connecticut ceded its rights of soil in the area to the company. Fourteen years later, in 1769, the first large contingent of Connecticut settlers came to stay in the Wyoming Valley. They built Forty Fort and Fort Durkee to help them in defending their claims. Meanwhile, in 1768, at the treaty of Fort Stanwix, the Penn family purchased preemption rights to the same land from the Six Nations. From the time that Connecticut settlers arrived in numbers there was open warfare in the valley between these Yankees and the Pennamites. The situation had in no way calmed down when Pickering arrived in the valley in the summer of 1786. See *SP,* VIII, xv–xxxix; Julien P. Boyd, "Attempts to Form New States in New York and Pennsylvania, 1786–1796," *New York State Historical Quarterly Journal,* XII (July 1931): 257–70; Shaw Livermore, *Early American Land Companies (New York: Oxford University Press, 1938), pp. 82*–90.

25. Robert J. Taylor, "Trial at Trenton," *William and Mary Quarterly,* ser. 3, XXVI (Oct. 1969): 521–47; Pickering to Rawle, Mar. 6, 1790, *PP,* reel 58.

26. Pickering to Hamilton, Mar. 25, 1825, Pickering Papers, Houghton Library.

27. Pickering to H. Pickering, Dec. 31, 1818, *PP,* reel 38.

28. Ibid.

29. Ibid.; Rush to Price, Oct. 27, 1786, *Letters of Benjamin Rush,* ed. Lyman Butter-

field (Princeton: Princeton University Press, 1951), I, 408–09; Robert L. Brunhouse, *Counter-Revolution in Pennsylvania* (Harrisburg: Pennsylvania Historical Commission, 1942), pp. 191–93.

30. Pickering to Clarke, Oct. 11, 1786, *PP,* reel 5; Pickering to J. Pickering, Nov. 15, 1786, *PP,* reel 35; Pickering to H. Pickering, Dec. 31, 1818, *PP,* reel 38.

31. *Minutes of the 10th General Assembly of the Commonwealth of Pennsylvania,* sess. II, Sept. 23, 1786; Franklin to Pettit, Oct. 10, 1786, *The Writings of Benjamin Franklin,* ed. Albert H. Smyth (New York: Macmillan, 1907), IX, 544.

32. Pettit to Wadsworth, May 27, 1786, in *Letters of Members of the Continental Congress,* ed. E. C. Burnett (Washington, D.C.: Carnegie Institution; 1921–36), VIII, 368–71; *SP,* VIII, xxviii–xxxiv.

33. Sprague to Pennsylvania Council, Nov. 25, 1786; Smith to Biddle, Dec. 18, 1786, *SP,* VIII, 420, 425.

34. Handbill, Jan. 10, 1787, endorsed by Pickering and Butler, *SP,* IX, 2; Pickering to Hodgdon, Jan. 12, 1787, ibid., pp. 7–8.

35. Journal of a trip from Philadelphia to Wyoming, Jan. 3 to Feb. 5, 1787, see esp. Jan. 11, *PP,* reel 57.

36. Ibid.

37. Taylor, "Trial at Trenton," pp. 545–46; Wilson to Pickering, Jan. 21, 1787, *PP,* reel 57.

38. Pickering's Journal, Jan. 22, 1787, *PP,* reel 58.

39. Judd to Butler, Jan. 11, 1787, *PP,* reel 57.

40. Ibid.; Hosmer to Schott, Feb. 2, 1787, ibid.; Judd to Butler, Feb. 26, Mar. 19, 1787, *SP,* IX, 70–71, 75–76.

41. Pickering's Journal, Jan. 26, 1787, *PP,* reel 57.

42. Ibid., Jan. 11, 13, 1787.

43. Anonymous to Pickering, Jan. 22, 1787, ibid.

44. Smith to Pickering and Butler, Jan. 30, 1787, *SP,* IX, 13.

45. Election returns, Feb. 1, 1787, *SP,* IX, 18–21.

46. Franklin to Speaker of Pennsylvania Assembly, Feb. 24, 1787, *PP,* reel 57.

47. Debate on Repeal of Confirming Act, Mar. 18, 1790, *SP,* X, 84–89; Pickering's Journal of a trip into the Pennsylvania wilderness, Aug. and Sept. 1786, *PP,* reel 57; Pickering to Peters, Mar. 29, 1790, *PP,* reel 58. A published copy of the petition may be found in *SP,* IX, 23–27.

48. Address to the Pennsylvania legislature, Feb. 5, 1787, *SP,* IX, 23–26.

49. Sprague to Pickering, Feb. 20, 1787; Smith to Pickering, Feb. 21, 1787, *SP,* IX, 63–65, 66–68.

50. Proceedings of the Susquehannah Co. Commissioners, March 1–May 1, 1787, ibid., pp. 119–22.

51. Sprague to Pickering, Feb. 20, 1787, ibid., pp. 63–65.

52. Denison to Speaker of the Assembly, Mar. 5, 1787; report of the legislative committee considering the petition, Mar. 17, 1787, ibid., pp. 72, 73–75.

53. Denison to Butler, Mar. 5, 1787, ibid., p. 71.

54. Denison to Butler, March. 9, 1787, ibid., p. 73.

55. Report of the legislative committee, Mar. 17, 1787, ibid., pp. 73–75.

56. *Proceedings and Debates of the Twelfth General Assembly of the Commonwealth of Pennsylvania,* sess. I, 128–31, Nov. 16, 1787.

57. Confirming Law, *SP,* IX, 82–86.

58. Pickering to J. Pickering, Mar. 27, 1787, *PP,* reel 40.

59. Circular Letter, Apr. 2, 1787, *PP,* reel 57.

60. Pickering to Butler, Apr. 2, 1787, ibid.

61. Ibid.; Franklin to Huntington, Apr. 14, 1787; Huntington to Franklin, May 5, 1787, *SP*, IX, 101, 126.

62. Sprague to Pennsylvania Council, Nov. 25, 1786, *SP*, VIII, 4; Judd to Butler, Jan. 11, 1787; Hosmer to Schott, Feb. 2, 1787, *PP*, reel 57. Scholars do not agree on whether there was actually a separatist conspiracy in the Wyoming area. See Boyd, "Attempts to Form New States," pp. 257–70; *SP*, IX, xxv–xxxiv.

63. Franklin to Hamilton, Apr. 29, 1787, *SP*, IX, 116–18.

64. Gore to Pickering, Smith to Smith, Apr. 20, 1787, *PP*, reel 57; Denison to Pickering, Apr. 26, 1787, *SP*, IX, 115.

65. Pickering to Hodgdon, Apr. 28, 1787, *PP*, reel 57; Denison to Biddle, May 4, 1787, *SP*, IX, 124–25.

Chapter 8. Kidnaped

1. Hodgdon to Pickering, June 10, 1787, *PP*, reel 57; Resolutions, remonstrance, and circular letter from Easton, May 21, 1787, *SP*, IX, 133–38.

2. Wadsworth to Pickering, June 10, 1787, *PP*, reel 57; Resolution of Connecticut General Assembly, May 1787, *SP*, IX, 141–43.

3. Pickering to Hodgdon, May 29, 1787, *PP*, reel 57.

4. Remonstrance of Luzerne Inhabitants against Joseph Montgomery, May 1787, *SP*, IX, 139–40.

5. Hodgdon to Pickering, July 30, 1787, *PP*, reel 57.

6. Pickering to Hodgdon, Aug. 9, 1787, ibid.

7. Pickering to B. Franklin, Aug. 13, 1787, *SP*, IX, 162–63.

8. Rush to Pickering, Aug. 30, 1787, *Letters of Benjamin Rush,* ed. Lyman Butterfield (Princeton: Princeton University Press, 1951), I, 439–40.

9. Pickering to Hodgdon, Aug. 26, 1787, *PP*, reel 57.

10. Dyer to Pickering, Aug. 18, 1787; J. Hamilton to J. Franklin, Sept. 8, 10, 1787; Gray to Butler, Sept. 12, 1787, *SP*, IX, 162, 184, 186–88, 189—90.

11. Pickering to Hodgdon, Aug. 26, 1787, *PP*, reel 57; Julien Boyd, "Attempts to Form New States in New York and Pennsylvania 1786–1796," *New York State Historical Quarterly Journal,* XII (July 1931): 257–70; *SP*, IX, xxv–xxxiv.

12. Hodgdon to Pickering, Aug. 16, 1787, *PP*, reel 57.

13. Pickering to Hodgdon, Aug. 26, 1787 (two letters), ibid.

14. Deposition of Tunes Dalson, Sept. 4, 1787; affidavit of Thomas Wigton, Sept. 8, 1787, ibid.

15. Biddle to Commissioners, Sept. 1, 1787, ibid.; Pickering to Rush, Sept. 13, 1787, *SP*, IX, 190–92.

16. Pickering to B. Franklin, Sept. 5, 1787, ibid., p. 180.

17. Minutes of Pennsylvania Council, Sept. 22, 1787; B. Franklin to Clinton, Sept. 22, 1787; proclamation for the arrest of John Franklin and others, Sept. 25, 1787; instructions to John Craig, in Council, Sept. 26, 1787, *SP*, IX, 202–05, 207.

18. Franklin to J. Franklin, Sept. 29, 1787; Kingsley to Butler, Sept. 29, 1787, *SP*, IX, 209–10.

19. Hodgdon to Pickering, Oct. 5, 1787, *PP*, reel 57; Pickering to H. Pickering, Dec. 31, 1818, *PP*, reel 38.

20. Pickering to Sill, June 18, 1788, *PP*, reel 58.

21. Pickering to H. Pickering, Dec. 31, 1818, *PP*, reel 38. Stephen Balliot, who had just gone on a visit to Philadelphia, was not present when the rioting broke out.

22. Pickering to Swift, Oct. 5, 1787, *PP*, reel 57; Swift to Pickering, Oct. 6, 1787, *SP*, IX, 224–25.

23. Extract of minutes of Pennsylvania Council, Oct. 10, 1787, *SP*, IX, 237–38.

24. Pickering to Swift, Oct. 9, 1787; Pickering to Hodgdon, Mar. 16, 1788, *PP*, reel 57.

25. Ibid.

26. Pickering to Clymer, Nov. 1, 1787, ibid.

27. *Proceedings and Debates of the Twelfth General Assembly,* sess. I, Nov. 10, 15, 16, 1787, pp. 90, 111–31.

28. Smith to Pickering, Dec. 7, 1787, *PP*, reel 57; Pickering to Peters, Nov. 22, 1787, *PP*, reel 5.

29. Clymer to Pickering, Mar. 15, 1788, *PP*, reel 19; Hodgdon to Pickering, Mar. 15, 1788, *PP*, reel 58.

30. Clymer to Pickering, Mar. 15, 1788, ibid.

31. *Proceedings and Debates of the Twelfth General Assembly,* sess. II, Mar. 20, 25, 1788, pp. 179–91.

32. Hodgdon to Pickering, Mar. 20, 1788; Coxe to Pickering, Mar. 29, 1788, *PP*, reel 58.

33. Rush and McKean to Pickering, May 10, 1788, *PP*, reel 58.

34. Pickering to McKean and Rush, May 25, 1788; Pickering to Hodgdon, May 30, 1788, ibid.; Pickering to Muhlenberg, May 27, 1788, *SP*, IX, 276–77; *Proceedings and Debates of the Twelfth General Assembly,* sess. II, Feb. 26, 1788, pp. 18–19.

35. Hodgdon to Pickering, May 18, 31, 1788, *PP*, reel 58.

36. Journal of Timothy Pickering during his captivity, June 26–July 15, 1788, ibid.; Pickering to H. Pickering, Dec. 31, 1818, *PP*, reel 38.

37. Earle's confession, July 19, 1788; Wigton's deposition, Aug. 1, 1788, *PP*, reel 58.

38. Testimony of Phelps, Aug. 26, 1788, ibid.

39. Deposition of Ellicott, July 8, 1788, *SP*, IX, 394–96.

40. Balliot and Armstrong to B. Franklin, July 9, 1788, *SP*, IX, 401; Ellicott to Pickering, Aug. 8, 1788, *PP*, reel 19.

41. Butler et al. to B. Franklin, July 9, 1788, *SP*, IX, 399–401.

42. Journal of Pickering during captivity, June 26–July 15, 1788, *PP*, reel 58.

43. Pickering to R. Pickering, July 3, 1788, *PP*, reel 2.

44. Journal of Pickering during captivity, June 26–July 15, 1788, *PP*, reel 58.

45. Pickering to Benjamin Franklin, July 19, 1788, *SP*, IX, 415–16.

46. Pickering to B. Franklin, July 28, 1788, with memo, *PP*, reel 58.

47. Ibid.; Pickering to Muhlenberg, Aug. 9, 1788, ibid.

48. Butler to Muhlenberg, July 29, 1788, *SP*, IX, 438–40.

49. Muhlenberg to Pennsylvania delegates in Congress, Aug. 6, 1788; Biddle to Pickering, Aug. 7, 1788, *SP*, IX, 451–52, 455; McKean and Bryan to governor of Pennsylvania, Aug. 7, 1788, Pickering Papers, *EI;* Bradford to Pickering, Aug. 23, 1788, *PP*, reel 58.

50. Pickering to Hodgdon, Nov. 9, 1788, ibid.

51. Hodgdon to Pickering, Aug. 28, 1788, ibid.

52. Pickering's notes for his appearance before the Rawle Committee, Feb. 23, 1790; deposition from Mrs. B. Flower, Feb. 23, 1790; Pickering's notes on further testimony before the Rawle Committee, Pickering to Rawle, Mar. 6, 1790; Pickering to Peters, Mar. 29, 1790; Minutes for a protest, Apr. 1790, ibid.; Pickering to the Rawle Committee, Mar. 2, 1790, *SP*, X, 41–58; Pickering to Johnson, Mar. 16, 1790, ibid., pp. 83–84.

Chapter 9. "Civilizing" the Iroquois

1. Pickering to J. Pickering, Apr. 21, 1789, *PP*, reel 3; Pickering to Williams, Apr. 24, 1789, *PP*, reel 6; Pickering to Hodgdon, June 4, 1789, Pickering Papers *EI.*

2. Pickering to Williams, Apr. 24, 1789, *PP*, reel 6.

3. Pickering to Williams, Nov. 24, 1789, ibid.

4. Pickering to R. Pickering, Nov. 4, 1789, *PP*, reel 2.

5. Ibid., Sept. 6, 1790.

6. Reginald Horsman, *Expansion and American Indian Policy* (East Lansing: Michigan State University Press, 1967), pp. 16–66; Anthony F. C. Wallace, *The Death and Rebirth of the Seneca Nation* (New York: Knopf, 1970), pp. 150–59; Francis Paul Prucha, *The Sword of the Republic: The United States Army on the Frontier* (New York: Macmillan, 1968).

7. Washington to Pickering, Sept. 4, 1790, *PP*, reel 61.

8. For diplomats and Indians, *treaty* meant a gathering where negotiations took place. The word will be used thus in discussing negotiations with the Indians.

9. Pickering to R. Pickering, Nov. 15, 1790, *PP*, reel 2; Edward H. Phillips, "Timothy Pickering at His Best," *Essex Institute Historical Collections*, CII (July 1966): 163–202.

10. Pickering to Washington, Dec. 4, 1790, *PP*, reel 61.

11. Speech by Farmer's Brother, Nov. 21, 1790, ibid.

12. Speech by Red Jacket, ibid.

13. Speech by Pickering, Nov. 20, 1790, ibid.

14. Pickering to King, June 1, 1785, *The Life and Correspondence of Rufus King*, ed. Charles R. King (New York: G. P. Putnam's Sons, 1894), I, 104–05.

15. Pickering to Washington, Dec. 4, 1790, *PP*, reel 61.

16. Pickering's certificate, July 1791, ibid.; Pickering to Chapin, Apr. 29, 1792, *PP*, reel 62.

17. Pickering to Washington, Dec. 31, 1790, *GWPLC*, reel 100; Washington to Pickering, Jan. 20, 1791, *PP*, reel 61.

18. Pickering to Hodgdon, Feb. 28, 1791, *PP*, reel 35.

19. Pickering to Knox, Aug. 21, 1791, *PP*, reel 60.

20. Pickering's narrative of the treaty of Newtown Point, July 17, 1791, ibid.; Wallace, *Death and Rebirth*, p. 200.

21. Pickering to Chapin, Apr. 29, 1792, *PP*, reel 62.

22. Pickering to Washington, Jan. 8, 1791; Pickering to Kirkland, Dec. 4, 1791, *PP*, reel 61; Pickering's plan for civilizing the Six Nations, n.d. but placed in March 1792, *PP*, reel 62.

23. Bernard Sheehan, *Seeds of Extinction* (Chapel Hill: University of North Carolina Press, 1974); A. Grenfell Price, *White Settlers and Native Peoples* (Melbourn: Georgian House, 1949); Roy H. Pearce, *The Savages of America: A Study of the Indian and the Idea of Civilization* (Baltimore: Johns Hopkins University Press, 1953).

24. Ibid.

25. Pickering to Knox, Aug. 16, 1791, *PP*, reel 61; Horsman, *Expansion and American Indian Policy*, pp. 53–65.

26. Knox to Wayne, Jan. 5, 1793, in *Anthony Wayne, A Name in Arms*, ed. Richard C. Knopf (Pittsburgh: University of Pittsburgh Press, 1959), pp. 164–67.

27. Knox to Washington, Dec. 27, 1790, *GWPLC*, reel 100.

28. Ibid.

29. Cornplanter's second speech, Jan. 10, 1791, *ASPIA*, I:1, 143–44.

30. Washington to Knox, Jan. 14, 1791, *GWPLC*, reel 100.

31. Washington to Pickering, Dec. 31, 1790, *PP*, reel 61; Pickering to Anspack, Jan. 12, 1791, Pickering Papers, *EI*.

32. Cornplanter to Washington, Mar. 17, 1791, *GWPLC*, reel 100.

33. Knox to Washington, Mar. 27, Apr. 10, 1791, ibid.

34. Ibid.

35. Knox to Washington, Dec. 27, 1790; Washington to Hamilton, Apr. 4, 1791, ibid.; Knox to St. Clair, Apr. 19, 1791, *PP*, reel 60.

36. Knox to Washington, Apr. 10, 1791, *GWPLC,* reel 100.
37. Pickering to J. Pickering, Apr. 23, 1791, *PP,* reel 35.
38. Knox to Washington, Aug. 17, 1791, *GWPLC,* reel 100.
39. Memo on preparations for holding a treaty with the Six Nations, Apr. 20–May 7, 1791; questions asked of Knox at conference, Apr. 1791, *PP,* reel 60.
40. Ibid.
41. Knox to Pickering, May 1, 1791, ibid.
42. Knox to Washington, May 30, 1791, *GWPLC,* reel 100.
43. Morris to Pickering, June 12, 1791, *PP,* reel 61.
44. Bowman to Pickering, May 11, 1791; Parrish to Pickering, May 19, 1791; Smith to Pickering, May 24, 1791, ibid.
45. Pickering to R. Pickering, July 1, 1791, *PP,* reel 2.
46. Pickering to Knox, Aug. 21, 1791, *PP,* reel 60; Wallace, *Death and Rebirth,* p. 199.
47. Ibid.
48. Pickering to Knox, July 16, 1791; Newtown Point narrative, July 4, 5, 10, 1791, *PP,* reel 60.
49. Newtown Point narrative, July 10, 1791, ibid.
50. Ibid.
51. Newtown Point narrative, July 13, 14, 1791, ibid.
52. William L. Stone, *The Life and Times of Red Jacket* (New York: Wiley & Putnam, 1841), pp. 64–65.
53. Ibid.
54. Newtown Point narrative, July 16, 1791, *PP,* reel 60.
55. Newtown Point narrative, July 17, 1791; Pickering to Knox, Aug. 16, 1791, *PP,* reel 61.
56. Ibid.
57. Ibid.
58. Pickering to R. Pickering, Aug. 12, 1791, *PP,* reel 2.

Chapter 10. A Diplomat Among the Indians

1. Clarke to Pickering, Oct. 26, Nov. 19, 1791, *PP,* reel 19; Pickering to Osgood, Nov. 30, 1791; Pickering to Clarke, Dec. 1, 1791, *PP,* reel 6.
2. Pickering to Bush, Oct. 21, 1791, Records of the Post Office Department, National Archives, R.G. 28, reel 1.
3. Pickering to R. Pickering, Mar. 16, 1792, *PP,* reel 2; Pickering to Hamilton, Mar. 9, 1792, *PP,* reel 6.
4. Pickering to R. Pickering, Dec. 5, 8, 1791, *PP,* reel 2; James R. Jacobs, *The Beginnings of the United States Army* (New York: Kennakat Press, 1972), pp. 115–16; Frances Paul Prucha, *The Sword of the Republic* (New York, Macmillan, 1969), pp. 25–26.
5. Pickering to R. Pickering, Dec. 5, 8, 1791, *PP,* reel 2; Knox to Pickering, Dec. 20, 1791, *PP,* reel 61; Knox to Kirkland, Dec. 20, 1791, *ASPIA,* I, 226; Barton to Ogdon, Jan. 19, 1792, Knox Papers, reel 30, *MHS.*
6. Pickering to Knox, July 16, 1791; Newtown Point narrative, June 26–July 17, 1791, *PP,* reel 60.
7. Washington to Morris, June 21, 1792, *GWPLC,* reel 102; Knox to Wayne, Sept. 7, 1792, in *Anthony Wayne, A Name in Arms,* ed. Richard C. Knopf (Pittsburgh: University of Pittsburgh Press, 1959), pp. 83–86.
8. *National Gazette* (Philadelphia), Jan. 9, 1792; *Connecticut Courant* (Hartford), Jan. 16, 1792; *Philadelphia Aurora,* Jan. 4, 1792; Stevenson to Simcoe, Jan. 3, 7, 1792, in *The Correspondence of Lieut. Governor John Graves Simcoe,* ed. E. A. Cruikshank (Toronto: The Society, 1923), I, 95–96, 100–01.

9. Hawkins to Washington, Feb. 10, 1792; Washington's memo for a reply to Hawkins, Feb. ?, 1792; Washington to Knox, Jan. 16, 1792, *GWPLC,* reel 101.

10. Pickering to R. Pickering, Jan. 7, 1792, *PP,* reel 2.

11. Reginald Horsman, *Expansion and American Indian Policy* (East Lansing: Michigan State University Press, 1967), p. 48; Anthony F. C. Wallace, *The Death and Rebirth of the Seneca Nation* (New York: Knopf, 1970), p. 159.

12. Proctor to Pickering, May 15, 1791; Knox to Pickering, June 13, 1791, *PP,* reel 61; Pickering to Chapin, May 14, 1792, *PP,* reel 59.

13. Brant to Kirkland, Mar. 8, 1791, *PP,* reel 61.

14. Captain Hendrick's narrative of his mission to Niagara and Grand River, Feb. 1792, *PP,* reel 59.

15. Knox to Clinton, Apr. 12, 1791; Knox to Brant, Feb. 25, 1792, *ASPIA,* I, 167, 228; Washington to Knox, Apr. 4, 1794, *GWPLC,* reel 105.

16. Pickering to R. Pickering, Mar. 22, 1792, *PP,* reel 2.

17. Pickering to Washington, Mar. 21, 1792, *PP,* reel 62.

18. Jefferson's memo, Mar. 9, 1792, Jefferson Papers, reel 25, *LC.*

19. Pickering to Washington, Mar. 21, 1792, *PP,* reel 62.

20. Pickering to R. Pickering, Mar. 22, 1792, *PP,* reel 2; Pickering to Hamilton, May 8, 1792, *PP,* reel 35.

21. Washington's speech to the assembled chiefs of the Six Nations, Mar. 23, 1792, *ASPIA,* I, 229.

22. Washington to Senate, Mar. 26, 1792, ibid., p. 225.

23. Good Peter's narrative, Apr. 1792, *PP,* reel 60; memo on New York land purchase, Apr. 1792, *PP,* reel 61.

24. Memo on conference with chiefs of the Five Nations, Apr. 26, 1792; Pickering's speech to the chiefs, Apr. 30, 1792, *PP,* reel 62.

25. *Philadelphia Aurora,* Aug. 11, 1792.

26. Ibid., Sept. 20, 1792.

27. Brant to Clinton, Dec. 11, 1792, Brant Papers, Draper Collection.

28. Proceedings of Indian council at the Glaize, Sept. 30–Oct. 9, 1792, *Simcoe Correspondence,* I, 218–31.

29. Brant to Clinton, July 26, 1792, Brant Papers, Draper Collection; Record of a council of the Six Nations at Buffalo Creek, Nov. 13, 14, 1792, *Simcoe Correspondence,* I, 256–60.

30. Knox to Wayne, Dec. 7, 1792, *Anthony Wayne,* pp. 148–51.

31. Morgan to Pickering, Apr. 17, 1793, *PP,* reel 59; Knox to Wayne, Mar. 5, 1793, *Anthony Wayne,* pp. 198–200.

32. Hull to Hamilton, Feb. 6, 1793, *PP,* reel 59.

33. Hammond to Grenville, June 13, July 3, 1792; Hammond to Simcoe, July 11, 1792, Hammond-Simcoe Correspondence, *CL;* Simcoe to McKee, Aug. 30, 1792; Proceedings of Indian Council at the Glaize, Sept. 30–Oct. 6, 1792, *Simcoe Correspondence* I, 207–09, 218–31.

34. Jefferson's memo, Feb. 25, 1793, *Simcoe Correspondence,* I, 297.

35. Heckewelder's journal of this trip may be found in *Thirty Thousand Miles with John Heckewelder,* ed. Paul A. W. Wallace (Pittsburgh: University of Pittsburgh Press, 1958), pp. 294–333.

36. McKee to Littlehales, Apr. 11, 1793 (copy), *PP,* reel 60.

37. Pickering's memo, n.d. *PP,* reel 60.

38. Pickering's memo, n.d., ibid.

39. Memo on a conversation between Simcoe and Duffy, n.d., *PP,* reel 59.

40. Simcoe to Clarke, June 14, July 26, 1793, *Simcoe Correspondence,* I, 354–55, 399–400.

41. Lincoln's analysis of failure, 1793, Lincoln Papers, reel 10, *MHS*.

42. Memo by the three envoys, June 1, 3, 1793, *PP*, reel 60.

43. Pickering's instructions to Captain Hendrick, June 4, 1793, ibid.

44. Parrish et al. to Lincoln, Pickering, and Randolph, June 17, 1793; Wilson to Lincoln, Pickering, and Randolph, June 17, 1793, ibid.

45. Minutes of a council at Freemason's Hall, July 7–8, 1793, *Simcoe Correspondence*, I, 377–82.

46. Ibid.; Lincoln, Pickering, and Randolph to Washington, July 10, 1793, *PP*, reel 59.

47. Brant's Journal, *Simcoe Correspondence*, II, 5–17.

48. McKee to Simcoe, July 1, 1793, ibid., I, 374.

49. *Thirty Thousand Miles with Heckewelder*, p. 312.

50. Simcoe to Clarke, July 10, 1793, *Simcoe Correspondence*, I, 383.

51. Pickering, Lincoln, and Randolph to Knox, July 10, 1793, *PP*, reel 6; Pickering, Lincoln, and Randolph to Washington, *PP*, reel 59.

52. Memo, July 30, 1793, *PP*, reel 60; *Thirty Thousand Miles with Heckewelder*, pp. 315–16.

53. Lincoln, Pickering, and Randolph to the Indians, July 3, 1793, *PP*, reel 60.

54. *Thirty Thousand Miles with Heckewelder*, p. 318.

55. A. L. Burt, *The United States, Great Britain, and British North America* (New Haven: Yale University Press, 1940), p. 131; Reginald Horsman, *Matthew Elliott* (Detroit: Wayne State University Press, 1964), p. 85; Wayne to Knox, Sept., 17, 1793, *Anthony Wayne*, pp. 272–75.

56. *Thirty Thousand Miles with Heckewelder*, pp. 315–19; Heckewelder's memo, July 1793, *PP*, reel 59.

57. Pickering, Lincoln, and Randolph to Wayne, Aug. 23, 1793, *PP*, reel 60.

58. Pickering to R. Pickering, Aug. 21, 1793, *PP*, reel 2.

Chapter 11. The War Department, Securing the Peace

1. North Callahan, *Henry Knox: General Washington's General* (New York: Rinehart, 1958), p. 295.

2. John H. Powell, *Bring Out Your Dead* (Philadelphia: University of Pennsylvania Press, 1949), pp. 29–113.

3. Pernick, "Politics, Parties, and Pestilence," *William and Mary Quarterly*, ser. 3, XXIX (Oct. 1972): 565.

4. Powell, *Bring Out Your Dead*, pp. 80–84.

5. Ibid.; Pernick, "Politics and Pestilence," pp. 573–75.

6. Ibid.

7. Ibid.

8. Pickering to Clarke, Oct. 1, 1793, *PP*, reel 35; Pernick, "Politics and Pestilence," pp. 563–65.

9. Pickering to Washington, Oct. 21, 23, 1793, *PP*, reel 6.

10. Powell, *Bring Out Your Dead*, p. 136.

11. Octavius Pickering and Charles W. Upham, *The Life of Timothy Pickering* (Boston: Little Brown, 1867), IV, 396.

12. Douglas S. Freeman, et al., *George Washington* (New York: Scribner's, 1948–57), VII, 131–35; Pickering to Washington, Oct. 14, 1793, *PP*, reel 6.

13. Pickering to Washington, Oct. 21, 1793, *PP*, reel 6.

14. Pickering to Washington, Oct. 28, 1793, *PP*, reel 35; Freeman et al., *Washington*, VII, 131–35.

15. J. L. Wright, *Britain and the American Frontier* (Athens: University of Georgia Press, 1975), pp. 87–93; Francis Philbrick, *The Rise of the West* (New York: Harper & Row, 1965), pp. 156–57.

16. William L. Stone, *The Life of Joseph Brant* (New York: A. V. Blake, 1838), II, 371–74.

17. Collection of newspaper clippings, Aug.–Sept. 1794, *PP*, reel 62.

18. Chapin to Knox, July 9, 1794; Brant to Smith, July 19, 1794, cited in Stone, *Brant*, II, 379–80; Jack Gifford, "The Northwest Indian War" (Ph.D. dissertation, UCLA, 1964), p. 376.

19. Pickering to Knox, Sept. 20, 1794, *PP*, reel 60.

20. Pickering to Knox, Oct. 15, 1794, ibid.

21. Ibid.

22. Knox to Pickering, Oct. 25, 1794, *PP*, reel 62.

23. Pickering to R. Pickering, Oct. 15, 1794, *PP*, reel 2.

24. Pickering to the Six Nations, n.d. (approx. Oct. 20, 1794); Pickering to Knox, Oct. 28, 1794, *PP*, reel 60.

25. Anthony F. C. Wallace, *The Death and Rebirth of the Seneca Nation* (New York: Knopf, 1970), pp. 175–76.

26. Pickering's speech to the Oneidas, Oct. 18, 1794, *PP*, reel 60.

27. Wallace, *Death and Rebirth*, p. 173; Reginald Horsman, *Expansion and American Indian Policy* (East Lansing: Michigan State University Press, 1967), pp. 17–20; "Indian Land Cessions in the United States," *Annual Report, Bureau of American Ethnology*, 1896–1897, pt. II, p. 648, pl. CLIV.

28. Charles J. Kappler, ed., *Indian Affairs, Laws and Treaties* (Washington, D.C.: U.S. Government Printing Office, 1903–13), II, 18–19, 27–29.

29. Pickering to Knox, Nov. 7, 1794, *PP*, reel 60; Kappler, *Indian Affairs*, II, 27–29.

30. Kappler, *Indian Affairs*, II, 27–29.

31. William L. Stone, *The Life and Times of Red Jacket* (New York: Wiley & Putnam, 1841), p. 134.

32. Pickering to Brant, Nov. 20, 1794, *PP*, reel 62.

33. Wayne to Knox, Dec. 23, 1794, in *Anthony Wayne, A Name in Arms*, ed. Richard C. Knopf (Pittsburgh: University of Pittsburgh Press, 1959), pp. 369–74; Pickering to Washington, Feb. 27, 1795, *GWPLC*, reel 12; Wayne to Knox, Dec. 14, 1794, Wayne Papers, *CL;* Gifford, "Northwest Indian War." pp. 423, 460.

34. Pickering to Dandridge, Feb. 27, 1795; Dandridge to Pickering, Feb. 27, 1795, *GWPLC*, reel 12.

35. Pickering's Report to the Speaker of the House, Jan. 26, 1795, *ASPIA*, I, 547; Pickering to Washington, Feb. 17, 1795, *GWPLC*, reel 12; *AC*, 3d Cong., 2d sess., p. 1221; Richard H. Kohn, *Eagle and Sword: The Federalists and the Creation of the Military Establishment in America* (New York: Free Press, 1975), pp. 176–78.

36. Pickering to Wayne, Apr. 15, 1795, *Anthony Wayne*, pp. 404–07.

37. Freeman et al., *Washington*, VII, 233.

38. Ibid., p. 239.

39. James Moneghan, *John Jay* (Indianapolis: Bobbs Merrill, 1935), p. 390; Freeman et al., *Washington*, VII, 256.

40. Pickering to Wayne, June 17, 1795, *Anthony Wayne*, pp. 423–24.

41. Pickering to Brickell, Nov. 19, 1793, Records of the Postmaster General's Office, National Archives, R.G. 28, microfilm, M. 601, reel 3.

42. Pickering to Wayne, Aug. 1, 1795, *Anthony Wayne*, pp. 440–42.

43. "Instructions to British Ministers in the U.S.," ed. Bernard Mayo, *Annual Report of the American Historical Association*, 1936, III, 83n.

44. Pickering to Wayne, June 17, 1795, *Anthony Wayne*, pp. 423–24.

45. Ibid.

46. Wayne to Pickering, Mar. 8, 1795, *Anthony Wayne*, pp. 386–90; Wright, *Britain and the American Frontier*, pp. 98–100; Gifford, "Northwest Indian War," p. 462.

47. Pickering to Wayne, June 17, 1795, *Anthony Wayne*, pp. 423–24.

48. Pickering to Wayne, June 27, 1795, ibid., pp. 429–30.

49. Freeman et al., *Washington*, VII, 261; James T. Flexner, *Washington* (Boston: Little Brown, 1972), II, 214.

50. Freeman et al., *Washington*, VII, 261.

51. Ibid., p. 260; Samuel Flagg Bemis, *John Quincy Adams and the Foundations of American Foreign Policy* (New York: Knopf, 1949), pp. 67–68; Bradford Perkins, *The First Rapproachement* (Philadelphia: University of Pennsylvania Press, 1956), pp. 34–35.

52. Freeman et al., *Washington*, VII, 261; Flexner, *Washington*, II, 214.

53. Flexner, *Washington*, II, 214.

54. Pickering to Wayne, June 17, Aug. 1, 1795, *Anthony Wayne*, pp. 423–24, 440–42.

55. Pickering and Upham, *Pickering*, III, 216.

56. Smith to Monroe, Aug. 6, 1795, Monroe Papers, reel 1, *LC*.

57. Donald H. Steward, *The Opposition Press of the Federalist Period* (Albany: State University of New York Press, 1969), p. 201; Freeman et al., *Washington*, VII, 266–69.

58. Higginson to Pickering, July 14, 1795; Williams to Pickering, July 17, 1795, *PP*, reel 20.

59. Ames to Wolcott, in *The Administrations of Washington and Adams*, ed. George Gibbs (New York: W. Van Norden, 1846), I, 210–11; Sturgis to Perkins, July 12, 1795, cited in Freeman et al., *Washington*, VII, 265n.

60. Pickering to Higginson, July 24, 1795, *PP*, reel 6.

61. Monaghan, *Jay*, pp. 388–404; Freeman et al., *Washington*, VII, 268–70.

62. Pickering to Washington, July 27, 1795, *PP*, reel 6.

63. Washington to Pickering, July 31, 1795, *PP*, reel 20.

64. Grenville to Hammond, May 9, 1795, in "Instructions to British Ministers," III, 83; Moncure Conway, *Omitted Chapters of History Disclosed in The Life and Papers of Edmund Randolph* (New York: G. P. Putnam's Sons, 1888), p. 23.

65. The dispatch with Pickering's translation and Hamilton's corrections may be found in *PP*, reel 41; Brant, "Edmund Randolph, Not Guilty!" *William and Mary Quarterly*, ser. 3, VII (April 1950): 182–83; Freeman et al., *Washington*, VII, 279–98.

66. Pickering to Washington, July 31, 1795, *PP*, reel 6; Pickering to Wayne, Aug. 1, 1795, *Anthony Wayne*, pp. 430–32.

67. Freeman et al., *Washington*, VII, 268.

68. Pickering to Washington, July 31, 1795, *PP*, reel 6.

69. Pickering to Wayne, Aug. 1, 1795, *Anthony Wayne*, pp. 440–42.

70. Pickering and Upham, *Pickering*, III, 217.

71. Flexner, *Washington*, III, 229.

72. Ibid.

73. Freeman et al., *Washington*, VII, 294–97; Pickering and Upham, *Pickering*, III, 216–*19*.

74. Ibid.; John J. Reardon, *Edmund Randolph* (New York: Macmillan, 1975), pp. 307—12.

75. Brant, "Edmund Randolph," p. 194n.

76. Pickering to J. Q. Adams, Sept. 10, 1795, *PP*, reel 6.

77. Ibid.

78. Pickering insisted to the last that Randolph had been a traitor. See Pickering's memo on a conversation with William Tilghman, Jan. 19, 1822, *PP*, reel 51.

Chapter 12. Secretary of State

1. Hamilton to Washington, Nov. 5, 1795, in *The Works of Alexander Hamilton,* ed. Henry C. Lodge (New York: G. P. Putnam's Sons, 1904), X, 129–32.

2. Pickering to Higginson, Sept. 22, 1795; Pickering to Hamilton, Nov. 17, 1795, *PP,* reel 6.

3. Ibid.; Douglas S. Freeman et al., *George Washington* (New York: Scribner's, 1948–57), VII, 324–25; James T. Flexner, *Washington* (Boston: Little Brown, 1972), II, 250.

4. J. Adams to A. Adams, Jan. 7, 1796, in *The Works of John Adams,* ed. C. F. Adams (Boston: Little Brown, 1850), I, 483.

5. Bingham to Pickering, June 5, 1798, *PP,* reel 63.

6. Pickering to Higginson, Dec. 12, 1795, *PP,* reel 6.

7. Jefferson to Monroe, Sept. 6, 1795; Beckley to Monroe, Sept. 23, 1795, Monroe Papers, *LC.*

8. *The Memoirs of John Quincy Adams,* ed. C. F. Adams (Philadelphia: Lippincott, 1874), Dec. 1, 1795, I, 143.

9. Hammond to Grenville, Jan. 5, 1795, F.O. 116, photostats in *LC.*

10. Pickering to Bond, Sept. 2, 1795, *PP,* reel 35; Pickering to J. Q. Adams or Deas, Sept. 12, 1795, *DIDSNA,* reel 3; Freeman et al., *Washington,* VII, 301–02.

11. Pickering to Bond, Oct. 12, 1795, *DLDSNA,* reel 8; Pickering to Pinckney, Oct. 22, 1795, *DIDSNA,* reel 3; *Philadelphia Aurora,* Jan. 6, Feb. 6, Mar. 27, Oct. 8, 1795. See also *Philadelphia Minerva,* June 27, 1795.

12. James F. Zimmerman, *Impressment of American Seamen* (New York: Columbia University Press, 1925), pp. 43–47.

13. *Philadelphia Aurora,* Aug. 8, 1795.

14. Pickering to J. Q. Adams, Sept. 12, 1795, *DIDSNA,* reel 3.

15. Pickering to J. Q. Adams or Deas, Sept. 12, 1795, ibid.

16. Grenville to Bond, Jan. 7, May 19, 1796, "Instructions to British Ministers," ed. Bernard Mayo, *Annual Report of the American Historical Association,* 1936, III, 104–05, 118–19.

17. J. Q. Adams to Pickering, Dec. 5, 1795, *The Writings of John Quincy Adams,* ed. W. C. Ford (New York: Macmillan, 1913), I, 434–36; Samuel Flagg Bemis, *John Quincy Adams and the Foundations of American Foreign Policy* (New York: Knopf, 1949), I, 75–76.

18. Pickering to Crawford, Apr. 21, 1796, *PP,* reel 36; Pickering to Bond, Mar. 19, 1796, *DLDSNA,* reel 9; Joanne L. Neel, *Phineas Bond: A Study in Anglo-American Relations* (Philadelphia: University of Pennsylvania Press, 1968), p. 136.

19. Pickering to Pinckney, Feb. 27, 1796, *DIDSNA,* reel 3; Pickering to Deas, Mar. 9, 1796, ibid.; Bemis, *John Quincy Adams,* I, 70n.

20. Pickering to Pinckney, Feb. 27, 1796, *DIDSNA,* reel 3.

21. Washington to the Senate and House, Mar. 1, 1796, *The Writings of George Washington,* ed. John C. Fitzpatrick (Washington, D.C.: U.S. Government Printing Office, 1939), XXXIV, 481; Freeman et al., *Washington,* VII, 348.

22. Stephen Kurtz, *The Presidency of John Adams: The Collapse of Federalism* (Philadelphia: University of Pennsylvania Press, 1957), pp. 39–77.

23. *AC,* 4th Cong., 1st sess., pp. 786, 802–10; Zimmerman, *Impressment,* pp. 55–59.

24. Pickering to Bond, Mar. 19, 1796, *PP,* reel 36.

25. Pickering to Lincoln, Mar. 22, 1796; Pickering to Bond, Mar. 25, 1796, *PP,* reel 36; Pickering to Collectors of Customs, Mar. 25, 1796, *DLDSNA,* reel 9.

26. Grenville to Bond, Jan. 18, 1796, "Instructions to British Ministers," III, 106–09; Neel, *Phineas Bond,* pp. 139–42.

27. Hamilton to Wolcott, Apr. 20, 1796, *The Papers of Alexander Hamilton,* ed. Harold

C. Syrett et al. (New York: Columbia University Press, 1974), XX, 128; Grenville to Bond, Jan. 18, 1796, "Instructions to British Ministers," III, 106–10; Neel, *Phineas Bond*, p. 140.

28. Pickering to Washington, Mar. 29, 1796, *GWPLC*, reel 109.

29. Hamilton to Washington, Mar. 29, 1796, *Hamilton Papers*, XX, 86–103.

30. Freeman et al., *Washington*, VII, 354.

31. Madison to Jefferson, Apr. 4, 1796, Madison Papers, *LC*.

32. *Philadelphia Aurora*, Apr. 1, 1796.

33. Pickering to Innes, Apr. 6, 1796, *PP*, reel 36.

34. Sedgwick to Williams, Apr. 9, 13, 1796, Sedgwick Papers, *MHS*.

35. *Gazette of the United States*, Apr. 20, 1796.

36. Pickering to Pinckney, Apr. 23, 1796, *DIDSNA*, reel 13.

37. Samuel E. Morison, *The Life and Letters of Harrison Gray Otis* (Boston: Houghton Mifflin, 1913), I, 57; Freeman et al., *Washington*, VII, 362–64.

38. Kurtz, *Presidency of John Adams*, pp. 68–69; Winfred E. Bernhard, *Fisher Ames* (Chapel Hill: University of North Carolina Press, 1965), pp. 262–74; Freeman et al., *Washington*, VII, 371–75.

39. Pickering to Pinckney, May 2, 1796, *DIDSNA*, reel 3.

40. Albert H. Bowman, *The Struggle for Neutrality* (Knoxville: University of Tennessee Press, 1974), pp. 237–38.

41. Gerard H. Clarfield, *Timothy Pickering and American Diplomacy* (Columbia: University of Missouri Press, 1969), pp. 41–44.

42. Ibid., pp. 52–56; Harry Ammon, *James Monroe: The Quest for National Identity* (New York: McGraw-Hill, 1971), pp. 150–56; Bowman, *Struggle for Neutrality*, pp. 257–60.

43. Pickering to Adet, Nov. 1, 1796, *ASPFA*, I:1, 578.

44. Pickering to Otis, June 30, 1796, *PP*, reel 36.

45. Pickering to Lowell, June 30, 1796; Pickering to Otis, July 12, 1796; Pickering to Washington, July 15, 1796, ibid.

46. Pickering to Adet, July 19, 1796, *DLDSNA*, reel 9.

47. Reprinted, *Philadelphia Aurora*, July 16, 1796.

48. Pickering to Clarke, July 22, 1796, *PP*, reel 6.

49. Ibid.

50. Harry Ammon, *Monroe*, p. 147; Bowman, *Struggle for Neutrality*, pp. 237–38; Kurtz, *Presidency of John Adams*, pp. 126–27.

51. Noble Cunningham, *The Jeffersonian Republicans* (Chapel Hill: University of North Carolina Press, 1957); Kurtz, *Presidency of John Adams*, pp. 179–90.

52. Kurtz, *Presidency of John Adams*, p. 178.

53. Adet to Pickering, Oct. 27, 1796, *ASPFA*, I:1, 577, Kurtz, *Presidency of John Adams*, pp. 127–32; Bowman, *Struggle for Neutrality*, pp. 264–67.

54. Washington to Hamilton, Nov. 2, 1796, *Writings of Washington*, XXXV, 252.

55. Ibid.

56. Liston to Grenville, Nov. 15, 1796, F.O. 115.

57. Adet to Pickering, Oct. 27, 1796, *ASPFA*, I:1, 577.

58. Pickering to Adet, Nov. 1, 1796, *ASPFA*, I:1, 578.

59. *Boston Independent Chronicle*, Nov. 17, 1796.

60. Ibid.

61. Pickering to Adet, Nov. 1, 1796, *ASPFA*, I:1, 578.

62. Bingham to King, Nov. 29, 1796; Goodhue to King, Dec. 12, 1796, *The Life and Correspondence of Rufus King*, ed. C. R. King (New York: G. P. Putnam's Sons, 1894), II, 124, Kurtz, *Presidency of John Adams*, pp. 184–90.

63. *Philadelphia Aurora,* Dec. 13, 1796.

64. Hamilton to Washington, Nov. 5, 1796, Hamilton Papers, *LC.*

65. Adet to the people of the U.S., Nov. 15, 1796, *ASPFA,* I:1, 583.

66. Hamilton to Washington, Nov. 19, 1796, Hamilton Papers, *LC.*

67. Washington to Pickering, Jan 4, 1797, *PP,* reel 21.

68. Pickering to Pinckney, Jan. 21, 1797, *PP,* reel 37.

69. Cabot to Pickering, Feb. 2, 1797; Hamilton to Pickering, Feb. 7, 1797; Jay to Pickering, Jan. 31, 1797, *PP,* reel 21.

70 *Philadelphia Aurora,* Feb. 2, 1797.

71. Ibid., Feb. 6, 1797.

72. James M. Banner, *To the Hartford Convention* (New York: Knopf, 1970), pp. 25–27.

73. Liston to Grenville, Apr. 18, 1797, F.O. 115.

Chapter 13. Pickering and Adams

1. No evidence connects Pickering to the alleged conspiracy against Adams in 1796. See John C. Miller, *Alexander Hamilton: Portrait in Paradox* (New York: Harper, 1959), pp. 446–48.

2. Adams to Rush, Apr. 22, 1811, *AP,* reel 118.

3. Manning J. Dauer, *The Adams Federalists* (Baltimore: Johns Hopkins University Press, 1953), p. 114; Page Smith, *John Adams* (Garden City, N.Y.: Doubleday, 1962), p. 922; Stephen Kurtz, *The Presidency of John Adams: The Collapse of Federalism* (Philadelphia: University of Pennsylvania Press, 1957), p. 271.

4. Quite obviously Hamilton set out to cultivate Pickering only after he took over the State Department. For confirmation, note that serious correspondence between the two begins in 1795. See *The Papers of Alexander Hamilton,* ed. Harold C. Syrett et al. (New York: Columbia University Press, 1974), XVIII, XIX.

5. Hamilton to Washington, Nov. 5, 19, 1796, Hamilton Papers, *LC;* Hamilton to Wolcott, Nov. 22, 1796, *The Works of Alexander Hamilton,* ed. Henry C. Lodge (New York: G. P. Putnam's Sons, 1904), X, 208–09.

6. Sayre to Adams, Mar. 30, 1797; Gerry to Adams, Feb. 3, 1797, *AP,* reel 383; George Billias, *Elbridge Gerry, Founding Father and Republican Statesman* (New York: McGraw-Hill, 1976), pp. 250–51.

7. Adams to Rush, Apr. 22, 1811, *Ap,* reel 118; Dauer, *Adams Federalists,* p. 114; Kurtz, *Presidency of John Adams,* p. 271.

8. J. Adams to J. Q. Adams, June 2, 1797, *AP,* reel 117; Samuel Flagg Bemis, *John Quincy Adams and the Foundations of American Foreign Policy* (New York: Knopf, 1949), I, 88.

9. Peter Hill, *William Vans Murray* (Syracuse: Syracuse University Press, 1971), pp. 36–40, 48.

10. Pickering to Hamilton, Mar. 30, 1797, Hamilton Papers, *LC.*

11. Thomas Jefferson, *The Complete Anas of Thomas Jefferson,* ed. F.B. Sawvel (New York: Round Table Press, 1903), pp. 184–85; Oliver Wolcott, *Memoirs of the Administrations of Washington and Adams,* ed. George Gibbs (New York: W. Dan Norden, 1846), I, 462–66; Smith, *John Adams,* II, 924–25; Dauer, *Adams Federalists,* pp. 124–25.

12. Pickering to J. Q. Adams, Mar. 17, 1797, *AP,* reel 383.

13. Hamilton to Pickering, Mar. 22, 29, 1797, *PP,* reel 21.

14. Pickering to Hamilton, Mar. 26, 1797, Hamilton Papers, *LC.*

15. Hamilton to Smith, Apr. 5, 10, 1797, Papers of William L. Smith, *LC.*

16. Ames to Wolcott, Apr. 7, 24, 1797, in Wolcott, *Administrations of Washington and Adams,* II, 477, 497–98; Cabot to Wolcott, Apr. 17, 1797, *Life and Letters of George Cabot,* ed. H. C. Lodge (Boston: Little Brown, 1877), pp. 128–30; Hamilton to Pickering, Mar. 29, May 11, 1797, *PP,* reel 21; Hamilton to Wolcott, Apr. 5, 1797, Hamilton Papers, *LC.*

17. King to Pickering, Mar. 5, 1797, *The Life and Correspondence of Rufus King,* ed. C. R. King (New York: G. P. Putnam's Sons, 1894), II, 152; Hamilton to Pickering, May 11, 1797; Hamilton to Wolcott, Apr. 5, 1797, *Hamilton Papers,* XXI, 22–23, 81–84; Miller, *Alexander Hamilton,* pp. 451–58; Robert Ernst, *Rufus King* (Chapel Hill: University of North Carolina Press, 1968), pp. 219–73.

18. Pickering to Hamilton, Apr. 29, 1797, Hamilton Papers, *LC.*

19. Pickering to Adams, May 1, 1797, *PP,* reel 6; Wolcott to Adams, Apr. 21, 1797, *AP,* reel 384.

20. *Messages and Papers of the Presidents,* ed. James D. Richardson (Washington, D.C.: U.S. Government Printing Office, 1896), I, 233–39.

21. Dauer, Adams Federalists, pp. 124–26; Smith, *John Adams,* II, 924–25.

22. J. Adams to A. Adams, Jan. 9, 1797, *AP,* reel 383.

23. A. Adams to J. Q. Adams, June 22, 1797, ibid., reel 384; Billias, *Elbridge Gerry,* pp. 260–63.

24. Pickering to McHenry, July 27, 1813, *PP,* reel 14.

25. Pickering to King, Feb. 8, 1798, *PP,* reel 8.

26. Adams to heads of departments, Jan. 25, 1798, *PP,* reel 22.

27. Sedgwick to ?, Jan. 29, 1798, Sedgwick Papers, *MHS.*

28. Pickering to Murray, Feb. 26, 1798, *PP,* reel 8.

29. Pickering to William Smith, Mar. 4, 1798, ibid.

30. Marshall et al. to Pickering, Jan. 8, 1798, *ASPFA,* I:2, 150–51.

31. Sedgwick to Van Schaack, Mar. 17, 1798, Sedgwick Papers, *MHS:* Smith, *John Adams,* II, 952–55; Albert H. Bowman, *The Struggle for Neutrality* (Knoxville: University of Tennessee Press, 1974), pp. 326–38; Kurtz, *Presidency of John Adams,* pp. 297–305.

32. Pickering to Murray, Mar. 28, 1798, *DIDSNA,* reel 4; Pickering to Ellicott, Apr. 1, 1798, *PP,* reel 8.

33. A. Adams to Cranch, Mar. 20, 1798, *New Letters of Abigail Adams,* ed. Stewart Mitchell (Boston: Houghton Mifflin, 1947), pp. 146–47; Pickering to Hamilton, Mar. 25, 1798, Hamilton Papers, *LC.*

34. *Messages and Papers of the Presidents,* I, 264–65.

35. Pickering to Marshall et al., Mar. 23, 1798, *PP,* reel 8; Clement Humphreys Letterbook, Historical Society of Pennsylvania.

36. Adams to heads of departments, Jan. 24, 1798, *PP,* reel 22; Smith, *John Adams,* II, 954.

37. Pickering to Higginson, Mar. 6, 1798, *PP,* reel 8; Pickering to Adams, Mar. 17, 1798, *DIDSNA,* reel 4.

38. Ibid.

39. Liston to Grenville, May 2, 1798, F.O. 115.

40. Adams to Pickering, Jan. 24, 1798, *PP,* reel 22.

41. Hamilton to Pickering, Mar. 17, 1798, ibid.

42. Pickering to Hamilton, Mar. 25, 1798 (two letters), PP, reel 8.

43. Hamilton to Pickering, Mar. 27, 1798, ibid., reel 22.

44. Pickering to King, Apr. 2, 1798, ibid., reel 8.

45. Liston to Grenville, May 2, Aug. 31, 1798, F.O. 115.

46. Hamilton to Pickering, Mar. 17, 1798, *PP,* reel 22; Pickering to Hamilton, Mar. 25, 1798, *PP,* reel 8.

47. Jefferson to Monroe, Mar. 21, 1798, Monroe Papers, reel 2, *LC.*

48. *AC*, 5th Cong., 1st sess., Mar. 29, 1798, pp. 1353–55.
49. Liston to Grenville, Apr. 11, 1798, F.O. 115.
50. Sedgwick to Van Schaak, Mar. 12, 18, 1798, Sedgwick Papers, *MHS*.
51. Smith, *John Adams*, II, 956–59.
52. Pickering to King, Apr. 2, 1798, *PP*, reel 8.
53. Tilton to Pickering, Apr. 17, 1798, *PP*, reel 22.
54. Pickering to Jay, Apr. 9, 1798, *PP*, reel 8.
55. Pickering to Humphreys, Apr. 13, 1798; Pickering to Adams, May 26, 1798, ibid.; Webster to Pickering, May 12, 1798, *PP*, reel 22; Pickering to Adams, Apr. 10, 1798, *AP*, reel 388.
56. Adams's notes on Dispatch #1, Mar. 5, 1798, *AP*, reel 386; Smith, *John Adams*, II, 953.
57. Adams to Peabody, June 22, 1798, Shaw Family Papers, *LC*.
58. Pickering to Adams, May 26, 1798, *PP*, reel 8.
59. Tracy to Hamilton, May 17, 1798, Hamilton Papers, *LC*.
60. Griswold to Griswold, May 29, 1798, Griswold Papers, Yale University Library.
61. Ames to Pickering, June 4, 1798, *PP*, reel 13.
62. Adams to Adams, May 29, 1798, *AP*, reel 388.
63. Pickering to Ellicott, June 1, 1798, *PP*, reel 8; Billias, *Elbridge Gerry*, pp. 280–82.
64. Cabot to Adams, June 22, 1798, *AP*, reel 389.
65. Pinckney to Pickering, June 29, 1798, *PP*, reel 22.
66. Adams to Peabody, June 22, 1798, Shaw Family Papers, *LC*.
67. Murray to King, Apr. 12, 1798, Murray Papers, Pierpont Morgan Library.
68. Pickering to King, June 12, 1798, *PP*, reel 11 (misplaced in 1799).
69. Gerry to Adams, Apr. 6, 1797, *AP*, reel 388; Gerry to Gerry, Mar. 26, Apr. 16, 20, 1798, Gerry Papers, *LC*.
70. *Messages and Papers of the Presidents*, I, 266.
71. Pickering to Gerry, June 25, 1798, *DIDSNA*, reel 4.
72. Jefferson to Stuart, June 8, 1798, Jefferson Collection, *MHS*.
73. *Philadelphia Aurora*, June 16, 1798.
74. *New York Timepiece*, June 11, 20, 1798.
75. Hamilton to Pickering, June 7, 8, 1798, *PP*, reel 22.
76. Hamilton to King, June 6, 1798, Papers of Rufus King, New York Historical Society.
77. Liston to Grenville, May 2, 1798, F.O. 115.
78. Pickering to J. Pickering, June 16, 1798, *PP*, reel 8; Liston to Grenville, July 9, 1798, F.O. 115.
79. Higginson to Pickering, June 9, 1798, *PP*, reel 22.
80. Ames to Pickering, July 10, 1798, ibid.
81. Adams to Cranch, June 19, 1798, *New Letters of Abigail Adams*, pp. 193–94; A. Adams to J. Q. Adams, July 14, 1798, *AP*, reel 390.
82. Pickering to Meyer, June 27, 1798, *PP*, reel 8.
83. Pickering to Marshall, July 24, 1798; Pickering to Carrington, Aug. 8, 1798, *PP*, reel 9.

Chapter 14. Schism

1. Richard H. Kohn, *Eagle and Sword: The Federalists and the Creation of the Military Establishment in America* (New York: Free Press, 1975), p. 222; Pickering to Hamilton, June 9, 1798, *PP*, reel 8.
2. Adams to McHenry, Oct. 22, 1798, McHenry Papers, *LC*.

3. Pickering to Hamilton, June 9, 1798, *PP*, reel 8.

4. Pickering to Humphreys, Feb. 1, 1797; Pickering to Pinckney, Feb. 25, 1797, *PP*, reel 37; Pickering to Hamilton, Mar. 25, 1798; Pickering to King, Apr. 2, 1798, *PP*, reel 8.

5. Pickering to King, Mar. 12, 1799; Pickering to Harper, Mar. 21, 1799; Pickering to Stevens, Apr. 20, 1799, *PP*, reel 10.

6. McKee to McHenry, June 7, 1797; anonymous to Adams, May 5, 1797; McHenry to McKee, July 25, Nov. 8, 1797, *AP*, reel 386.

7. Memo, confidential papers, Sept. 13, 1798; Pickering to Adams, Oct. 4, 11, 1798, *PP*, reel 9; James M. Smith, *Freedom's Fetters: The Alien and Sedition Laws and American Civil Liberties* (Ithaca: Cornell University Press, 1956), pp. 175–76.

8. Pickering to King, Apr. 6, July 16, 1797, *PP*, reel 6; Pickering to Tichenor, Apr. 1, 1797, *PP*, reel 37.

9. Pickering to Washington, July 6, 1798, ibid., reel 9.

10. Stephen Kurtz, *The Presidency of John Adams: The Collapse of Federalism* (Philadelphia: University of Pennsylvania Press, 1957), pp. 234–39; Page Smith, *John Adams* (Garden City, N.Y.: Doubleday, 1962), II, 972–74; Douglas S. Freeman et al., *George Washington* (New York: Scribner's, 1948–57), VII, 403–12; Gerard H. Clarfield, *Timothy Pickering and American Diplomacy* (Columbia: University of Missouri Press, 1969), pp. 165–79; Ralph A. Brown, *The Presidency of John Adams* (Lawrence: University of Kansas Press, 1975), pp. 63–71.

11. Pickering to Washington, July 6, 1798, *PP*, reel 9; McHenry to Adams, July 12, 1798, *AP*, reel 390; Washington to McHenry, July 22, 1798, *The Writings of George Washington*, ed. John C. Fitzpatrick (Washington, D.C.: U.S. Government Printing Office, 1939), XXXVI, 356–60.

12. Pickering to Washington, Sept. 13, 1798, *PP*, reel 9.

13. Washington to Adams, Sept. 16, 1798, *AP*, reel 391.

14. Hamilton to Washington, June 2, 1798, Hamilton Papers, *LC*.

15. Hamilton to Pickering, July 17, 1798, ibid.

16. Pickering to Hamilton, Aug. 21, 1798, *PP*, reel 9.

17. Ibid.

18. Ibid.

19. Pickering to Jay, July 20, 1798, ibid.

20. McHenry to Washington, Aug. 6, 1798, McHenry Papers, *CL*.

21. Pickering to J. Q. Adams, Mar. 17, 1798; Pickering to Ellicott, June 1, 1798, *PP*, reel 8; Pickering to Cabot, Feb. 4, 1799, *PP*, reel 10.

22. Gerry to Gerry, July 12, 1798, Gerry Papers, *LC;* Albert H. Bowman, *The Struggle for Neutrality* (Knoxville: University of Tennessee Press, 1974), pp. 340–50; George Billias, *Elbridge Gerry, Founding Father and Republican Statesman* (New York: McGraw-Hill, 1976), pp. 282–84.

23. *Philadelphia Aurora*, Aug. 31, Sept. 1, 1798.

24. Ibid.

25. Pickering to Marshall, Sept. 4, 1798, *PP*, reel 9.

26. Pickering to King, Sept. 15, 1798, ibid.

27. *Philadelphia Aurora*, Nov. 6, 1798.

28. Marshall to Pickering, Oct. 15, 1798, *PP*, reel 23.

29. Ibid.

30. Cabot to Pickering, Oct. 6, 26, Nov. 7, 1798, *PP*, reel 23.

31. Ibid.; Ames to Pickering, Nov. 22, 1798, ibid.

32. Adams to Pickering, Oct. 26, 1798, *AP*, reel 119.

33. Pickering to Adams, Nov. 5, 1798, *PP*, reel 9.

34. Adams to Gerry, Nov. 5, 1798, Gerry Papers, *LC*.

35. Shaw to A. Adams, Nov. 25, 1798, *AP*, reel 392.

36. Liston to Grenville, Nov. 7, 1798, F.O. 115, *LC*.

37. Marshall to ?, Aug. 11, 1798, Marshall Papers, *LC*; Pickering to Marshall, Oct. 4, 19, 1798, *PP*, reel 9.

38. Leonard Baker, *John Marshall* (New York: Macmillan, 1976), pp. 302–06.

39. Marshall to Pickering, Nov. 12, 1798, Marshall Papers, *LC*.

40. Ibid.; Pickering to Cabot, Nov. 10, 1798, *PP*, reel 9; Pickering to Adams, Dec. 11, 1798, *PP*, reel 10; Adams to Gerry, Dec. 15, 1798, *AP*, reel 117.

41. Adams to McHenry, Oct. 22, 1798, McHenry Papers, *LC*.

42. Manning J. Dauer, *The Adams Federalists* (Baltimore: Johns Hopkins University Press, 1953), pp. 233–37; McHenry to Smith, Oct. 20, 1798, McHenry Papers, *CL*; Liston to Grenville, Nov. 7, 1798, F.O. 115, *LC*.

43. Shaw to Adams, Dec. 18, 1798, *AP*, reel 392; Adams to Adams, Jan. 10, 1799, *AP*, reel 393; Frederick B. Tolles, *George Logan* (New York: Oxford University Press, 1953), pp. 153–84.

44. Bowman, *Struggle for Neutrality*, pp. 345–50.

45. Kurtz, *Presidency of John Adams*, pp. 334–73; Peter Hill, *William Vans Murray* (Syracuse: Syracuse University Press, 1971), pp. 132–46.

46. Pickering to Adams, Nov. 27, 1798, *PP*, reel 9; Adams to Congress, Dec. 12, 1798, *AC*, 5th Cong., 3d sess., pp. 2420–24; Brown, *Presidency of John Adams*.

47. Pickering to Cabot, Feb. 4, 1799, *PP*, reel 10.

48. Adams to Shaw, Jan. 25, 1799, Shaw Family Papers, LC; Gerry's memo, Mar. 26, 1798, Gerry Papers, *LC*.

49. Adams to Cunningham, Mar. 20, 1809, *AP*, reel 407.

50. Ibid.

51. Ibid.

52. Ibid.; Gerry's memo, Mar. 26, 1799, Gerry Papers, *LC*.

53. Pickering to Washington, Feb. 2, 1799; Pickering to Jay, Feb. 1, 1799, *PP*, reel 10.

54. Pickering to King, Feb. 19, 1799, ibid.; Brown, *Presidency of John Adams*, p. 96.

55. Sedgwick to Hamilton, Feb. 25, 1799, Hamilton Papers, *LC*; Stockton to Pickering, Jan. 11, 1822; Ross to Pickering, Feb. 5, 1822, *PP*, reel 31; Richard E. Welch, *Theodore Sedgwick, Federalist* (Middletown: Wesleyan University Press, 1965), pp. 187–88; Brown, *Presidency of John Adams*, pp. 95–100.

56. Stockton to Pickering, Jan. 11, 1822; Ross to Pickering, Feb. 5, 1822, *PP*, reel 31.

57. Hill, *Murray*, pp. 132–46; Stephen Kurtz, "The French Mission of 1799–1800: Concluding Chapter in the Statecraft of John Adams," *Political Science Quarterly*, LXXX (Dec. 1965): 543–57; Kohn, *Eagle and Sword*, pp. 256–59.

58. Ellsworth to Pickering, Sept. 20, 1799, *PP*, reel 25; Brown, *Presidency of John Adams*, p. 101.

59. Pickering to Campbell, May 3, 1799, *PP*, reel 11.

60. Cabot to Pickering, Mar. 7, 1799, *PP*, reel 24.

61. Ames to Pickering, Mar. 12, 1799, ibid.

62. Pickering to Murray, June 14, July 10, 1799, "The Letters of William Vans Murray," in ed. W. C. Ford, *American Historical Association Annual Report for 1912* (Washington, D.C.: U.S. Government Printing Office, 1914), pp. 562, 573–74.

63. McHenry to Murray, July 1, 1799, McHenry Papers, *CL*.

64. Pickering to Washington, Aug. 2, 1799, *PP*, reel 11; Hill, *Murray*, pp. 152–53.

65. Murray to Pickering, May 19, 1799, *PP*, reel 120.

66. Adams to Pickering, Aug. 6, 1799, *AP*, reel 120.

67. Pickering to Adams, Sept. 10, 1799, *PP,* reel 12.
68. Ibid.
69. Pickering to King, Feb. 19, 1799, ibid.
70. Pickering to Adams, Sept. 10, 1799, ibid.
71. Adams to Pickering, Sept. 16, 1799, *AP,* reel 396.
72. Ellsworth to Pickering, Sept. 26, 1799, *PP,* reel 25; Pickering to Cabot, Sept. 29, 1799, *PP,* reel 12.
73. Pickering to Murray, Oct. 14, 1799, ibid.
74. Stoddert to Adams, Aug. 29, Sept. 13, 1799, *AP,* reel 396.
75. Pickering to Murray, Oct. 14, 1799, *PP,* reel 12; Brown, *Presidency of John Adams,* pp. 110–12.

Chapter 15. Humiliations

1. Pickering to Cabot, Oct. 22, 1799; Pickering to Goodhue, Oct. 22, 1799; Pickering to Bingham, Oct. 23, 1799; Pickering to Ames, Oct. 24, 1799, *PP,* reel 12.
2. Griswold to Fanny Griswold, Mar. 27, 1800, Griswold Papers, Yale University Library.
3. Stephen Kurtz, *The Presidency of John Adams: The Collapse of Federalism* (Philadelphia: University of Pennsylvania Press, 1957), pp. 354–408.
4. John C. Miller, *Alexander Hamilton: Portrait in Paradox* (New York: Harper, 1959), pp. 511–14.
5. Bernard C. Steiner, *Life and Letters of James McHenry* (Cleveland: Arthur H. Clark Co., 1907), pp. 453–54; Howard Mattison-Boze, "James McHenry, Secretary of War, 1796–1800" (Ph.D. dissertation, University of Minnesota, 1965), pp. 258–63.
6. Adams to Pickering, May 10, 1800; Pickering to Adams, May 12, 1800; Adams to Pickering, May 12, 1800, *PP,* reel 13.
7. Goodhue to Pickering, May 19, 1800, *PP,* reel 26; Pickering to C. C. Pinckney, May 25, 1800, *PP,* reel 13.
8. James M. Smith, *Freedom's Fetters: The Alien and Sedition Laws and American Civil Liberties* (Ithaca: Cornell University Press, 1956), pp. 182–84, 283–84, 311; John C. Miller, *Crisis in Freedom* (Boston: Little Brown, 1951), pp. 73, 88–90, 99–102; Kurtz, *Presidency of John Adams,* pp. 391–93.
9. Pickering to Smith, May 7, 1800; Pickering to J. Pickering, May 7, 1800; Pickering to King, May 7, 1800, *PP,* reel 13.
10. Miller, *Alexander Hamilton,* pp. 515–24; Marvin Zahniser, *Charles C. Pinckney, Founding Father* (Chapel Hill: University of North Carolina Press, 1967), pp. 215–33.
11. Pickering to Williams, May 19, 1800; Pickering to C. C. Pinckney, May 25, 1800; Pickering to Goodhue, May 26, 1800, *PP,* reel 13; Pickering to Humphreys, May 26, 1800, *PP,* reel 11.
12. Pickering to W. L. Smith, June 7, 1800, *PP,* reel 13.
13. Pickering to Williams, May 19, 1800; Pickering to J. Pickering, May 27, 1800, ibid.
14. Sedgwick to Hamilton, May 7, 1800, Hamilton Papers, *LC.*
15. Dwight to Hillhouse, Mar. 1, 1800, Hillhouse Papers, Yale University Library.
16. Kurtz, *Presidency of John Adams,* p. 400.
17. Goodhue to Pickering, June 2, 1800, *PP,* reel 26.
18. Pickering to J. Pickering, May 27, 1800, *PP,* reel 13.
19. Pickering to Timothy Williams, May 19, 1800; Pickering to Goodhue, May 26, 1800; Pickering to Samuel P. Gardner, June 21, 1800, ibid.
20. Ibid.

21. Williams to Pickering, May 25, 1800; Goodhue to Pickering, May 26, 1800; Cabot to Pickering, May 26, 1800; Lyman to Pickering, May 26, 1800, *PP*, reel 26; Pickering to Goodhue, May 31, 1800; Pickering to J. Pickering, June 7, 1800, *PP*, reel 13.

22. Pickering to T. Pickering, Jr., June 27, 1800, ibid.

23. Pickering to J. Pickering, June 7, July 30, 1800, *PP*, reel 4:II.

24. Pickering to R. Pickering, Nov. 2, 1800 *PP*, reel 2.

25. Pickering to J. Pickering, Dec. 27, 1800, *PP*, reel 4:II.

26. Ibid.

27. Pickering to R. Pickering, Feb. 16, 1801, *PP*, reel 2; Octavius Pickering and Charles W. Upham, *The Life of Timothy Pickering* (Boston: Little Brown, 1867), IV, 24–29.

28. Ibid.

29. All told, thirty-four investors purchased shares of Pickering's holdings. Theodore Lyman and William Gray each subscribed $2,000. Most of the rest subscribed between $500 and $1,000.

30. David H. Fischer, *The Revolution of American Conservatism* (New York: Harper and Row, 1965), pp. 1–28, 255; James M. Banner, *To the Hartford Convention* (New York: Knopf, 1970), pp. 142–43, 219–21.

31. *Salem Gazette*, Oct. 18, 1802; James H. Robbins, "Voting Behavior in Massachusetts, 1800–1820: A Case Study" (Ph.D. dissertation, Northwestern University, 1970), pp. 146–47.

32. Pickering to R. Pickering, Apr. 4, 1806, *PP*, reel 2.

33. *Salem Gazette*, Oct. 18, 1802; Robbins, "Voting Behavior," pp. 146–47.

34. William Bentley, *Diary* (Salem: Essex Institute, 1907), II, 455; Robbins, "Voting Behavior," pp. 154–58.

35. *Salem Register*, Oct. 4, 11, 25, 1802.

36. Robbins, "Voting Behavior," pp. 154–58; Gordon Ross, "The Crowninshield Family in Business and Politics, 1790–1830" (Ph.D. dissertation, Claremont Graduate School, 1965), pp. 98–109.

37. *Salem Gazette*, Oct. 1, 1802.

38. Ibid., Oct. 8, 18, 1802.

39. Ibid., Nov. 2, 1802.

40. *Memoirs of John Quincy Adams*, ed. F. C. Adams (Philadelphia: Lippincott, 1874), I, 257–59.

41. Ibid.

Chapter 16. Hysteria, the First Secessionist Conspiracy

1. James Sterling Young, *The Washington Community* (New York: Columbia University Press, 1966), pp. 41–48; Pickering to J. Pickering, Oct. 17, 1803, *PP*, reel 4:II.

2. Pickering to R. Pickering, Nov. 7, 1803, *PP*, reel 2; Robert A. McCaughey, *Josiah Quincy* (Cambridge: Harvard University Press, 1974), pp. 46–47.

3. James R. Venza, "Federalists in Congress" (Ph.D. dissertation, Vanderbilt University, 1967), pp. 49–50; *The Memoirs of John Quincy Adams*, ed. C. F. Adams (Philadelphia: Lippincott, 1874), I, 256–57; Winfred E. Bernhard, *Fisher Ames* (Chapel Hill: University of North Carolina Press, 1965), pp. 338–39; David H. Fischer, *The Revolution of American Conservatism* (New York: Harper and Row, 1965).

4. For the Pickering-Adams feud in the Senate see T. B. Adams to J. Q. Adams, Dec. 15, 1803, *AP*, reel 403; Shaw to Adams, Jan. 7, 1804, *AP*, reel 403; *Memoirs of J. Q. Adams*, XX, 288; Pickering to Higginson, Jan. 6, 1804, *PP*, reel 14.

5. William Plumer, Diary, Feb. 28, 1806, Plumer Papers, *LC*.

6. Pickering to Peters, Apr. 13, 1806, Pickering Papers, *EI.*

7. Pickering to Caleb Strong, Nov. 22, 1803; Pickering to Truxton, Nov. 25, 1803; Pickering to Rufus Putnam, Dec. 6, 1803, *PP,* reel 14.

8. Pickering to Strong, Nov. 22, 1803, ibid.

9. Pickering to Putnam, Dec. 6, 1803, ibid.

10. Ralph K. White, *Nobody Wanted War* (Garden City, N.Y.: Doubleday, 1968), pp. 14–16.

11. Noble Cunningham, Jr., *The Jeffersonian Republicans in Power* (Chapel Hill: University of North Carolina Press, 1963), pp. 12–70.

12. Pickering to Cabot, Jan. 29, 1804, *PP,* reel 14.

13. Pickering to Pickering, Jan. 19, 1806, *PP,* reel 4: I.

14. Plumer, Diary, entries for Jan. 14, Feb. 10, Mar. 18, 1806, Plumer Papers, *LC;* Young, *Washington Community,* pp. 98–106.

15. Pickering to Cabot, Jan. 29, 1804, *PP,* reel 14.

16. Pickering to J. Pickering, Dec. 5, 1803, *PP,* reel 4:II.

17. Pickering to Cabot, Jan. 29, 1804, *PP,* reel 14.

18. Higginson to Pickering, Nov. 22, 1803; Cabot to Pickering, Dec. 10, 1803, *PP,* reel 26.

19. Ellicott to Pickering, Dec. 27, 1803, ibid.; James M. Banner, *To the Hartford Convention* (New York: Knopf, 1970), pp. 43–49.

20. Laussure to Pickering, Feb. 26, 1804, *PP,* reel 27.

21. Plumer to Mason, Jan. 14, 1804, Plumer Papers, *LC;* Plumer to J. Q. Adams, Dec. 20, 1828, in *Documents Relating to New England Federalism,* ed. Henry Adams (New York: B. Franklin, 1877), p. 145; Lynn Turner, *William Plumer of New Hampshire* (Chapel Hill: University of North Carolina Press, 1962), pp. 133–50.

22. Pickering to Cabot, Jan. 29, 1804, *PP,* reel 14.

23. Pickering to J. Pickering, Feb. 18, 1804, *PP,* reel 4:II; Hall to Pickering, May 26, 1800, *PP,* reel 26.

24. Pickering to J. Pickering, Feb. 18, 1804, *PP,* reel 4:II.

25. Pickering to J. Pickering, Dec. 23, 1803, ibid.

26. Pickering to J. Pickering, Jan. 12, 1804, pp. reel 3.

27. Hillhouse to Hillhouse, Dec. 23, 1803, Hillhouse Papers, Yale University Library.

28. Pickering to J. Pickering, Jan. 12, 1804, *PP,* reel 3; Pickering to J. Pickering, Jan. 20, Feb. 18, *PP,* reel 4:II. William never recovered. He died in a mental institution on June 16, 1814.

29. Peters to Pickering, Jan. 9, 1804, *PP,* reel 27.

30. Higginson to Pickering, Mar. 17, 1804, ibid.

31. Cabot to Pickering, Feb. 14, 1804, ibid.

32. Fischer, *Revolution of American Conservatism,* p. 176; Banner, *To the Hartford Convention,* pp. 116–21.

33. Pickering to King, Mar. 4, 1804, *PP,* reel 14.

34. Griswold to Wolcott, Mar. 11, 1804, *Documents Relating to New England Federalism,* pp. 354–57.

35. Ibid.

36. John C. Miller, *Alexander Hamilton: Portrait in Paradox* (New York: Harper, 1959), p. 565.

37. Ibid.

38. Hervey P. Prentiss, "Timothy Pickering and the Federalist Party, 1801–1804," *Essex Institute Historical Collections,* LXIX (Jan. 1933): 1–35; idem, "Pickering and the Embargo," ibid. (April 1933): 97–136; idem, "Timothy Pickering and the War of 1812," ibid., LXX (April 1934): 105–46.

Chapter 17. Battling the Embargo

1. Pickering to R. Pickering, Dec. 9, 1805, *PP,* reel 3.

2. Bradford Perkins, *Prologue to War* (Berkeley: University of California Press, 1961), pp. 79–82; Reginald Horsman, *The Causes of the War of 1812* (New York: A. S. Barnes, 1962), pp. 38–39; Curtiss Nettles, *The Emergence of a National Economy* (New York: Holt, Rinehart and Winston, 1962), p. 396.

3. Lyman to Pickering, Jan. 27, 1806, *PP,* reel 27.

4. Goodhue to Pickering, Feb. 12, 1806, ibid.; Crowninshield to Oliver, Dec. 22, 1805; Crowninshield to Silsbee, Jan. 17, 1806, Crowninshield Family Papers, Peabody Museum; Gordon Ross, "The Crowninshield Family in Business and Politics" (Ph.D. dissertation, Claremont Graduate School, 1965), pp. 111–68.

5. Pickering to Lowell, Dec. 28, 1805; Pickering to Ames, Dec. 29, 1805, *PP,* reel 38.

6. *AC,* 9th Cong., 1st sess., Feb. 3, 1806, p. 81.

7. Ibid.; Pickering to Putnam, Jan. 4, 1806, Putnam Papers, *MHS.*

8. Dumas Malone, *Thomas Jefferson, the President* (Boston: Little Brown, 1974), V, 110–11; Irving Brant, *James Madison, Secretary of State* (Indianapolis: Bobbs Merrill, 1953), pp. 312–14; John Pancake, *Samuel Smith and the Politics of Business* (Tuscaloosa: University of Alabama Press, 1972), p. 176.

9. Pickering to Ames, Feb. 2, 1806, *PP,* reel 38; Pickering to J. Pickering, Feb. 2, 1806, *PP,* reel 4:II.

10. Pickering to J. Pickering, Dec. 20, 1806, *PP,* reel 4:II; Pickering to Ames, Apr. 1, 1806, *PP,* reel 14; Pickering to Peters, Apr. 13, 1806, Pickering Papers, *EI.*

11. Rutledge to Otis, Aug. 3, 1807, Otis Papers, *MHS:;* Webster to King, July 6, 1807; King to Gore, Sept. 11, 1807, *Life and Correspondence of Rufus King,* ed. C. P. King (New York: G. P. Putnam's Sons, 1894), V, 38, 40; Samuel Flagg Bemis, *John Quincy Adams and the Foundations of American Foreign Policy* (New York: Knopf, 1949), I, 140–41; Samuel E. Morison, *The Life and Letters of Harrison Gray Otis* (Boston: Houghton Mifflin, 1913), I, 276–77; *New York Evening Post,* June 29, 1807; *Boston Columbian Centinel,* July 8, 1807; *Salem Gazette,* July 3, 1807.

12. IMPARTIALIS, draft in *PP,* reel 68; Pickering to Gardner, Nov. 18, 1807, *PP,* reel 38.

13. Liston to Grenville, Aug. 30, 1797, F.O. 115, photostats in *LC;* Pickering to Liston, Sept. 7, 1797, *DLDSNA,* R.G. 59, reel 10.

14. Pickering to King, July 14, 1799, *DIDSNA,* reel 1.

15. Undated memo, *PP,* reel 50.

16. Ibid.

17. J. Q. Adams to J. Adams, Oct. 27, 1807, *AP,* reel 405.

18. For Monroe's negotiations see Perkins, *Prologue to War,* pp. 82–83; Harry Ammon, *James Monroe: The Quest for National Identity* (New York: McGraw-Hill, 1971), pp. 248–69.

19. Truxton to Pickering, Oct. 26, 1807, *PP,* reel 28.

20. Ibid.

21. IMPARTIALIS, Nov. 17, 1807, *PP,* reel 68; Lowell to Pickering, Nov. 27, 1807, *PP,* reel 28.

22. Pickering to Gardner, Dec. 10, 1807; Pickering to Williams, Dec. 13, 1807, *PP,* reel 38; J. Q. Adams to T. B. Adams, Dec. 14, 1807, *AP,* reel 405.

23. Ibid.

24. Gray to Pickering, Jan. 8, 1808, *PP,* reel 28; Pickering to Sullivan, Feb. 16, 1808, *PP,* reel 14.

25. Pickering to Williams, Dec. 20, 24, 1807, ibid.; Brant, *Madison, Secretary of State,* pp. 405–16; Malone, *Jefferson,* V, 567–70; Perkins, *Prologue to War,* p. 196.

26. Undated memo, *PP,* reel 54; Pickering to Williams, Dec. 31, 1807, *PP,* reel 38; Pickering to R. Pickering, Jan. 1, 1808, *PP,* reel 3; Pickering to Cabot, Jan. 8, 1808, *PP,* reel 4:II.

27. Pickering to McHenry, Dec. 26, 1807, McHenry Papers, *LC;* Pickering to R. Pickering, Jan. 1, 1808, *PP,* reel 3; Pickering to J. Pickering, Feb. 28, 1808, *PP,* reel 4:II.

28. James M. Banner, *To the Hartford Convention* (New York: Knopf, 1970), pp. 295–97.

29. Pickering to Van Rensselaer, Sept. 26, 1808, *PP,* reel 14.

30. Pickering to Sullivan, Feb. 16, 1808, ibid.

31. Banner, *To the Hartford Convention,* pp. 44–45.

32. Dwight to Otis, Mar. 16, 1808, Otis Papers, *MHS;* Pickering to Cabot, Mar. 11, 1808, *PP,* reel 14; Pickering to R. Pickering, Mar. 15, 1808, *PP,* reel 3.

33. *Salem Gazette,* Mar. 25, 1808.

34. Wagner to Pickering, Mar. 21, 1808; Rose to Pickering, May 8, 1808, *PP,* reel 28.

35. T. B. Adams to J. Q. Adams, Mar. 15, 1808, *AP,* reel 405.

36. Lincoln to Adams, Apr. 18, 1808, *AP,* reel 406.

37. *Salem Register,* Mar. 26, 1808.

38. Ibid.

39. Ibid., Mar. 30, 1808.

40. Ibid., Apr. 2, 1808.

41. Sullivan to Pickering, Mar. 18, 1808, *PP,* reel 68.

42. Strong to Pickering, Apr. 6, 1808, *PP,* reel 28.

43. Hillhouse to Pickering, June 11, 1808, ibid.; James H. Robbins, "Voting Behavior in Massachusetts, 1800–1820: A Case Study" (Ph.D. dissertation, Northwestern University, 1970), pp. 85–86.

44. Peters to Pickering, Feb. 26, 1808, *PP,* reel 28.

45. Crowninshield to Bentley, Apr. 14, 1808; Crowninshield to Crowninshield, Mar. 19, 1808, Box 6, Crowninshield Family Papers, Peabody Museum.

46. Dearborn to Dearborn, Mar. 20, 1808, Box 6, Dearborn Papers, *MHS.*

47. Brant, *Madison, Secretary of State,* p. 450.

48. Rose to Pickering, May 8, 1808, *PP,* reel 28.

49. Brant, *Madison, Secretary of State,* p. 450.

50. Randolph to Pickering, Nov. 1, 1809, *PP,* reel 29; O. Pickering to J. Pickering, Feb. 28, 1815, *PP,* reel 38.

51. Pickering to Pickering, Apr. 4, 1808, *PP,* reel 3.

52. Brant, *Madison, Secretary of State,* pp. 443–46; Malone, *Jefferson,* V, 575.

53. Carroll to Harper, Aug. 11, 1808, reel 2, Harper Family Papers, Maryland Historical Society (microfilm).

54. Cooke to Chase, Mar. 19, 1808; McHenry to Pickering, Mar. 29, 1808, *PP,* reel 28.

55. Brant, *Madison, Secretary of State,* pp. 445–46; Malone, *Jefferson,* V, 575.

56. Adams to Bacon, Nov. 17, 1808; Adams to Giles, Nov. 15, 1808; Adams to Parker, Dec. 5, 1808, *AP,* reel 135.

57. Adams to Quincy, Dec. 23, 1808, *AP,* reel 118.

58. Gallatin to Nicholson, Dec. 29, 1808, in Henry Adams, *The Life of Albert Gallatin* (New York: Peter Smith, 1943), p. 385.

59. Hanson to Pickering, Jan. 10, 1809, *PP,* reel 29.

60. Marshall to Pickering, Dec. 19, 1808, *PP,* reel 28.

61. Washington to Pickering, Dec. 27, 1808, ibid.

62. Stoddert to Pickering, Dec. 27, 1808; Cabot to Pickering, Dec. 15, 1808, ibid.; Lowell to Pickering, Jan. 5, 1809, *PP,* reel 29.

63. Peters to Pickering, Jan. 11, 1809, *PP,* reel 29.

64. *AC,* 10th Cong., 2d sess., Dec. 2, 1808, p. 230.

65. Ibid., pp. 238–39; Adams, *Life of Gallatin,* pp. 381–82; Raymond Walters, *Albert Gallatin, Jeffersonian Financier and Diplomat* (New York: Macmillan, 1957), p. 209.

66. *AC,* 10th Cong., 2d sess., Dec. 17, 1808, p. 241.

67. Ibid., p. 249.

68. Ibid., p. 276.

69. Giles to Adams, Dec. 25, 1808, *AP,* reel 406.

70. *AC,* 10th Cong., 2d sess., Dec. 30, 1808, pp. 950–60.

71. Pickering to Jay, Jan. 13, 1809; Pickering to Mason, Jan. 4, 1809, *PP,* reel 14; Pickering to Pickering, Jan. 8, 1809 *PP,* reel 4:II.

72. Pickering to Jay, Jan. 13, 1809, *PP,* reel 14.

73. Pickering to Pickering, Jan. 30, 1809, *PP,* reel 4:II.

74. Pickering to Pickering, Feb. 7, 1809, ibid.

75. Williams to Pickering, Feb. 12, 1809, *PP,* reel 29.

76. Adams to Bacon, Nov. 17, 1808, *AP,* reel 135.

Chapter 18. The Crucible of War

1. *AC,* 11th Cong., 1st sess., May 23, 1809, pp. 11–12.

2. Pickering to R. Pickering, June 19, 1809, *PP,* reel 4:I.

3. Ibid.

4. Bacon to J. Q. Adams, June 29, 1809, *AP,* reel 407.

5. Pickering to R. Pickering, Dec. 3, 1809, *PP,* reel 4:I.

6. David H. Fischer, *The Revolution of American Conservatism* (New York: Harper and Row, 1965), p. 255.

7. Handbill, Feb. 6, 1809, *PP,* reel 4:I.

8. Handbill, Mar. 24, 1810, Pickering Papers, *EI.*

9. Pickering to Wagner, Mar. 26, 1810, *PP,* reel 14; Pickering to Gallatin, Apr. 3, 1810, *PP,* reel 38.

10. Pickering to Peters, Feb. 18, 1809, *PP,* reel 14.

11. Irving Brant, *Madison the President* (Indianapolis: Bobbs Merrill, 1956), pp. 90–101.

12. Pickering to Pratt, Dec. 6, 1809, Pickering Papers, *EI.*

13. Pickering to R. Pickering, Dec. 3, 1809, *PP,* reel 4:I; Evans to Pickering, Dec. 12, 1809; Hanson to Pickering, Dec. 11, 1809; Stoddert to Pickering, Jan. 10, 1809, *PP,* reel 29; Dwight to Pitkin, Dec. 6, 1809, Pitkin Family Papers, Huntington Library.

14. Pickering to Pratt, Dec. 6, 1809, Pickering Papers, *EI.*

15. Pickering to Gardner, Dec. 22, 1809, *PP,* reel 38; Pickering to Teackle, Dec. 30, 1809, Rufus King Papers, Huntington Library; Erskine to ?, Aug. 1, 1809 (copy), *PP,* reel 43.

16. T. B. Adams to J. Q. Adams, Mar. 27, 1810, *AP,* reel 409.

17. James H. Robbins, "Voting Behavior in Massachusetts, 1800–1820: A Case Study" (Ph.D. dissertation, Northwestern University, 1970). p. 198.

18. For an alternative view see Hall to J. Q. Adams, May 16, 1810; Plumer to J. Q. Adams, May 18, 1810, *AP,* reel 409.

19. Octavius Pickering and Charles W. Upham, *The Life of Timothy Pickering* (Boston: Little Brown, 1867), IV, 172; Morison, *The Life and Letters of Harrison Gray Otis* (Boston: Houghton Mifflin, 1913), II, 20–21.

20. Pickering to R. Pickering, Apr. 8, 1810, *PP*, reel 3.
21. Brant, *Madison, the President*, pp. 184–87.
22. *AC*, 11th Cong., 3d sess., Dec. 31, 1809, p. 65.
23. Ibid., pp. 65–66, 75, 78; Pickering to R. Pickering, Jan. 1, 1811, *PP*, reel 3.
24. Memo, Jan. 11, 1811, *PP*, reel 54.
25. Waterhouse to Adams, *AP*, reel 411.
26. Ibid.
27. "Letters Addressed to the People of the United States of America . . . ," *PP*, reel 68.
28. A. Adams to J. Q. Adams, Mar. 30, Apr. 8, 1811, *AP*, reel 411.
29. J. Adams to Rush, Apr. 22, 1811, *AP*, reel 118.
30. Waterhouse to Adams, May 20, 1811, *AP*, reel 411.
31. Lee to Pickering, May 12, 1811, *PP*, reel 29.
32. A. Adams to J. Q. Adams, Mar. 30, Apr. 8, 1811, *AP*, reel 411.
33. Morison, *Otis*, II, 32–36; Robert A. McCaughey, *Josiah Quincy* (Cambridge: Harvard University Press, 1974), pp. 71–72.
34. Pickering to Dana, Jan. 16, Feb. 7, 1812; Pickering to Reed, Jan. 31, Mar. 3, 1812, *PP*, reel 14.
35. Reed to Pickering, Nov. 12, 1811, *PP*, reel 29.
36. Pickering to Dana, Jan. 16, 1812, *PP*, reel 14.
37. Pickering to Rose, Apr. 7, 1812; Pickering to Jackson, Apr. 8, 1812, ibid.
38. *Salem Register*, May 5, 1812; Hervey Prentiss, "Timothy Pickering and the War of 1812," *Essex Institute Historical Collections*, LVV, no. 2 (Apr. 1934): 110–11.
39. Pickering to Pennington, July 12, 1812, *PP*, reel 14.
40. *Salem Gazette*, July 28, 1812; Pickering's draft of his address to the convention along with draft resolutions, n.d., *PP*, reel 52.
41. Pickering to Pennington, July 12, 1812, *PP*, reel 14.
42. *Boston Columbian Centinel*, Aug. 8, 1812; James M. Banner, *To the Hartford Convention* (New York: Knopf, 1970), pp. 262–63.
43. Morison, *Otis*, II, 61; Banner, *To the Hartford Convention*, pp. 309–10.
44. *Salem Gazette*, Mar. 8–April 16, 1813.
45. Pickering to R. Pickering, Jan. 9, 1814, *PP*, reel 3; Pickering to Putnam, Feb. 7, 1814, *PP*, reel 15.
46. Gerry to Gerry, June 16, 1813, Gerry Papers, *MHS*.
47. Pickering to Pickering, May 19, 1812, cited in Pickering and Upham, *Pickering*, IV, 225.
48. Gerry to Gerry, June 16, 1813, Gerry Papers, *MHS*.
49. Pickering to R. Pickering, May 24, 1813, cited in Pickering and Upham, *Pickering*, IV, 224.
50. Pickering to R. Pickering, May 19, 1813, ibid.
51. Pickering to R. Pickering, June 6, 1813, ibid., p. 227.
52. Pickering to Lowell, Nov. 7, 1814, *PP*, reel 15.
53. Pickering to Söderström, Aug. 27, 1813, *PP*, reel 14; Söderström to Pickering, Sept. ?, 1813, *PP*, reel 30.
54. T. B. Adams to J. Q. Adams, Feb. 9, 1814, *AP*, reel 417.
55. Degrand to Adams, Feb. 7, 1814, ibid.
56. Samuel Dexter, an "Adams Federalist," challenged the incumbent Caleb Strong for the governorship but was defeated by a wide margin.
57. Pickering to R. Pickering, Jan. 6, 1814, *PP*, reel 3.
58. Ibid.
59. *AC*, 13th Cong., 1st sess., Jan. 10, 1814, p. 855.

60. Pickering to Putnam, Feb. 7, 1814, *PP*, reel 15.

61. *AC*, 13th Cong., 1st sess., Jan. 18, 1814, pp. 1054–60.

62. Pickering to Putnam, Feb. 7, 1814, *PP*, reel 15.

63. Ibid. See also Putnam to Pickering, Feb. 12, 1814, *PP*, reel 30; Banner, *To the Hartford Convention*, pp. 313–19.

64. Harry Coles, *The War of 1812* (Chicago: University of Chicago Press, 1965), p. 172.

65. Pickering and Upham, *Pickering*, IV, 253.

66. Degrand to Adams, Oct. 16, 1814, *AP*, reel 420.

67. Ibid.; Waterhouse to Adams, Oct. 13, 1814, ibid.

68. Ibid.; Adams to Adams, Oct. 14, 1814, ibid.

69. Degrand to Adams, Oct. 16, 1814, ibid.

70. Pickering to Peter, Sept. 14, 1814, *PP*, reel 15.

71. Irving, Brant, *Madison, Commander in Chief* (Indianapolis: Bobbs Merrill, 1961), pp. 334–35; Samuel Flagg Bemis, *John Quincy Adams and the Foundations of American Foreign Policy* (New York: Knopf, 1949), I, 200–05; Bradford Perkins, *Castlereagh and Adams* (Berkeley: University of California Press, 1964), pp. 67–80.

72. *AC*, 13th Cong., 3d sess., Oct. 10, 1814, pp. 381–82.

73. Pickering to Strong, Oct. 12, 1814, *PP*, reel 15.

74. Jay to Pickering, Nov. 1, 1814, *PP*, reel 30.

75. Morris to Pickering, Oct. 17, Nov. 1, 1814, ibid.

76. For brief descriptions of the caucus see Pickering to Morris, Oct. 21, 1814, *PP*, reel 15; Dana to Eustis, Nov. 2, 1814, Eustis Papers, *LC*.

77. Pickering to Morris, Oct. 21, 1814, *PP*, reel 15.

78. Ibid.

79. Pickering to Lowell, Nov. 7, 27, 1814; Pickering to Hillhouse, Dec. 15, 1814, ibid.

80. Pickering to Putnam, Feb. 3, 1814; Pickering to Lowell, Oct. 15, 1814, ibid.

81. Pickering to Lowell, Nov. 27, 1814, ibid.; Banner, *To the Hartford Convention*, pp. 318–31.

82. Pickering became obsessed with the idea that the English would win the war for Federalism. See Pickering to Hodgdon, Dec. 25, 1814, *PP*, reel 15; Pickering to R. Pickering, Jan. 8, 1815, *PP*, reel 3; Pickering to Cutler, Jan. 9, 1815, *PP*, reel 38.

83. Pickering to Hillhouse, Dec. 15, 1815 *PP*, reel 15.

84. Pickering to Lowell, Jan. 23, 1815, ibid.

85. Pickering to Strong, Jan. 7, 1815, ibid.

86. Pickering to Gardner, Nov. 23, 1814, *PP*, reel 38; Pickering to Marshall, Jan. 7, 1829, *PP*, reel 16.

87. *National Intelligencer*, Feb. 6, 1815; Pickering to Strong, Jan. 28, 1815, Papers of Caleb Strong, *MHS*.

88. Pickering to R. Pickering, Feb. 5, 1815, *PP*, reel 3.

89. Ibid.

90. Ibid.; Pickering to Lowell, Jan. 24, 1815, *PP*, reel 15.

Chapter 19. Epilogue

1. Pickering to R. Pickering, Dec. 3, 1815, Jan. 14, 23, 1816, *PP*, reel 3.

2. Pickering to R. Pickering, Jan. 29, 1816, ibid.

3. Pickering to Cabot, Dec. 14, 1815, *PP*, reel 15; anonymous to Pickering, Feb. 20, 1816, *PP*, reel 55; Williams to Pickering, Feb. 28, 1816; Bowditch to Pickering, Feb. 29, 1816; Thorndike to Pickering, Mar. 20, 1816; Pickman to Pickering, Mar. 23, 1816, *PP*, reel 31.

4. Pickering to Yard, Jan. 31, 1817, *PP*, reel 15.

5. Congress enacted a law establishing a regular salary of $1,500 a year for congressmen and senators. This replaced the older system of per diem payment.

6. Pickering to Brooke, Dec. 14, 18, 1816, *PP*, reel 38.

7. James M. Banner, *To the Hartford Convention* (New York: Knopf, 1970), p. 73.

8. David H. Fischer, *The Revolution of American Conservatism* (New York: Harper and Row, 1965), pp. 190–94.

9. Octavius Pickering and Charles W. Upham, *The Life of Timothy Pickering* (Boston: Little Brown, 1867), IV, 276–79; Ashton to Pickering, Oct. 31, 1816, *PP*, reel 31.

10. Pickering and Upham, *Pickering*, IV, 334.

11. Memo, July 4, 1826, *PP*, reel 46.

12. Pickering to the inhabitants of Salem, Mar. 24, 1828; Pickering to Inches, Apr. 4, 1828, *PP*, reel 16.

13. Pickering and Upham, *Pickering*, IV, 316–17.

14. Pickering to Jefferson, Feb. 12, 1821, *PP*, reel 38; Jefferson to Pickering, Feb. 27, 1821, *PP*, reel 15.

15. Pickering to Mead, Sept. 12, 1819, ibid.; Pickering to Gardner, Sept. 23, 1819, *PP*, reel 38; Pickering to Randolph, Dec. 24, 1819; Pickering to Mercer, Jan. 15, 1820, *PP*, reel 15.

16. Pickering to Marshall, Jan. 17, 1826, *PP*, reel 16.

17. Ibid.

18. "Negro Slavery," Apr. 1826, *PP*, reel 46.

19. Pickering to Stevenson, Apr. 10, 1826, *PP*, reel 16.

20. Pickering's notebook, Aug. 19, 1818, *PP*, reel 46; Pickering to Marshall, Feb. 14, 1827, *PP*, reel 16; Pickering to Peters, Jan. 21, 1811, Peters Papers, Historical Society of Pennsylvania.

21. Pickering to Coleman, Jan. 19, 1827, *PP*, reel 38; notes on a visit to New York and Philadelphia, July–August 1827, *PP*, reel 50.

22. Pickering to Peters, Jan. 21, 1811, Peters Papers, Historical Society of Pennsylvania.

23. Memo, Nov. 15, 21, 27, 1821, *PP*, reel 51.

24. Gardner to Pickering, Sept. 27, 1822, *PP*, reel 31; Coleman to Pickering, Aug. 1, 1824, *PP*, reel 32.

25. Memo, July 26, 1822., *PP*, reel 52.

26. *Correspondence between the Hon. John Adams, . . . and Wm. Cunningham*, ed. E. M. Cunningham (Boston, 1823).

27. Ibid., p. iii.

28. Adams to Cunningham, Nov. 25, 1808, ibid., p. 56.

29. Pickering to Peters, Oct. 21, 1823; Pickering to Lowell, Oct. 20, 1823, *PP*, reel 15.

30. Pickering, *Review of the Correspondence between the Hon. John Adams . . . and . . . Wm. Cunningham Esq.* (Salem, 1824).

31. *Salem Gazette*, May 21, 1824; clipping in *PP*, reel 68.

32. *Baltimore Patriot*, May 17, 1824, *PP*, reel 68.

33. *Salem Gazette*, July 16, 1824; Adams to Sprague, May 16, 1824; Adams to Davis, May 20, 1824, *AP*, reel 147.

34. Pickering to Bowman, June 10, 1824, *PP*, reel 15.

35. Pickering to Coleman, Apr. 30, 1827, *PP*, reel 38.

36. Pickering to Livingston, Dec. 19, 1827; Pickering to Randolph, Mar. 25, 1828, *PP*, reel 16.

37. Pickering to Lyman, Apr. 7, 1828, ibid.; Lyman to Pickering, Apr. 16, 1828, *PP*, reel 32.

38. Pickering to Van Cortlandt, Apr. 18, 1828, ibid.

39. Ibid.; Van Cortlandt to Pickering, Apr. 7, 1828, ibid.

40. Lyman to Pickering, Sept. 3, 1828, ibid.

41. Pickering to Peters, Nov. 12, 1828, *PP,* reel 16.

42. The Hamilton family turned Hamilton's papers over to Pickering, even paying him an advance of $500 for the biography. See a contract between Pickering and Mrs. E. Hamilton, Aug. 1, 1827, *PP,* reel 55.

43. Pickering and Upham, *Pickering,* IV, 393–94.

44. Ibid., pp. 358–59.

45. Ibid., p. 360. See also Henry Pickering's memo on his father's death, Feb. 2, 1829; Pickering to Coleman, Feb. 4, 1829, Pickering Papers, *EI.*

A Note on the Sources

AT HIS DEATH Timothy Pickering left an extraordinarily rich manuscript collection. The bulk of it, preserved and more recently microfilmed by the Massachusetts Historical Society, has formed the basis of this biography. But other smaller collections of Pickering's writings also proved useful, particularly those at the Essex Institute, the Houghton Library, the Library of Congress, the New York Historical Society, the New York City Public Library, and the New York Society Library. Unhappily, most of Pickering's offical correspondence as secretary of war no longer exists. But the Papers of the Continental Congress, the General Records of the Postmaster General's Office, and the General Records of the State Department, all preserved in the National Archives and on microfilm have been invaluable. The British Foreign Office Records, preserved on film and available at the Library of Congress, have also proved extremely useful.

Pickering was involved in so much during his half-century in public life that it was impossible to rely entirely upon his own personal and official correspondence in reconstructing his public career. The following manuscript collections were therefore also consulted:

The American Philosophical Society Library
  The Papers of Nathanael Greene.
The Boston Public Library
  The Papers of Dwight Foster.
The Clements Library, University of Michigan
  The Papers of Thomas Gage, Nathanael Greene, James McHenry, and Anthony Wayne. The Hammond-Simcoe Correspondence, the Northwest Territory Papers, the War of 1812 Papers.
Columbia University Library
  The Papers of Alexander Hamilton.
The Essex Institute
  The Crowninshield Family Papers, the Goodhue Family Papers, the Papers of Samuel Putnam, the Salem Social Library Records, the Salem Town Records (transcripts).
Harvard University Archives
  Faculty Records.

The Historical Society of Pennsylvania
>The Diary of John Heckewelder, the Papers of George M. Dallas, Peter Duponceau, George Logan, Thomas McKean, Richard Peters, and Anthony Wayne. Clement Humphreys letterbook, the Gratz Collection, and the Society Collection.

The Houghton Library, Harvard University
>The Papers of Joseph Dennie, Timothy Pickering, Jr., and Paine Wingate.

The Huntington Library
>The Papers of William Eaton, Nathanael Greene, Rufus King, James McHenry, and the Pitkin Family Papers.

The Library of Congress
>The papers of Elias Boudinot, William Eaton, Andrew Ellicott, William Eustis, Sir Augustus John Foster, Elbridge Gerry, Nicholas Gilman, Alexander Hamilton, Robert G. Harper, Harry Innes, Thomas Jefferson, Tobias Lear, Levi Lincoln, James McHenry, James Madison, John Marshall, James Monroe, William Vans Murray, Charles C. Pinckney, William Plumer, the Shaw Family, Samuel Smith, William L. Smith, Benjamin Stoddert, and George Washington.

Maryland Historical Society
>The Harper Family Papers (microfilm).

Massachusetts Historical Society
>The Adams Family Papers, the papers of Henry Dearborne, Thomas Jefferson, Henry Knox, Benjamin Lincoln, Harrison Gray Otis, Samuel Putnam, Theodore Sedgwick, and Caleb Strong.

National Library of Scotland
>Papers of Sir Robert Liston (microfilm made available through the auspices of the University of California—Berkeley Library).

New York City Public Library
>Papers of James Monroe.

New York Historical Society
>Papers of Horatio Gates and Rufus King.

The Peabody Museum
>The Crowninshield Family Papers.

Pierpont Morgan Library
>Papers of Elbridge Gerry and William Vans Murray.

Stanford University Library
>The Ames Family Papers.

State Historical Society of Wisconsin
>The Draper Collection (microfilm in the University of California—Berkeley Library).

Yale University Library
>The papers of Roger Griswold and James Hillhouse.

Space limitations make it impossible for me to acknowledge all of the published sources, including documents, correspondence, secondary works, and unpublished dissertations that have been used in preparing this biography. The more important sources are of course to be found in the notes. But my understanding of Pickering's role in early American history has been shaped in a thousand ways by many scholars whose works are cited nowhere in the text. I owe them a debt of gratitude.

Index